"As a philosopher, I found it fascinating to read these new employments of concepts of epistemic injustice in the sphere of social work—its theory and its practice. In their developments of theoretical ideas energized through application in a range of contexts and perspectives across professional social work, these contributions are testament to the practical power of abstract ideas."

Miranda Fricker, *Professor at New York University, USA and author of* Epistemic Injustice: Power and the Ethics of Knowing

"Social work, even in its most radical versions, cannot claim to promote social justice without taking an honest look at its own assumptions. In particular, it must scrutinize the underlying processes of knowledge production. From multiple personal, political, and professional viewpoints, this collection powerfully invites us to do precisely that: to engage with uncomfortable questions that may unsettle the self-images of anti-oppressive and critical social work practitioners. Doing so enables us to open up important and timely avenues for revisiting and strengthening the emancipatory potential of the profession."

Jasna Russo, *Professor at Alice Salomon University of Applied Sciences, Berlin, Germany*

"This timely and seminal volume offers a powerful exploration of what counts as knowledge for equitable and socially just social work. It should be essential reading for students, practitioners, and researchers seeking to understand what knowledge matters in social work and how it should be developed and applied in practice."

Reima Ana Maglajlic, *Reader in Social Work, Head of Department of Social Work and Social Care at University of Sussex, UK*

Epistemic Injustice and Resistance in Social Work

This book explores epistemic injustice in various aspects of social work practice, research, and education, and how those in the field can address issues of power, oppression, and institutionalized prejudice.

This edited volume invites social work scholars, educators, practitioners, and students to deeply engage in the conversation about social justice and human rights on epistemic grounds. It begins with a simple but profound question: *Whose knowledge counts, and whose voices are silenced?* Bridging the gap between theory and practice, this book contextualizes epistemic injustice concepts such as testimonial, hermeneutical, and contributory justice across diverse social work settings to help readers better recognize when and how these concepts manifest in the profession and how to address them from an epistemic justice lens. The chapters span a range of issues relevant to the field, including health and mental health, transformative social work, and the inclusion of systemically marginalized voices in practice and research such as LGBTQIA+, disabled communities, and street-involved. Contributors draw on their first-hand experience teaching social work students and practicing and researching with culturally diverse communities across settings. Each chapter invites readers to consider and reimagine ways of resisting epistemic injustice in their work and how social workers can join in collective resistance in the epistemic domains of the profession.

With case studies and practical examples throughout, this book is essential for social work students, educators, researchers, and practitioners of all levels. This guide serves both as a mirror to reflect the challenges within the profession and as a roadmap to chart pathways toward a more just, inclusive, and epistemically responsible field.

Eunjung Lee, PhD, MSW, RSW, is Professor and Endowed Chair in Mental Health & Health at the Factor-Inwentash Faculty of Social Work, University of Toronto, Canada.

Andrea Greenblatt, PhD, MSW, is Assistant Director at Ontario SPOR Support Unit, Toronto, Canada.

Ran Hu, PhD, MSW, MA, is Assistant Professor at The Ohio State University College of Social Work, USA.

Epistemic Injustice and Resistance in Social Work

Rethinking Social Justice in Practice, Education, and Research

Edited by Eunjung Lee, Andrea Greenblatt, and Ran Hu

Routledge
Taylor & Francis Group
NEW YORK AND LONDON

Designed cover image: Getty Images © Colors Hunter – Chasseur de Couleurs

First published 2027
by Routledge
605 Third Avenue, New York, NY 10158

and by Routledge
4 Park Square, Milton Park, Abingdon, Oxon, OX14 4RN

Routledge is an imprint of the Taylor & Francis Group, an informa business

ISBN: 978-1-041-07146-4 (hbk)
ISBN: 978-1-041-07144-0 (pbk)
ISBN: 978-1-003-63904-6 (ebk)

DOI: 10.4324/9781003639046

Typeset in Times New Roman
by Deanta Global Publishing Services, Chennai, India

Contents

Figures

Contributors

Karen Bell, PhD, is Associate Professor of Social Work at Charles Sturt University (CSU), and she is located on Ngunnawal/Ngambri Country in regional New South Wales, Australia. Karen's record of research and publication demonstrates her interest in post-conventional philosophy of social work, critical posthumanism, post-anthropocentrism, and feminist qualitative research. Many of her publications explore the transformative capacity of post-conventional theories in relation to the philosophy of social work and epistemic justice. Her research also encompasses qualitative research, gender, interprofessional partnerships, and the multidimensional impacts of climate change. Karen's current research collaborations include projects on professional identity, menstrual justice, gender, ecosocial approaches to disaster practice, social work in libraries, and research capacity building.

Peter Beresford OBE is Visiting Professor at the University of East Anglia and Co-Chair of Shaping Our Lives, the UK disabled people's and user-led organization. He is also Emeritus Professor of Social Policy at Brunel University London and Emeritus Professor of Citizen Involvement at the University of Essex. He has a longstanding involvement in issues of participation and service user involvement in research and evaluation, as a writer, researcher, and educator. His areas of particular interest are disability, mental health, palliative care, social work and social care, welfare reform, social work education, and participatory research. He has published widely in his fields of interest, most recently, *The Antidote: How People-Powered Movements Can Renew Politics, Policy and Practice* (2025) and *At the Heart of a Mad Movement: The Life and Work of Peter Campbell, Psychiatric System Pioneer* (coedited with Peter Barham and Ker Wallwark (2026)).

Jackie Bolton, BA, is Independent Social Worker and Co-Founder of the Romani and Traveller Social Work Association. Through research and leadership of a Traveller-led charity, where she is Chair of Trustees, Jackie works to reduce inequalities of outcomes and life chances and promote the wellbeing and safeguarding of all Romani and Travelling people. Jackie achieves this by promoting the use of trauma-informed, relationship-based, and person-centered practice which is culturally informed and reduces the impact of Anti-Gypsyism (structural and institutional racism). Jackie has worked with Gypsies, Roma, and Travellers in the East of England and survivors of child sexual abuse/exploitation/criminal exploitation across England and Wales, and more recently with children and families affected by serious youth violence in London. In her most recent research, she completed a document analysis of serious child safeguarding case reviews with Romani and Traveller communities in England, and she seeks to contribute to the knowledge and learning base for social workers and other professionals working with Romani and Traveller children, families, and communities.

Wendy Bowles, PhD, is a white settler woman and Professor of Social Work at Charles Sturt University (CSU) living and working on Wiradjuri Country, New South Wales, Australia. Wendy is a founding member of the social work team who pioneered teaching social work online in Australia, with the aim of opening the social work profession to those previously excluded. Her research, publications, and teaching interests include being an ally to the Wiradjuri nation, to people with disabilities, eco-social work, social work ethics with a focus on relational ethics, rurality, and how these intersect.

Andrea Greenblatt, PhD, is interested in how youth experience can impact health policy, practice, and research. Her work has spanned healthcare and community settings, and she explores how social workers can work to center youth voices and promote epistemically just practice. She completed her post-doctoral fellowship at the Hospital for Sick Children in the Child Health Evaluative Sciences program and most recently holds the role of Assistant Director at Ontario SPOR Support Unit.

Ran Hu, PhD, is Assistant Professor at The Ohio State University College of Social Work. Through research, Hu is committed to promoting the health, safety, and wellbeing of sex workers and survivors of GBV and/or trafficking through developing culturally safe services and exploring non-carceral anti-violence policies. Hu has worked with migrant women in sex work and survivors of trafficking in New York City and with rural-to-urban migrant sex workers in Beijing. In her most recent postdoctoral research, she studied socio-structural inequities impacting migrant sex workers' occupational health and safety in Metro Vancouver. Informed by her transnational work, her current scholarship explores and addresses intersecting social-structural and epistemic inequities that contribute to violence against sex workers, human trafficking, and gender-based violence.

Christina Hyland, PhD, is a graduate of the University of Toronto Factor-Inwentash School of Social Work PhD program. Hyland's critical qualitative research explores how eating struggles and body image challenges are experienced by diverse populations, and the epistemic injustices they endure, particularly within social services and other clinical encounters. Hyland's work is founded on her passionate commitment to deepening her understanding of trauma, eating struggles, and the impact of structural oppression on the lives of disadvantaged populations. In addition to working in the community in various social justice/advocacy-oriented roles, Hyland has had a clinical private practice since 2014, supporting youth and young adults who are struggling in their relationship with food, sense of self, and body image-related concerns.

Gio Iacono is Assistant Professor at the University of Connecticut School of Social Work. He completed his PhD and MSW from the University of Toronto. Iacono's research and scholarship consist of two interconnected aims, rooted in advancing social justice: (1) Promoting the holistic well-being of LGBTQIA+ young people and (2) Transforming social work education and training to sustain culturally responsive practice and advocacy. He has worked as a psychotherapist, clinical social worker, educator, community organizer, and researcher in a variety of health and community-based settings for over 15 years. His community organizing and advocacy work have primarily focused on diverse LGBTQIA+ communities. Iacono is funded by the Mind & Life Institute.

Bibiana D. Koh, PhD, LCSW-C (she/her), joined the School of Social Work at Salisbury University as Associate Professor in Fall 2021. She was previously at Augsburg University (Minneapolis, Minnesota), where she held a three-year university appointment (2018–2021) as the Batalden Scholar in Applied Ethics. At Salisbury, Koh has served as the Justice, Equity, Diversity, & Inclusion (JEDI) Coordinator for the College of Health and Human Services. She currently serves as an Office of Diversity and Inclusion (ODI) Faculty Fellow. Koh is the author of *Anti-Oppressive Social Work Ethics* (expected release Fall 2026). Her scholarship focuses on the intersections of ethics, diversity, and critical pedagogy.

Eunjung Lee, PhD, MSW, RSW, is Professor and Endowed Chair in Mental Health & Health at the Factor-Inwentash Faculty of Social Work, University of Toronto, Canada. She has served as Associate Editor of the *Clinical Social Work Journal* and as Cultural Competence Track Chair for the *Council on Social Work Education* in the United States. Drawing on critical theories of language, discourse, and power, and grounded in epistemic injustice and feminist scholarship, her research focuses on everyday interactions in clinical practice and simulation-based learning in social work education. Her work interrogates the praxis of cross-cultural practice, social policy, and regulation, analyzing how policies and their underlying politics shape dominant discourses that affect immigrants and refugees in a global neoliberal era, and theorizes Canadian and Korean multiculturalism and the welfare state.

Jacqueline McNamara (BSW, MHlthSc) is a PhD candidate at Charles Sturt University and Lecturer at Central Queensland University. She is located on Darumbal Country, Rockhampton, Queensland, Australia. She teaches social work field education and is currently exploring the professional identity of women social workers through her PhD research. McNamara teaches, researches, and is involved with community development projects and local partnerships that are focused on challenging the intersecting systems of oppression that disadvantage women and girls, especially as experienced by First Nations communities. In all of these areas, McNamara centers radical feminist and phenomenological approaches, alongside First Nations research methodologies and decolonizing social work practice.

Bernadette Moorhead, PhD, is Senior Lecturer in Social Work at Charles Sturt University (CSU). She is located on Wiradjuri Country, Wagga Wagga, New South Wales, Australia. Moorhead is a member of the CSU Environmental and Social Justice Research Group and the Future of the Professions Group. Her membership in these groups is reflective of her research agenda that is driven by interpretive phenomenological, feminist, and critical research methodologies. Moorhead currently leads an international team of researchers who critically examine professional identity in social work across the globe. Moorhead has also published in the areas of newly qualified social work and short-term study abroad programs, with the latter having a particular focus on embedding reciprocity into exchange relationships.

Noam Ringer, PhD, is a researcher and licensed clinical psychologist affiliated with Stockholm University and the psychiatric healthcare services in Stockholm, Sweden. Ringer holds a PhD in Health Education, with research focusing on coping with psychiatric illness and processes of meaning-making among children, adolescents, and families. Integrating research and clinical practice, Ringer's work aims to advance knowledge about the preconditions that support children's healthy development and psychological wellbeing in the context of mental health challenges. Ringer's research emphasizes children's lived experiences and the psychosocial, familial, and educational contexts shaping wellbeing. Current research interests include child and adolescent mental health, family and school environments, and how children and young people understand and navigate psychiatric conditions in everyday life.

Vivien Roman-Hampton, MSW, LICSW, is a doctoral student at the University of Connecticut's School of Social Work with over a decade of experience as a clinical social worker. She founded and operates a group mental health practice focused on increasing accessibility for historically marginalized communities and serves as Director of Outreach and Teacher Development for the Mindfulness Institute for Emerging Adults. Roman-Hampton's research focuses on the role of mindfulness as an intervention to foster resilience and flourishing within historically marginalized communities and combat systems of oppression. Her research interests include contemplative practices, diversity, equity, inclusion, community-engaged research, and the intersection of artificial intelligence and social justice. Through her work, Roman-Hampton aims to advance social justice and empower marginalized communities using innovative interventions and approaches.

Ulla-Karin Schön is a social worker and Professor in Social Work whose research is centrally concerned with epistemic injustice in mental health and disability services. Her work critically examines how knowledge, voice, and credibility are distributed in social work practice, with a particular focus on recovery-oriented care, user participation, and shared decision-making. Co-production with experts by experience is a core principle of her research, serving as a foundation for addressing epistemic injustice and promoting epistemic justice in both research and practice. She has led interdisciplinary projects on user involvement, person-centered social practices, digital support for participation, and the implementation of new interventions in social and health services. She also conduct research on supporting young people not in employment or education in transitions toward work, social participation, and belonging.

Manaal Syed is Assistant Professor in Social Work at Renison University College, affiliated with the University of Waterloo. Syed's areas of expertise include social work with older adults, community-based models of social work practice, social policy, qualitative research, and social work education. Her research program focuses on critical approaches for working with diverse aging populations, and she has published in the areas of transnational aging, age-friendly communities, social isolation and loneliness in older adults, and knowledge transfer and exchange for gerontological social work initiatives. Syed is currently leading a Tri-Council-funded SSHRC project focused on intergenerational relations in multi-generational families.

Catalina Tang Yan 趙嘉蓮, PhD, is Assistant Professor and PhD Director at Lesley University. Tang Yan is a transdisciplinary scholar who uses a decolonial and racial equity lens to study the narratives that create epistemic justice at the intersection of health, language, disability, and education. Her research focuses on the ways critical youth and community-based participatory action research approaches can create equitable social policy, unsettling pedagogy, and applied research. As an educator, she approaches her teaching as a continuous praxis to humanize the classroom with students and integrate defiant pedagogies shaped by decolonial, critical race, and feminist theories. She is committed to co-creating anti-oppressive and brave communities of learning inside and outside the classroom to facilitate critical reflection, challenge individual worldviews, and embody systemic and liberatory approaches to justice. As a former immigrant youth leader, organizer, and youth worker in various Out of School Time youth programs in the Greater Boston Area, she seeks to partner with community stakeholders locally and transnationally to support their community organizing efforts in achieving social change and transformation.

Peter Unwin, PhD, is a qualified social worker who has held a variety of practice, managerial, and inspectoral posts across UK social work. His practice, research, and publications revolve around the voices of marginalized communities and are all characterized by a commitment to co-production and a search for social justice. Unwin has been a foster carer and has a particular professional interest in the fields of fostering and adoption, where he has argued for greater inclusivity. Unwin is an ally member of the Romani and Traveller Social Work Association, the Chair of Worcestershire's (England) British Association of Social Workers Branch, Trustee of a Gypsy, Roma, and Traveller charity, and is Principal Lecturer in Social Work at the University of Worcester. In recent years, Unwin has become aware of the extensive epistemic injustices suffered by the UK's Gypsy, Roma, and Traveller populations and has led a number of large scale co-produced research projects designed to right such injustices. He has also introduced teaching about Gypsy, Roma, and Traveller issues into the curriculum.

Luissa Vahedi is a social epidemiologist whose interdisciplinary research examines the intersection of gender, health, and socio-political inequality in global contexts. Her work focuses on advancing the health and socio-economic rights of women and girls, particularly in settings affected by conflict and state fragility, drawing on syndemic theory and mixed-methods approaches to generate policy-relevant evidence. She has contributed to international research initiatives and published in leading peer-reviewed journals on topics including gender-based violence, health inequities, and structural determinants of wellbeing. In addition to her research, she is an experienced educator committed to equity-oriented teaching, and she actively engages in knowledge translation to inform policy and practice in global health and development.

Introduction

Interrogating Epistemic Injustice in Social Work Practice, Education, and Research

Eunjung Lee, Ran Hu, and Andrea Greenblatt

This book is an invitation to our social work community – scholars, educators, practitioners, students, and service users – to deeply engage in conversations about social justice and human rights on epistemic grounds. It begins with a simple but profound question: *Whose knowledge counts, and whose voices are silenced?* Contemporary epistemic injustice scholarship has addressed and deepened this fundamental question: How does it feel to have one's experiences and stories discredited (Fricker, 2007)? How do individuals access the resources they need to make sense of their experiences when their identities are disrespected and devalued in the social order (Dotson, 2012; Fricker, 2007)? How does a person resist such injustice to their existence, rights, and identities? (Medina, 2013). This book attempts to critically interrogate and understand these pervasive phenomena in society, particularly in the context of social work encounters with individuals, families, communities, and organizations. We also endeavor to reimagine and explore ways of promoting epistemic justice while addressing epistemic injustice across social work practice, education, and research.

Epistemic justice is fundamental to all types of justice, including social justice and distributive justice (Lakeman, 2010; Miller, 1999), yet it has gained limited attention in social work. We, as the editors of and contributors to this book, are among a small but growing group of scholars in social work who have been actively publishing and presenting on topics related to epistemic injustice (Bell, 2014; Beresford, 2022; Beresford & Rose, 2023; Greenblatt et al., 2024; Iacono, 2017; Johnstone & Lee, 2018, 2021, 2024a, 2024b; Koh, 2023; Lee, 2022; Lee et al., 2022a, 2022b; Lee et al., 2019a, 2019b; Maleku, 2025; Newbigging et al., 2024; Russo & Beresford, 2015; Tang Yan, 2023). This collective body of work demonstrates the critical role of epistemic injustice in social (justice) work across practice, teaching, and research settings. In clinical practice, for example, epistemic injustice can occur when a clinician's institutional power and presumed authority determine whose voice predominates within a therapeutic dyad, risking the discrediting of the client as a knower of their lived reality. This type of injustice is often inherently embedded in the power hierarchies and structure of clinical interactions; the potential silencing of clients during clinical

DOI: 10.4324/9781003639046-1

assessment and service delivery is not necessarily intended maliciously or consciously. Correspondingly, it becomes even more critical to closely understand how epistemic injustice is produced in everyday social work practice with clients, as well as in research and teaching activities. At various conferences and lecture presentations to which we were invited, we noticed that attendees often identified the importance of epistemic (in)justice and its relevance to their own areas of social (justice) work. Many expressed a desire for an edited book or special journal issues on epistemic injustice to support their practice, teaching, and research.

Several recently published books and/or chapters focus on key concepts in epistemic injustice, including its implications for social science research, medicine, healthcare, and mental illness (Brady & Fricker, 2016; Catala, 2025; Giladi & McMillan, 2022; Kidd et al., 2017; Lund et al., 2024; McGlynn, 2026; Santos, 2014; Sherman & Goguen, 2019: Wood, 2020). While examining similar topics, our book is uniquely situated in the field of social work, focusing specifically on a wide range of key issues across practice, teaching, and research. To our knowledge, no edited volume on epistemic injustice in social work currently exists; this book will be the first of its kind. Principles of epistemic justice are fundamental to all kinds of social work encounters and actions. Issues of power, oppression, and institutionalized prejudice are embedded in the systems within which social workers and clients, social work educators and students, and social work researchers and research participants interact. Drawing on the diverse experiences and scholarship of our contributors, this book brings to light how epistemic questions manifest in our field through empirical examples, case studies, and critical reflections. It also guides social work practitioners, researchers, and educators to embody epistemically just ways when working with a range of clients, students, and research participants, including those facing mental health concerns, systemic barriers, and oppressive policies and institutional practices.

0.1 Organization of the Book

This edited volume consists of fourteen chapters. Most contributors are experienced social work practitioners, researchers, and educators. Drawing on their first-hand experience teaching social work students, and practicing and researching with diverse, marginalized communities across various settings, they critically reflect on how the construct of epistemic injustice has impacted their inter/actions in teaching, research, and practice.

The book's opening chapter – Chapter 1, "Understanding the Epistemic Domain in Social Work to Foster Social Justice" (Lee) – invites readers to view our social work profession from an epistemic lens, encouraging us to foreground epistemic discussions and questions as a foundational pillar of social justice. This chapter introduces the epistemic injustice scholarship and its precursors in Black feminist works, outlining why the epistemic domain matters to social work, and especially, "why now", given the rise in authoritarian politics and attacks on social justice and diversity-focused scholarship both within and beyond the social work profession. This chapter argues that attending to epistemic *injustice* (not merely promoting epistemic *justice*) is essential to advancing social justice. It further elaborates how we, as social work practitioners, educators, and researchers, can embody epistemic resistance against epistemic injustice by developing testimonial sensibilities and expanding epistemic resources for the people we serve.

This book is organized into two parts, each addressing the multifaceted ways epistemic injustice intersects with social work ethics, theory, research, and practice. Part I, "Imagining Social Work Ethics, Theory, Research and Practice toward Epistemic Justice", brings together four chapters that explore ethical, conceptual, and practical pathways for embedding epistemic justice into the foundations of social work. More specifically, Chapter 2, "Epistemic Ethics Justice in Social Work: Developing a Critical Consciousness" (Koh), examines the gaps in how social work codes of ethics operationalize "justice" and argues that epistemic injustice and critical consciousness can bridge these gaps. The author introduces practical tools – such as decentering, bias identification, and power analysis – to foster anti-oppressive ethics and cultivate epistemically just communities. Chapter 3, "Transformative Social Work and Epistemic Justice" (Bell, Moorhead, McNamara, and Bowles), critiques the Euro-Western, modernist, androcentric paradigm underpinning conventional social work, and its perpetuation of hierarchical knowledge systems. Drawing on feminist, Indigenist, and critical posthumanist perspectives, the authors propose a transformative framework grounded in relationality, equity, and liberation, illustrating how diverse epistemologies can advance epistemic justice. Chapter 4, "Epistemic Injustice in Community-Based Participatory Research: Toward Embodying Decolonial Ethical Relationality, Sentipensante, and Accountable Praxis in Social Work" (Tang Yan), interrogates power hierarchies and epistemic injustice within community-based participatory research collaborations. Anchored in decolonial and sentipensante frameworks, the chapter calls for accountable, relational praxis that disrupts colonial knowledge structures and co-creates counterspaces for participatory inquiry in social work research. Chapter 5, "Confronting Epistemic Injustice in Everyday Social Work Practice" (Lee), attends to social workers' seemingly mundane practice at the micro, mezzo, and macro levels, showing how epistemic injustice emerges in everyday practice realities. By analyzing turn-by-turn interactions between social workers, individuals, and families, and by elaborating on community-level examples, this chapter underscores the importance of remaining vigilant in confronting our own enactments that perpetuate epistemic injustice, moving toward practices that honor clients as knowers and uphold human dignity.

With this conceptual groundwork in place, Part II, 'Interrogating Epistemic Injustice in Social Work Practice with the Marginalized', invites readers to witness proactive efforts to critically reflect on and challenge epistemic injustice across diverse populations and contexts. Chapter 6, "Epistemic Injustice and Youth Mental Health: The Role of Social Workers in Promoting Epistemically Just Practice" (Greenblatt), explores how youth with mental health concerns experience testimonial and hermeneutical injustice in their interactions with the mental health system and with mental health professionals in Canada. By providing first-person accounts of youth-reported experiences of epistemic injustice and justice in mental health service settings, this chapter offers strategies for validating youth knowledge and embedding epistemic justice in clinical practice. Chapter 7, "Epistemic Injustice in the Context of Contested Diagnoses: Dismissal and Delegitimation in the Face of Complex Evidence" (Schön and Ringer), examines families in Sweden navigating contested diagnoses – such as Pediatric Acute-Onset Neuropsychiatric Syndrome (PANS) – to reveal how skepticism and systemic barriers undermine care. This chapter shares how children with PANS and their parents seek, claim, and validate their knowledge about the condition. The authors advocate for person-centered approaches that recognize patients and caregivers as legitimate knowers and underscore social workers' critical roles in fostering epistemic justice in health care. Chapter 8, "'Not Sick Enough': How Willful Hermeneutical Ignorance and Agential Testimonial Injustice Shape the Clinical Care of Street-Involved and Homeless Youth with Eating Struggles" (Hyland), exposes how biomedical models dominate the knowledge base around eating disorders. Correspondingly, these models can perpetuate epistemic erasure and punitive treatment practices for marginalized youth in Canada, such as street-involved homeless youth, especially when they seek support for eating struggles and body image distress. The chapter calls for trauma-informed, epistemically honoring care tailored to these vulnerable populations who are dealing with multiple axes of oppression. Chapter 9, "The Absence of Gypsy, Roma, and Traveller Voices and Knowledge in UK Health and Social Work" (Unwin and Bolton), addresses the historical and ongoing silencing of Gypsy, Roma, and Traveller communities, and outlines social work's complicity in this process. Highlighting contemporary social work initiatives, such as the Romani and Traveller Social Work Association, this chapter proposes co-productive and trauma-informed strategies to counter epistemic injustice against this marginalized group. Chapter 10, "Reflecting on the Epistemic Silencing of People in the Sex Trades Within the Anti-Trafficking Movement in the United States" (Hu), interrogates how the epistemic silencing of people, especially women, in the sex trades manifests as pre-emptive dismissal and objectification in the anti-trafficking movement. Drawing on an analysis of historical anti-trafficking policymaking and building upon community-based knowledge from the author's direct work with migrant women in anti-trafficking service provision, the author advocates for the recognition and intentional promotion of epistemic agency among people in the sex trades in anti-trafficking work. Chapter 11, "Stigma as a Fundamental Cause of Epistemic Injustice" (Vahedi), identifies stigma as a root cause of epistemic injustice. Drawing on case studies of forcibly displaced populations, people with disabilities, and LGBTQ+ communities, this chapter demonstrates how social devaluation undermines the capacity of marginalized groups to be recognized as knowers and leads to testimonial and hermeneutical harms. The author calls for structural interventions to dismantle stigma and promote inclusive knowledge production to advance epistemic justice and ensure equitable participation in global health research and policy. Chapter 12, "Unrecognized Truths: The Impact of Epistemic Injustice on LGBTQIA+ Communities" (Roman-Hampton and Iacono), examines how societal norms and biases perpetuate epistemic injustice against LGBTQIA+ individuals. The authors propose intersectional strategies, along with diversity, equity, and inclusion (DEI)-informed practices, to dismantle these barriers and foster belonging by highlighting the significance of education and practice in mitigating these injustices. This chapter offers pedagogical and professional practice approaches that strengthen LGBTQIA+ visibility and inclusion, and suggests directions for creating more inclusive environments, along with practical steps to engage more ethically with marginalized groups. Chapter 13, "Tracing the Layers of Epistemic Injustice in Social Constructions of Aging and Older Adults: Implications for Gerontological Social Work" (Syed), offers a conceptual analysis of the epistemological foundations informing major aging perspectives and their impact on the contemporary knowledge and discourse on aging. The author critically interrogates the dominant aging frameworks and media representations that marginalize older adults. This chapter advocates for new and reformed epistemic resources that amplify their voices and resist exclusionary narratives to diversify the knowledge base on aging through rich, alternative forms of epistemic representation by diverse older adults. Chapter 14, "Challenging Epistemic Injustice Through More Inclusive Discourse: A Standpoint from Service Users' Lived Experiences" (Beresford), invites critical reflection on potential "epistemic injustice within epistemic injustice" scholarship and practice, especially from the perspective of service users and disabled people. The author illustrates how epistemic injustice discourse developed, tracing its connections to earlier experiential movements, such as the disabled people's and psychiatric system survivor movements. This chapter proposes ways to advance a more inclusive narrative that centers lived experience to epitomize the original meaning of epistemic justice.

Across the chapters, the authors share the common construct of epistemic injustice, its subtypes (such as testimonial injustice, hermeneutical injustice, and contributory injustice), and related terms (such as epistemic objectification, epistemic agency, and willful hermeneutical ignorance). It is noteworthy to see how each scholar understands, makes meaning, augments, and applies each construct to various populations and fields in their own unique ways. This diversification of understanding epistemic injustice, we believe, broadens our understanding of the magnitude and scope of injustice. It also enriches our orientation and commitment toward fostering epistemic justice in various fields of the social work profession. We also want to note that different authors use different terminology throughout the book. In some chapters, authors use the phrase "people with disabilities" and in others, the term "disabled people" is used. Each contributor chose their terms with intentionality and purpose, reflecting their own lived experiences and ideological stances.

0.2 Toward Epistemic Justice in Social Work

As the chapters in this volume demonstrate, epistemic injustice is neither peripheral nor incidental; it is deeply woven into the fabric of social work practice, education, and research. Across diverse contexts, the book contributors reveal how testimonial and hermeneutical exclusions undermine the dignity and agency of the people and communities we claim to serve, and how dominant paradigms and institutional structures perpetuate these harms. Yet, the chapters also offer hopeful pathways: relational, participatory, and decolonial approaches that expand epistemic resources and center marginalized voices.

Several common themes emerge. First, epistemic justice is inseparable from social justice; without recognizing people as knowers, our commitments to equity and human rights remain incomplete. Second, advancing epistemic justice requires reflexivity and humility, necessitating an honest recognition and reflection on how professional norms and power hierarchies across teaching, practice, and research shape whose knowledge counts. Third, transformation is possible when social workers: embrace plural epistemologies and uplift diverse ways of knowing; cultivate testimonial sensibilities and honor lived experience; and proactively promote the epistemic agency of structurally silenced communities so that they can contribute as leaders in knowledge production.

This book invites readers to reflect deeply on how our professional roles and positionalities may sustain or resist epistemic injustice. As you engage with each chapter, we invite you to consider these guiding questions: How do our everyday practices, research agendas, and teaching methods reproduce dominant narratives or silence diverse voices? What strategies can we adopt to create epistemic spaces that amplify marginalized knowledge rather than erase it? How might intersectionality inform our efforts to achieve epistemic justice among diverse communities and across different settings? What structural changes are needed to dismantle stigma, bias, and systemic barriers that undermine epistemic agency and the development of diverse hermeneutical resources?

We also invite readers to join us – the editors and contributors – in brainstorming practical ways to advance epistemic justice in social work. As practitioners, we can adopt trauma-informed, culturally responsive, and participatory approaches that validate clients' lived experiences while practicing reflexivity to identify and disrupt epistemic harms in everyday interactions. As educators, we can embed epistemic justice into curricula by foregrounding marginalized knowledge systems, fostering critical dialogue, and equipping students with tools for anti-oppressive ethics and epistemic resistance. As researchers, we can employ inclusive and co-productive methodologies that challenge dominant knowledge production practices and prioritize community-driven epistemologies, while ensuring knowledge dissemination efforts that amplify voices historically silenced in academic and policy spaces.

> Ultimately, epistemic justice is not an abstract ideal but a practical necessity for advancing equity and human dignity. Epistemic justice is not optional, but the foundation of ethical, inclusive, and transformative social (justice) work. We hope this book serves as both a mirror to reflect the challenges within our profession, and a roadmap to chart pathways toward a more just, inclusive, and epistemically responsible social work.

References

Bell, K. (2014). Exploring epistemic injustice through feminist social work research. *Affilia: Journal of Women and Social Work*, *29*(2), 165–177.

Beresford, P. (2022). User involvement. In S. Torres & S. Donnelly (Eds.), *Critical gerontology for social workers* (pp. 161–176). Policy Press. https://doi.org/10.51952/9781447360476.ch011

Beresford, P., & Rose, D. (2023). Decolonising global mental health: The role of mad studies. *Cambridge Prisms: Global Mental Health*, *10*, e30. https://doi.org/10.1017/gmh.2023.21

Brady, M. S., & Fricker, M. (Eds.). (2016). *The epistemic life of groups: Essays in the epistemology of collectives*. Oxford University Press.

Catala, A. (2025). *The dynamics of epistemic injustice: Situating epistemic power and agency*. Oxford University Press.

Dotson, K. (2012). A cautionary tale: On limiting epistemic oppression. *Frontiers: A Journal of Women's Studies*, *33*(1), 24–47. https://doi.org/10.5250/fronjwomestud.33.1.0024

Fricker, M. (2007). *Epistemic injustice: Power and the ethics of knowing*. Oxford University Press.

Giladi, P., & McMillan, N. (Eds.). (2022). *Epistemic injustice and the philosophy of recognition*. Routledge.

Greenblatt, A., Lee, E., Ashcroft, R., & Muskat, B. (2024). Epistemic justice and injustice among youth with mental health concerns. *Children & Society*, *38*(4), 1039–1058.

Iacono, G. (2017). Epistemic injustice: Towards uncovering knowledge of bisexual realities in social work research. *Advances in Social Work*, *18*(2), 563–582.

Johnstone, M., & Lee, E. (2018). State violence and the criminalization of race: Epistemic injustice and epistemic resistance as social work practice implications. *Journal of Ethnic and Cultural Diversity in Social Work*, *27*(3), 234–252. https://doi.org/10.1080/15313204.2018.1474826

Johnstone, M., & Lee, E. (2021). Epistemic injustice and Indigenous women: Toward centring indigeneity. *Affilia: Journal of Women and Social Work*, *36*(3), 376–390. https://doi.org/10.1177/0886109920985265

Johnstone, M., & Lee, E. (2024a). A colonial legacy of cultural and epistemic genocide: Limited education access, family dislocation and premature death of Indigenous youth in Northern Ontario, Canada. *Whiteness and Education*, *9*(1), 36–50. https://doi.org/10.1080/23793406.2022.2136581

Johnstone, M., & Lee, E. (2024b). Repositioning our understanding of trauma through the lens of epistemic injustice and hermeneutic omissions. In C. Brown (Ed.), *Talking trauma talk: Resisting the politics of mainstream trauma discourse* (pp. 43–56). Routledge.

Kidd, I. J., Medina, J., & Pohlhaus G., Jr. (Eds.). (2017). *The Routledge handbook of epistemic injustice*. Routledge.

Koh, B. D. (2023). Epistemic ethics justice: A "radical imaginary." *Journal of Ethnic & Cultural Diversity in Social Work*, *34*(5–6), 286–294.

Lakeman, R. (2010). Epistemic injustice and the mental health service user. *International Journal of Mental Health Nursing*, *19*(3), 151–153. https://doi.org/10.1111/j.1447-0349.2010.00680.x

Lee, E. (2022). Fact construction and categorization in assessment: Cultivating epistemic justice and resistance in social work assessment. *Social Service Review*, *96*(3), 534–571. https://doi.org/10.1086/721273.

Lee, E., Greenblatt, A., Hu, R., Johnstone, M., & Kourgiantakis, T. (2022a). Developing a model of broaching and bridging in cross-cultural psychotherapy: Toward fostering epistemic and social justice. *American Journal of Orthopsychiatry*, *92*(3), 322–333. https://doi.org/10.1037/ort0000611

Lee, E., Greenblatt, A., Hu, R., Johnstone, M., & Kourgiantakis, T. (2022b). Micro-skills of broaching and bridging in cross-cultural psychotherapy: Locating therapy skills in the epistemic domain toward fostering epistemic justice. *American Journal of Orthopsychiatry*, *92*(3), 310–321. https://doi.org/10.1037/ort0000610

Lee, E., Herschman, J., & Johnstone, M. (2019a). How to convey social workers' understanding to clients in everyday interactions? Toward epistemic justice. *Social Work Education: International Journal*, *38*(4), 485–502. https://doi.org/10.1080/02615479.2018.1539070

Lee, E., Tsang, A. K. T., Bogo, M., Johnstone, M., Herschman, J., & Ryan, M. (2019b). Honoring the voice of the client in clinical social work practice: Negotiating with epistemic injustice. *Social Work*, *64*(1), 29–40. https://doi.org/10.1093/sw/swy050

Lund, R., Blackmore, J., & Rowlands, J. (Eds.). (2024). *Epistemic injustice: Governing research practice within academic knowledge production*. Routledge.

Maleku, A. (2025). Toward epistemic justice in social work research: (Re) imagining global knowledge production. *The British Journal of Social Work*, *55*(2), 613–620. https://doi.org/10.1093/bjsw/bcaf052

McGlynn, A. (2026). *Epistemic injustice: An introduction*. Routledge.

Medina, J. (2013). *The epistemology of resistance: Gender and racial oppression, epistemic injustice, and resistant imaginations*. Oxford University Press.

Miller, D. L. (1999). *Principles of social justice*. Harvard University Press.

Newbigging, K., Salla, A., Schön, U. -K., & King, C. (2024). Editorial: Addressing epistemic injustice in mental health. *Frontiers in Psychiatry*, *15*, 1–3. https://doi.org/10.3389/978-2-8325-4658-1

Russo, J., & Beresford, P. (2015). Between exclusion and colonisation: Seeking a place for mad people's knowledge in academia. *Disability & Society*, *30*(1), 153–157.

Santos, B. D. S. (2014). *Epistemologies of the South: Justice against epistemicide*. Paradigm Publishers and Routledge.

Sherman, B. R., & Goguen, S. (Eds.). (2019). *Overcoming epistemic injustice: Social and psychological perspectives*. Rowman & Littlefield.

Tang Yan, C. (2023). Narratives and discourses of epistemic justice, power, and oppression in community-based participatory research collaborations. *Journal of the Society for Social Work and Research, 16*(1), 61–90. https://doi.org/10.1086/725433

Wood, D. A. (2020). *Epistemic decolonization: A critical investigation into the anticolonial politics of knowledge*. Springer.

Chapter 1

Understanding the Epistemic Domain in Social Work to Foster Social Justice

Eunjung Lee

1.1 Introduction

The social work profession has long been characterized by a fundamental tension between two core imperatives: the pursuit of professionalization and the commitment to social justice. This dual mission is not merely a historical artifact but a persistent and contested feature of the field, shaping its identity, practices, and ontological, epistemological, and ethical foundations. Historically, social work in North America emerged at the intersection of two distinct traditions: the Charity Organization Societies, which emphasized individual casework and moral reform, and the Settlement House movement, which prioritized community engagement and structural change. This duality created a tension within the profession, where practitioners are often caught between the demands of helping individuals adjust to existing social structures and the imperative to challenge and transform those very structures (Abramovitz, 1998).

In contemporary discourse, this tension is often framed as a conflict between the *professional project* and the *social justice project* (Olson, 2007). The professional project seeks to establish social work as an accountable, evidence-based discipline with standardized practices and institutional legitimacy. This includes the development of formal credentials, adherence to regulatory frameworks, and alignment with nation states and their sanctioned models of service delivery. In contrast, the social justice project is rooted in a transformative vision that seeks to address systemic inequities, amplify marginalized voices, and advocate for structural change through progressive re-imagination and creative participatory approaches.

Critical scholars have argued that the professionalization of social work, while enhancing its status and influence, has at times diluted its commitment to social justice. Olson (2007) warns that social justice discourses risk becoming instrumentalized, serving primarily to legitimize the profession rather than to challenge entrenched power structures. Similarly, Abramovitz (1998) emphasizes that the process of professionalization can constrain the radical potential of social work by prioritizing technical expertise over sociopolitical engagement

DOI: 10.4324/9781003639046-2

for activism and advocacy. This enduring tension has significant implications for how social workers understand their roles, responsibilities, and ethical commitments. It also raises critical questions about the epistemological foundations of the profession: Whose knowledge counts? How is it validated? And, to what ends is it mobilized? These questions are particularly salient in light of contemporary discussions of epistemic injustice, which foreground the ways in which marginalized groups are systematically excluded from knowledge production and recognition.

To explore these issues, this chapter begins by examining the historical and contemporary debates surrounding social work's dual mission of professionalization and social justice, with particular attention to how evidence-based practice (EBP) has shaped and dominated the profession's epistemological foundations. The chapter then considers the scholarship on epistemic injustice, highlighting its precursors in both the antislavery movement and the work of Black feminists. It also details the contemporary contributions of Miranda Fricker (2007), Kristie Dotson (2012), and José Medina (2013), showing how these scholars unpack key constructs such as epistemic agency, testimonial injustice, hermeneutical resources, and epistemic resistance. Building on this foundation, the chapter explores how epistemic injustice intersects with social work's knowledge base and practices, and how these intersections impact the profession's social justice commitments. Finally, the chapter concludes by proposing a framework for epistemic responsibility and resistance, offering pathways for social workers to foster testimonial sensibilities and expand hermeneutical resources in practice, education, and research.

1.2 Social Work Professionalization and Social Justice within Social Work

Social justice is a core value in social work. The International Federation of Social Workers (IFSW, 2024) has a *Global Social Work Statement of Ethical Principles* that includes "promoting social justice" as a core principle (along with human rights, collective responsibility, and respect for diversities, all of which are central to the profession). Promoting justice is also a core value identified by the Canadian Association of Social Workers (CASW, 2024), which further outlines how social workers can enact these principles in practice. Similarly, the Canadian Association for Social Work Education (CASWE) places social justice in its mission statement, while its educational policies and accreditation standards identify 13 learning objectives within the curricular framework for the Bachelor of Social Work (BSW) and Master of Social Work (MSW) programs that focus on social justice (CASWE, 2021). The National Association of Social Workers (NASW, 2024) in the United States focuses on several pillars of social justice, including immigration and economic justice. Further, the *Educational Policy and Accreditation Standards* (EPAS) from the American

Council of Social Work Education (CSWE) adopted a competency-based education framework; among nine social work competencies listed in the 2022 EPAS, there are two directly related to social justice – "Competency 2: Advance Human Rights and Social, Racial, Economic, and Environmental Justice" (p. 9) and "Competency 3: Engage Anti-Racism, Diversity, Equity, and Inclusion (ADEI) in Practice" (p. 9). These two competencies urge social work educators to integrate social justice-oriented pedagogy into their curricula for social work students. Social work programs across the world are expected to include social justice explicitly and implicitly in their professional training. How to articulate and demonstrate the embodiment of social justice in social work practice, education, and research has been an ongoing focus of the social work profession more generally.

Despite this focus on social justice, however, the centering and highlighting of it in social work practice, education, and research have been, ironically and pervasively, ongoing challenges and struggles. At times, social justice has had to compete with a professionalization agenda, and more often than not, negotiate with pervasive Euro-centric, colonial, and neoliberal agendas of the nation states and institutions which operate outside of, but powerfully govern, the profession. These multiple conflicts have positioned social workers within arm's reach of these states and institutions, making social workers complicit in their wrongdoings, and concealing harms done to oppressed populations, all while diverting our minds and actions toward the other polarized end – professionalization (Brady et al., 2019; Butler-Warke et al., 2020; Wahab, 2020).

Debate surrounding the dual professional missions of social work – professionalization versus social justice – dates back to the early twentieth century. Abraham Flexner, an Assistant Secretary at the General Education Board of New York City, delivered a speech entitled "Is Social Work a Profession?" on May 17, 1915, at the National Conference of Charities and Correction in Baltimore; his answer was "No" (Flexner, 1915). Despite his own doubts about his competency to comment on this topic as a non-social work professional, Flexner's speech became a fulcrum, driving the social work field to focus on its professionalization efforts – from Mary Richmond's *Social Diagnosis* (1917) to the recent prevalence of evidence-based practice (EBP) scholarship – seeking to cultivate its own theoretical and epistemological legitimacy over the next century (Olson, 2007). More specifically, the profession pursued increased efficiencies and measurable outcomes rooted in positivistic, modern empiricism, and neoliberal ideologies (Butler-Warke et al., 2020). This professionalization led to the development of professional authority and power to position social work as an independent discipline of science. However, I think it also left two critical and interrelated imprints on the profession: first, it not only widened the gap between the dual missions of professionalization and social justice, but also silenced efforts for social justice in social work; and second, it narrowed the epistemic domain of the profession. To elaborate, I will use EBP as an example.

1.3 The Impacts of EBP on the Social Justice Mission and the Epistemic Domain of Social Work

In 1973, Joel Fischer published an article entitled "Is Case Work Effective? A Review" in *Social Work,* NASW's journal, critically reflecting on our own professional practice in terms of the effects of social work interventions. This paper ignited a long-standing debate on the dual missions of the profession, subsequently sparking a turn toward and boom in EBP in social work in the following decades, "creating and cementing a scientifically based profession" (Reid, 1994, p. 180). In reflection, Fischer's prediction in 1993 proved to be correct: "by the year 2000, empirically based practice – the new social work – may be the norm, or well on the way to becoming so" (p. 55). Indeed, there has been a burgeoning scholarship and wide interest in EBP in social work over the past several decades. Proponents include institutional actors, such as the NASW, which jointly hosted symposia with the National Institute of Mental Health (NIMH) to promote EBP integration (e.g., 2007 NIMH–NASW Symposium: NASW, 2025). Journals, such as *Research on Social Work Practice* and the *Journal of Evidence-Based Social Work* have served as key platforms for disseminating EBP scholarship. As Webb (2001) articulated, "the idea that good practice is ultimately to be delivered by research informed evidence which is underpinned by rigorous and effective methodologies is deeply appealing to our contemporary technocratic culture" (p. 58).

Along with the dominance and prevalence of EBP in social work, there have been critical reflections on and critiques of EBP from both its supporters and opponents, as well as scholars seeking to integrate both the benefits and limitations of EBP. For example, Gambrill (2016) highlights the tendency to value questionable EBP-oriented practices – especially in the name of professional authority – over client experiences, as well as a prevalent rhetorical use of EBP without substantive scientific rigor and fidelity as major concerns. Main critiques of EBP focus on its epistemic foundations which center positivistic conceptions of knowledge, valuing objective reality and rationality. EBP opponents note that this epistemic approach may fit well in the natural sciences and to some extent, medicine, but it is not in line with social work, with its social justice value-oriented, sociopolitical context-dependent, and practice-oriented approaches to knowledge creation and use (Olson, 2007; Webb, 2001). Challenges with applying EBP into practice (such as practitioners' time-constraints and their limited access to scientific findings) and concerns about reducing professional judgments and critical decision-making into narrowly rigid guidelines resulting in cookie-cutter practice have also been raised and contested (Lin, 2023). Nonetheless, the hierarchy of evidence which positions the randomized controlled trial at the top of the EBP ladder, along with the concerns about EBP's limited applicability to practice, are ongoing issues yet to be resolved. While recognizing both the importance and limitations of EBP, several scholars propose various means of including different ways of knowing to reconcile conflictual epistemological foundations, respect clients' experiences, and consider contextual factors (Drisko & Grady, 2015; Lin, 2023; Regehr et al., 2007).

Utilizing empirical evidence to develop a scientific knowledge base and to guide practical applications in practice is both timely and necessary for critically reflecting on our own work, moving the profession forward, and claiming our turf among other helping professions in the mental health, health, social, and policy fields. However, I am also concerned about the potential long-term impact or imprint of EBP discourse on the nature of the social work profession. By marking EBP and its underlying epistemological assumptions as the norm, studies not based on randomized controlled trials are discursively constructed as less rigorous, and at times, even degraded or dismissed. Webb (2001) argues that the problematic epistemological assumption of EBP is that reality is "out there" to be discovered and that its methods can translate critical concepts and complex human experiences into logical classifications; correspondingly, EBP's categorical yet limited variables, or so-called effective outcomes are then regarded as "inherently insuperable" (p. 58), especially when the EBP epistemology is allied with neoliberal ideas of new managerialism.

Both neoliberalism (e.g., management) and EBP (e.g., scientism) underscore effectiveness, forming what Webb called "scientific management" in social work where EBP "entraps professional practice within an instrumental framework… and manages social work within a technocratic framework of routinized operations" (p. 71). Rather than promoting professionalization, critical scholars argue that social work has been de-professionalized under neoliberalism, fragmenting social services and transforming social workers into technocrats or managers. These series of changes have been legitimized under the very claim of professionalization and the detrimental effects of neoliberal management on the social work profession have been well studied (see Brown et al., 2025; Butler-Warke et al., 2020; Dustin, 2007; Hyslop, 2018; Ferguson, 2007; Lee et al., 2019). Meanwhile, excluded are those clients who do not fit within controlled trial conditions, whose needs and experiences are not neatly measured or hypothesized to change in the short-term to show effective outcomes, and/or whose individual conditions are shaped by systemic inequities and oppressions that are not easily measured by experimental studies. Thus, Olson (2007) argues that by grounding its identity in pursuing professionalization, "social work actively works to avoid taking responsibility for the social justice project and… actively destroys the possibility to be part of creating a just world" (p. 62).

In fact, several studies found that after completing their degrees, social work students began using more codified and standard responses (Fazzi, 2016), were motivated to be compliant with rules and managerial procedures primarily (Whittaker & Reimer, 2017), and scored lower in critical thinking capacities compared to the general population (Sheppard et al., 2018). Others found that social work practitioners, once in the field, become more compliant with dominant discourses (e.g., the neoliberal ethos of individualism and managerialism), express punitive attitudes toward marginalized people rather than upholding social justice values (Fenton & Smith, 2019), and tend not to use the language of social justice (Hawkins et al., 2001). Altogether, critical scholars have underlined the insuperable conflict between professionalization (nested within the context of neoliberalism and scientific managerialism: e.g., EBP) and social justice ideals. What has happened, I argue, is that by highlighting professionalization, the very value of social justice is buried. When these dual (or even multiple) professional objectives are acknowledged, they become normalized, marked as plural aims with equal weight. As a result, real-world structural power imbalances are undermined, group-based privileges are overlooked, and oppressed groups are systemically marginalized. I echo Olson's (2007) proposal that professionalization should serve the goal of social justice. Further, I argue that the social work mission should be singular, not the conflictual dual. In this regard, considering the epistemic domain in social work, especially now, is critical.

1.4 Why Epistemic Domain in Social Work and Why Now?

While focusing on professionalization, scholars explicitly and implicitly change academic discourses on the very nature of epistemology – i.e., positioning positivism and modern empiricism as the norm, while discursively dismissing and degrading other ways of knowing, at times, acknowledging them only in a tokenistic manner. For example, Lin (2023) discusses the ideological and epistemological divides around EBP, noting that the arguments of EBP supporters (e.g., Gambrill, 2019) do not actually address skeptics' questions regarding multiple ways of knowing, and whether they are included within EBP epistemology. Lin articulates that "simply clarifying that EBP process includes client engagement is not equivalent to defining the *client's lived experiences as itself a form of legitimate knowledge*" (p. 189, italics added). In reviewing developments in empirically based practice perspectives in social work in a paper entitled "Empirically-Based Practice: The End of Ideology?", Fischer (1993) acknowledges the importance of epistemology as the basis for determining the methods and types of knowledge development and ultimately, the actual practice of the profession. However, he proceeds to argue that the ongoing epistemological debates in social work around "logical positivism versus other philosophies" are "actually a red herring" (p. 23). Here, Fischer discursively positions logical positivism as the epistemological norm/mainstream while otherizing the rest altogether (i.e., "other philosophies") and furthermore, explicitly erases the debate itself. As the paper title implies, the discursive erasure of the epistemological debate as "ideology" is notable, but most of the paper details and highlights EBP developments in social work, marking EBP as objective and non-ideological. This attitude, I argue, has resulted in shrinking the epistemic domain of the profession; by narrowing the epistemological framework into a positivistic, empirical approach, subjective experiences are neglected and structural and contextual factors ignored, thereby marginalizing multiple ways of knowing and silencing marginalized persons as knowers. That is why it is imperative to critically reflect on the epistemic domain of social work knowledge.

Critical scholarship – such as anti-oppressive practice (AOP) and antiracist, diversity, equity, and inclusion (ADEI) approaches, which value diverse and/or marginalized experiences that are often challenging to categorize or quantify – has long been characterized in our profession as "non-scientific" and "ideological", and this trend has intensified recently. For example, the backlash was noteworthy when the CSWE's 2022 EPAS explicitly included ADEI to describe core competencies in social work education. Similarly, we might also consider the recent special issue of the *Journal of Teaching in Social Work* (JTSW) entitled "Beyond Ideological Mandates: Critical Reflections on Anti-Racist and Anti-Oppressive Social Work Education" from March 2025. The issue editors, Lens et al. (2025), explain that the special issue call was inspired by the CSWE's elevation of "a singular 'means' in the form of antiracist and antioppressive social work practice" (p. 179) in the 2022 EPAS and the required implementation of these approaches in the curriculum for accreditation beginning in 2025. There were many valid points and useful recommendations made throughout the special issue, such as highlighting humanitarian approaches (Twis, 2025) and educating students to tackle complex social issues by employing evidence-based and competent social work practice (Gambrill, 2025; Thyer, 2025). However, I also found several themes unsettling and alarming.

Some scholars in the special issue characterize anti-racism and anti-oppressive approaches as being opposed to social work professional ethics, values, and scientifically guided interventions, contrasting them with scientific liberal approaches (Gambrill, 2025). Mills (2025) argues that "social work education has become skewed, prejudiced, and distorted in its obsessive fixation on race, ethnicity, sexual and gender inclusiveness, intersectional positionality, and the need to accuse White populations for all the ills of human suffering" (p. 403). Mills explicitly notes that "exposure to DEI principles actually increase agreement with fascist attitudes from Adolf Hitler" (p. 399). Similarly, others in the special issue describe critical scholarship on anti-racism and anti-oppressive approaches as "harmful social work ideologies" (Thyer, 2025, p. 303), an "injection of 'neoracism'" (Cantú, 2025, p. 194), "tribalism and hostility by their doctrine of divisiveness" (van Zyl, 2025, p. 357), "very different from the recognition of universal human rights" (p. 357), and even frame such approaches as "anti-liberal and anti-universal" (p. 354). This view creates a binary division within social work – as though individuals using critical approaches are harmful to the profession, oppose liberal ideas, and do not value universal human rights.

Many of us can sympathize with some authors in the special issue who shared vivid examples, especially personal experiences, of how social justice related theories and approaches become weaponized to oppress their personal experiences and divide people. Examples include the observation of grouping students by race and shaming of students (Gambrill), an agonizing journey as a MSW student (Jordan the Social Worker, pseudonym, 2025) or as a doctoral student (Cantú). However, discursively framing entire critical approaches alongside antisemitism and neoracism goes too far. This binary split is taken to the extreme when scholars describe anti-racism and anti-oppressive approaches as "elevating propaganda" (Cantú, 2025, p. 182), "the new orthodoxy" (Lens et al., 2025, p. 180), and – according to Mills (2025) – "philosophically unsophisticated, embarrassing, and naïve" (p. 409), "pejoratively as 'woke' ideology" (p. 396), "a cult of indoctrination" (p. 403), "not science but religion", "EDI Gospel", "antiracist snake oil", "toxicity", and "race hysteria" (p. 410). They add that such approaches are thus "an unethical form of pedagogy and clinical praxis that will likely damage members of society by producing incompetent mental health professionals" (Mills, 2025, p. 393), and pose "a direct threat to the wellbeing of clients" (Lens et al., 2025, p. 185). Finally, they propose that critical approaches be abandoned altogether, basically "cancelling" the whole of critical scholarship: "It must be openly challenged at all" (Mills, 2025, p. 399); "I reject this framing wholesale" (Twis, 2025, p. 455); "ought to be fully abandoned within social work" (pp. 460–461). In the editorial, Lens et al. (2025) describe "the deeply troubling presence of a chilling effect of ideological singularity within social work academia" (p. 179) in the responses to their call for papers. To me, witnessing the level of disrespect toward fellow social work scholars who engage with critical approaches, along with the wholesale rejection of ADEI and critical scholarship in one of social work education's flagship journals in 2025, is beyond belief and was itself chilling.

Within the political context of Trump's executive orders (EOs) from January 2025 banning social justice and diversity initiatives within the federal government and among federal contractors – such as EO No. 14151 (2025), *Ending Radical and Wasteful Government DEI Programs and Preferencing*, and EO No. 14173 (2025), *Ending Illegal Discrimination and Restoring Merit-Based Opportunity* – and given their ongoing threats to human rights, it is difficult to dismiss the implicit and explicit ontological stance and political views contained in the special issue. Most articles call for the abandonment of anti-racism, anti-oppressive, and DEI approaches, invoking the same logic underlying the EOs (i.e., characterizing critical approaches as ineffective or citing the need to save finite resources instead of allocating them to ADEI). For example, in this special issue, Strom and Lieberman (2025) write, "The wholesale mandate to center ADEI, by definition, means that other material, foci, and priorities are moved to the margins" (p. 389). Opposing the addition of ADEI mandates, Gambrill (2025) similarly comments, "…whenever something is added to a curriculum, something must be detracted. There is only so much time. What will be reduced? Thus, there are opportunity costs" (p. 277). Thyer (2025) similarly questions the Society for Social Work Research's annual convention prioritizing anti-oppressive and antiracist themes, which "appears to minimize the value of many other social work fields, theories and perspectives. Isn't mental health also really important?", and suggests that a critical discussion "silences the high-quality work in these areas which do not have such a focus" (p. 306).

These discourses – "how about others?" – are similar to the arguments made by some when the Black Lives Matter (BLM) movement became more prominent (i.e., "how about White lives?"). Significantly, the BLM movement does not ignore the lives of White, Indigenous, or other people of color, but highlights the systemic and daily occurrences of brutal violence against the Black community. Similarly, highlighting ADEI does not mean ignoring other important matters in social work, but rather encouraging us to center an ADEI lens and include a social justice mandate across social work education. According to their logic of "opportunity costs", it is really telling that ADEI, as a focus, was not featured until the 2022 EPAS, although social work has valued social justice since its inception.

While critiquing anti-racism and AOP as unscientific (Gambrill, 2025), most articles in the special issue argue that universal liberalism has progressed human rights. However, we must not forget the complicity of our profession in the harms done to many people – especially equity-deserving populations – in the name of science, help, and professionalism, approaches that are often disguised as civilized, neutral, universal, and liberal. One example, among many others, is eugenics and the sterilization of people who were disabled, mentally ill, Black, Indigenous, and people of color where social workers were actively involved (Kaniecki et al., 2023; Kennedy, 2008; Stubblefield, 2007). In invoking certain epistemic domains – such as "liberalism" and "scientific empiricism" – and/or using a neoliberal ethos of "opportunity costs", many authors in the special issue painstakingly prove their rationale for boldly proposing the total abandonment of social justice-related knowledge, practice, and activism. This answers the "why now" question: We must deeply engage with and consider the epistemic domain in social work so that we do not knowingly or unknowingly fall into silencing the social justice mission of our profession, or side with wrongdoing and complicity. Instead, we must endlessly ask, "Whose knowledge is recognized and respected while another's is discredited, silenced, and even oppressed?" Further, we must also interrogate how the result of this economy of epistemic power at both interpersonal and systemic levels impacts clients, social work practitioners/educators/researchers, and the social work profession as a whole.

1.5 In Search of Epistemic Inquiry to Re-Center Social Justice in Social Work

When I first encountered the concept of epistemic injustice at an international social work conference in 2014, I felt pure joy and excitement for various reasons. At that time, I struggled to articulate how systemic trauma and structural oppressions can injure one's fundamental experience of being human. An oft-cited social work emphasis on the person-in-environment (PIE), however, appeared inadequate to capture the deep entanglement of and complex layers between persons and systems. Since my scholarship has focused on social justice-oriented research, practice, and education, I have engaged with constructs such as social justice, cultural competence, AOP, critical feminist scholarship, anti-racism, Indigenous, and anti-colonial approaches to illustrate how systems can permit or limit the doing, becoming, and being of individuals. Some of these concepts – such as cultural competence and social justice scholarship – while crucial to social justice work, have been taken in various directions. At times, these critical ideas have lost their original noble foundations and become mainstreamed, interpreted as static, or even viewed as outdated (e.g., cultural competence), attracting few fresh perspectives (for an in-depth discussion, see Lee, 2024; Lee et al., 2024). Other bodies of scholarship – such as critical feminism, anti-racism, Indigenous, and anti-colonial approaches – have often encountered challenges and barriers in reaching students, practitioners, and researchers who are not explicitly interested in topics on sexual and gender diversity, racism, colonialism and/or Indigenous matters. I felt a strong need to identify the construct that speaks to all doing, learning/teaching, and researching in social work.

My program of research consists of three inter-related areas: (1) theorizing socially just cross-cultural social work; (2) translating anti-oppressive, social justice-oriented approaches into micro dyadic and institutional social work praxis; and (3) critically interrogating the profession of social work – its knowledge, power, practice, and education – as a site of investigation. Since all these themes center on social justice, when others ask about my research focus, I answer "social justice" either briefly or at length, depending on the context. More often than not, I am then asked again, "So what area are you researching?" as if social justice is not a legitimate research focus (i.e., "Since we all do social justice related work as social work scholars!"), or as if it has already been achieved (e.g., "Our profession has come a long way for that!"), so there is no need to focus on social justice as a distinct field of scholarly attention (Postan-Aizik et al., 2020). This experience is also echoed by many students who specialize in social justice and diversity in their advanced year of the MSW program at my institution. They shared their frustration when asked about this specialization, especially during interviews for field practicum sites. Also, my colleague and I observed a pattern in which some students immerse themselves in pursuing marketable clinical approaches that provide "recognizable certificates for lucrative employment options, while others engage with social justice-related work advocating for marginalized populations in the community and seeking employment at often low wage grassroots agencies" (Lee & Johnstone, 2024, p. 1385).

These experiences – demonstrating how social justice research and scholarships are sidelined and how social justice-related practice is undervalued, discredited, and silenced in individual interactions, institutional practice, academia (e.g., the JTSW special issue), and society (e.g., Trump's EOs) – are undeniably pervasive. Having worked in the United States and Canada as a social work practitioner, educator, and researcher for nearly three decades, I agree with critical scholars who assert that it is a myth to assume that "the profession's organizing value is social justice" (Olson, 2007, p. 46) or that our profession is radical in upholding social justice more than others (Brady et al., 2019). In recent years, we faced the COVID-19 pandemic, and now its endemic, along with an upsurge in anti-Asian racism; a heightened awareness of police and state brutality with the BLM movement; ongoing efforts and struggles for Truth and Reconciliation with Indigenous Peoples around the world; and emerging Madness and (Dis) ability Rights movements. Further, there have been some disturbing turns toward authoritarianism in the United States, Europe, and East and South Asia, where post-truth politics undermine social justice efforts and increase identity politics. In this current context, social work scholars urgently need to debunk the myths of our profession; critically analyze our historic and current complicity in structural oppressions and inequities; and rethink social justice matters and issues, including how to respond to and resist pervasive injustice locally and globally. I believe that it is particularly important at this time to re-examine how we understand our own profession and clients' experiences/knowledge, as well as to re-envision the concept of the "social" for social workers through the lens of the epistemic domain.

1.5.1 What Is Epistemic Injustice

Questioning the domain of epistemology in human interactions and social practices has a long history dating back to Aristotle (Fricker, 2007). In the modern era, scholars trace work on epistemic injustice – theorizing how marginalized speakers are dismissed and silenced due to unjust power relations and structural inequities – back to early feminist and critical race scholars, especially Black feminists (McWilliams, 2025). Isabella Baumfree, commonly known as Sojourner Truth, was a former enslaved woman who became an outspoken advocate for the abolition, temperance, and women's rights movements in the nineteenth century. Her famous speech, "Ain't I a Woman?" (Truth, 1851), delivered at the Women's Rights Convention in Ohio, vividly testified how Black women's experiences were ignored and dismissed, and that all women – Black or White – should be treated as equal to men. Truth, known as a historical precursor who crystallized intersectionality (Bickell, 2023; Crenshaw, 1989), speaking in 1867, observed the silence surrounding Black women's rights after the Fifteenth Amendment to the U.S. Constitution, noting that men – including Black men – appeared unable to hear women, especially Black women. She commented: "I was amused how men speak up for one another. They cannot bear that a woman should say anything about the man, but they will stand here and take up the time in man's cause" (cited in McWilliams, 2025, p. 3). This sharp observation, based on the experiences of Black women about 150 years ago, clearly conceptualized what we now understand as epistemic injustice. Since then, the inequity of epistemic power has been challenged in many areas, such as mad studies, the Hearing Voices Network, the critical disability movement, and Indigenous scholarship.

Within this ripe context, critical feminist scholar Miranda Fricker (2007) invigorated this construct in her book, *Epistemic Injustice: Power and the Ethics of Knowing*. She elaborated two types of epistemic injustice: *testimonial injustice* and *hermeneutical injustice*. Fricker (2007) argues that testimonial injustice occurs when a speaker's credibility as the knower of their own experiences is questioned and denied because of the hearer's bias and prejudice against the speaker's marginalized identity. Here, testimony does not refer to a statement made during legal proceedings, but rather the very inter/action of conveying one's knowledge/experience. Hermeneutical injustice occurs when individuals or communities are denied access to resources which can help them to make sense of their experiences. Consequently, they are unable to convey their understanding to others, preventing them from sharing their experiences and/or contributing to the construction of shared resources. Fricker's work has inspired many fields, including social work, medicine, psychiatry, education, correctional and legal systems, and others, encouraging both scholars and activists to engage deeply with the epistemic domain and the power dynamics embedded within them.

In explaining this noble construct, Fricker (2007) begins her book by discussing power, especially *social power*. She defines power as "a capacity on the part of social agents (individuals, groups, or institutions) exercised in respect to other social agents" (p. 10) and power-in-operation as "purely structural" (p. 11). Anderson (2012) similarly notes that testimonial injustice and exclusion become "structural when institutions are set up to exclude people without anyone having to decide to do so" (p. 166). Indeed, social work focuses on the "social" of workings, interrogating how structures shape and address social issues, rather than problematizing individuals for their suffering or blaming individual service providers and managers for systemic problems. I found Fricker's position closely aligned with the professional beliefs of many social workers: (1) acknowledging and respecting someone as a whole human being truly begins with good listening; (2) "being ethical" is "being political"; and (3) interrogating inter/actions between interlocutors as situated within structural conditions and social power. In social work, when we critically reflect on the workings of power in relation to access barriers, assessment criteria, and intervention selection, we cannot scrutinize individual clients, social workers, and/or agencies out of their contexts (such as funding bodies or regulatory state power). Other epistemic injustice scholars also highlight the multi-layered sites where social workers have been deeply engaged: "…social injustice is always embedded in a range of attitudinal, individual, institutional, and societal processes, and thus epistemic injustice is generated by a range of macro and micro social forces" (Dore, 2019, p. 378).

Thus, Lakeman (2010) rightfully argues that epistemic justice is the foundation of all forms of justice, including social justice.

1.5.2 Why Focus on Injustice rather than Justice?

I have been sharing my understanding of epistemic injustice in social work practice through presentations and publications for about a decade. I also incorporate the readings on epistemic injustice into my teaching in doctoral courses. Several students have asked why I focus on injustice rather than justice, at times commenting that, like other critical scholars, I highlight the "negative" aspects of social work rather than celebrating the "positive" (such as the progress achieved toward social justice despite ongoing wrongdoings and complicity, for example). This offers a good opportunity for me to invite them to consider decoupling the notion of injustice from justice and to critically reflect on what we mean by "justice" and "social justice", in particular.

Several critical scholars illuminate the paradoxical nature of justice-injustice, suggesting that the pursuit of justice does not automatically resolve injustice. Johnstone and Lee (2018) comment on this paradox in interrogating Canadian approaches to racial discrimination and exclusion – especially with respect to the Toronto police carding debate – despite a prevailing national pride in inclusive, multicultural policy discourse. The Metro Toronto Police established a practice known as "carding", which was intended to be a proactive crime-prevention policy. It involved randomly stopping and questioning persons and then recording the data onto a card. Proponents described this practice as "criminal profiling" (i.e., identifying criminal types, thus representing a legitimate police practice), and sought to differentiate it from "racial profiling". However, a recurring series of reports and analyses conducted by a national newspaper, the *Toronto Star*, highlighted the racial implications of carding beginning in 2002 and onward, igniting academic debates over criminal versus racial profiling. The debate centered on whose truth and experiences are credited and whose human rights are valued, respected, or ignored. According to their 2013 findings:

> the number of Blacks who were stopped and documented was higher than the actual number of young Black males (ages 15 to 24) who lived in Toronto. This was higher than the number of Blacks who were stopped and frisked by police in New York City, a situation that resulted in lawsuits and settlements.
>
> (Johnstone & Lee, 2018, p. 242)

The carding example underscores the significance of racial exclusion despite the discursive claims that Toronto is a multicultural city where diversity and inclusion are promoted.

Critical scholars argue that, although it is often assumed that inclusion offers a solution to exclusion, and that the two occupy opposite ends of a single continuum, this is not the case; in reality, they are separate phenomena (Galabuzi, 2008). The introduction of social inclusion measures – such as equal representation of race and gender in organizations and organizational diversity policies – does not necessarily address the issue of social exclusion (Ahmed, 2012; Richmond & Saloojee, 2005). These scholars highlight the importance of addressing pervasive social exclusion and discrimination that continue to be troubling social problems, in addition to efforts for inclusive policy and practice.

According to a recent conceptual review on the operationalization of social justice (Atteberry-Ash, 2023), the field of social work has relied heavily on John Rawls's definition of the concept, which highlights *distributive justice* – valuing fairness and equal access to resources, rights, and opportunities. In fact, his book, *A Theory of Justice* (1971), powerfully monopolized debates about justice not only in social work but also across disciplines for years. However, in the early 1990s, Iris Young shifted our attention from "justice" to the social forms of "injustice" to critically examine the very meaning of social justice. In *Justice and the Politics of Difference* (1990), Young critiques the limitations of a Rawlsian framework, suggesting that his liberal approach to justice is inadequate in explaining the contexts of social justice and fails to capture the conditions underlying social injustice. She identifies three reasons for its limitations: (1) its commitment to an "ideal" (liberal and rational) theory that diverts attention from the irrational and inequitable conditions that shape unjust political decisions; (2) its narrow focus on a distributive paradigm that reduces "rights" to "resources" and "goods", thus constraining the multifaceted construct of justice into economic terms; and (3) "its obfuscation of relations of power" (Aubert et al., 2019, p. 104), as if liberal assumptions are inherently impartial. Problematizing justice-as-distribution, Young highlights structures of injustice – such as domination, oppression, and exclusion – that were often overlooked in liberal frameworks. She broadens the focus beyond individuals to include the "social" – the systems, institutions, and social processes that produce harms at both local and global levels through large networks of persons and organizations that share varying degrees of responsibility, calling for a *social connection model of responsibility* (Young, 2006, 2011). Young's critique of the liberal ideal of justice and her focus on social responsibility underline the very nature of justice and how I understand "social justice": social justice is not a static, ideal state to be attained and "checked off" once complete, but an ongoing process/practice/action and forward-looking perspective/imagination which aims to bring about changes in the structural processes that created suffering in the first place. While we strive for "social justice-to-come" (Lee & Johnstone, 2024, p. 1393), we need to continue interrogating and addressing injustice in the past and present.

A recent edited volume, *Social Work's Histories of Complicity and Resistance,* also includes a collection of articles discussing our profession's role in some of the more troubling actions of the past when engaging with marginalized communities – for example, the Jewish community in Nazi Germany (Kuhlmann, 2023); the oppressive mental health system in England (Moth, 2023); the Black community in apartheid South Africa (Harms-Smith & Turton, 2023); and adoption social work practice in Ireland (McGettrick, 2023), among others. Critical social work scholars Vasilios Ioakimidis and Aaron Wyllie (2023), the editors of this volume, share their rationale for examining the plight of marginalized communities. They write that they have witnessed not only "truly inspiring empowering and emancipatory practice that kept fuelling our desire to be part of a 'profession worth fighting for'" but also "the impact of oppressive and often alienating social work practices" (p. 4) that persist in the present. I agree with their assertion that "[H]istories of oppression act as a constant reminder of the social catastrophes that can occur, should social workers stop defending and prioritising fundamental human rights" (p. 4). In this regard, pausing and reflecting critically on what social workers have done in their practice is not past-oriented but future-oriented. Similarly, considering epistemic domains – especially examinations of epistemic injustice in social workers' inter/actions with individuals, families, and communities – is not intended to "point fingers" at social work practices in the past. Rather, it aims to inform our future practice by learning from their – and our own – mistakes and remaining vigilant about how easily we may fall into epistemic oppression in our daily practice.

1.6 Epistemic Responsibilities for Social Workers: Ways of Fostering Epistemic Resistance

Epistemic injustice calls for epistemic resistance. Medina (2013) refers to *epistemic resistance* as a space in which multiple voices are encouraged, friction among opinions is fostered, and dissent is expected and respected with equity. In such a space, a range of viewpoints is valued over an insisted-upon consensus and/or a forced integration toward a single voice, as a unified perspective often reifies dominant views and, by default, privileges people with power. I think this is closely linked to social work values of respect for diversity and different perspectives. Both epistemic resistance and social work values urge practitioners, educators, and researchers to foster and respect multiple viewpoints in clinical encounters, community organizations, and policy contexts, as well as in teaching and mentoring students and conducting research with diverse participants and communities.

To respect others, we need to recognize them as knowers whose testimonies should be fairly and credibly valued. Foregrounding a client as an "epistemic agent" or "knower" of their own experiences is pivotal in social work. It means we truly recognize clients as "knowing subjects", not as "knowable objects" to be examined through a professional gaze, while respecting their epistemic authority. In this regard, it is critical for social work practitioners, educators, and researchers to develop *testimonial sensibilities*. To prevent testimonial injustice, Fricker (2007) argues that we must cultivate epistemic virtue – particularly, testimonial sensibilities – to counteract the influence of stereotypes and enable hearers to process testimony ethically and credibly. She writes that, "our idea of testimonial sensibility is an idea of a spontaneous critical sensitivity that is permanently in training and continuously adapting according to individual and collective experience" (p. 84). Here, I think Fricker highlights two key points: first, the significance of ongoing training so "the hearer can respond to the word of another with the sort of critical openness" (p. 84); and second, the social responsibility of fostering testimonial sensibility, since it "presents us with a rational capacity… which is inculcated in the subject through a process of socialization, which permits ongoing correction and adjustment in the light of experience and critical reflection" (p. 85). Since Fricker views testimonial injustice as fundamentally systemic, addressing it requires not only individual but also systemic and social efforts to change the prevalent prejudices and biases that underlie these habitual distorted judgments. When I reflect on this point, I am reminded of Young's (2011) concept of social responsibility: we all hold different degrees of responsibility for injustice and wrongdoings against marginalized individuals and groups; therefore, we must participate in efforts to mend harms *together*. In this regard, the chapters in Part I of this book examine how to take epistemic responsibility in reimagining social work ethics (Chapter 2), theories (Chapter 3), research (Chapter 4), and practice (Chapter 5).

While continuously fostering testimonial responsibility both individually and collectively within the social work community, it is also critical to identify, develop, and expand *hermeneutical resources* across multiple levels of social work practice, education, and research. Fricker (2007) describes a lack of hermeneutical resources at both the individual and systemic levels, which can prevent speakers from understanding and communicating their experiences to others. She underscores that hermeneutical injustice is a more fundamental form of injustice and urges us to consider "the gap in collective hermeneutical resources" (p. 151), which places marginalized people at an unfair disadvantage in comprehending and/or communicating their social experiences. Alternatively, Dotson (2012) argues that multiple hermeneutical resources exist and further suggests that marginalized groups possess hermeneutical resources of their own, which enable them to fully comprehend and communicate their experiences. However, hermeneutical injustice arises when a hearer – especially one with power – willfully refuses to recognize a speaker's hermeneutical resources, often belonging to a marginalized group, thereby systematically excluding that speaker from contributing to shared hermeneutical resources.

Given the complex situations encountered by social work practitioners, educators, and researchers, the accounts of both Fricker and Dotson could be useful for understanding and addressing the issues at hand. A common theme from both theorists' work is the significance of collective hermeneutical resources – namely, expanding these resources to address structural gaps (Fricker) and acknowledging, respecting, and valuing multiple sets of collective hermeneutical resources to address exclusion from and oppression in epistemic participation (Dotson). Throughout the chapters in Part II of this book, the authors discuss how to expand hermeneutical resources to fill a gap or to share epistemic authority so that hermeneutical resources may be shaped. For example, in Chapter 6, Greenblatt illustrates how her research provides a space for youth to "know" their own mental health experiences while also "shaping" shared epistemic authority to understand and make meaning of those experiences. Reading and reflecting on the experiences of people suffering from contested diagnoses (Chapter 7), street-involved homeless youth (Chapter 8), Gypsies, Romani, and Travellers (Chapter 9), people in the sex-trade (Chapter 10), people with HIV (Chapter 11), LGBTQIA+ communities (Chapter 12), older adults (Chapter 13), and service users (Chapter 14), the authors carefully conduct their analyses on the hermeneutical injustice which occurs due to collective hermeneutical resource gaps and dismissals, intentionally making friction and resisting against them. In so doing, the authors seek to create hermeneutical resources that allow us to expand our views, challenge habitual perceptions, and question pervasive dominant perspectives on these marginalized populations. I hope this book may also inspire readers to reflect on how to foster testimonial sensibility and hermeneutical resources for the clients and communities we serve.

References

Abramovitz, M. (1998). Social work and social reform: An arena of struggle. *Social Work, 43*(6), 512–526. https://www.jstor.org/stable/23717767

Ahmed, S. (2012). *On being included: Racism and diversity in institutional life*. Duke University Press.

Anderson, E. (2012). Epistemic justice as a virtue of social institutions. *Social Epistemology, 26*(2), 163–173. https://doi.org/10.1080/02691728.2011.652211

Atteberry-Ash, B. E. (2023). Social work and social justice: A conceptual review. *Social Work, 68*(1), 38–46. https://doi.org/10.1093/sw/swac042

Aubert, I., Garrau, M., & de Latour, S. G. (2019). Iris Marion Young and responsibility. *Critical Horizons, 20*(2), 103–108. https://doi.org/10.1080/14409917.2019.1596200

Bickell, L. (2023). The epistemological asymmetry of framing "woman" via US women's rights pioneers. *Hypatia, 38*(4), 683–706. https://doi.org/10.1017/hyp.2023.84

Brady, S. R., Sawyer, J., & Perkins, N. H. (2019). Debunking the myth of the 'radical profession': Analysing and overcoming our professional history to create new pathways and opportunities for social work. *Critical and Radical Social Work, 7*(3), 315–332. https://doi.org/10.1332/204986019X15668424193408

Brown, C., Baines, D., Doll, K., & Johnstone, M. (2025). The impact of neoliberalism on social justice-based social work practice in mental health. *Canadian Social Work Review, 42*(1), 71–92.

Butler-Warke, A., Yuill, C., & Bolger, J. (2020). The changing face of social work: Social worker perceptions of a neoliberalising profession. *Critical and Radical Social Work, 8*(1), 59–75. https://doi.org/10.1332/204986019X15633629305936

Canadian Association for Social Work Education. (2021). *CASWE-ACFTS educational policies and accreditation standards for Canadian social work education.* https://caswe-acfts.ca/wp-content/uploads/2021/08/EPAS-2021-1.pdf

Canadian Association of Social Workers. (2024). *CASW code of ethics, values and guiding principles.* https://www.casw-acts.ca/files/attachements/CASW_Code_of_Ethics_Values_Guiding_Principles_2024.pdf

Cantú, A. (2025). A case for intellectual humility, tolerance, and humanism: Perspectives from an ethnically "minoritized" graduate student. *Journal of Teaching in Social Work, 45*(2), 188–215.

Council of Social Work Education. (2022). *The 2022 educational policy and accreditation standards.* https://www.cswe.org/accreditation/policies-process/2022epas/

Crenshaw, K. (1989). Demarginalizing the intersection of race and sex: A Black feminist critique of antidiscrimination doctrine, feminist theory, and antiracist politics. *University of Chicago Legal Forum, 1989*(8), 139–67.

Dore, I. (2019). Doing knowing ethically – where social work values meet critical realism. *Ethics and Social Welfare, 13*(4), 377–391. https://doi.org/10.1080/17496535.2019.1598458

Dotson, K. (2012). A cautionary tale: On limiting epistemic oppression. *Frontiers: A Journal of Women's Studies, 33*(1), 24–47. https://doi.org/10.5250/fronjwomestud.33.1.0024

Drisko, J. W., & Grady, M. D. (2015). Evidence-based practice in social work: A contemporary perspective. *Clinical Social Work Journal, 43*(3), 274–282. https://doi.org/10.1007/s10615- 015- 0548-z

Dustin, D. (2007). *The McDonaldization of social work.* Routledge.

Executive Order No. 14151, 3 C.F.R. (2025). https://www.federalregister.gov/documents/2025/01/29/2025-01953/ending-radical-and-wasteful-government-dei-programs-and-preferencing

Executive Order No. 14173, 3 C.F.R. (2025). https://www.federalregister.gov/documents/2025/01/31/2025-02097/ending-illegal-discrimination-and-restoring-merit-based-opportunity

Fazzi, L. (2016). Are we educating creative professionals? The results of some experiments on the education of social work students in Italy. *Social Work Education, 35*(1), 89–99.

Fenton, J., & Smith, M. (2019). "You can't say that!": Critical thinking, identity politics and the social work academy. *Societies, 9*(3), 1–14. https://www.mdpi.com/2075-4698/9/4/71.

Ferguson, I. (2007). *Reclaiming social work: Challenging neo-liberalism and promoting social justice.* SAGE.

Fischer, J. (1973). Is Case Work Effective? A Review. *Social Work, 18*(1), 5–20. http://www.jstor.org/stable/23712511

Fischer, J. (1993). Empirically based practice: The end of ideology? In M. Bloom (Ed.), *Single-system designs in the social services: Issues and options for the 1990s* (pp. 21–39). Haworth.

Flexner, A. (1915). Is social work a profession? *Social Welfare History Project.* https://socialwelfare.library.vcu.edu/social-work/is-social-work-a-profession-1915/

Fricker, M. (2007). *Epistemic injustice: Power and the ethics of knowing*. Oxford University Press.

Galabuzi, G. E. (2008). Daily struggles: The deepening racialization and feminization of poverty in Canada. In M. Wallis & S. -M. Kwok (Eds.), *Social exclusion: Socio-economic and political implications of the racialized gap* (pp. 81–94). Canadian Scholars Press Inc.

Gambrill, E. (2016). Is social work evidence-based? Does saying so make it so? Ongoing challenges in integrating research, practice and policy. *Journal of Social Work Education, 52*(Suppl. 1), S110–S125. https://doi.org/10.1080/10437797.2016.1174642

Gambrill, E. (2019). The promotion of avoidable ignorance in the British Journal of Social Work. *Research on Social Work Practice, 29*(4), 455–469. https://doi.org/10.1177/1049731518763953

Gambrill, E. (2025). How strategic ignorance contributes to missed opportunities to enhance social justice. *Journal of Teaching in Social Work, 45*(2), 276–297.

Harms-Smith, L. & Turton, Y. (2023). Colonial and apartheid South Africa: Social work complicity and resistance. In V. Ioakimidis & A. Wyllie (Eds.), *Social work's histories of complicity and resistance: A tale of two professions* (pp. 73–94). Policy Press. https://doi-org.myaccess.library.utoronto.ca/10.56687/9781447364306-008

Hawkins, L., Fook, J., & Ryan, M. (2001). Social worker's use of the language of social justice. *British Journal of Social Work, 31*(1), 1–13.

Hyslop, I. (2018). Neoliberalism and social work identity. *European Journal of Social Work, 21*(1), 20–31.

International Federation of Social Workers (IFSW). (2024). *Global social work statement of ethical principles*. https://www.ifsw.org/global-social-work-statement-of-ethical-principles/

Ioakimidis, V., & Wyllie, A. (Eds.). (2023). *Social work's histories of complicity and resistance: A tale of two professions*. Policy Press. https://doi.org/10.56687/9781447364306

Johnstone, M., & Lee, E. (2018). State violence and the criminalization of race: Epistemic injustice and epistemic resistance as social work practice implications. *Journal of Ethnic & Cultural Diversity in Social Work, 27*(3), 234–252. https://doi.org/10.1080/15313204.2018.1474826

Jordan the Social Worker (pseudonym). (2025). Out of balance: Moving beyond anti-racist & anti-oppressive education. *Journal of Teaching in Social Work, 45*(2), 216–232. https://doi.org/10.1080/08841233.2025.2469538

Kaniecki, M., Novak, N. L., Gao, S., Lira, N., Treviño, T. A., O'Connor, K., & Stern, A. M. (2023). Racialization and reproduction: Asian immigrants and California's twentieth-century eugenic sterilization program. *Social Forces, 102*(2), 706–729. https://doi.org/10.1093/sf/soad060

Kennedy, A. C. (2008). Eugenics, "degenerate girls," and social workers during the progressive era. *Affilia, 23*(1), 22–37.

Kuhlmann, C. (2023). Social services in Nazi Germany and the role of social workers between complicity and rare resistance. In V. Ioakimidis & A. Wyllie (Eds.), *Social work's histories of complicity and resistance: A tale of two professions* (pp. 97–108). Policy Press. https://doi-org.myaccess.library.utoronto.ca/10.56687/9781447364306-009

Lakeman R. (2010). Epistemic injustice and the mental health service user. *International Journal of Mental Health Nursing, 19*(3), 151–153. https://doi.org/10.1111/j.1447-0349.2010.00680.x

Lee, E. (2024). Unsettling discourses of cross-cultural social work practice: Moving from theoretical debates to interrogating and transforming praxis. *British Journal of Social Work, 54*(3), 905–921. https://doi.org/10.1093/bjsw/bcad163

Lee, E., & Johnstone, M. (2024). Critical pedagogy to promote critical social work: Translating social justice into direct social work practice. *Social Work Education: International Journal, 43*(5), 1384–1397. https://doi.org/10.1080/02615479.2023.2185602

Lee, E., Johnstone, M., Kourgiantakis, T., Hu, R., & Leung, V. (2024). Praxis of cross-cultural social work practice (CCSWP): A critical discourse analysis of graduate student and faculty perspectives on cultural competence and relevant constructs. *Qualitative Social Work, 23*(3), 458–481. https://doi.org/10.1177/14733250231153047

Lee, E., Tsang, A. K. T., Bogo, M., Johnstone, M., & Herschman, J. (2019). Clients and case managers as neoliberal subjects? Shaping session tasks and everyday interactions with severely mentally ill (SMI) clients. *European Journal of Social Work, 22*(2), 238–251. https://doi.org/10.1080/13691457.2018.1529662

Lens, V., Farber, N., & Fram, M. (2025). Editorial. *Journal of Teaching in Social Work, 45*(2), 179–187.

Lin, N. (2023). Moving beyond either-or debates: An invitation to reconcile ideological divides in evidence-based practice. *Clinical Social Work Journal, 51*, 188–197. https://doi.org/10.1007/s10615-023-00863-5

McGettrick, C. (2023). Adoption social work practice in Ireland: Critical reflections on present-day injustices. In V. Ioakimidis & A. Wyllie (Eds.), *Social work's histories of complicity and resistance: A tale of two professions* (pp. 261–277). Policy Press. https://doi-org.myaccess.library.utoronto.ca/10.56687/9781447364306-020

McWilliams, E. C. (2025). Testimonial injustice and the nature of epistemic injustice. In K. Sylvan, E. Sosa, J. Dancy, & M. Steup (Eds.), *The Blackwell companion to epistemology* (3rd ed.). Wiley-Blackwell. https://philpapers.org/archive/MCWTIA-2.pdf

Medina, J. (2013). *The epistemology of resistance: Gender and racial oppression, epistemic injustice, and the social imagination.* Oxford University Press. https://doi.org/10.1093/acprof:oso/9780199929023.001.0001

Mills, J. (2025). A critique of antiracist ideology. *Journal of Teaching in Social Work, 45*(2), 393–415.

Moth, R. (2023). Institutionalisation and oppression within the mental health system in England: Social work complicity and resistance. In V. Ioakimidis & A. Wyllie (Eds.), *Social work's histories of complicity and resistance: A tale of two professions* (pp. 165–182). Policy Press. https://doi-org.myaccess.library.utoronto.ca/10.56687/9781447364306-014

National Association of Social Workers. (2024). *Social justice.* https://www.socialworkers.org/Advocacy/Social-Justice

National Association of Social Workers. (2025). *Evidence-based practice.* https://www.socialworkers.org/News/Research-Data/Social-Work-Policy-Research/Evidence-Based-Practice

Olson, J. J. (2007). Social work's professional and social justice projects: Discourses in conflict. *Journal of Progressive Human Services, 18*(1), 45–60. https://doi.org/10.1300/J059v18n01_04

Postan-Aizik, D., Shdaimah, C. S., & Strier, R. (2020). Positioning social justice: Reclaiming social work's organising value. *British Journal of Social Work, 50*(6), 1652–1668. https://doi.org/10.1093/bjsw/bcz111

Rawls, J. (1971). *A theory of justice*. Harvard University Press.

Regehr, C., Stern, S., & Shlonsky, A. (2007). Operationalizing evidence-based practice: The development of an institute for evidence-based social work. *Research on Social Work Practice, 17*(3), 408–416.

Reid, W. J. (1994). The empirical practice movement. *Social Service Review, 68*(2), 165–84.

Richmond, M. E. (1917). *Social diagnosis*. Russell Sage Foundation.

Richmond, T., & Saloojee, A. (Eds.). (2005). *Social inclusion: Canadian perspectives*. Fernwood Publishing.

Sheppard, M., Charles, M., Rees, P., Wheeler, M., & Williams, R. (2018). Inter-personal and critical-thinking capabilities in those about to enter qualified social work: A six-centre study. *British Journal of Social Work, 48*(2), 1855–1873. https://doi.org/10.1093/bjsw/bcx143.

Strom, K., & Lieberman, A. (2025). Deck chairs on the Titanic. *Journal of Teaching in Social Work, 45*(2), 384–392.

Stubblefield, A. (2007). "Beyond the pale": Tainted whiteness, cognitive disability, and eugenic sterilization. *Hypatia, 22*(2), 161–181.

Thyer, B. A. (2025). Mandated ideologies are harmful to social work practice and research. *Journal of Teaching in Social Work, 45*(2), 298–316.

Truth, S. (1851). Ain't I a woman? In P. C. McKissack & F. McKissack (Eds.), *Sojourner Truth: Ain't I a woman?* (pp. 99–115). Scholastic.

Twis, M. (2025). "So, you're a Zionist?": Reflections on philosophy, theory, ethics and values in social work education and social justice advocacy. *Journal of Teaching in Social Work, 45*(2), 441–472.

van Zyl, M. A. (2025). A philosophical liberal critique of the postmodern definition of social justice in social work education competency standards. *Journal of Teaching in Social Work, 45*(2), 348–361.

Wahab, S. (2020). Teaching social justice in dangerous times: Practices of hope. *Social Work and Policy Studies: Social Justice, Practice and Theory, 3*(2), 1–13. https://socialwork.ubc.ca/news/teaching-justice-in-dangerous-times-practices-of-hope/

Webb, S. A. (2001). Some considerations on the validity of evidence-based practice in social work. *British Journal of Social Work, 31*(1), 57–80.

Whittaker, L., & Reimer, E. (2017). Students' conceptualisations of critical reflection. *Social Work Education, 36*(8), 946–958. https://doi.org/10.1080/02615479.2017.1383377.

Young, I. M. (1990). *Justice and the politics of difference*. Princeton University Press.

Young, I. M. (2006). Responsibility and global justice: A social connection model. *Social Philosophy and Policy Foundation, 23*(1), 102–130.

Young, I. M. (2011). *Responsibility for justice*. Oxford University Press.

Part I

Imagining Social Work Ethics, Theory, Research, and Practice toward Epistemic Justice

Chapter 2

Epistemic Ethics Justice in Social Work

Developing a Critical Consciousness

Bibiana D. Koh

2.1 Introduction: Commitment to Social Justice

In North America, both the National Association of Social Workers (NASW, 2017) and Canadian Association of Social Workers (CASW, 2024) *Codes of Ethics* underscore their commitment to social justice. In NASW's *Code of Ethics* (2021), social justice is one of six core values and is accompanied by the ethical principle that "Social workers challenge social injustices". In CASW's *Code of Ethics* (2024), "promoting social justice" is one of seven core values. Both are consistent with Principle 3 of the International Federation of Social Workers' (IFSW) (2018) *Global Statement of Ethical Principles*: promoting social justice.

Yet, neither professional code clearly defines the concept of justice. The NASW's (2021) *Code* does not operationalize justice (Atteberry-Ash, 2023). Likewise, while Value 2 of the CASW's *Code* (2024) focuses on "promoting social justice" through Guiding Principles 2.1 through 2.4, "justice" itself is not defined. While the *13 Grand Challenges for Social Work* (GCSW: 2019, 2020) outline a cluster of initiatives aimed at creating a "just society", this cannot be established without a clear definition of justice. Moreover, an objective to "achieve equal opportunity and justice" (Uehara et al., 2013) can only be advanced with a clear operationalization. Ultimately, a commitment to social justice cannot be promoted without clearly understanding the theoretical underpinnings of social justice in social work.

North American educational accreditation standards also underscore the importance of social justice. Specifically, both the Canadian Association for Social Work Education (CASWE)'s and the Council on Social Work Education (CSWE)'s respective Educational Policies and Accreditation Standards (EPAS) (CASWE, 2021; CSWE, 2022) include commitments to justice in both their program mission statements[1] and practice standards (CASWE, 2021; CSWE, 2022). Both also situate social justice in the context of oppression or anti-oppression. CASWE's (2021) EPAS defines social justice as follows:

DOI: 10.4324/9781003639046-4

> Social justice (AS 1.1.1): For the purposes of these Educational Policies and Accreditation Standards social justice is broadly understood as ideas, values, processes, policies, and practices that advance the vision of CASWE-ACFTS.
>
> (p. 22)

It continues with the following:

> CASWE-ACFTS envisions an economically, socially, environmentally just world based on humanitarian and democratic ideals that demonstrate respect for the worth, agency, and dignity of all beings. Achieving such a vision calls for critical analysis of power relations, the dismantling of inequitable social structures and solidarity with populations that experience poverty, oppression, and exploitation.
>
> (p. 23)

CSWE's (2022) EPAS does not explicitly define social justice. Instead, it situates justice in the context of several core social work values – adding "an anti-racist and anti-oppressive perspective" – and "a quest for social, racial, economic, and environmental justice" (p. 14).

Taken together, there is a clear professional mandate for a commitment to social justice in the context of anti-oppressive practice; they mutually enforce democratic and humanitarian ideals in the context of social welfare. A clear definition of justice and a cogent conceptualization will strengthen this mandate. While this chapter will later expound on the importance of *praxis* (versus practice), social justice will first be defined, the limitations of these definitions next outlined, and finally, clear alternatives to fill the conceptual gaps presented.

2.1.1 Defining Social Justice

An analysis of social justice in social work revealed that the concept was largely defined by the philosophy of John Rawls, Amartya Sen, and Martha Nussbaum (Atteberry-Ash, 2023). All three philosophers view justice as part of a social contract. This is important in the context of the social contracts among social workers, those whom we serve, and the serving institutions (per Sen, 2012, "ideal social institutions", p. 101). Such a social contract also denotes a collaborative, reciprocal relationship committed to seeking justice.

If justice in social work is largely conceptualized in the theoretical frameworks of Rawls, Sen, and Nussbaum, it is important to have a basic understanding of their viewpoints.[2] For Rawls (2001), justice is rooted in the principles of fairness and equality. Fairness involves the equal distribution of goods, while equality is about equal rights to "basic liberties" (Rawls, 2001, p. 375). Fairness is guided and tested by the objectivity inherent in the "veil of ignorance", which suggests that we cannot fully know either our own identities or those of others. For Rawls (2001), the equal distribution of goods is meant to benefit those with fewer social and economic resources.

In response to Rawls's focus on goods and resources, Sen (2009) proposed an alternative: the distribution of capabilities – what he called "the freedom-based capability approach" (p. 231). Capabilities are either distributed or shared. For Sen, there is a movement away from the fairness espoused by Rawls to a consideration of capabilities from an equity lens with a focus on "what people are actually able to do and to be" (Nussbaum, 2003, p. 33). Rather than allocating equal resources per Rawls (see Nussbaum, 2003), capabilities (e.g., goods and tools) are distributed based on equity to provide equal access for all (Atteberry-Ash, 2023). Sen's conceptual shift from equality to equity is an important distinction in the consideration of social justice in social work. Capabilities are also regarded as necessary to achieving the political goal of social justice in the social contract and are actively crafted by the individual via free will (Nussbaum, 2002).

For both Sen and Nussbaum, gender justice is also important. Nussbaum (2002, 2003), for instance, introduces care to her definition of the capabilities approach. Nussbaum (2002) inquires not only about women's capabilities but also their satisfaction. These additions are important because they highlight human relationships (Shah et al., 2023) in both social and gender justice; capabilities and satisfaction in the context of human relationships are even more important when considering epistemic injustices and suffering.

Despite these important contributions by Rawls, Sen, and Nussbaum, none of the philosophical underpinnings of social justice (per Rawls, Sen, or Nussbaum) offer a clear appraisal of structural power, which is an important component of anti-oppressive practice. As an ideal theorist[3] Rawls's (2001) theory of justice asks us to view justice with neutrality "behind a veil of ignorance" (p. 363). Sen (2012) focuses on both examples of injustices (e.g., famines, etc.) and "just institutions" (p. 103); he does not examine the role of structural power in either. Similarly, while Nussbaum (2002) comes closest to examining power vis-à-vis domination, her gender justice also falls short of a structural power analysis of inequalities in her capabilities approach. In fact, one might argue that her discussion of women lies behind a Rawlsian "veil of ignorance" because there is no racial analysis of structural discrimination and power in her gender justice.

Taken together, these philosophical limitations (i.e., not critiquing justice from a power lens) fall short of how justice should be operationalized in social work. Power, justice, and oppression are intertwined. To combat the "five faces of oppression" (violence, exploitation, marginalization, powerlessness, and cultural imperialism per Young, 2009, p. 55), justice is needed. Toward this end, the inclusion of an analysis of justice through the lens of structural power is particularly important in the context of operationalizing justice in anti-oppressive social work ethics.

Feminist philosopher Fricker's (2007) conceptualization of testimonial and hermeneutical epistemic injustices can partially fill these philosophical gaps. Mills's (2017) non-ideal justice theory rounds out the gaps needed to operationalize epistemic justice. Specifically, his analysis of racist ideology in the context of "epistemic exclusions" (Fricker, 2017, p. 109) illuminates the imperfections of justice (and non-ideal institutions) in practice (Mills, 1997). Taken together, both Fricker's (epistemic injustices) and Mills's (epistemic exclusions) justice conceptualizations fill the conceptual gaps left by Rawls, Sen, and Nussbaum.

This chapter next focuses on how Fricker's (2007) concepts of testimonial and hermeneutical epistemic injustices are central to our profession's commitment to promoting a just society (per the GCSW, 2019, 2020) in the context of anti-oppressive ethics praxis. In describing justice, two specific kinds of epistemic *in*justices (testimonial and hermeneutical) will be defined. Examples of epistemic injustices in social work ethics will be discussed in the context of anti-oppressive ethics.

2.1.2 *Key Terminology*

Given that the premise of this chapter centers on a need for conceptual clarity and operationalization of justice in anti-oppressive social work ethics, this section will clearly define the following terms: social work ethics, ethics praxis, and anti-oppressive ethics. Thereafter, epistemic injustices will be discussed.

Social Work Ethics. Social work ethics are defined as a body of institutions[4] including licensing and regulatory bodies and ethics mandates. Examples of licensing bodies include the State Boards of Social Work in the United States and the British Columbia College of Social Workers (BCCSW) in Canada. The Association of Social Work Boards (ASWB) oversees social work licensing exams in North America. Examples of North American accrediting bodies include the Council for Social Work Education and the Commission on Accreditation. Examples of ethical mandates include codes of ethics (e.g., NASW's and CASW's *Codes of Ethics*) and state/provincial statutes and legislation.

Ethics Praxis. This chapter distinguishes ethics *practice* from ethics *praxis*. Praxis is defined as a "theory of change" (Roberts, 2019, p. 6) – achieved through iterative cycles of theoretical engagement and reflective practice to achieve transformation and liberation (Freire, 1970). In this chapter, there are two kinds of praxes: anti-racist and anti-oppressive. The first kind, anti-racist, has four goals: (1) to know oneself, (2) to make racism and systemic oppression explicit, (3) to challenge the denial of racism and oppression, and (iv) to transform society via praxis (Kendi, 2019; Lynch et al., 2017; Utt & Tochluk, 2020). The second kind, anti-oppressive, also has four goals: (1) to identify social differences, (2) to use critical reflection (i.e., reflexivity), (3) to analyze the historical context of social systems/infrastructures, and (4) to analyze power (Clifford & Burke,

2005). BSnti-racism and anti-oppression make up, inform, and are inherently embedded in ethics praxis. Anti-racist praxis should strive for anti-oppressive goals. Both praxes inform social justice and anti-oppressive ethics.

To promote change, both praxes are operationalized as anti-racist and anti-oppressive ethics practices that include ethical analysis, ethical deliberation, ethical decision-making, and the application of ethics mandates (e.g., codes of ethics). Reinforcing the notion of praxis as change, Haaz (2019) argues for the importance of disrupting the status quo to move toward "initiative and empowerment" (p. 268).

Critical Consciousness. Critical consciousness is the discovery vis-à-vis self-reflection that one is engaging in oppressive practices. Freire (1970) emphasizes the importance of educating the oppressor. This may include raising our *social consciousness* (per Shelby, as cited in Mills, 2017) which includes these following forms : (1) widely shared beliefs, (2) networks that explain or justify power, (3) collective perspectives that are "common sense", and (4) significantly impact interactions and institutions (p. 103).

This chapter argues that accessible language is inherently anti-racist and anti-oppressive. Using accessible, everyday language can break down barriers between academia (those with high levels of privilege and education) and the general population (those with varying levels of education). Due to educational inequities, language is intertwined with race and educational levels (Inoue, 2021) and therefore, structural racism. Indeed, language biases are embedded in issues of power, domination (Bourdieu, 1993; Fairclough, 1989), and race (Inoue, 2021). In recognition of this power, accessible terminology (e.g., ethics practice as defined by the two praxes) will be used in this chapter while also informing the reader of how epistemic injustices are defined in the literature.

Epistemic Injustices. Epistemics involves knowledge and ways of knowing; it is linked to the philosophical branch of epistemology. Epistemic *in*justices are inherently discriminatory (Fricker, 2017). They happen when people are discriminated against as "knowers" (Stock et al., 2023) – meaning people who hold knowledge. Two kinds of epistemic injustices – testimonial and hermeneutical injustice – are situated in the contexts of structural power and domination (Fricker, 2007).

Testimonial injustice is one kind of epistemic injustice (Fricker, 2007; Byskov, 2021) whereby a "knower" (i.e., an individual) may be questioned or discredited (Lee, 2022) based on their social identity categories (i.e., race, ethnicity, gender, etc.). This undermining of the knower's credibility is inherently discriminatory and underscores the structural inequalities embedded in intersectionality (Crenshaw, 1989, 1991; Collins & Bilge, 2016; Collins, 2019). As such, the positionality of the knower is important because testimonial injustices involve questioning the knower's credibility. This questioning could be conscious or unconscious, implicit or explicit. Prejudice, discrimination, implicit biases, and racism – all concepts with a neurological basis (Amodio, 2014;

Molenberghs, 2013; Sapolsky, 2017) – contribute to the discrimination embedded in testimonial injustice. The neurobiological basis of bias, however, does not absolve responsibility for those who do the "questioning". Thus, critical reflexivity is crucial in epistemic ethics justice.

For example, consider how a White social worker may question the experiences of a non-dominant colleague or client, such as an African immigrant. This questioning may be compounded by intersectionality, adding structural layers of epistemic oppression (Collins, 2017). What if the African immigrant is female identified? What if she speaks English with an accent? What if she is Muslim and wears a hijab? What if she were a client versus a colleague? And how would the White social worker's credibility discrimination be different if they were male, female, or transgender? In other words, credibility discrimination (i.e., testimonial injustice) may play out differently based on the different social identities of those involved and the social structures in which these identities are embedded.

Another example of credibility discrimination may involve a White social worker who is working with a low-income, queer-identified Latine client struggling with depression and substance use. In their work, a therapeutic relational rupture occurs because the social worker dismisses and ignores the client's suffering – suffering which is compounded by the client's intersectionality and epistemic oppression. Given the interlocking layers of oppression that the client experiences based on their social identity categories (i.e., intersectionality), epistemic oppression is embedded within the client's intersectionality and subsequently highlights how the client may be harmed as a knower. Per Collins (2017), epistemic oppression "relies on specific strategies that reproduce social inequality" (p. 118). Thus, intersectionality and epistemic oppression are inextricably intertwined and contribute to the client's credibility discrimination.

While this is one example of credibility discrimination, it is important to highlight the fact that regardless of social identities, any knower can perpetuate epistemic oppression. That is, a non-White social worker may also partake in credibility discrimination (i.e., testimonial discrimination) with the same queer-identified Latine client. Interrupting this unjust practice and credibility discrimination requires both critical reflexivity and a power analysis. Together, both represent movements toward epistemic ethics justice and ethics *praxis*.

The other kind of epistemic injustice is called hermeneutical injustice (Fricker, 2007, 2013). In this case, injustices are situated in discriminatory practices whereby an individual may come to feel silenced, isolated, or misheard so that the injustice is not explicitly verbalized (Medina, 2017). These "hermeneutical harms can run so deep as to annihilate one's self, so as to produce hermeneutical death" (Medina, 2017, p. 41). As Guenther (2017) argues, this annihilation may be akin to Fanon's (1952) notion of "psychic alienation": "the estrangement of separating off a person from some of the essential attributes of personhood" (Fricker, 2007, p. 58). Thus, hermeneutical injustices may rob an individual of making sense of their own internal and lived experiences from a phenomenological perspective (Guenther, 2017).

Consider, for instance, a Black transgender social worker (they/them) who is repeatedly misgendered in their place of employment by both colleagues and clients. By feeling "psychic alienation", they may experience systemic silencing which causes a kind of existential harm that, over time, disrupts their sense of self (Guenther, 2017). Although Love (2019) does not explicitly talk about epistemic injustice in her book, *We Want to Do More Than Survive,* she refers to being "spirit murdered" (p. 34), which is akin to Fanon's (1952) idea of "psychic alienation" and the points made by Fricker (2007) and Guenther (2017). Taken together, there may be a feeling that by being unheard and/or silenced, one's being and/or internal experiences are erased over time. Once again, both critical reflexivity and power analyses are needed to interrogate occurrences of hermeneutical ethics injustices.

While Fricker's feminist philosophy may pick up where Rawls, Sen, and Nussbaum leave off, important aspects of justice – and thereby injustice – are omitted. Specifically, Glass and Newman (2015) argue that Fricker fails to highlight the importance of the role of critical consciousness in epistemic injustices. In their critique of Fricker's (2007) epistemic injustices, they draw a parallel to Freire (1970): just as one must understand that they are being oppressed to seek liberation (through the development of a critical consciousness, see earlier definition in the chapter), so, too, must one understand that they are being discriminated against to experience epistemic oppression. In other words, one can only experience an epistemic injustice (testimonial or hermeneutical) if one is aware (through the development of their own critical consciousness) of their discrimination and oppression. To build this awareness, the next section outlines specific tools (introduced by Koh, 2025b, but expanded below) that can help to develop a critical consciousness. Pedagogical examples of each tool follow.

2.2 Epistemic Ethics Justice in Social Work: Developing a Critical Consciousness

A critical consciousness is fostered through critical reflexivity (Garlough & Savitz, 2023). To fight discriminatory epistemic injustices, one must cultivate tools to develop a critical consciousness, thereby increasing our awareness and countering injustices. These tools include the following: decentering, identifying biases, and conducting power analyses. Because ethics is a practice (Koh, 2025a), these critically reflexive tools can be practiced in an anti-racist and anti-oppressive ethics classroom; pedagogical examples for each critical consciousness tool are also provided. In using these tools, we can simultaneously develop a critical consciousness *and* fight for epistemic ethics justice in the context of *ethics praxis*. Indeed, the cultivation of a critical consciousness fills the final gap in this chapter's operationalization of justice in anti-oppressive ethics.

2.2.1 *Critical Consciousness Tool 1: Decentering*

Decentering involves four metacognitive and critically reflexive processes which can be used to promote epistemic ethics justice: (1) developing a meta-awareness, (2) disidentification from one's internal experiences, (3) disrupting the dominant social construct of "Whiteness" as an infrastructure (across social identities), and (4) reducing one's reactivity to cognitive content (Bernstein et al., 2019; Crudup et al., 2021). Missing from Bernstein et al. (2019), a proposed fifth metacognitive and critically reflexive process should include analyses of various intersectional oppressions including (but not limited to) class, patriarchy/heteropatriarchy, misogynoir, queer, trans, and indigenous peoples.

Decentering is an attempt to disrupt, displace, or deconstruct our metacognitive processes; it offers us an opportunity to step outside ourselves. Thus, disruption requires us to shift our internal (i.e., cognition) and external (i.e., dominant White culture as a social construct) perspectives and experiences (Bernstein et al., 2015). Through displacing – or decentering – we can shift our perspectives in terms of one's (and others') lived experiences (May, 2015) in the context of understanding epistemic injustices. Doing this may compel us to know who we are ethically (Abramson, 1996) – and to first *center* our moral lived experiences. Thus, the pedagogical examples below include both centering and decentering pedagogical examples.

Pedagogical Examples to Facilitate Critical Consciousness Tool 1: Decentering. A concrete example to help students cultivate critical consciousness tool 1 includes allowing students sufficient time (e.g., pauses in class) to self-reflect (e.g., written first, verbal second) during class in all formats (in-person, synchronous/asynchronous online, hybrid). First, in the context of ethics case-based learning, providing students an opportunity to self-reflect (and center) before engaging in classroom dialogue is important.

One cannot *decenter* themself before *centering*. Assignments that help students *center* their values, beliefs, and positionality may be needed. Using Kitchener's (1984) ethical genogram, for instance, students can create a three-generational ethical genogram (and critically analyze it) to center (i.e., meta-awareness) their moral lived experiences. The ethical genogram can include relevant social identities (e.g., gender, culture, ethnicity, spirituality, etc.) that have informed the values/beliefs that shaped their moral compass. Similarly, with respect to outside (i.e., non-familial) societal moral influences, students can also create an "ethical ecomap" which may help to illustrate these influences.

For instance, consider an ethical situation that involves a client who is undocumented and seeking services at a walk-in opioid crisis center. This client is a recent political refugee; they are unhoused, unemployed, and speak limited English. In their heritage country, they were a radiologist for 15 years at a well-respected hospital. Decentering immediately requires us to step outside of ourselves and see the client through another non-dominant perspective – first, internal (e.g., emotion, cognition, etc.) and second, external (e.g., dominant "White" structures, dominant social identities, etc.). Internally, we must develop a meta-awareness to step outside of our own experience. Doing so requires first centering and then engaging in a tuning in process to see ourselves as "other" (i.e., decentering). Ideally, this decentering reduces our reactivity to emotional and cognitive content that emerges in the ethical situation because we develop the ability to see things outside of ourselves. In this way, decentering is also about perspective taking and empathy building.

Finally, in another centering exercise, students can write their own positionality statements to situate themselves in their ethics practice. This will include students identifying important social identities (e.g., age, race, ethnicity, gender, citizenship, etc.), roles, and/or lived experiences to situate their "position" (Kinefuchi & Orbe, 2008) in entering into *ethics praxis*. This is essential to entering into analyses of power (critical consciousness tool 2). These concrete pedagogical suggestions not only support the cultivation of critical consciousness tool 1 (decentering), but they are also consistent with a Freireian approach (McLaren & da Silva, 1993).

2.2.2 *Critical Consciousness Tool 2: Identifying Biases*

Epistemic injustices cannot be fought without understanding the role of bias in discriminatory epistemic practices. As such, ethics education needs to focus on developing our critical consciousness about bias. This critical consciousness includes both increasing our ability to identify bias as well as understanding how our own biases impede our ethical deliberations. This is a significantly overlooked area in social work ethics education.

Part of developing a critical consciousness of bias includes starting with an understanding of its neurobiological basis. Implicit biases are unconscious or conscious responses to others that are embedded in our stereotypes (Berger, 2020; Greenwald & Banaji, 1995; Greenwald et al., 2003); they are conceptually distinct from both stereotype threat and epistemic injustice (Saul, 2017). To aid in our basic understanding of implicit biases, it is important to understand that the neurological response is adaptive. For instance, neuroception (part of polyvagal theory) suggests we subconsciously view others as either safe or threatening (Porges, 2011). Thus, one might surmise that neuroception, coupled with an increased awareness of our implicit biases, may provide a starting point to developing a critical consciousness about the role of both in our ethical decision-making.

It may also be helpful to understand research which suggests that both implicit bias (Terbeck, Kahane, et al., 2012; Terbeck, Savulescu, et al., 2016) and emotions (via the amygdala) play a role in moral decision-making (Glick, 2022). Because emotion is intertwined with a neurological response referred to as the flight-fight-freeze response (LeDoux, 2015), we should understand the role of emotion in our ethical deliberation processes. For instance, a social worker may make a fear-based decision (e.g., mandated reporting) because their amygdala is activated (Fox & Shackman, 2019) and they worry about potential repercussions such as being sued or reported to their licensing board. Teachers also share similar concerns about mandated reporting: "fear of getting into trouble" (Allen, 2023, p. 31). Given the role of emotions in implicit biases and ethical decision-making, "centering" is crucial.

This neurobiological framework has important implications for epistemic injustice. Consider, for instance, how epistemic oppression manifests when a social worker reports suspected abuse due to a culturally specific coining healing ritual (performed by a Hmong Shaman) out of a fear of getting into trouble; this worker engages in epistemic oppression compounded by intersectionality (Collins, 2017). Research suggests that the Hmong experience discrimination in the child welfare system (Huynh-Hohnbaum, 2024). The Hmong literature also underscores the following: "Do not confuse the regular patterns of coining or cupping for abuse" (Purnell, 2019, p. 207). Thus, if the coining ritual were reported as suspected abuse, would the Hmong family experience credibility discrimination? If so, does the social worker's duty to protect the public in this case result in an epistemic injustice? These are examples of important epistemic injustice questions. Cultural knowledge and awareness are needed to combat bias.

We can cultivate a critical consciousness of our own biases. Centering ourselves and slowing down our thinking (i.e., Kahneman, 2011) may help in this developmental process. For instance, one might have implicit biases about Black African immigrants – e.g., if they are undocumented, unemployed, and seeking services for an addiction. Most likely, we may respond with our own biases about any of these factors. Yet, if we (first center and) then decenter our own experiences from dominant discourses to foster our critical consciousness, might we see this individual in a different light? One possible way to do this might be to use Rawls's neutral "veil of ignorance" to first *center*. Thereafter, we might *decenter* to consider possibilities outside our own lived experience. Is it possible that by doing so we may learn that this individual is experiencing structural barriers (e.g., lack of medical license, English as a second language, being undocumented) that have prevented them from obtaining employment in their area of expertise, internal medicine? How might our own (and others') implicit biases and structural barriers impact this individual's experience of epistemically just treatment? Our reactivity may be embedded in our biases. By increasing awareness of them, policies and procedures can be implemented to inhibit the ability to act on them.

Pedagogical Examples to Facilitate Critical Consciousness Tool 2: Identifying Biases. Consistent with the examples shared with tool 1 (decentering), sufficient time to self-reflect is important in all ethics case-based learning. Three other strategies may also help. First, integrating curriculum on implicit bias and the neuroscience of race/racism (e.g., learned fear responses to skin color and status – see Sapolsky, 2017; Kubota et al., 2012; Mattan et al., 2018; Stevens & Abernethy, 2018) is important. Such curricular integration will assist in boosting our meta-awareness and aid in developing a critical consciousness and promoting epistemic ethics justice. If approached collaboratively in a way that encourages peer review and team-building, this collective critical consciousness raising can elevate the curriculum.

Second, students can take implicit association tests (IAT; Greenwald et al., 2003) to help them develop a meta-awareness and critical consciousness about bias. IATs (free and available online, see Project Implicit) indirectly assess stereotypes and attitudes about difference (Buttrick et al., 2020). The IATs, however, are not without their limitations and thus a caveat is noteworthy. Importantly, Gawronski, Ledgerwood, and Eastwick (2022) have differentiated the construct of implicit bias from its actual measurement. As such, the process of actually taking any one of the numerous tests available may set the stage for a discussion to increase critical awareness and develop a critical consciousness. Importantly, the IATs may also set the stage for increasing critical awareness and engaging in prejudice-habit-breaking programs to reduce implicit biases (Devine et al., 2012).

Finally, integrating the cultivation of critical consciousness about bias in our ethical deliberation processes in assignments will also support the development of this tool. Specifically, case-based ethical decision-making assignments (individual or group, in-class or submitted online) allow students to critically reflect on their biases and the potential impacts on their deliberation processes. A community-based approach to ethics and ethical deliberation (Koh, 2026, in press) may also facilitate peer feedback, foster collective responsibility, and encourage meta-cognition among community members. Moreover, discussing how specific IAT results may help students use reflexivity to gain insight into how their biases may impact their ethical deliberations can be helpful. To move toward epistemic ethics justice and praxis, it is necessary to raise our critical consciousness about the neuroscience of ethical decision-making (e.g., Sapolsky, 2017) and the role of emotions in ethics (Koh, 2025b).

2.2.3 Critical Consciousness Tool 3: Power Analyses Using Positional Reflexivity

Atteberry-Ash (2023) underscored that social justice in social work is largely defined by Rawls, Sen, and Nussbaum; yet none of these justice theories fully examine or critique power. To develop a critical consciousness, power analyses are needed. Foucault offers a solid starting point for this, as he conceptualized power as residing in neither individuals nor institutions (Fricker, 2007; Rabinov, 1994).

Building on Foucault, Fricker (2007) identified an important aspect of power: the potential to exercise control over others. Fricker (2007) provided the following definition of social power:

> [A] practically socially situated capacity to control over others' actions, where this capacity may be exercised (actively or passively) by particular social agents, or alternatively, it may operate purely structurally.
>
> (p. 13)

Social workers undoubtedly have the potential to exercise power over others. Thus, the use of a self-discovery tool (e.g., heuristics) to conduct a critical analysis of the power involved in an ethical situation may help slow down the deliberation process. For instance, a heuristic founded on the social theory of intersectionality (Crenshaw, 1989, 1991; Collins & Bilge, 2016; Collins, 2019) could invite probing, discovery, critical reflection, and power analyses. "Positional reflexivity" (Cousin, 2010, p. 11) may be another analytic tool (more on this below).

Structural power analyses may also reveal a deeper systemic understanding of the structural and institutional barriers (e.g., national medical licensing exams, state licensing, language, access to health insurance, etc.) faced by certain individuals. Let us return to the Black African person who is undocumented and an immigrant. If we decenter and examine our own biases, we may learn that they are seeking services for one of their children who has an addiction problem. Moreover, if the client is treated poorly (e.g., enduring testimonial or hermeneutical injustice) due to their lack of power, they may not report their unjust ethical experience. In fact, it is quite likely that they *lack* the systemic knowledge to report an ethics complaint. One could argue that the closer one is to dominant White culture, the easier it may be to navigate its ethics institutions and mandates. Thus, a lack of power and the inability to communicate and convey injustice *is* a hermeneutical injustice – one that is embedded in layers of subjugated epistemic oppression.

Pedagogical Examples to Facilitate Critical Consciousness Tool 3: Conducting Power Analyses. Consistent with the examples shared for tools 1 (decentering) and 2 (identifying bias), reflective pauses and different approaches to critical self-reflection are the cornerstones of critical consciousness development via tool 3 (power analyses) to support epistemically just ethics. Three other concrete pedagogical strategies can facilitate critical analyses of power.

One of these strategies is the use of a heuristic to invite critical discovery and analysis. Koh (2024), for instance, developed a six-question intersectional ethics heuristic for this purpose. In a case-based ethics classroom, students can individually or collectively analyze an ethically challenging situation using the heuristic. For example, asking the following questions can facilitate power analyses: "What unequal, oppressive systems of power should be considered in the context of this given ethical situation?" and "How can we make an ethical decision that considers intersectionality, anti-oppressive ethics, and our professional mandates" (Koh, 2024, p. 53). To learn more about the intersectional ethics heuristic, see Koh (2024).

Another way to cultivate critical consciousness tool 3 (power analyses) is by facilitating dialogue in a community-based ethics model (Koh, 2025a; Koh, 2026, in press) that is consistent with a Freirean (1970) approach. Ethics is abstract and can be difficult for students to grasp. As such, providing platforms for students to critically self-reflect and be in dialogue with one another allows them the opportunity to learn from each other as they examine power (and potentially use the intersectional ethics heuristic). Community-based ethics shifts learning away from the individual to assist students with collectively analyzing how power may be used (and misused) to create epistemic ethics justice. Using a community-based ethics model, for instance, groups of students may deliberate over a "mock" ethics complaint submitted to a licensing board. This discussion should include an anti-oppressive power analysis to support epistemically just ethics.

Finally, using "positional reflexivity" (Cousin, 2010, p. 11) is an important grounding and centering tool before engaging in an analysis of power. Cousin (2010) states that this concept "concerns the examination of 'place, biography, self and other to understand how they shape the analytic exercise'" (p. 11). Thus, Cousin (2010) suggests that by engaging in identity-based "positional reflexivity", one considers specific positionalities such as "class positionality" (p. 11) and "coloured positionality" (p. 12). Each type of identity-specific positionality comes with a "special pair of glasses" (p. 11). Using positional reflexivity to examine power in an ethics situation may assist with both centering and decentering. Additionally, it may help raise awareness of potential biases. These critical consciousness tools are interconnected and collectively support the development of a critical consciousness.

2.3 Implications for Social Work Ethics Education

Taken together, these tools are essential components to developing our own critical consciousness utilizing critical reflexivity – to look inward, hold ourselves accountable, and critically analyze power (Badwell, 2016; Collins, 2019). These three critical consciousness tools – decentering, identifying biases, and conducting power analyses – need pedagogical support in an epistemically just ethics classroom. The concrete examples discussed offer such support. Developing these tools to fight epistemic injustices and epistemic oppression requires us to utilize an anti-oppressive *ethics praxis* education approach that centers critical reflexivity (which is also a principle of anti-oppressive praxis per Koh, 2026, in press).

Importantly, cultivating critical consciousness tools runs counter to the notion of the "banking" (p. 53) model approach to education – that is, one where educators make informational "deposits" (p. 53) and learners make "withdrawals" – that Freire (1970) critiqued. This transactional view of education leaves little room for critical thinking, let alone the cultivation of a much-needed critical consciousness. As Freire (1970) argued, the stronger the "banking" model approach to education, the less likely we are to develop a critical consciousness. In addition to the Freirean (1970) goals of education,[5] anti-oppressive ethics education that promotes epistemic justice requires both ethics educators and learners to be in a critical dialogue – one that supports critical reflexivity – in the ethics classroom.

Strategies to disrupt a "banking" model of education are centered on ways to slow down deliberation in the ethics classroom. Avoiding a "grind culture" (Hersey, 2022, p. 79) – that is, one which promotes the need to cram ethics concepts into the curriculum and make a designated number of Freirean "deposits" in a given class period – is a good start. From there, allowing students time to first critically self-reflect and *then* to be in dialogue with others provides an opportunity to not only dismantle epistemic injustices in an ethics classroom but also to foster the previously discussed critical consciousness tools. The use of critically reflective pauses in the classroom undoubtedly encourages meta-awareness.

For Freire (1970), dialogue was an important part of critical consciousness, and thus key to our liberation and transformation. Correspondingly, opening learning spaces for community-based ethics dialogues that center Freirean educational goals (anti-oppressive practice approaches which may include anti-racism and raising class consciousness) also supports the development of a critical consciousness. In these community and dialogic learning spaces, case-based learning (e.g., deliberating over an ethics case) provides an optimal opportunity to practice all three critical consciousness tools. Developing an understanding of epistemic injustices in anti-oppressive ethics praxis places diverse, moral, lived experiences at the forefront of just ethics communities. In these epistemically just communities, we can build upon and consult with one another in a way that makes ethical deliberation reflexive, collaborative, and grounded in collective care.

This chapter challenges us to use anti-oppressive ethics praxis to move toward an epistemically just ethics society. Three educational tools (decentering, identifying biases, and conducting power analyses) that can be integrated into case-based ethics education were discussed. Eliminating epistemic injustices to promote anti-racist and anti-oppressive ethics praxis is both inclusive and humanizing; it further places community care at the forefront, which is sorely needed to create an epistemically just society.

The slow pace of desired incremental change cannot be overlooked, particularly when impeded by dominant "White thinking" and infrastructures. No doubt, collaboration and community work are slower. Yet, as a community of change agents, we must believe we need to be liberated (Freire, 1970). Collectively, we must see this new vision of epistemically just ethics education as a moral imperative to bring this vision into fruition. Changes in our approach to social work ethics are long overdue (Koh, 2025b). As social work professionals, we must contemplate the possibility that oppression can be reinforced even by well-intentioned action; thus, critical reflective praxes should be central to anti-oppressive social work ethics education. It is time to "disrupt" social work ethics education (O'Leary & Tsui, 2023), to use our moral imagination, and to consider the possibilities that will help create an ethically just society.

Notes

1 CASWE's (2021, p. 5) EPAS includes "a commitment to equity and social justice" (Educational Policy 1.1: Mission and Goals, SB/M 1.1.1); CSWE's (2022, p. 13) EPAS includes "the purpose of social work is actualized through its quest for social, racial, economic, and environmental justice" (Educational Policy 1.0: Program Mission).
2 A thorough examination is beyond the scope of this chapter. For more on these philosophical perspectives, the reader is referred to Rawls (2001), Sen (2006, 2012), and Nussbaum (1999, 2002, 2003).
3 For more on Rawlsian ideal theory, see Herzog (2012) and Hendrix (2013).
4 As cited in Chambon et al. (1999), Foucault stated that "…social work has become programmatic and institutionalized" (p. 91).
5 (1) reflection and knowing oneself, (2) awareness of the forces that have shaped our consciousness, and (c) laying down the conditions for producing a new kind of educational life.

References

Abramson, M. (1996). Reflections on knowing oneself ethically: Toward a framework for social work practice. *Families in Society*, *3*, 195–202.

Allen, A. J. (2023). *Prevention in schools: Examining school personnel's attitudes and knowledge of mandated reporting* (Publication No. 616). [Doctoral Dissertation, Philadelphia College of Osteopathic Medicine]. PCOM Psychology Dissertations. https://digitalcommons.pcom.edu/psychology_dissertations/616/

Amodio, D. M. (2014). The neuroscience of prejudice and stereotyping. *Nature Reviews Neuroscience*, *15*(10), 670–682. https://doi.org/10.1038/nrn3800

Atteberry-Ash, B. (2023). Social work and social justice: A conceptual review. *Social Work*, *68*(1), 38–46. https://doi.org/10.1093/sw/swac042

Badwell, H. (2016). Critical reflexivity and moral regulation. *Journal of Progressive Human Services*, *27*, 1–20. https://doi.org/10.1080/10428232.2016.1108169

Berger, J. (2020). Implicit attitudes and awareness. *Synthes*, *197*, 1291–1312. https://doi.org/10.1007/s11229-018-1754-3

Bernstein, A., Hadash, Y., & Fresco, D. M. (2019). Metacognitive processes model of decentering: Emerging methods and insights. *Current Opinion in Psychology*, *28*, 245–251.

Bernstein, A., Hadash, Y., Lichtash, Y., Tanay, G., Shepherd, K., & Fresco, D. M. (2015). Decentering and related constructs: A critical review and metacognitive processes model. *Perspectives on Psychological Sciences*, *10*(5), 599–617. https://doi.org/10.1177/1745691615594577

Bourdieu, P. (1993). *Language and symbolic power*. Harvard University Press.

Buttrick, N., Axt, J., Ebersole, C. R., & Huband, J. (2020). Re-assessing the incremental predictive validity of implicit association tests. *Journal of Experimental Social Psychology*, *88*, 1–30. https://doi.org/10.1016/j.jesp.2019.103941

Byskov, M. F. (2021). What makes epistemic injustice an "injustice"? *Journal of Social Philosophy*, *52*(1), 116–133. https://doi.org/10.1111/josp.12348

Canadian Association of Social Workers (CASW). (2024). *Canadian Association of Social Workers code of ethics, values and guiding principles*. https://www.casw-acts.ca/en/casw-code-ethics-2024

Canadian Association for Social Work Education (CASWE). (2021). *Educational policies and accreditation standards for Canadian social work education*. https://caswe-acfts.ca/wp-content/uploads/2021/08/EPAS-2021.pdf

Council on Social Work Education (2022). *Educational policy and accreditation standards for baccalaureate and masters social work programs*. https://www.cswe.org/getmedia/bb5d8afe-7680-42dc-a332-a6e6103f4998/2022-Educational-Policy-and-Accreditation-Standards-(EPAS).pdf

Chambon, A. S., Irving, A., & Epstein, A. (1999). *Reading Foucault for social work*. Columbia University Press.

Clifford, D., & Burke, B. (2005). Developing anti-oppressive ethics in the new curriculum. *Social Work Education*, *24*(6), 677–692. doi: https://doi.org/10.1080/02615470500185101

Collins, P. H. (2017). Intersectionality and epistemic injustice. In I. J. Kidd, J. Medina, & G. Pohlhaus (Eds.), *The Routledge handbook of epistemic injustice* (pp. 115–124). Routledge.

Collins, P. H. (2019). *Intersectionality as critical social theory*. Duke University Press.

Collins, P. H., & Bilge, S. (2016). *Intersectionality*. Polity.

Cousin, G. (2010). Positioning positionality: The reflexive turn. In M. Savin-Bade & C. Howell Major (Eds.). *New approaches to qualitative research: Wisdom and uncertainty* (pp. 9–18). Routledge.

Crenshaw, K. (1989). Demarginalizing the intersection of race and sex: A Black feminist critique of antidiscrimination doctrine, feminist theory and antiracist politics. *University of Chicago Legal Forum*, 139–168.

Crenshaw, K. (1991). Mapping the margins: Intersectionality, identity politics, and violence against women of color. *Stanford Law Review*, *43*(2), 1241–1299.

Crudup, C., Fike, C., & McLoone, C. (2021). De-centering whiteness through revisualizing theory in social work education, practice, and scholarship. *Advances in Social Work*, *21*(2/3), 654–671. https://doi.org/10.18060/24120

Devine, P. G., Forscher, P. S., Austin, A. J., & Cox, W. T. L. (2012). Long-term reduction in implicit race bias: A prejudice habit breaking intervention. *Journal of Experimental Social Psychology*, *48*(6), 1267–1278. https://doi.org/10.1016/j.jesp.2012.06.003

Fairclough, N. (1989). *Language and power*. Longman.

Fanon, F. (1952). *Black skins, White masks*. Grove Press.

Fox, A. S., & Shackman, A. J. (2019). The central extended amygdala in fear and anxiety: Closing the gap between mechanistic and neuroimaging research. *Neuroscience Letters*, *693*, 58–67. https://doi.org/10.1016/j.neulet.2017.11.056

Freire, P. (1970). *The pedagogy of the oppressed*. Continuum Publishing Co.

Fricker, M. (2007). *Epistemic injustice: Power and ethics of knowing*. Oxford University Press.

Fricker, M. (2013). Epistemic justice as a condition of political freedom? *Synthese, 190,* 1317–1332. doi: https://doi.org/10.1007/s11229-012-0227-3

Fricker, M. (2017). Evolving concepts of epistemic injustice. In I. J. Kidd, J. Medina, & G. Pohlhaus (Eds.), *The Routledge handbook of epistemic injustice* (pp. 53–60). Routledge.

Garlough, D. K., & Savitz, R. S. (2023). White teachers developing racial identity awareness and critical consciousness through critical reflexivity. *Whiteness and Education, 8*(2), 283–312. https://doi.org/10.1080/23793406.2022.2100818

Gawronski, B., Ledgerwood, A., & Eastwick, P. W. (2022). Reflections on the difference between implicit bias and bias on implicit measures. *Psychological inquiry, 33*(3), 219–231. https://doi.org/10.1080/1047840X.2022.2115729

Glass, R. D., & Newman, A. (2015). Ethical and epistemic dilemmas in knowledge production: Addressing their intersection in collaborative, community-based research. *Theory and Research in Education, 13*(1), 23–37. https://doi.org/10.1177/1477878515571178

Glick, S. M. (2022). *The emotions in bioethical decision-making. Yale Journal of Biology and Medicine, 95,* 355–358.

Grand Challenges for Social Work. (2019, February). *Grand challenges for social work: Vision, mission, domain, guiding principles, & guideposts to action.* http://grandchallengesforsocialwork.org/

Grand Challenges for Social Work. (2020, June). *Grand challenges for social work announce grand challenge to eliminate racism.* https://grandchallengesforsocialwork.org/grand-challenges-for-social-work/announcing-the-grand-challenge-to-eliminate-racism/

Greenwald, A. G., & Banaji, M. R. (1995). Implicit social cognition: Attitudes, self-esteem, and stereotypes. *Psychological Review, 102*(1), 4–27.

Greenwald, A. G., Nosek, B. A., & Banaji, M. R. (2003). Understanding and using the implicit association test: I. An improved scoring algorithm. *Journal of Personality and Social Psychology, 85,* 197–216. doi: 10.1037/0022-3514.85.2.197

Guenther, L. (2017). Epistemic injustice and phenomenology. In I. J. Kidd, J. Medina, & G. Pohlhaus (Eds.). *The Routledge handbook of epistemic injustice* (pp. 195–204). Routledge.

Haaz, I. (2019). Inclusive education and epistemic value in the praxis of ethical change. In. O. F. Ike, J. Mbae, & C. Onyia (Eds.), *Mainstreaming ethics in higher education research ethics in administration, finance, education, environment and law* (Vol. 1, pp. 259–290). https://globethics.net/

Hendrix, B. A. (2013). Where should we expect social change in non-ideal theory? *Political Theory, 41*(1), 116–143. https://doi.org/10.1177/0090591712463201

Hersey, T. (2022). *Rest is resistance: A manifesto.* Little, Brown Spark.

Herzog, L. (2012). Ideal and non-ideal theory and the problem of knowledge. *Journal of Applied Philosophy, 29*(4), 271–288. https://doi.org/10.1111/j.1468-5930.2012.00577.x

Huynh-Hohnbaum, A. L., (2024). Asian American children in the child welfare system. In Y. R. Harris & G. J. O. Carpenter (Eds.), *Children of color in the child welfare system: Psychological research and best practices* (pp. 119–133). American Psychological Association. https://doi.org/10.1037/0000369-006

International Federation of Social Workers (IFSW) (2018, July 2). *Global social work statement of ethical principles*. https://www.ifsw.org/global-social-work-statement-of-ethical-principles/
Inoue, A. (2021). *Above the well: An antiracist literacy argument from a boy of color*. The WAC Clearinghouse.
Kahneman, D. (2011). *Thinking fast and slow*. Farrar, Straus and Giroux.
Kendi, I. (2019). *How to be an anti-racist*. Penguin Random House.
Kinefuchi, W., & Orbe, M. P. (2008). Situating oneself in a racialized world: Understanding student reactions to *Crash* through standpoint theory and context-positionality frames. *Journal of International and Intercultural Communication*, *1*(1), pp. 70–90. https://doi.org/10.1080/17513050701742909
Kitchener, K. S. (1984). Intuition, critical-evaluation and ethical principles: The foundation for ethical decision in counseling psychology. *Counseling Psychologist*, *12*(3), 43–55.
Koh, B. D. (2026, in press). *Anti-oppressive social work ethics*. New York, NY: Columbia University Press.
Koh, B. D. (2025a). Insights from the lived experience of Buddhist ethics: Implications for social work education. *Social Work Education*, 1–16. https://doi.org/10.1080/02615479.2024.2368174
Koh, B. D. (2024). Intersectional ethics: A pedagogical heuristic for ethical deliberation. *Social Work Education*, *43*(1), 46–59. https://doi.org/10.1080/02615479.2022.2069746
Koh, B. D. (2025b). Epistemic ethics justice: A "radical imaginary." *Journal of Ethnic & Cultural Diversity in Social Work*, 1–9. 10.1080/15313204.2023.2291658
Kubota, J. T., Banaji, M. R., Phelps, E. A. (2012). The neuroscience of race. *Nature Neuroscience*, *15*(7), 1–18. https://doi.org/10.1038/nn.3136
LeDoux, J. (2015). *Anxious*. Penguin Books.
Lee, E. (2022). Fact construction and categorization in assessment: Cultivating epistemic justice and resistance in social work assessment. *Social Service review*, *96*(3), 534–571. https://doi.org/10.1085/721273
Love, B. (2019). *We want to do more than survive*. Beacon Press.
Lynch, I., Swartz, S., & Isaacs, D. (2017). Anti-racist moral education: A review of approaches, impact and theoretical underpinnings from 2000 to 2015. *Journal of Moral Education*, *46*(2), 129–144. https://doi.org/10.1080/03057240.2016.1273825
Mattan, B. D., Wei, K. Y., Cloutier, J., Kutoba, J. T. (2018). The social neuroscience of race-based and status-based prejudice. *Current Opinions in Psychology*, *24*, 27–34.
May, V. M. (2015). *Pursuing intersectionality, unsettling dominant imaginaries*. Routledge.
McLaren, P., & da Silva, T. T. (1993). Decentering pedagogy. In P. McLaren & P. Leonard (Eds.), *Paulo Freire: A critical encounter* (pp. 47–89). Routledge.
Medina, J. (2017). Varieties of hermeneutical injustice. In I. J. Kidd, J. Medina, & G. Pohlhaus (Eds.), *The Routledge handbook of epistemic injustice* (pp. 41–52). Routledge.
Mills, C. (2017). Ideology. In I. J. Kidd, J. Medina, & G. Pohlhaus (Eds.). *The Routledge handbook of epistemic injustice* (pp. 100–111). Routledge.
Mills, C. (1997). *The racial contract*. Ithaca, NY: Cornell University Press.

Molenberghs, P. (2013). The neuroscience of in-group bias. *Neuroscience and Biobehavioral Reviews*, *37*, 1530–1536. https://doi.org/10.1016/j.neubiorev.2013.06.002

National Association of Social Workers (NASW). (2021). *Code of ethics of the National Association of Social Workers*. https://www.socialworkers.org/About/Ethics/Code-of-Ethics/Code-of-Ethics-English

Nussbaum, M. C. (1999). Women and equality: The capabilities approach. *International Labour Review*, *138*(3), 227–245.

Nussbaum, M. C. (2002). Capabilities and social justice. *International Studies Review*, *4*(2), 123–235. 131.118.206.8

Nussbaum, M. C. (2003). Capabilities as fundamental entitlements: Sen and social justice. *Feminist economists*, *9*(2–3), 33–59. https://doi.org/10.1080/1354570022000077926

O'Leary, P., & Tsui, M. (2023). Disrupting social work ethics. *International Social Work*, *1–3*. https://doi.org/10.1177/00208728231170078

Porges, S. W. (2011). *The polyvagal theory: Neurological foundations of emotions, attachment, communication, and self-regulation*. W.W. Norton & Company, Inc.

Purnell, L. D., & Fenkl, E. A. (2019). *Handbook for Culturally Competent Care*. Springer.

Rabinov, P. (1994) *Foucault: Ethics*. The New Press.

Rawls, J. (2001). A theory of justice. In J. P. Sterba (Ed.), *Ethics: Classical Western texts in feminist and multicultural perspectives* (pp. 363–378). Oxford University Press.

Roberts, D. E. (2019). Abolition constitutionalism. *Harvard Law Review*, *133*(1), 1–81.

Sapolsky, R. (2017). *Behave*. Penguin Books.

Saul, J. (2017). Implicit bias, stereotype threat, and epistemic injustices. In I. J. Kidd, J. Medina, & G. Pohlhaus (Eds.), *The Routledge Handbook of Epistemic Injustice* (pp. 235–242). Routledge.

Sen, A. (2006). What do we want from a theory of justice? *The Journal of Philosophy*, *103*(5), 215–238.

Sen, A. (2009). *The idea of justice*. Belknap Press of Harvard University Press.

Sen, A. (2012). Values and justice. *Journal of Economic Methodology*, *19*(2), 101–108.

Shah, R., Ahluwalia, S., & Spicer, J. (2023). Relational care and epistemic injustice. *Primary Health Care Research & Development*, *24*(e62), 1–4. https://doi.org/10.1017/S1463423623000555

Stevens, F. L., & Abernethy, A. D. (2018). Neuroscience and racism: The power of groups for overcoming implicit bias. *International Journal of Group Psychotherapy*, *68*(4), 561–584. https://doi.org/10.1080/00207284.2017.1315583

Stock, T., Schlehofer, M., Nyland, J. (2023). *What is philosophical enfranchisement? Community ethics and the role of the university in public practice*. Precollege Philosophy and Public Practice.

Terbeck, S., Kahane, G., McTavish, S., Savulescu, J., Cowen, P. J., Hewstone, M. (2012). Propranolol reduces implicit negative racial bias. *Psychopharmacology*, *222*, 419–424. https://doi.org/10.1007/s00213-012-2657-5

Terbeck, S., Savulescu, J., Chesterman, L. P., & Cowen, P. J. (2016). Noradrenaline effects on social behavior, intergroup relations, and moral decisions. *Neuroscience and Biobehavioral Reviews*, *66*, 54–60. 10.1016/j.neubiorev.2016.03.031

Uehara, E., Flynn, M., Fong, R., Brekke, J., Barth, R. P., Coulton, C., Davis, K., DiNitto, D., Hawkins, J. D., Lubben, J., Manderscheid, R., Padilla, Y., Sherraden, M., &

Walter, K. (2013). Grand challenges for social work. *Journal of the Society for Social Work and Research*, *4*, 165–170. https://doi.org/10.5243/jsswr.2013.11

Utt, J. & Tochluk, S. (2020). White teacher, know thyself: Improving anti-racist praxis through racial identity development. *Urban Education*, *55*(1), 125–152. https://doi.org/10.1177/0042085916648741

Young, I. M. (2009). Five faces of oppression. In G. Henderson & WaterstoneM. (Eds.), *Geographic thought: A praxis perspective* (pp. 55–71). Routledge.

Chapter 3

Transformative Social Work and Epistemic Justice

Karen Bell, Bernadette Moorhead, Jacqueline McNamara, and Wendy Bowles

3.1 Introduction

This chapter draws on transformative theories to explore how social workers contribute to epistemic justice, a concept introduced by Miranda Fricker (2007, 2008). Fricker (2007) argued that "there are areas where injustice is normal" (viii) and so "the only way to reveal what is involved in epistemic justice … is by looking at the negative space that is epistemic injustice" (pp. viii–vix). Epistemic injustice involves recognizing how some groups are discredited, ignored, and silenced as legitimate knowers. As a foundation for this exploration into how social workers contribute to epistemic justice, we first discuss the dominant discourses from which conventional Euro-Western forms of social work have emerged and outline some ways in which they perpetuate oppression, including epistemic injustice.

To move beyond the constraints of conventional social work, we present our vision for a transformative social work paradigm by drawing on feminist, Indigenist, post-anthropocentric, and critical posthumanist theories. Transformative social work is a broad term encompassing a range of paradigms including feminism, Indigenism, post-anthropocentrism, and critical posthumanism.

For the purposes of this chapter, we broadly define feminism as "a movement to end sexism, sexist exploitation, and oppression" (hooks, 2014, p. 1). We draw on Fejo-King's (2014) description of Indigenism as "a way of claiming space within social work research and practice for Aboriginal knowledge systems and ways of knowing, doing and being" (p. 55), which are "led by Indigenous researchers, academics and practitioners" (p. 64). We position post-anthropocentrism and critical posthumanism as holistic approaches to understanding the interconnectedness of all beings with the natural world; while post-anthropocentrism helps us to unravel the myth of human exceptionalism and androcentric thinking, critical posthumanism disrupts the human male as a central reference point for humanity itself (Bell, 2023; Pease, 2021).

DOI: 10.4324/9781003639046-5

Taken together, post-anthropocentrism and critical posthumanism also enable us to expose the entanglements of systems of oppression and their mutually reinforcing socio-political, cultural, environmental, and economic inequities (Bell, 2023). Thus, at its ontological core, transformative social work is founded on principles of collectivity, relationality, equity, decolonization, and justice (Chigangaidze et al., 2022). Through multilevel transformational action, the various intersecting systems of oppression are addressed with the aim of achieving fair and just outcomes for all, and not only for a privileged few. Therefore, we contest that transformative social work may serve as a foundation to guide social work actions for epistemic justice and provide illustrative examples from our own feminist participatory social work action research later.

In alignment with our overarching transformative approach and as a foundation for the chapter ahead, we as situated co-authors, first introduce ourselves and acknowledge the complexities of our positionality using first-person nouns to centre who we are in our writing. We are all White women from Anglo-European colonial ancestry, based in varying regional locations across Australia on the unceded First Nations lands of the Wiradjuri, Ngunnawal, Ngambri, and Darumbal people. We are united by our commitment to equity and justice in all its forms and to transformative approaches in social work theory and practice.

3.1.1 Key Terminology

Critical Posthumanism and Post-Anthropocentrism. These transformative approaches have the conceptual capacity to explore the impacts of intersecting systems of oppression and expose the myths of human exceptionalism and male supremacy. These approaches position humans as intrinsically interconnected with one another and all living things, including the natural environment (Bell, 2023).

Epistemic Injustice. Recognizes how intersecting systems of oppression resulting in a negative space whereby some groups are systematically discredited, ignored and silenced as legitimate holders of knowledge (Fricker, 2007).

Epistemic Justice. Epistemic justice is a positive space within which all people and groups are recognized as legitimate bearers of diverse knowledge with agency, context, and valuable knowledge to share (Fricker, 2007).

Euro-Western Social Work. The dominant form of Euro-Western social work emerged from the Western Enlightenment and is founded on modernist, androcentric, colonialist perspectives. These oppressive systems create and sustain sociocultural, political and economic inequities, along with underpinning ethical dilemmas in relation to social workers as agents of social control or social care (Burt, 2022).

Feminism. Broadly, feminism comprehensively critiques male supremacist perspectives and decentres male humans as a central reference point. Feminism is emancipatory as it aims to end patriarchal systems of oppression and promote diversity and equity for all (hooks, 2014).

Indigenism. Led by First Nations people, Indigenist approaches involve sharing knowledge systems about "ways of knowing, being, and doing" and working towards emancipation for all by "claiming space within social work research" (Fejo-King, 2014, pp. 55 & 64).

Transformative Social Work. Is a collective approach addressing the disempowering constraints of Euro-Western social work by drawing together concepts from critical posthumanism, post-anthropocentrism, feminism and Indigenism to unravel intersecting systems of oppression. The aim of transformative social work is to achieve fairness, equity and emancipation for all, with humans recognized as diverse and intrinsically embedded within the natural environment (Chigangaidze et al., 2022).

3.2 Dominant Discourses in Conventional Euro-Western Social Work

The origins of Euro-Western social work are often attributed to settlement movements and charity organization societies across the United Kingdom and United States of America in the late 19th and early 20th centuries (Burt, 2022). Analysis of documents from this period shows that while the term "social work" was applied to a broad range of human activities, even leisure, the meaning evolved to capture workers, both paid and unpaid, in social reform, charity, and philanthropic contexts (Burt, 2022). Social workers have emerged from industrial and capitalist-based Western societies that inherently produced social problems, especially poverty and inequality, and saw the shift of welfare needs being met by the state onto the individual (Beckett, 2018). As schools of social work were established to train the new workforce and seek professional status, theoretical and practice tensions within and between individualist and collectivist ideologies, including radical traditions, dominated debates and produced contested notions of the purpose of the emerging profession (Burt, 2022; Bussey et al., 2021; Ioakimidis & Trimikliniotis, 2020). Along with the pursuit of professional status and recognition, these differing streams have underpinned a complex and nuanced legacy which is characterized by social liberation and social control functions that have seen social workers to strive for social change on one hand and act complicitly in the oppression of many groups on the other (Beckett, 2018; Ioakimidis & Trimikliniotis, 2020; McGregor, 2019).

Despite these conflicting ideas, the origins and much of Euro-Western social work's expansion across the globe in the 20th century has emerged from a colonial Euro-centric modernist paradigm that incorporates patriarchal and anthropocentric thinking (Bell, 2021; Green, 2023; Laing, 2021; Panagiotaros et al., 2022). Underpinned by the Western Enlightenment period, legitimate knowledge is constructed as rational, disembodied, linear, and positivist – all qualities ascribed to the hegemonic archetypical White male – with the aim of uncovering universal truth (Bell, 2012). Drawing largely from Western male philosophers, the ideals and principles of modernism create and reproduce hierarchical binaries and "Cartesian dualisms" (Bell, 2012, p. 412) that centre on the primacy of humans, especially males, over all species and the natural environment (Boetto, 2017; Braidotti, 2019; Laing, 2021; Yadav, 2021). Further, this modernist ethos reflects a nature/culture binary (Richter, 2023), and establishes dualisms across human groups, such as "Male/female, Black/White and able-bodied/disabled" (Beckett, 2018, p. 969). The "divisive metaphysics" (Hanrahan, 2011, p. 275) and polarized ontology of Western modernism produces epistemologies characterized by inequities, partiality, and privilege, which are then reproduced by colonized imaginations (Blackstock, 2009; Noble, 2021).

In terms of professional knowledge, the positivist facets of modernism have often been embraced by Euro-Western social work, including early key figures like Mary Richmond (Healy, 2022). Embedding positivist approaches into social work theory and practice, including the pursuit of professional status, has come at the cost of pathologizing and regulating the behaviour of individuals and communities, actions which are carried out under the illusion of being objective and value-free (Haraway, 1988; Martinez-Brawley, 2019). This has seen Euro-Western social work often align with pseudo-scientific ideals of social eugenics that have reinforced White supremacy (Hall, 2021; Ioakimidis & Trimikliniotis, 2020) and male dominance (Noble, 2021). Further, such thinking has ignored structural and intersecting causes of inequalities and oppression (Bell, 2021; Bussey et al., 2021), the subjective and constructivist elements of social work knowledge (Beckett, 2018; Martinez-Brawley, 2019), and the interconnectedness of living and non-living elements on the planet (Bell, 2023; Boetto, 2017; Richter, 2023).

These dominant paradigms are imbued with divisive hierarchies, disembodiment, and domination; they have reproduced epistemic injustices, where the voices, worldviews, and knowledge paradigms of many groups and species that are not human have been ignored, rendered invisible or marginalized as "other" (Bell, 2023; Laing, 2021; Yadav, 2021). These epistemic injustices are even more stark when revisiting social work's troubled legacy; radical traditions and diversity of knowledge and worldviews, especially within Indigenous communities, have always existed and influenced the profession, but are often relegated to the periphery (Clarke, 2022; Ioakimidis & Trimikliniotis, 2020; McGregor, 2019; Panagiotaros et al., 2022), with Indigenous knowledges often being appropriated (Chigangaidze et al., 2022; Fejo-King, 2014; Green & Bennett, 2018).

The epistemic consequences of Euro-Western modernism contradict the core values and principles of social justice and the emancipatory aims of social work (Bell, 2012; Boetto, 2017; Bussey et al., 2021). There is a profound need for fundamental transformation in social work knowledge (Bell, 2023; Clarke, 2022; Green, 2023; Noble, 2021), especially as modernism continues to thrive within contemporary neoliberalism while the planet faces ecological collapse (Panagiotaros et al., 2022). To add momentum to social work's "collective professional shift" (Morgenshtern et al., 2022, p. 2), we must all consciously work to transcend injustice in all its forms – including epistemic injustice (Morgenshtern et al., 2022).

Having described the origin story of the dominant forms of Euro-Western social work as a product of modernism, we now consider the challenges and possibilities of transcending the constraints of the profession's androcentric and colonialist traditions. The multidimensional nature of the social work domain effectively situates the profession as part of a collective effort to resist "business as usual" and continue working towards justice, health, and equity (Ioakimidis & Maglajlic, 2022).

3.3 Transformative Social Work and Epistemic Justice

At its ontological core, transformative social work is founded on principles of collectivity, relationality, equity, decolonization, and justice (Chigangaidze et al., 2022) (Figure 3.1). Through multilevel transformational action, the various intersecting systems of oppression are addressed with the aim of achieving fair and just outcomes for all, instead of for only a privileged few.

Transformative social work is also informed by feminism in its rejection of conventional humanist dualisms, including the positioning of some humans above others (specifically male above female, White above non-White, Western above non-Western, traditional gender categories above fluidity of gender, and so on) (Braidotti, 2019; Crenshaw, 2017; Noble, 2021). Indeed, feminist theory has an extensive influence on transformative social work, providing a systematic critique of hegemonic male dominance, heteronormativity, and human exceptionalism (Noble, 2021). Further, transformative social work draws on feminism and critical posthumanism to bring patriarchal oppression into sharp focus as it de-centres the hegemonic human male as the standard "neutral" reference point for all humankind and as the dominant epistemic agent and legitimate knowledge-bearer (Code, 1991; Haraway, 1988; Plumwood, 1994).

The marginalization of "others," including ignoring or silencing them as incapable of knowing (Fricker, 2007) in favour of reproducing the myth of male exceptionalism (Fricker, 2008; Harding, 2007; Plumwood, 1994) has long been detrimental to the quality, richness, and pace of knowledge production. In contrast, within a transformative social work paradigm there is a focused effort to seek out marginalized groups as epistemic agents and legitimate bearers of knowledge for the benefit of all. Acknowledging the hard-fought campaigns of groups that have been previously excluded as knowers (for instance, First Nations peoples, women, or people with disabilities), it is important that social workers seek opportunities to work in solidarity "with" and not "for" people; this is expressed eloquently in the disability slogan "nothing about us without us" (Charlton, 1998, p. 3). Doing so involves striving for humble acceptance and appreciation of difference, leading to more equal, respectful relationships, and

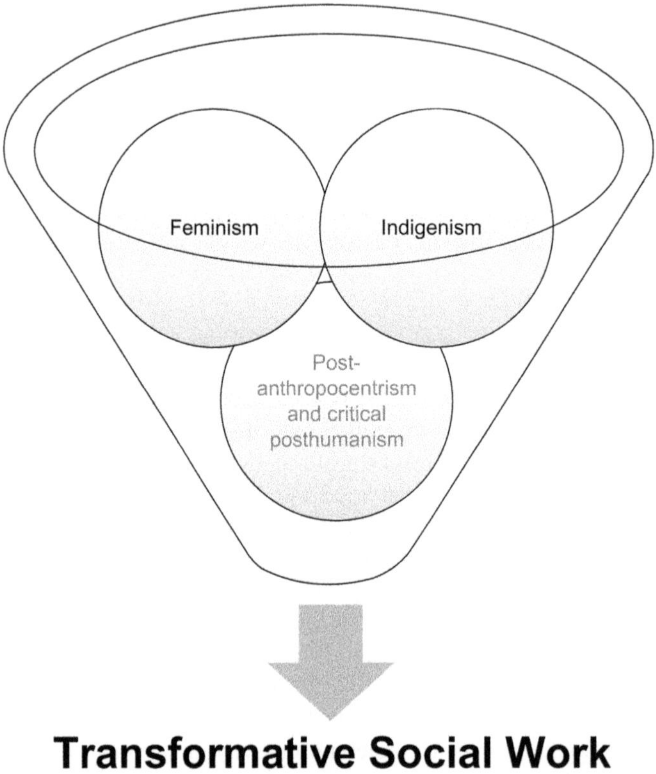

Figure 3.1 Transformative Social Work Model.

the transformation of traditional "professional" unequal relationships (Bowles & Hugman, in press); relational and feminist political ethics of care are at the heart of this transformation (see McAuliffe, 2023; Tronto, 2015).

Thus, transformative social work draws on feminist, Indigenist, post-anthropocentric, and critical posthumanist thinking as it situates humans as interdependent, embodied, and mutually co-existent with the natural environment and other non-human living entities rather than transcendent, exceptional, disembodied or above (Braidotti, 2019; Fejo-King, 2014; Ungar, 2002). A key strength of this form of transformative thinking is its capacity to encompass and articulate the entangled, fluid interconnections between all living and non-living things (Bell, 2023; Plumwood, 1994). In addition, through the deconstruction of androcentrism, consumerism, and humans' "supreme entitlement" (Braidotti, 2019, p. 68), transformative approaches have the capacity to decentre capitalist market economies and human interests as central to material existence (Webb,

2021) in favour of other relational priorities, including the natural environment. Transformative approaches also pose fundamental challenges for us all to address ingrained systems of oppression and privilege, including gendered hierarchies and environmental degradation. In addition, a challenge for non-Indigenist social workers in enacting transformation is to work in critical allyship (Gates et al., 2023) with Indigenous colleagues to respectfully privilege Indigenous knowledges, rather than appropriating them.

3.3.1 *Epistemology: Epistemic Justice, Standpoint Theory, and Situated Knowledges*

The ontological foundations of transformative social work weave post-anthropocentrism and critical posthumanism into an epistemological base. This creates a transformative social work paradigm characterized by epistemic justice, which values all as bearers of knowledge (discussed in the previous section); standpoint theory, which aims for "a politics of engaged, accountable positioning" (Haraway, 1988, p. 590); and situated knowledges, which involve understanding knowledges as coming from particular contexts, such as communities or bodies (Haraway, 1988). Drawing from Braidotti (2019), Harding (2007), Fricker (2007, 2008), and Haraway (1988), these ideas honour the agency of living and non-living species as knowledge bearers. By centring diverse sources of knowledge that are experiential, interpretive, embodied, relational, reflective, and dialogic (Bell, 2023; Braidotti, 2019; Clarke, 2022; Fricker, 2008; Haraway, 1988), social workers can reclaim "subjective value-laden" (Beckett, 2018, p. 971), constructivist elements of social work knowledge (Martinez-Brawley, 2019).

Social inequities are reflected in what counts as knowledge and among those recognized as credible sources of knowledge (Daukas, 2019; Wylie, 2011). Epistemic injustice is a "negative space" (Fricker, 2008, p. vix) due to the failure of powerful individuals or groups to recognize or value marginalized individuals or groups as legitimate bearers of knowledge (Bell, 2014; Daukas, 2019; Fricker, 2008). In alignment with social work's radical aims for justice in all forms, epistemic justice is a "positive space" (Fricker, 2008, p. 71) within which all entities are legitimate bearers of knowledge with epistemic agency. Epistemic justice thus positions knowledge bearers and sources of knowledge as socially situated through partiality that unfolds within sociocultural, temporal, relational, and embodied contexts (Braidotti, 2019; Fox & Alldred, 2020; Haraway, 1988; Harding, 2007).

An embodied stance dissolves conventional hierarchical binaries, such as mind/body, object/subject, and nature/culture, by seeing them as fundamentally entwined and in constant motion (Braidotti, 2019; Fox & Alldred, 2020). It also acknowledges the interconnectedness of lived experience that occurs within and through the bodies we inhabit (van Rhyn et al., 2021). These epistemological ideas call on social workers to position ourselves as curious and creative knowledge bearers, knowledge seekers, knowledge advocates, and knowledge observers; we must become embodied empathizers who can be attuned to both ourselves and others as active and non-judgemental listeners. Inherent in this is the capacity to develop shared intersubjective understandings, while accepting that we cannot completely fathom the totality of another's experience (Johnstone & Lee, 2021; van Rhyn et al., 2021).

Transformative social work provides a framework for working within "pockets of resistance" (Bell, 2014, p. 173) that is to work in alliance with marginalized groups, to scope, explore, and embrace non-dominant, marginalized knowledge, and the experiential knowledge of previously "illegitimate" epistemic agents. In feminist social work research, this cultivates a dynamic participatory process of collective organizing and consciousness-raising, resulting in outcomes of acts of resistance (Bell, 2023; Noble, 2021). As recursive and interdependent, this process leads to disrupting and subverting the anthropocentric ideas that have pervaded dominant epistemic standpoints, namely, the Eurocentric and patriarchal knowledge that has informed the professional project of social work (Bell, 2023; Jara, 2024; Noble, 2021). The possibilities and challenges of enacting transformative social work through Feminist Participatory Action Research (FPAR) will now be illustrated by sharing selected findings from Jacqueline's (third author) Doctoral work (university ethics approval number H202371), which explored the experience of women social workers in Australia in developing and maintaining their social work professional identity (McNamara, 2025).

3.4 Enacting Transformative Social Work through Feminist Participatory Action Research

The research project was guided by a radical feminist paradigm with disruptive, decolonizing, and transformative aims. To realize these aims, Patricia Maguire's (2000) FPAR methodology was employed, using a focus group approach informed by collectivist, dialogic, and democratic principles. It is recognized in FPAR that women, as one of the many sexually minoritized groups oppressed by sexism, require a space of their own to collectivize and centre their epistemic positions to foster consciousness-raising and acts of resistance to achieve epistemic justice (Dutta et al., 2023; Maguire, 2000; Woolf, 1929).

The focus group, comprising ten women social workers from across Australia, was established in 2021 and met six times over the course of nine months. In keeping with the democratized approach of FPAR, Jacqueline was a member of the group and worked in partnership with a co-facilitator, Jamie Anderson, who identifies as an Aboriginal Gungaloo woman from the Dawson River areas in Central Queensland. The meetings were recorded, transcribed, and analysed using a thematic-informed narrative production method (Haraway, 1988; Sadurní-Balcells, 2023). This culminated in three process-focused themes: collective organizing, consciousness-raising, and acts of resistance. These themes exemplify the activation of epistemic agency and justice through the group's engagement.

The focus group participants came from various locations across Australia. All participants were women, representing varying age groups, cultural backgrounds, and levels of experience as social workers. Four participants were from the non-government sector, and the other four were employed by government agencies. Most were in non-social work generalist human services roles, and while all participants expressed an interest in feminism at the outset of their involvement in the focus groups, they did not overtly identify as feminists.

Throughout the focus group sessions, the centrality of *collective organizing* as a theme was recognized, with members regularly highlighting solidarity as necessary in identifying and critically considering oppression and inequity experienced by women in the professional domain. Correspondingly, the members defined the focus group as a collegiate feminist process fostering reflexive collective action. Establishing the focus group as a safe space for exploring women's experiences was imperative in nurturing the foundations for the recursive and interdependent process outcomes of consciousness-raising and acts of resistance. This hinged on a critically reflexive group process and dynamics, where the co-constructed values and goals were broadly encompassed by an embodied, relational, communitarian, and intersectional emphasis, reflective of the transformative praxis of FPAR (Lykes & Hershberg, 2012).

Indeed, the participants discussed the lack of opportunity within the dominant professional domain to engage in a safe collective of woman-centric critical reflexivity. In this, they critically discussed the primacy of neoliberalism and managerialism in their workplaces, with hierarchical, disembodied, individualist, and technocratic approaches to social work supervision. For instance, one participant stated this form of supervision enforced "doing the job" over "thinking about the profession." In addition, the group concluded that a feminist lens was central to a holistic critique of their workplace experiences as women. Participants explained that the neoliberal context siloed efforts to collaborate and develop inter- and transdisciplinary affirmative partnerships between women for the purposes of consciousness-raising and collective action, all of which are central to the relational approach of the profession (Moorhead, 2021).

Participants also expressed feeling othered and silenced by the prevailing professional culture and, as a result, their ability to recognize and name injustice had been stymied; this demonstrates the pervasive and insidious presence of testimonial quieting and smothering in perpetuating hegemonic standpoints (Dotson, 2011; Fricker, 2007). The group concluded that in the current professional landscape, the only tools on offer for women and marginalized others to deconstruct and respond to oppression were predominantly those of the oppressor. This is interpreted as a hermeneutical injustice and was evident in the participants' recounted experiences of feeling complicit with service delivery that reinforced neocolonial, patriarchal social policies, and through this, their own gender-based oppression in the Australian context. The group co-reflected during these earlier meetings on this complicity, and connected the lack of opportunities for meaningful supervision, critical reflexivity, and collective context resultant of neoliberalism in preventing their standpoint as women for transformative focused consciousness. This was poignant, and reflective of Audre Lorde's (1984) famous quote, "what does it mean when the tools of a racist patriarchy are used to examine the fruits of that same patriarchy? It means that only the most narrow parameters of change are possible and allowable" (p. 110). These insights and experiences confirmed that as a fluid and interconnected process, FPAR-informed action promoting the position of women at structural levels must be informed by microcosms of safe, woman-centric, collective organizing; efforts should be focused on power, participation, and relationality to decolonize imagination (Blackstock, 2009) and activate epistemic agency and awareness (Baines, 2024; Fricker, 2007; Goessling, 2024).

As illustrated earlier in this chapter, efforts to enact a transformative framework are often derailed by the intersecting systems of oppression that perpetuate and reinforce the colonial-patriarchal hegemony of dominant standpoints that govern and inform human service delivery (Bell, 2023; Noble, 2021). These standpoints are embedded in the knowledge paradigms of institutions within which social workers are located, reinforcing barriers to developing resources for perceiving and responding to epistemic injustice (Dworkin, 1974, 1983; hooks, 2014). Collective organization can be immobilized when enduring neoliberal contexts – which the participants termed "emotional labour" – pose the risk of engaging in and colluding with the silencing of narratives (Kostecki, 2024; Showden et al., 2022). This was identified by group *consciousness-raising* in discussing the androcentric social construction of women in the professional domain and, in turn, the participants identified how they had been reproducing this through their professional identity and frameworks for practice. In these conversations, the group referred to the sexual division of labour and how this shaped their identities. Deconstructing this as a group through consciousness-raising highlighted the patriarchal culture of human services, where the word "feminism" is often censored or absorbed into a vacuum of "contexts of privilege," and women's knowledges and discourses are ignored, silenced or manipulated as part of the everyday experiences of sexism, misogyny, and discrimination.

Over the course of focus group sessions, participants also recounted instances where they had attempted to respond to more overt acts of epistemic violence in their workplaces; they used "humour" to defuse such situations or chose to "pick their battles" accordingly. When discussing consciousness-raising in later focus group sessions, the participants reflected on the embedded Indigenist approach introduced by co-facilitator Jamie Anderson. In knowledge sharing, Jamie put forward the use of the "talking stick" protocol and shared the First Nations cultural practice of Dadirri to foster a decolonized approach, involving deep listening and shedding biases (Miriam-Rose Ungunmerr, 1988), which is integral to consciousness-raising endeavours (hooks, 2014). Through this, the participants acknowledged that the talking stick protocol greatly resourced their ability to perceive epistemic injustice and think structurally about how this has been reinforced within not only their workplaces, but also through the profession of social work.

Additional *acts of resistance* emerged through the group's epistemic transition from inquirers to knowers, and the collective reclamation of women's discourses and knowledge in the professional domain. This transition facilitated a collective strategizing for how to privilege women's epistemic agency in constructing both the individual and broader professional identity of social work. To enact these collective strategies, members increasingly engaged in individual acts of resistance outside of the focus group, where they undertook disruptive and subversive activities. These activities included consciousness-raising, advocacy, covert-activism, communitarian approaches, and the employment of feminist frameworks in practice. Despite their challenges in enacting their focus group knowledge, participants talked about being persistent and empowered through the feminist focus group dynamic. This was symbolic of Donna Haraway's (2018) exhortation to realize transformation through the need for solidarity and collective action to "stay with the trouble" by adopting a "radical imagination" that fosters "creative visionaries" and "inventive practices," and not "game over cynicism" (p. 105). In summary, FPAR methodology employs collective organizing as a recursive and democratic process that creates spaces for consciousness-raising and acts of resistance to achieve transformative outcomes.

3.5 Discussion: Towards Transformative Social Work Epistemic Justice

In this chapter, we argued that as social workers striving for transformative change, we first need to recognize and engage with the "negative space" (Fricker, 2007, p. viii–ix) of epistemic injustice as it applies to all parts of our world, including the natural environment, not just human beings. Social workers must understand that, if we are to resist prevailing modernist, androcentric, positivist, colonial, Euro-centric, and neoliberal dominant discourses – which together, perpetuate epistemic injustice – we need to acknowledge how these intersecting injustices operate in our personal, community, professional, and work contexts. We also need to find ways to "see with new eyes" how these powerful discourses control what we know and how we experience reality, as shown in our example of FPAR.

For social workers to comprehensively embody epistemic justice, a richer, holistic epistemology is needed to transcend the conventional Euro-Western social work discourse that has dominated the profession. A fundamental imperative of transformative social work is to actively seek new ways of being in relationships which welcome, listen to, honour, and respect the knowledges of previously "silenced" knowers, recognizing that people's knowledges differ depending on their situation. All perspectives, especially those previously excluded, are needed. Transformative social work involves exploring how to work collectively and humbly, rather than from conventional hierarchical positions of professional or other forms of power. Only together can we develop the strength to "stay with the trouble" (Haraway, 2018, p. 105) in order to tackle the complex challenges confronting us and co-create effective solutions. Working in solidarity and learning from each other offers the hope that together, we will be able to work towards a more epistemically just and sustainable world.

References

Baines, D. (2024). Feminized care work, social work and resistance in the context of late neoliberalism. In C. Noble, S. Rasool, L. Harms-Smith, G. Muñoz-Arce, & D. Baines (Eds.), *The Routledge international handbook of feminisms in social work* (pp. 394–404). Routledge.

Beckett, J. P. (2018). The changing nature of social work. *International Social Work, 61*(6), 968–973.

Bell, K. (2012). Towards a post-conventional philosophical base for social work. *British Journal of Social Work, 42*(3), 408–423.

Bell, K. (2014). Exploring epistemic injustice through feminist social work research. *Affilia: Journal of Women and Social Work, 29*(2), 165–177.

Bell, K. (2021). A philosophy of social work beyond the anthropocene. In V. Bozalek & B. Pease (Eds.), *Post-anthropocentric social work: Critical posthuman and new materialist perspectives* (pp. 58–67). Routledge.

Bell, K. (2023). Post-anthropocentric social work: Transformative philosophy for contemporary theory and practice. In D. Hölscher, R. Hugman, & D. McAuliffe (Eds.), *Social work theory and ethics: Ideas in practice* (pp. 121–140). Springer.

Blackstock, C. (2009). The occasional evil of angels: Learning from the experiences of Aboriginal people and social work. *First Peoples Child and Family Review, 4*(1), 28–37.

Boetto, H. (2017). A transformative eco-social model: Challenging modernist assumptions in social work. *The British Journal of Social Work, 47*(1), 48–67.

Bowles, W., & Hugman, R. (in press). Ethical issues in social work research. In M. Alston, P. Buykx, W. Foote, & D. Betts (Eds.), *Handbook of social work research methods* (p. XXXX). Elgar Publishing.

Braidotti, R. (2019). A theoretical framework for the critical posthumanities. *Theory, Culture & Society, 36*(6), 31–61.

Burt, M. (2022). Introducing social workers: Their roles and training. *British Journal of Social Work, 52*(4), 2166–2182.

Bussey, S. R., Jemal, A., & Caliste, S. (2021). Transforming social work's potential in the field: A radical framework. *Social Work Education, 40*(1), 140–154.

Charlton, J. I. (1998). *Nothing about us without us: Disability oppression and empowerment.* University of California Press. http://www.jstor.org/stable/10.1525/j.ctt1pnqn9

Chigangaidze, R., Mafa, I., Simango, T., & Mudehwe, E. (2022). Establishing the relevance of the Ubuntu philosophy in social work practice: Inspired by the Ubuntu World Social Work Day, 2021 celebrations and the IFSW and IASSW's (2014) Global definition of social work. *International Social Work, 66*(1), 6–20. https://doi.org/10.1177/00208728221078374

Clarke, K. (2022). Reimagining social work ancestry: Toward epistemic decolonization. *Affilia: Feminist Inquiry in Social Work, 37*(2), 266–278.

Code, L. (1991). *What can she know? Feminist theory and the construction of knowledge*. Cornell University Press.

Crenshaw, K. (2017). *On intersectionality: Essential writings*. The New Press. https://scholarship.law.columbia.edu/books/255

Daukas, N. (2019). Epistemic justice and injustice. In M. Fricker, P. Graham, D. Henderson, & PedersenN. (Eds.), *The Routledge handbook of social epistemology* (pp. 327–334). Routledge.

Dotson, K. (2011). Tracking epistemic violence, tracking practices of silencing. *Hypatia, 26*, 236–257.

Dutta, U., Fernández, J. S., Galletta, A., & Langhout, R. D. (2023). Participatory action research as movement toward radical relationality, epistemic justice, and transformative intervention: A multivocal reflection. In H. Cooper, M. N. Coutanche, L. M. McMullen, A. T. Panter, D. Rindskopf, & K. J. Sher (Eds.), *APA handbook of research methods in psychology, research designs: Quantitative, qualitative, neuropsychological, and biological* (2nd ed., Vol. 2, pp. 305–327). American Psychological Association.

Dworkin, A. (1974). *Woman hating*. Penguin.

Dworkin, A. (1983). *Right-wing women: The politics of domesticated females*. The Women's Press.

Fejo-King, C. (2014). Indigenism and Australian social work. In NobleC. , H. Strauss, & B. Littlechild (Eds.), *Global social work: Crossing borders, blurring boundaries* (pp. 55–68). Sydney University Press.

Fox, N., & Alldred, P. (2020). Sustainability, feminist posthumanism and the unusual capacities of (post) humans. *Environmental Sociology, 6*(2), 121–131.

Fricker, M. (2007). *Epistemic injustice: Power and ethics of knowing*. Oxford University Press.

Fricker, M. (2008). Epistemic injustice précis. *Theoria, 61*, 69–71.

Gates, T. G., Bennett, B., & Baines, D. (2023). Strengthening critical allyship in social work education: Opportunities in the context of #BlackLivesMatter and COVID-19. *Social Work Education, 42*(3), 371–387.

Goessling, K. P. (2024). Learning from feminist participatory action research: A framework for responsive and generative research practices with young people. *Action Research, 23*(1), 48–70. https://doi.org/10.1177/14767503241228502

Green, S. (2023). Colonisation, post-colonialism and decolonisation. In D. Hölscher, R. Hugman, & D. McAuliffe (Eds.), *Social work theory and ethics: Ideas in practice* (pp. 1–20). Springer.

Green, S., & Bennett, B. (2018). Wayanha: A decolonised social work. *Australian Social Work, 71*(3), 261–264.

Hall, R. E. (2021). Social work's feminist façade: Descriptive manifestations of white supremacy. *The British Journal of Social Work, 52*(2), 1055–1069.

Hanrahan, C. (2011). Challenging anthropocentrism in social work through ethics and spirituality: Lessons from studies in human and animal bonds. *Journal of Religion and Spirituality in Social Work, 30*(3), 272–293.

Haraway, D. (1988). Situated knowledges: The science question in feminism and the privilege of partial perspective. *Feminist Studies, 14*(3), 575–599.

Haraway, D. (2018). Staying with the trouble for multispecies environmental justice. *Dialogues in Human Geography, 8*(1), 102–105. https://doi.org/10.1177/2043820617739208

Harding, S. (2007). Feminist standpoints. In Hesse-Biber (Ed.)S. , *Handbook of feminist research: Theory and praxis* (pp. 45–69). Sage Publications.

Healy, K. (2022). *Social work theories in context: Creating frameworks for practice* (3rd ed.). Bloomsbury.

hooks, b. (2014). *Feminism is for everybody: Passionate politics* (2nd ed.). Routledge.

Ioakimidis V., & Maglajlic, R. (2022). Global inequality, failed systems and the need for a paradigm shift. *British Journal of Social Work, 52*(2), 605–608.

Ioakimidis, V., & Trimikliniotis, N. (2020). Making sense of social work's troubled past: Professional identity, collective memory and the quest for historical justice. *The British Journal of Social Work, 50*(6), 1890–1908.

Jara, J. N. (2024). Ecofeminism and the popular solidarity economy in Latin American social work. In C. Noble, S. Rasool, L. Harms-Smith, G. Muñoz-Arce, & D. Baines (Eds.), *The Routledge international handbook of feminisms in social work* (pp. 587–597). Routledge.

Johnstone, M., & Lee, E. (2021). Epistemic injustice and Indigenous women: Toward centering Indigeneity in social work. *Affilia: Feminist Inquiry in Social Work, 36*(3), 376–390. https://doi.org/10.1177/0886109920985265

Kostecki, T. (2024). "We can't just sit back and say it's too hard": Older women, social justice, and activism. In C. Noble, S. Rasool, L. Harms-Smith, G. Muñoz-Arce, & D. Baines (Eds.), *The Routledge international handbook of feminisms in social work* (pp. 526–535). Routledge.

Laing, M. (2021). On being posthuman in human spaces: Critical posthumanist social work with interspecies families. *The International Journal of Sociology and Social Policy, 41*(3/4), 361–375.

Lorde, A. (1984). *Sister outsider: Essays and speeches*. Crossing Press.

Lykes, M. B., & Hershberg, R. M. (2012). Participatory action research and feminisms: Social inequalities and transformative praxis. In S. Hesse-Biber (Ed.), *Handbook of feminist research: Theory and praxis* (2nd ed., pp. 331–367). Sage.

Maguire, P. (2000). Feminist participatory research: Opportunities and challenges. *Feminist Review, 66*, 60–78.

Martinez-Brawley, E. E. (2019). Changing perspectives and changing goals: Constructivism in social work re-visited. *The British Journal of Social Work, 50*(1), 264–281.

McAuliffe, D. (2023). An ethic of care: Contributions to social work practice. In HölscherD. , R. Hugman, & D. McAuliffe (Eds.), *Social work theory and ethics: Ideas in practice* (pp. 349–366). Springer Nature.

McGregor, C. (2019). A paradigm framework for social work theory for early 21st century practice. *The British Journal of Social Work, 49*(8), 2112–2129.

McNamara, J. (2025). *A feminist approach for exploring and transforming the professional identity of women social workers in Australia*. PhD thesis, Charles Sturt University (under examination),

Miriam-Rose Ungunmerr. (1988). *Dadirri, inner deep listening and quiet still awareness: A reflection by Miriam-Rose Ungunmerr*. Retrieved July 2, 2024, from https://www.miriamrosefoundation.org.au/wpcontent/uploads/2021/03/Dadirri_Handout.pdf

Moorhead, B. (2021). Sustaining professional identity during the initial post-qualification period: Implications for retention strategies. *International Social Work, 64*(6), 1009–1021.

Morgenshtern, M., Schmid, J., & Yu, N. (2022). Interrogating settler social work with indigenous persons in Canada. *Journal of Social Work, 22*(5), 1170–1188. https://doi.org/10.1177/14680173211056823

Noble, C. (2021). Ecofeminism to feminist materialism: Implications for anthropocene feminist social work. In V. Bozalek & B. Pease (Eds.), *Post-anthropocentric social work: Critical posthuman and new materialist perspectives* (pp. 95–107). Routledge.

Panagiotaros, C. V., Boddy, J., Gray, T., & Ife, J. (2022). (Re-)Imagining social work in the anthropocene. *The British Journal of Social Work, 52*(8), 4778–4794.

Pease, B. (2021). Fostering non-anthropocentric vulnerability in men: Challenging the autonomous masculine subject in social work. In V. Bozalek & B. Pease (Eds.), *Post-anthropocentric social work: Critical posthuman and new materialist perspectives* (pp. 108–120). Routledge.

Plumwood, V. (1994). *Feminism and the mastery of nature*. Routledge.

Richter, M. (2023). Critical post-humanism and social work in the city: About being entangled as researcher and professional. *Social Inclusion, 11*(3), 210–219.

Sadurní-Balcells, N. (2023). The promise of agency in the narrative productions methodology: Thinking through decolonial feminisms. *Qualitative Research in Psychology, 20*(4), 565–578.

Showden, C. R., Nairn, K., & Matthews, K. R. (2022). 'So people wake up, what are we gonna do?': From paralysis to action in decolonizing activism. *Ethnicities, 22*(5), 663–684.

Tronto, J. C. (2015). *Who cares? How to reshape a democratic politics*. Cornell University Press.

Ungar, M. (2002). A deeper, more social ecological social work practice. *The Social Service Review, 76*(3), 480–497.

van Rhyn, B., Barwick, A., & Donelly, M. (2021). Embodiment as an instrument for empathy in social work. *Australian Social Work, 74*(2), 146–158.

Webb, S. (2021). What comes after the subject? Towards a critical posthumanist social work. In V. Bozalek & B. Pease (Eds.), *Post-anthropocentric social work: Critical posthuman and new materialist perspectives* (pp. 19–31). Routledge.

Woolf, V. (1929). *A room of one's own*. Harcourt, Brace and Company.

Wylie, A. (2011). Epistemic justice, ignorance, and procedural objectivity – editor's introduction, *Hypatia, 26*(2), 233–236.

Yadav, R. (2021). Conversation with the twenty-first century social work: Some 'post(s)' perspectives. *The British Journal of Social Work, 52*(5), 2966–2983.

Chapter 4

Epistemic Injustice in Community-Based Participatory Research

Toward Embodying Decolonial Ethical Relationality, Sentipensante, and Accountable Praxis in Social Work

Catalina Tang Yan

4.1 Introduction

Scholars have interrogated the ethics and politics of knowledge production in social science in general, and social work in particular (Macías, 2016). More specifically, they examine how competing neoliberal and psychological discourses of individuality and responsibility produce subjects of governance within research to maintain carceral logics (Leotti, 2020) and further reinforce human stratification (Orme, 2006). Thus, Strickland and Sharkey (2022) argue that knowledge is not inherently liberatory in the social work profession, but rather an exercise of power where social workers' professional "selves" are rooted in serving as "gatekeepers" who normalize settler-colonial white supremacist logics; correspondingly, we must begin to interrogate and confront our role as social control agents. Rather than engaging in research activities that maintain the status quo (i.e., constructing narratives that reproduce superiority, domination, and otherness), scholars highlight a need for researchers to define and know more about ourselves in ways that transcend descriptions of feelings to applications of critical thought in situating ourselves historically, geopolitically, and epistemologically in the context of modernity and knowledge production (Puebla, 2014; Quijano, 2007).

To contest embedded power hierarchies within knowledge production, scholars have increasingly adopted research methodologies and epistemological orientations that are committed to furthering the interests of exploited and oppressed groups, such as Community-Based Participatory Research (CBPR) or Participatory Action Research (PAR) (Fine et al., 2021; Johnson & Flynn, 2021; Wallerstein et al., 2017). Inspired by grassroots efforts in the Global South and working in solidarity with oppressed groups engaged in social movement struggles, PAR was described as a research method that combines activism, rigorous empiricism, and dissemination strategies that aim to unearth forgotten histories of ongoing political struggles and center collective historical analyses of power in knowledge production (Fals-Borda, 1979; Hall & Tandon, 2017; Lomeli & Rappaport, 2018). While scholars have integrated CBPR/PAR methodologies to increase community participation in research (Duke, 2020; Julian McFarlane et

DOI: 10.4324/9781003639046-6

al., 2022; Morrell et al., 2023), a critical self-examination and critique of their cooptation and misuse – particularly in terms of shifting PAR's radical impacts to mainstream academic social science, especially in higher education – has yet to be explored (Fals-Borda, 2001; Gaventa & Cornwall, 2006).

This chapter draws from decolonial (Mignolo & Escobar, 2013), sentipensante (Rendón, 2023), and radical relationality (Donald, 2016; Kerr & Adamov Ferguson, 2021) frameworks to theorize how power hierarchies and epistemic injustice can occur within PAR collaborations. Using situational analysis (A. E. Clarke, 2022) to examine social work scholars' and community-based stakeholders' narratives, this chapter interrogates epistemic injustice within participatory inquiry. Embodiments of disruption and refusal are presented as ways to contest epistemic injustice through the co-creation of counterspaces and counternarratives among social work scholars.

4.1.1 Key Terminology

Community-Based Participatory Research/Participatory Action Research. Epistemological orientation that aims to co-construct counter knowledge using participatory mechanisms in partnership with oppressed communities to engage in participatory inquiry, research, data collection, analysis, and action/dissemination initiatives toward the transformation of social realities and mobilization of political action (Wallerstein et al., 2017).

Carceral Logics. Systems that respond to social problems using surveillance, punishment, control, policing, and militarism that enforce racial capitalism, poverty, and prioritization of punishment over rehabilitation and transformative solutions (Kaba, 2021; Kaba & Ritchie, 2022).

Counternarratives. Narratives developed by the perspectives of individuals experiencing oppression that challenge dominant narratives and provide alternative viewpoints of social realities shaped by structural violence and oppression (Brooms et al., 2021; Case & Hunter, 2014; Schwartz, 2014).

Counterspaces. Affirming spaces that support psychological wellbeing of individuals experiencing oppression by challenging deficit-based societal narratives (Brooms et al., 2021; Case & Hunter, 2014; Schwartz, 2014).

Decolonial Framework. Analytical framework that critiques and seeks to dismantle Western colonial legacies and logics on knowledge, power, and culture (Mignolo & Escobar, 2013).

Epistemicide. Systematic violence and erasure of ecologies of knowledge, languages, cultures, and ancestral practices as a result of settler-colonial expansion and Eurocentric modernity (de Sousa Santos & Meneses, 2019).

Radical Relationality. Epistemological orientation that shifts away from colonial logics to prioritize interdependence, reciprocity, and collective responsibility among individuals and the environment (Donald, 2016; Kerr & Adamov Ferguson, 2021).

Sentipensante. A neologism and metaphorical framework that connects feeling and thinking to embody ways of being and possibilities of knowledge production and education (Fals-Borda & Mora-Osejo, 2003; Rendón, 2023).

Situational Analysis. An epistemological and qualitative methodological approach that incorporates grounded theory and map-making to examine structural analysis of major situations and discourses (A. E. Clarke, 2022).

4.2 Epistemic Injustice and Structural Violence in Social Work Knowledge Production

Epistemic injustice consists of the reproduction of testimonial and hermeneutical injustice, where individuals are discredited as knowers of their own lived experiences and social realities due to prejudice (Fricker, 2017). This concept has been further expanded by scholars integrating Black feminist and critical structural approaches; they theorize how epistemic injustice involves reducing collective experiences of discrimination to individual accounts and neglecting the dangers of perpetuating epistemic oppression and violence – namely, by reproducing settler-colonial epistemologies, participating in legacies of erasure and violence among systems and institutions by design, and promoting cultures of justification, silencing, exclusion, and exploitation (Berenstain et al., 2022; Dotson, 2011, 2012, 2014). Additionally, epistemic violence has been deeply entrenched in perpetuating *epistemicide*, which involves sustaining historical processes of the settler-colonial expansion and hegemonic Eurocentric modernity that maintain the destruction and dispossession of ecologies of knowledge, languages, cultures, and ancestral practices (de Sousa Santos & Meneses, 2019). While often-overlooked, epistemic violence may seem to occur in the absence of specific direct, indirect, or structural actors; yet, this form of structural violence is normalized through psychological violence (i.e., brainwashing and indoctrination) that blurs personal and structural violence (Barrientos, 2021; Galtung, 1969).

Cultivating a critical examination of epistemic injustice in knowledge production within the relational contexts between social work practitioners and community stakeholders is key to advancing justice in the profession (Lee, 2023). Scholars have interrogated clinical practices that perpetuate epistemic injustice, including fact construction and categorization in assessment, case formulation, listening empathetically, and conveying understanding of clients' experiences (Lee, 2022; Lee, Herschman et al., 2019; Lee, Tsang et al., 2019). By failing to acknowledge the epistemic authority and injustice present in institutionalized documents, procedures, and practices (such as child welfare and protection risk assessments, for example), human dignity can be undermined (Bostock & Koprowska, 2022; Johnstone, 2020). As the profession continues to be dominated by the hegemony of medical models that reinforce psychocentrism – where pathologies and views of madness are rooted individually rather than as the product of social structures and relations (LeBlanc & Kinsella, 2016)

– social workers are called upon to engage in a critical radical clinical approach that integrates epistemic justice principles, ethics of knowing, and relational collaboration (Johnstone, 2021).

While an emerging body of research has theorized and explored applications of epistemic justice within social work clinical practice, the analysis of epistemic justice in macro social work research and practice is limited. Drawing from relevant experiences and knowledges, scholars have theorized how postcolonial concepts can be translated to international social work practices that disrupt colonial assumptions in knowledge production and center reflexivity and critical discourse analysis (Willey-Sthapit, 2023). Similar articulations have theorized the importance of foregrounding Indigenous resistance, activism, and wisdom as approaches to address hermeneutical gaps in knowledge generation and dissemination (K. Clarke, 2022; Johnstone & Lee, 2021). Moreover, scholars have used critical feminist theory and epistemic injustice to examine women's experiences of agency in the realm of assisted reproduction to underscore power relationships therein (Bell, 2014). In addition to these collective efforts to apply epistemic justice to social work and to promote community wellbeing through macro social work systems-level interventions and partnerships, it is essential for social workers to develop a critical understanding of historical contexts and systems of power and oppression (Sousa et al., 2020). In particular, given the power imbalances inherent in the relationship between social work researchers and community members, (1) epistemic injustice and tokenistic partnerships can be avoided, (2) unconventional choices in and approaches to recognizing community members as knowers can be implemented, and (3) prioritizing relationship building may provide a means of restoring epistemic justice (Doherty et al., 2021; Skelton et al., 2023).

4.2.1 *Coloniality and Participatory Action Research*

Born of resistance struggles in the Global South, Community-Based Participatory Research (CBPR) or Participatory Action Research (PAR) is an epistemological approach that seeks to reclaim critical historical knowledges through the co-construction of counter knowledge; this is achieved by using participatory mechanisms that aim to disseminate information, transform social realities, and mobilize political action (Fals-Borda, 1987). Social workers have increasingly adopted CBPR/PAR approaches to research, training, and practice to challenge deficit-based constructions of oppressed communities and shift paradigms of knowledge expertise by affirming the profession's values (Teixeira & Kennedy, 2022). Social work scholars have partnered with youth and community stakeholders as co-researchers in all stages of the research process to collect, analyze, and disseminate knowledge in the margins and advance intersectional struggles, such as health equity, racial justice, community development, and education (Aldana et al., 2021; Tang Yan, Bachour et al., 2022; Tang Yan, Johnson et al., 2022). However, scholars have also voiced growing concerns about the need to redress power imbalances within the research collaboration (Tang Yan et al., 2023); researchers must increasingly navigate and subvert neoliberal and extractive academic structures that privilege scholarly productivity, the commodification of knowledge, and the development of standardized evidence-based practices over CBPR/PAR principles of participatory localized knowledge for social transformation (Kramer et al., 2021; Tang Yan, 2023).

While CBPR/PAR seeks to promote community participation and social change, scholars have examined the ways CBPR/PAR reproduces colonial modes of knowledge production and power relations; these tendencies are characterized by an emphasis on methodology (rather than the praxis of transforming social realities), privileging knowledge extraction, and limiting knowledge exchange and collaboration (Delgado-Baena et al., 2022). In reflecting upon these challenges, scholars have identified emerging tasks of transforming institutions, situating CBPR/PAR within a transdisciplinary lens, and recommitting to knowledge production that is accountable to bottom-up approaches and social, political, and cultural movements (Fals-Borda, 2005). More importantly, scholars are seeking to restore the values and creativity of CBPR/PAR and resist intellectual colonialism that favors Eurocentric forms of knowledge production that sustain political and economic systems of extraction, domination, and control of the Global North over the Global South (Fals-Borda & Mora-Osejo, 2003).

4.2.2 *Decolonial, Sentipensante, and Radical Relationality Frameworks*

To disrupt the ways in which hegemonic knowledge is – often unknowingly – reinforced and reproduced by well-intentioned social work researchers and practitioners, it is imperative to engage in a decolonial, sentipensante, and radical relationality praxis; doing so may allow individuals to contest social work's unexamined ontologies, epistemologies, and methodologies at the intersection of systems of power and oppression. Coloniality – namely, relationships of power and domination that reproduce racial and gender structures aligned with colonial, neoliberal, and imperialist systems of oppression and dispossession (Lugones, 2010; Quijano, 2007) – is deeply embedded in knowledge production, including CBPR/PAR (Fernández, 2022). Adopting a decolonial framework as an epistemic stance to cultivate and enact a radical (re)imagination and refusal of Western colonial epistemologies and gazes can generate knowledge that is transdisciplinary and grounded in histories and relationships of mutual and embodied co-existence and accountability (Fernández et al., 2021).

Additionally, to transgress colonial Eurocentric research standards rooted in the key pillars of reason and objectivity, sentipensante – namely, a neologism and metaphorical framework combining feeling (*sentimiento*) and thought (*pensamiento*) to embody ways of being and possibilities of knowledge production

– challenges normative whiteness and integrates an approach to understanding and transforming social realities where scientific reasoning is not enough (Fals-Borda, 2009).

Moreover, through an ethical and radical relationality framework, individuals are situated to unlearn colonial logics of knowledge production by understanding more deeply the histories and experiences of individuals and recognizing the responsibilities of being in interdependent ethical relationships beyond differences (Donald, 2016; Kerr & Adamov Ferguson, 2021). This process of unlearning and relearning the relational interdependent histories and experiences is essential as social work practice and values are increasingly compromised by neoliberal ideologies and policies that favor free market logics, individualism, and mass privatization (Abramovitz & Zelnick, 2021; Toft et al., 2023). Thus, it is essential for social workers to transform these structures through a radical relational praxis (Maree Stanley, 2020).

4.3 Case Study: Epistemic Injustice and Resistance in Participatory Action Research

4.3.1 *Background and Aims*

This study emerged from my lived experiences in interrogating and excavating the contradictions in praxis I witnessed complicitly and experienced personally with CBPR/PAR knowledge production processes as a doctoral student in a higher education institution in the United States. While I felt drawn to CBPR/PAR epistemological approaches to participatory forms of knowledge production and actively engaged in facilitating, organizing, and co-leading multiple CBPR/PAR collaborations as a community stakeholder and doctoral student, I felt conflicted; CBPR/PAR's values of radical relationality, political action, and transformation were often constrained and reduced to outputs and outcomes determined by the standards of neoliberal and colonial knowledge production. This study sought to explore *how* multiple positioned actors – namely social work faculty and community stakeholders with prior or current experience in CBPR/PAR collaborations – engage in knowledge production processes, contest interlocking systems of power and oppression, and resist epistemic violence. Rather than illustrating a comparative analysis of multiple perspectives, this study examines discourses of how multiple actors and protagonists conceptualize, contest, and redress epistemic oppression in CBPR/PAR social work collaborations (for more detailed information, see Tang Yan, 2023).

4.3.2 *Methodology*

Individual semi-structured interviews were conducted to gain an in-depth understanding (Jamshed, 2014) of epistemic injustice and power differentials among social work faculty (n = 13) and community stakeholders (n = 10) with prior or current experience in CBPR/PAR collaborations in the United States. Participants were recruited using non-probability sampling strategies including quota, snowball, and convenience sampling (Taherdoost, 2016). Interview transcripts were analyzed using thematic analysis (Braun & Clarke, 2021) and situational analysis (A. E. Clarke, 2022). Annotations of descriptive, linguistic, and conceptual comments were documented and subsequently coded to generate initial developing themes that were refined, defined, and named (Braun & Clarke, 2021). Characterized as a catalyst of the "critical-cartographic turn" (Grzanka, 2021, p. 11) to promote systems-level research, situational analysis is an epistemological and qualitative methodological approach that incorporates grounded theory and mapping techniques to illustrate critical and structural analysis of major situations and discourses (A. E. Clarke, 2022). Multiple readings of interview transcripts were completed, followed by memo-ing and map-making exercises to capture relevant human, nonhuman, discursive, and contextual elements (A. E. Clarke, 2022) relevant to epistemic justice and power in CBPR/PAR. Finally, member checking was conducted to increase trustworthiness, reflexivity, and transparency (Motulsky, 2021) where online individual meetings were held with all participants to share research findings, solicit feedback, and clarify any questions (McKim, 2023).

4.3.3 Positionality and Reflexivity

My identity as a researcher is profoundly shaped by my experiences growing up at the intersection of both the Global South (Colombia) and Global North (United States). I acknowledge that my ontological and epistemological approaches are influenced by a genealogy of critical feminist and decolonial scholars, activists, and community members committed to knowledge creation and ways of being aligned with principled struggles of resistance and justice. I identify as a person at the intersection of cultural, racial, and ethnic identities as an able-bodied, cis-gender woman born and raised by Chinese parents in Colombia. My experiences as a youth and community organizer, as well as a co-leader of CBPR/PAR collaborations situate me as both inside and in between social locations that confer both privilege and the status of "the other." I have also wrestled with feelings of indignation, disappointment, and anger where I have enacted oppressive practices and harm to community partners through violent institutional policies in CBPR/PAR collaborations. My socioeconomic class, education, affiliation with a university in the Global North, and the capacity to produce knowledge relevant to PAR afford me a status of privilege. While this privilege is shared with social work faculty who engaged in dialogical reflection as part of this study, I attempted to increase intersubjectivity and transparent and critical reflexive approaches in my communication with community stakeholders.

4.4 Findings: Epistemic Injustice and Epistemic Resistance in Participatory Action Research

Social work faculty (n = 13) and community stakeholders (n = 10) participated in two waves of in-depth individual semi-structured interviews via Zoom for a duration of 60 minutes each between 2020 and 2021. Over half of the faculty identified as female (77%). Racial identities reported by faculty included white (n = 5), Black/African American (n = 4), Asian, Southeast Asian, Pacific Islander (n = 2), and Latinx (n = 2). Nearly half of the faculty reported being involved in CBPR/PAR collaborations that had a minimum duration of 1–6 weeks (46%) and a maximum duration of 1–3 years (61%). Furthermore, half of the community stakeholders identified as male (n = 5), followed by female (n = 4), and gender nonconforming (n = 1). Racial identities reported by community stakeholders included Black/African American (n = 7), followed by Latinx (n = 2), and white (n = 1) (for more detailed demographic information, see Tang Yan, 2023).

Thematic and situational analysis illuminated discourses that normalized and replicated epistemic violence while also elucidating enactments of resistance and refusal within CBPR/PAR collaborations. Situational mapping underscored visible and invisible human and nonhuman elements, relationships, social worlds, and positions embedded in CBPR/PAR collaborations (Figures 4.1 and 4.2). While key actors (e.g., researchers, community partners, universities, community-based organizations, etc.) were visible and tended to be emphasized throughout scholarly literature and CBPR/PAR methodologies, invisible nonhuman elements and discourses, such as silent actors/actants (e.g., university gatekeeping, knowledge extraction, etc.), discursive constructions/major issues (e.g., structural violence, silencing, power imbalance, etc.), as well as temporal, historical, political, economic, sociocultural, and symbolic elements (e.g., predatory recruitment, structural racism, wealth strapping, white supremacy, etc.), have yet to be examined in relationship to epistemic violence (Figure 4.1). Additionally, mapping discourses that maintain colonial white supremacist paradigms of knowledge production against discourses promoting epistemic justice, embodied knowledge, and radical relationality illuminated visible and invisible positions of power enacted within PAR collaborations (Figure 4.3).

4.4.1 *Epistemic Violence: Colonial Knowledge Production and Othering*

While social work faculty facilitated participatory mechanisms to engage community stakeholders in knowledge co-creation within PAR collaborations, creating an egalitarian approach was constrained by institutional restrictions. One faculty member described:

Figure 4.1 Messy Situational Map.

Figure 4.2 Social Worlds/Arena Map.

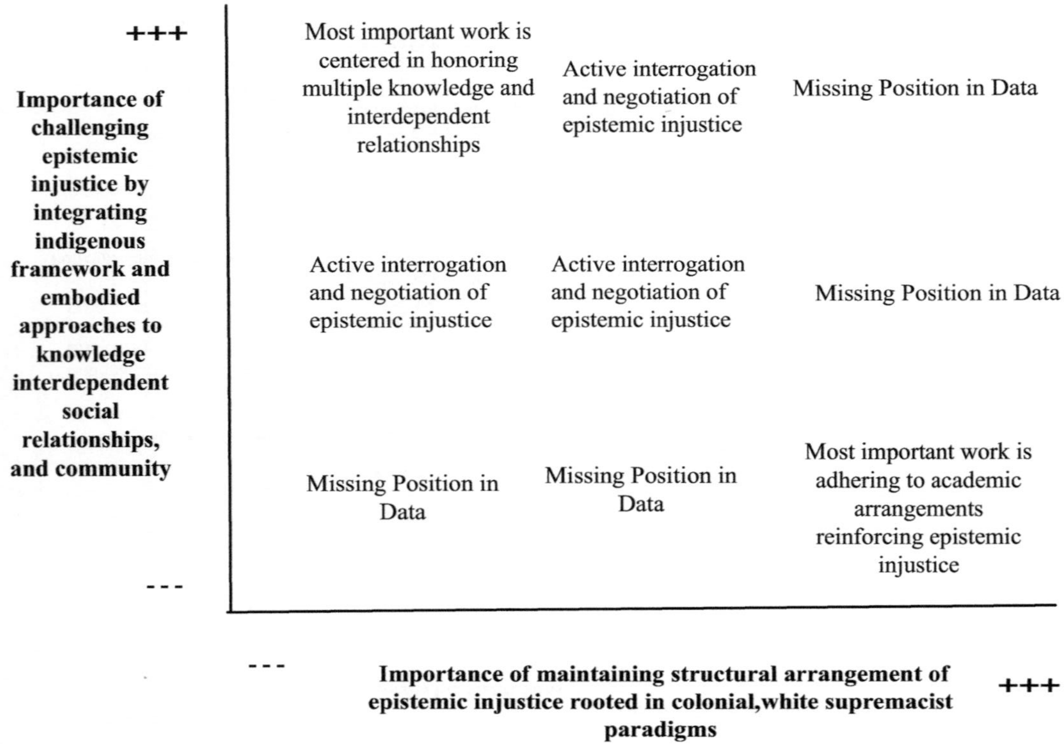

Figure 4.3 Positional Map.

> We live in social structures where that carries a lot of power and influence and even if I am intentionally trying to dismantle that and have an egalitarian approach to this research … when I enter a room full of young people … a question would be asked and everybody in the group would turn to me or ask me, *is this okay? can we do this?*, like permission seeking … some of that was necessitated by some of the processes required by the IRB (Institutional Review Board) and by my institution … we were following a protocol by my university that I had submitted … some of that is the result of us being socialized in these systems that even in environments where just because we intend to deconstruct these power dynamics doesn't mean they're deconstructed.
>
> (Chris, Faculty)

These constraints also resonated with the challenges another faculty experienced when trying to center Indigenous culture, traditions, and community wisdom throughout the CBPR/PAR collaboration. The faculty encountered obstacles in obtaining the IRB's approval to distribute kupu (i.e., gifts) to community elders: "That's how you enter an elder's home. You don't leave the gift when you leave. No, you enter with it. And what the pushback was, first of all, you have to call it compensation." Rather than viewing the researcher's Indigenous cultural knowledge as a valuable form of information and meaning-making in the research process with elders, institutional guidelines reinforced hermeneutical injustice; by invalidating gift-giving, this practice was instead defined through the gaze of knowledge transaction, whereby it was viewed as a potential source of coercion or undue influence. Additionally, the faculty noted challenges in requesting cash instead of gift cards: "I asked for cash ... They don't have credit cards … elders won't have any place to go to use gift certificates. And that was a pushback because we don't want to have the appearance of coercion or buying their story …" The faculty concluded: "Those are little things, but they were such barriers. It took forever to go back and forth..."

In addition to prioritizing institutional research policies over community partners' knowledges, traditions, and agency, discourses of testimonial injustice – specifically, othering – were generated through the discrediting and devaluing of community partners as knowers. The faculty explained how school district leaders denied Black youth researchers the opportunity to present their year-long research findings; viewing Black youth researchers in positions of influence and knowledge co-creation represented a threat to power and required surveillance:

> *Well, I think you need to make sure that you have hired security to watch them* – why do I have to hire a security guard? – *we just don't trust them.* They came to those meetings consistently, there was never an example of misbehavior, never … These young people have done nothing but perform exceptionally for me. … Their lives have changed. So, we missed an

> opportunity on that … that makes me very hesitant to continue my work because the last thing I need… as I'm pushing forward (is) for all the work to be undone. And then there are broken promises for young people. So … I'm operating as a true outsider, not a part of that district system. I don't get to change that discourse about the kids need security … I think there are some significant implications when you have that level of interlocking power and oppression. You know ultimately, we're talking about young people's development that is impacted.
>
> (Eastie, Faculty)

Finally, while higher education institutions provided financial resources to community partners and researchers to engage in PAR collaborations, university policies determined the range of financial compensation for stakeholders based on educational degrees obtained, contradicting PAR's egalitarian principles:

> How do you pay people … disparities in terms of salaries … it's a total contradiction and paradox to the work that we do … we want to blend the science in knowledge, and we don't want science to be valued more than experiential knowledge. But yet, when we are paying people, we are paying people based on their educational backgrounds, because that's what the university requires. They want to see their CVs and what they're able to do or not to do and then kind of like the rates that we're supposed to be paying. That's not equitable.
>
> (Mary, Faculty)

Community partners also reported additional financial barriers, including the need to submit required paperwork before being compensated, as well as payment delays. One youth co-researcher described:

> So, like, (Name of University) is a system of power that they have the resources to carry out things … and then at the same time, it can be a system of oppression … I'm gaining a lot of knowledge. I'm gaining the resources to carry out this research. But AT THE SAME TIME through … their HR department, trying to get hired, having to go through THAT many steps just to carry out the research is a way of, you know, it's a system of oppression in a way, because they're creating so many barriers, just for me to get paid, just for me to do this type of research. So, in a way, it's kind of like you have to go through, you know, ALL THESE steps, ALL these challenges to get to your final goal.
>
> (Lucas, Community Partner)

Despite the emancipatory and egalitarian approach of CBPR/PAR that prioritizes key community stakeholders' knowledge and experiences, faculty and community partners wrestled with compounding academic financial structures that limited their full participation in CBPR/PAR, reinforced dominant interpretive tools, and discounted community partners as knowledge producers.

4.4.2 *Enactments of Refusal, Sentipensante, and Radical Relationality*

Rather than merely integrating strategies to mitigate the negative impacts of unjust forms of knowledge co-creation in PAR, participants highlighted the importance of transforming fundamental structural issues that reinforce epistemic injustice. In particular, they described enactments of refusal to render more visible the seemingly invisible discourses of power which prioritize transactional partnerships over meaningful and reciprocal collaborations of knowledge co-creation and action:

> if on a grant … researchers are coming to you and saying, *hey, we want you to partner on this grant*. And they're not willing to tell you the grant … what their end is, that's a flag. I mean, it's not a comfortable conversation. We have researchers making all six figures … that's a hard conversation to talk to community partners, making 50 K and saying, *oh, yeah, I'm going to get $30,000 or 10% of my salary, $20,000 or $30,000 from this, and I'll give you $5,000 for stipends for young people*, that's a tough conversation, but like if you're not going to have that tough conversation, then you're not going for a partnership, you really just want someone to get the grant … that does not mean that what you're doing is CBPR, right? Like, CBPR is mutually beneficial, and even if it's not in funding, it's in resources. And even if it's not in resources, it's in relationships. And if you can't cross the dots around all those three things, then my recommendation to community partners is to walk away… you need to see someone who's invested being in the community.
>
> (U.J., Community Partner)

Additionally, discourses promoting epistemic justice called for sentipensante and radical ethical relationality approaches to commit to accountable relationships that combine reason with love, heart, and body to reclaim the harmony of truth. Participants described a need to cultivate "right" relationships, where individuals are emotionally attuned, participate in support networks, and are accountable for their actions at individual and institutional levels, particularly if they have enacted harm based on desires to gain more power at the expense of others. Another participant, a gender fluid spiritual healer, artist, and passionate youth worker and organizer with learning disabilities, explained:

> Everything should be rooted in the wellness of the physical, emotional, spiritual, and mental for everybody. That's the community approach. … Our

> circles in dynamics of people … I have a supervisor. I'm also supervising and those people are also getting supervised … different networks and intertwining of holding people accountable but also reminding people of why they're there. Professionalism and all these different things … that's just a made up thing to suppress people's nature … Everything that you do affects someone, every little thing that you do is affecting someone and if it's affecting one person, it's affecting the whole different, like how are you actually taking accountability or for the actions on an institutional level? How are you creating that bridge from institutional to personal and honoring in everything that you do? Because if you're not doing it, then you're playing a role in the maximum problem. It's about, like, reevaluating. It's about taking accountability, but on a more realistic level.
>
> (Mayinde, Community Partner)

Similarly, another faculty highlighted the role of radical relationality within PAR where researchers should be expected to work through relational processes, disconnections, and connections:

> I think that it's really important for people to understand that CBPR is not about you working with an advisory board. It's not about just asking people thoughts and going about doing what you always do. It's not about thinking that you know better than the people in your board … If your board is not participating and getting in conflict. And being involved and caring about it and doing the work. And you're having to bug the heck out of them to be involved. There's something wrong. So, you better fix it because if you're doing something that's really meaningful to that particular community when you are listening and trying to do the power and all of that, there's this magical process that happens that, that just makes the work very, very different.
>
> (Mary, Faculty)

Faculty and community partners described enactments of the epistemology of resistance, namely, the cultivation of specific practices to develop a social imagination that increases one's sensitivity to the oppression of marginalized individuals (Medina, 2013). To counteract how social insensitivity and imposed silences prevent community members from participating fully in knowledge production processes, it is necessary for faculty to be attuned and accountable to building meaningful relationships.

4.4.3 *Counterspaces and Counternarratives*

Faculty and community stakeholders reported engaging in a series of practices to shift away from supporting the ongoing development of damage-centered narratives-based research. These practices consisted primarily of creating counterspaces and counternarratives that prioritize being in "right" relationships with one another through attunement and re-envisioning collective purposes to achieve a shared theory of change. Drawing from Critical Race Theory (CRT), counterspaces are defined as affirming educational spaces where individuals interact in ways that challenge deficit-based notions of marginalization that were built upon social identities reinforced by racist institutionalized spaces (Brooms et al., 2021; Case & Hunter, 2014; Schwartz, 2014). These spaces were evident in the work of one of the faculty participants, a Chicana-*mestiza* junior faculty member with experience leading Youth Participatory Action Research (YPAR) with youth of color living in urban and rural settings. She shared her reflections on trying to create intentional and thoughtful counterspaces with youth researchers and to recognize how individuals are implicated with one another when examining racial, economic, and religious factors shaping segregation:

> I had to be … mindful of … facilitating the group because we were all from … different backgrounds … I had to be … conscientious of not really tokenizing our city youth. To make it a learning experience for the suburban youth so like our exchanges weren't about *Oh, let's examine how the city is messed up*. Instead … it's a suburb and city issue. How are we both implicated in this? People were really torn … well, whose responsibility is it? Should people in the suburbs also be providing funds for the inner city, if they are coming into the inner city to enjoy it outside of those institutions?
>
> (Ana, Faculty)

To facilitate and cultivate counterspaces, faculty described the "internal work" needed to critically examine individual, deeply held beliefs, particularly around faculty's positionality at the intersection of privilege and power. Ana further stated:

> there is a lot of work that needs to happen internally individually for myself and the staff on learning and unlearning our privilege, our power, or using our privilege as a leverage, right? Rather than as a tool of oppression. So that's that piece of like doing the work for yourself so that you can model … And if you haven't done the personal internal work, just because of the way privilege functions … so, in many ways it's a form of neglect … if you're not being conscientious of it.
>
> (Ana, Faculty)

Epistemic injustice erases social sensitivity, radical solidarity, and interconnections between interlocking systems of oppression, thus preventing individuals from different groups from engaging meaningfully in listening to and learning from one another (Medina, 2013). Faculty articulated the responsibility and commitment to co-create and sustain counterspaces and counternarratives as individual and collective practices that are deeply intertwined with and interdependent in resisting epistemic injustice within PAR.

4.5 Discussion: Social Work Implications and Actions

Findings reveal that when examining participatory knowledge production processes using decolonial, sentipensante, and embodied frameworks, discourses of epistemic violence – specifically, testimonial and hermeneutical injustice – are actively contested with enactments of refusal and the cultivation of counterspaces to foster epistemic justice. While social work researchers intend to create egalitarian community research partnerships, situational analysis mapping underscores the ways nonhuman elements and institutional policies and practices constrained these knowledge production efforts. While social work's value of the pursuit of justice aligns with participatory epistemologies of knowledge production (i.e., CBPR/PAR) that intend to democratize knowledge and promote epistemic justice, scholars challenge us to ask: "Is our research for the institution or for the community?" (Gutierrez et al., 2023, p. 294). Emphasizing the participatory nature of CBPR/PAR without acknowledging the ways interlocking systems of power and oppression are intertwined with colonial approaches to knowledge production can lead to performative enactments of knowledge co-creation (Burns et al., 2021). Thus, to engage in participatory knowledge production processes that support epistemic justice and resist epistemic oppression within colonial academic contexts, findings suggest it is necessary for social work scholars to engage in radical relationality and critical unsettling reflexivity to cultivate critical awareness of individual assumptions and disrupt systems of power within knowledge production processes.

This chapter presents relevant implications for social work practitioners, educators, scholars, and policymakers engaged in CBPR/PAR; we must interrogate the multilevel factors that maintain epistemic injustice and engage in the co-creation of counterspaces that embody enactments of refusal, radical relationality, and possibilities to resist institutional, dominant paradigms of knowledge production that prioritize colonialism and extraction. CBPR/PAR remains a site of re-training core epistemic values; we may shift away from Eurocentric approaches (Krueger-Henney & Ruglis, 2020) and guide prospective social work scholars to re-examine individual assumptions and consider the dangers seen, unseen, and foreseen associated with these epistemic dissonances. CBPR/PAR can also present possibilities to enhance individual competencies in confronting epistemic violence and to strengthen critical awareness and praxis grounded in radical relationality as well as decolonial and embodied frameworks (Almeida et al., 2019; Tang Yan, Johnson et al., 2022; Tang Yan, Orlandimeje et al., 2022; Volpe et al., 2023). Moreover, this chapter explicitly illustrates key ethical and epistemic issues in participatory research inquiry that a growing body of scholars are encouraging us to further interrogate, unsettle, and redefine as a praxis of engagement and redressing of historical trauma (Glass et al., 2018). Similarly, scholars suggest rendering visible critiques of Western epistemic violence in research, dismantling borderland epistemologies that prioritize the surveillance and policing of imposed forms of knowledge, and excavating possibilities for more expansive and fluid ways of being and knowing in research (Krueger-Henney et al., 2023).

This chapter focuses on theorizing power hierarchies and epistemic injustice within CBPR/PAR collaborations informed by decolonial, sentipensante, and radical relationality frameworks. It drew from relevant research exploring the perceptions of knowledge production processes and power dynamics among social work faculty and community partners with prior experience in CBPR/PAR collaborations. Situational mapping and thematic analysis illuminated the multiple discourses and narratives of epistemic injustice masked by participatory research narratives. By inviting social work faculty and community stakeholders to interrogate the ways participatory knowledge production is not exempt from colonial knowledge production shaping neoliberal and extractive research practices in higher education, we have gained a deeper understanding of epistemic injustice and generated community-level possibilities to embody and enact epistemic justice in CBPR/PAR.

References

Abramovitz, M., & Zelnick, J. (2021). Neoliberal managerialism and the human services. In *Encyclopedia of social work*. https://doi.org/10.1093/acrefore/9780199975839.013.1408

Aldana, A., Richards-Schuster, K., & Checkoway, B. (2021). "Down woodward": A case study of empowering youth to see and disrupt segregation using photovoice methods. *Journal of Adolescent Research, 36*(1), 34–67. https://doi.org/10.1177/0743558420933220

Almeida, R. V., Werkmeister Rozas, L. M., Cross-Denny, B., Lee, K. K., & Yamada, A.-M. (2019). Coloniality and intersectionality in social work education and practice. *Journal of Progressive Human Services, 30*(2), 148–164. https://doi.org/10.1080/10428232.2019.1574195

Barrientos, K. C. (2021). Turn white or disappear: Psychological colonialism as structural violence in the work of Johan Galtung and Frantz Fanon. *Academia Letters*. https://www.academia.edu/60828911/Turn_White_or_Disappear_Psychological_Colonialism_as_Structural_Violence_in_the_Work_of_Johan_Galtung_and_Frantz_Fanon

Bell, K. (2014). Exploring epistemic injustice through feminist social work research. *Affilia, 29*(2), 165–177. https://doi.org/10.1177/0886109913516457

Berenstain, N., Dotson, K., Paredes, J., Ruíz, E., & Silva, N. K. (2022). Epistemic oppression, resistance, and resurgence. *Contemporary Political Theory, 21*(2), 283–314. https://doi.org/10.1057/s41296-021-00483-z

Bostock, L., & Koprowska, J. (2022). 'I know how it sounds on paper' risk talk, the use of documents and epistemic justice in child protection assessment home visits. *Qualitative Social Work, 21*(6), 1147–1166. https://doi.org/10.1177/14733250221124217

Braun, V., & Clarke, V. (2021). One size fits all? What counts as quality practice in (reflexive) thematic analysis? *Qualitative Research in Psychology*, *18*(3), 328–352. https://doi.org/10.1080/14780887.2020.1769238

Brooms, D. R., Clark, J. S., & Druery, J. E. (2021). "We can redefine ourselves": Enhancing Black college men's persistence through counterspaces. *Journal of Black Studies*, *52*(3), 277–295. https://doi.org/10.1177/0021934720976410

Burns, D., Howard, J., & Ospina, S. M. (2021). *The SAGE handbook of participatory research and inquiry*. SAGE Publications.

Case, A. D., & Hunter, C. D. (2014). Counterspaces and the narrative identity work of offender-labeled African American youth. *Journal of Community Psychology*, *42*(8), 907–923. https://doi.org/10.1002/jcop.21661

Clarke, A. E. (2022). Situating grounded theory and situational analysis in interpretive qualitative inquiry. In A. E. Clarke, R. Washburn, & C. Friese (Eds.), *Situational analysis in practice* (2nd ed., pp. 3–48). Routledge.

Clarke, K. (2022). Reimagining social work ancestry: Toward epistemic decolonization. *Affilia: Feminist Inquiry in Social Work*, *37*(2), 266–278. https://doi.org/10.1177/08861099211051326

de Sousa Santos, B., & Meneses, M. (2019). *Knowledges born in the struggle: Constructing the epistemologies of the Global South*. Routledge. https://www.routledge.com/Knowledges-Born-in-the-Struggle-Constructing-the-Epistemologies-of-the/Santos-Meneses/p/book/9780367362072

Delgado-Baena, A., Serrano, L., Vela-Jiménez, R., López-Montero, R., & Sianes, A. (2022). Epistemic injustice and dissidence: A bibliometric analysis of the literature on participatory action research hosted on the web of science. *Action Research*, *20*(4), 318–342. https://doi.org/10.1177/14767503221126531

Doherty, M., McGuire, A., Martin, R., & Gillieatt, S. (2021). Disrupting 'expertise': Learnings from a grassroots lived experience and social work academic partnership. *Advances in Social Work and Welfare Education*, *22*(2), Article 2. https://journal.anzswwer.org/index.php/advances/article/view/72

Donald, D. (2016). From what does ethical relationality flow? An "Indian" act in three artifacts. *Counterpoints*, *478*, 10–16.

Dotson, K. (2011). Tracking epistemic violence, tracking practices of silencing. *Hypatia*, *26*(2), 236–257. https://doi.org/10.1111/j.1527-2001.2011.01177.x

Dotson, K. (2012). A cautionary tale: On limiting epistemic oppression. *Frontiers: A Journal of Women Studies*, *33*(1), 24–47. https://doi.org/10.5250/fronjwomestud.33.1.0024

Dotson, K. (2014). Conceptualizing epistemic oppression. *Social Epistemology*, *28*(2), 115–138. https://doi.org/10.1080/02691728.2013.782585

Duke, M. (2020). Community-based participatory research. In *Oxford research encyclopedia of anthropology* (pp. 1–17). https://doi.org/10.1093/acrefore/9780190854584.013.225

Fals-Borda, O. (1979). Investigating reality in order to transform it: The Colombian experience. *Dialectical Anthropology*, *4*(1), 33–55. https://doi.org/10.1007/BF00417683

Fals-Borda, O. (1987). The application of participatory action-research in Latin America. *International Sociology*, *2*(4), 329–347. https://doi.org/10.1177/026858098700200401

Fals-Borda, O. (2001). Guest editorial: From Cartagena to Ballarat: A report on the Joint Fifth World Congress on action learning, action research, and process management and Ninth World Congress on participatory action research. *Systemic Practice and Action Research, 14*(2), 125.

Fals-Borda, O. (2005). Participatory (action) research in social theory: Origins and challenges. In P. Reason & H. Bradbury (Eds.), *Handbook of action research: Concise paperback edition* (pp. 27–37). SAGE.

Fals-Borda, O. (2009). *Una sociología sentipensante para América Latina.*

Fals-Borda, O., & Mora-Osejo, L. E. (2003). Context and diffusion of knowledge: A critique of eurocentrism. *Action Research, 1*(1), 29–37. https://doi.org/10.1177/14767503030011003

Fernández, J. S. (2022). Decolonising participatory action research in community psychology. In KessiS. , S. Suffla, & M. Seedat (Eds.), *Decolonial enactments in community psychology* (pp. 29–51). Springer International Publishing. https://doi.org/10.1007/978-3-030-75201-9_3

Fernández, J. S., Sonn, C. C., Carolissen, R., & Stevens, G. (2021). Roots and routes toward decoloniality within and outside psychology praxis. *Review of General Psychology, 25*(4), 354–368. https://doi.org/10.1177/10892680211002437

Fine, M., Torre, M. E., Oswald, A. G., & Avory, S. (2021). Critical participatory action research: Methods and praxis for intersectional knowledge production. *Journal of Counseling Psychology, 68*(3), 344–356. https://doi.org/10.1037/cou0000445

Fricker, M. (2017). *Evolving concepts of epistemic injustice* (I. J. Kidd, J. Medina, & G. Pohlhaus Jr., Eds., pp. 53–60). Routledge. https://www.routledge.com/9781138828254

Galtung, J. (1969). Violence, peace, and peace research. *Journal of Peace Research, 6*(3), 167–191. https://doi.org/10.1177/002234336900600301

Gaventa, J., & Cornwall, A. (2006). Challenging the boundaries of the possible: Participation, knowledge and power. *IDS Bulletin, 37*(6), 122–128. https://doi.org/10.1111/j.1759-5436.2006.tb00329.x

Glass, R. D., Morton, J. M., King, J. E., Krueger-Henney, P., Moses, M. S., Sabati, S., & Richardson, T. (2018). The ethical stakes of collaborative community-based social science research. *Urban Education, 53*(4), 503–531. https://doi.org/10.1177/0042085918762522

Grzanka, P. R. (2021). The shape of knowledge: Situational analysis in counseling psychology research. *Journal of Counseling Psychology, 68*(3), 316–330. https://doi.org/10.1037/cou0000527

Gutierrez, R. A. E., Sonsteng-Person, M., King-Shaw, S., & Valmocena, M. T. (2023). For the institution or for the community?: Toward an anti-oppressive research praxis in conducting participatory action research. *Journal of Community Practice, 31*(3–4), 284–296. https://doi.org/10.1080/10705422.2023.2272162

Hall, B. L., & Tandon, R. (2017). Participatory research: Where have we been, where are we going? – A dialogue. *Research for All, 1*, 365–374. https://doi.org/10.18546/RFA.01.2.12

Jamshed, S. (2014). Qualitative research method-interviewing and observation. *Journal of Basic and Clinical Pharmacy, 5*(4), 87–88. https://doi.org/10.4103/0976-0105.141942

Johnson, H., & Flynn, C. (2021). Collaboration for improving social work practice: The promise of feminist participatory action research. *Affilia, 36*(3), 441–459. https://doi.org/10.1177/0886109920954424

Johnstone, M. (2020). Epistemic (in)justice in child welfare risk assessment. In C. Brown & J. E. MacDonald (Eds.), *Critical clinical social work: Counterstorying for social justice* (pp. 267–287). Canadian Scholars' Press.

Johnstone, M. (2021). Centering social justice in mental health practice: Epistemic justice and social work practice. *Research on Social Work Practice, 31*(6), 634–643. https://doi.org/10.1177/10497315211010957

Johnstone, M., & Lee, E. (2021). Epistemic injustice and indigenous women: Toward centering indigeneity in social work. *Affilia, 36*(3), 376–390. https://doi.org/10.1177/0886109920985265

Julian McFarlane, S., Occa, A., Peng, W., Awonuga, O., & Morgan, S. E. (2022). Community-based Participatory Research (CBPR) to enhance participation of racial/ethnic minorities in clinical trials: A 10-Year systematic review. *Health Communication, 37*(9), 1075–1092. https://doi.org/10.1080/10410236.2021.1943978

Kaba, M. (2021). *We do this 'til we free us: Abolitionist organizing and transforming justice*. Haymarket Books.

Kaba, M., & Ritchie, A. J. (2022). *No more police: A case for abolition*. The New Press.

Kerr, J., & Adamov Ferguson, K. (2021). Ethical relationality and indigenous storywork principles as methodology: Addressing settler-colonial divides in inner-city educational research. *Qualitative Inquiry, 27*(6), 706–715. https://doi.org/10.1177/1077800420971864

Kramer, C. S., Cosgrove, D., Mountz, S., & Lee, E. (2021). Finding a place for my research to belong: Experiences of early-career social work participatory action researchers in neoliberal academia. *Critical and Radical Social Work, 9*(2), 269–287. https://doi.org/10.1332/204986020X16031175005938

Krueger-Henney, P., Kress, T., & Amorim, S. (2023). This is not a research article: An invitation to mobilize knowledge from the epistemological borderlands of social science. *Cultural Studies of Science Education, 18*(2), 359–375. https://doi.org/10.1007/s11422-023-10178-z

Krueger-Henney, P., & Ruglis, J. (2020). PAR is a way of life: Participatory action research as core re-training for fugitive research praxis. *Educational Philosophy and Theory, 52*(9), 961–972. https://doi.org/10.1080/00131857.2020.1762569

LeBlanc, S., & Kinsella, E. A. (2016). Toward epistemic justice: A critically reflexive examination of 'sanism' and implications for knowledge generation. *Studies in Social Justice, 10*(1), Article 1. https://doi.org/10.26522/ssj.v10i1.1324

Lee, E. (2022). Fact construction and categorization in assessment: Cultivating epistemic justice and resistance in social work assessment. *Social Service Review, 96*(3), 534–571. https://doi.org/10.1086/721273

Lee, E. (2023). Resisting dogmatism in social work knowledge generation: Theorising, social justice and implications for social work doctoral education. *The British Journal of Social Work, 53*(2), 1142–1160. https://doi.org/10.1093/bjsw/bcac176

Lee, E., Herschman, J., & Johnstone, M. (2019). How to convey social workers' understanding to clients in everyday interactions? Toward epistemic justice. *Social Work Education, 38*(4), 485–502. https://doi.org/10.1080/02615479.2018.1539070

Lee, E., Tsang, A. K. T., Bogo, M., Johnstone, M., Herschman, J., & Ryan, M. (2019). Honoring the voice of the client in clinical social work practice: Negotiating with epistemic injustice. *Social Work, 64*(1), 29–40. https://doi.org/10.1093/sw/swy050

Leotti, S. M. (2020). The discursive construction of risk: Social work knowledge production and criminalized women. *Social Service Review, 94*(3), 445–487. https://doi.org/10.1086/710562

Lomeli, J. D. R., & Rappaport, J. (2018). Imagining Latin American social science from the Global South: Orlando Fals Borda and participatory action research. *Latin American Research Review*, *53*(3), 597–612. https://doi.org/10.25222/larr.164

Lugones, M. (2010). The coloniality of gender. In L. De Souza Lima, E. Otero Quezada, & J. Roth (Eds.), *Feminisms in movement* (pp. 35–58). Routledge.

Macías, T. (2016). Editorial: "The ethics and politics of knowledge production," critical reflections on social work and social sciences research. *Intersectionalities: A Global Journal of Social Work Analysis, Research, Polity, and Practice*, *5*(1), Article 1.

Maree Stanley, J. (2020). Intersectional and relational Frameworks: Confronting anti-blackness, settler colonialism, and neoliberalism in u.s. social work. *Journal of Progressive Human Services*, *31*(3), 210–225. https://doi.org/10.1080/10428232.2019.1703246

McKim, C. (2023). Meaningful member-checking: A structured approach to member-checking. *American Journal of Qualitative Research*, *7*(2), 41–52.

Medina, J. (2013). Resistant imaginations and radical solidarity. In J. Medina (Ed.), *The epistemology of resistance: Gender and racial oppression, epistemic injustice, and the social imagination* (pp. 250–312). Oxford University Press. https://doi.org/10.1093/acprof:oso/9780199929023.003.0006

Mignolo, W. D., & Escobar, A. (2013). *Globalization and the decolonial option.* Routledge.

Morrell, M. A., Willis, T. R., Brown, D. R., O'Brian, C. A., Post, S. L., Woloschak, G. E., Bonini, M. G., Paunesku, T., Popovic, J., Manning, T. M., Henley, C., Girotti, J., Rogers, R., Velásquez, C., López, J., Glenn, J., & Simon, M. A. (2023). Lessons learned in the practice of community-based participatory research with community partner collaboration in study design and implementation: The community scientist model. *Cancer Causes & Control*, *34*(7), 621–624. https://doi.org/10.1007/s10552-023-01699-7

Motulsky, S. L. (2021). Is member checking the gold standard of quality in qualitative research? *Qualitative Psychology*, *8*(3), 389–406. https://doi.org/10.1037/qup0000215

Orme, J. (2006). What are we producing knowledge for? *Journal of Social Policy and Social Work*, *2*, 196–208.

Puebla, C. A. C. (2014). Indigenous researchers and epistemic violence. In Denzin, Norman K. & M. D. Giardina (Eds.), *Qualitative inquiry outside the academy* (pp. 387–401). Routledge.

Quijano, A. (2007). Coloniality and modernity/rationality. *Cultural Studies*, *21*(2–3), 168–178. https://doi.org/10.1080/09502380601164353

Rendón, L. I. (2023). *Sentipensante (Sensing / Thinking) pedagogy: Educating for wholeness, social justice, and liberation.* Routledge. https://www.routledge.com/Sentipensante-Sensing--Thinking-Pedagogy-Educating-for-Wholeness-Social/Rendon/p/book/9781642675771

Schwartz, J. (2014). Classrooms of spatial justice: Counter-spaces and young men of color in a GED program. *Adult Education Quarterly*, *64*(2), 110–127. https://doi.org/10.1177/0741713613513632

Skelton, D., Coyne, B., Monje Barón, B., & Blunschi Ackermann, M. -R. (2023). 'Taking knowledge on a journey': Creating conditions for epistemic justice. *Action Research*, *1*. https://doi.org/10.1177/14767503231205235

Sousa, C. A., Yutzy, L., Campbell, M., Cook, C., & Slates, S. (2020). Understanding the curricular needs and practice contexts of macro social work: A community-based process. *Journal of Social Work Education, 56*(3), 533–547. https://doi.org/10.1080/10437797.2019.1656686

Strickland, C. A., & Sharkey, C. N. (2022). Power knowledge in social work: Educating social workers to practice racial justice. *Journal of Ethnic & Cultural Diversity in Social Work, 31*(3–5), 240–247. https://doi.org/10.1080/15313204.2022.2070897

Taherdoost, H. (2016). Sampling methods in research methodology; How to choose a sampling technique for research. *International Journal of Academic Research in Management, 5*(2), 18–27. https://doi.org/10.2139/ssrn.3205035

Tang Yan, C. (2023). Narratives and discourses of epistemic justice, power, and oppression in community-based participatory research collaborations. *Journal of the Society for Social Work and Research.* https://doi.org/10.1086/725433

Tang Yan, C., Bachour, A., Pérez, C. J., Ansaldo, L. P., Santiago, D., Jin, Y., Li, Z., Mok, Y. S., Weng, Y., & Martinez, L. S. (2022). Partnering with immigrant families to promote language justice and equity in education. *American Journal of Community Psychology, 70*(3–4), 433–457. https://doi.org/10.1002/ajcp.12604

Tang Yan, C., Jin, Y., Chalfin, E., & Sprague Martinez, L. (2023). Interrogation, negotiation, and subversion of power differentials in community-based participatory research: A scoping review. *Progress in Community Health Partnerships: Research, Education, and Action, 18*(2), 295–305. https://preprint.press.jhu.edu/pchp/preprints/interrogation-negotiation-and-subversion-power-differentials-community-based

Tang Yan, C., Johnson, K., Kwesele, C., Araujo Brinkerhoff, C., & Sprague Martinez, L. (2022). Critical reflections from doctoral students engaging in local and transnational community-based participatory research (CBPR) approaches to health promotion. *Journal of Social Work Education, 58*(2), 245–258. https://doi.org/10.1080/10437797.2021.1883491

Tang Yan, C., Orlandimeje, R., Drucker, R., & Lang, A. J. (2022). Unsettling reflexivity and critical race pedagogy in social work education: Narratives from social work students. *Social Work Education, 41*(8), 1669–1692. https://doi.org/10.1080/02615479.2021.1924665

Teixeira, S., & Kennedy, H. (2022). Social work and youth participatory action research (YPAR): Past, present, and future. *Social Work, 67*(3), 286–295. https://doi.org/10.1093/sw/swac016

Toft, J., Lightfoot, E. B., Calhoun, M., Choy-Brown, M., Merighi, J. R., Renner, L. M., Soffer-Elnekave, R., Mendel, J., & Marsalis, S. (2023). Effects of neoliberalism on social work practice in the United States: A scoping review. *Social Work Research, 47*(2), 99–110. https://doi.org/10.1093/swr/svad003

Volpe, V. V., Hope, E. C., Mosley, D. V., Javidi, H., Sosoo, E. E., & Benson, G. P. (2023). How we get free: graduate training as an opportunity for equitable participation and liberation. *Perspectives on Psychological Science, 18*(2), 428–444. https://doi.org/10.1177/17456916221096086

Wallerstein, N., Duran, B., Oetzel, J. G., & Minkler, M. (2017). *Community-based participatory research for health: Advancing social and health equity.* John Wiley & Sons.

Willey-Sthapit, C. (2023). Epistemic justice in international social work research: Postcolonial theory and analytic strategies. *International Journal of Social Welfare.* https://doi.org/10.1111/ijsw.12613

Chapter 5

Confronting Epistemic Injustice in Everyday Social Work Practice

Eunjung Lee

5.1 The Perils/Strengths of Listening as Epistemic In/Justice in Social Work Practice

Building a strong working relationship with clients is fundamental at all levels of social work practice. In clinical work, the therapeutic alliance is not merely a conditional element but a key factor for facilitating transformative changes in clients (Norcross, 2011; Sudbery, 2002; Tosone, 2004). In community organizations, alliance is also a prerequisite to activating desirable change (Lauer et al., 2025). To build relationships with clients and communities, we as social workers must carefully listen to their stories – their values, viewpoints, struggles, and strengths. Such attentive and intentional listening will allow us to gain the information we need to guide our professional actions (e.g., assessment and subsequent intervention).

Yet, what if we cannot hear their stories as they were intended? Perhaps this mishearing may occur due to our pre-conceived notions of certain groups of people – that is "identity prejudice" (Fricker, 2007, p. 1)? Furthermore, what if we *question* the experiences of others as if their stories are not trustworthy or credible – that is "testimonial injustice" (p. 1)? Or maybe we even give the impression to clients and communities that we are no longer interested in or available to hear their experiences – that is "epistemic silencing" (p. 6)? Despite our good intentions to help others, what if we are lacking the relevant information (i.e., hermeneutical resources) needed to understand their experiences? And when this lack occurs, what if it can be attributed to our habitual reliance on dominant discourses or a pervasive and systemic absence of efforts to develop a shared understanding of their experiences – that is "hermeneutical injustice" (p. 1)? Even with ample evidence of their marginalized experiences, what if we fail to recognize these clients and communities as valid and, correspondingly, decline to integrate them into a socially shared understanding and our professional decision making – that is "willful hermeneutical ignorance" (Pohlhaus, 2012, p. 715)? All these questions fall within the epistemic domain – territories of knowledge – and form the focus of this chapter.

DOI: 10.4324/9781003639046-7

These "what if" scenarios are sadly more common than not, including in my own practice. In the hopes of countering and preventing the reoccurrence of such unjust incidents, this chapter aims to both unveil and illustrate how these moments can happen in our everyday practice. Doing so is critical in order to pause, reflect upon, and change the *modus operandi* of our day-to-day activities; as Garfinkel (1967) notes, the epistemic domain forms "an essential part of the background features of everyday interactional scenes" (Lee, Herschman et al., 2019, p. 488). Indeed, epistemic attacks are layered into multiple levels of social work practice in "more mundane, ordinary and less obvious ways," yet "subtly conditioning our shifting view of human beings" and their marginalized communities (Watts & Hodgson, 2019, p. 93).

To achieve this aim, I am guided by critical feminist scholars' work on the ethics of knowing, power, and social discrimination. In particular, I find Fricker's concept of what she calls *epistemic injustice* pivotal in social work practice. Fricker (2007) explains that "a distinctively epistemic kind of injustice" occurs when "a wrong is done to someone specifically in their capacity as a knower" (p. 1). When one's capacity as a knower of their own experiences is denied and silenced, and their lived experience/knowledge is not recognized as a contribution to our shared knowledge, she argues that epistemic injustice ensues. Consequently, the experiences and knowledge of these clients and communities continue to be relegated to the margins and they must carry the burden of explaining their experiences over and over to those with social power (e.g., social workers and other professionals). Notably, these individuals and groups encounter ongoing systemic discrimination, since their experiences are buried in a void. What happens to the clients and communities (i.e., their epistemic injuries/trauma) is profound since one's capacity to be recognized as a trustworthy conveyer of knowledge is essential to achieving a sense of human value and worth (Fricker, 2007). Thus, knowledge, power, and social discrimination are intrinsically intertwined, which is why social work practitioners should care about epistemic injustice.

Before illustrating how we may stumble into epistemic injustice in our everyday practice, this chapter will briefly highlight key terms to guide readers. This terminology will also outline how these philosophical concepts emerged to unsettle and advance our understanding of human actions and interactions (hereafter, inter/actions) and how these inter/actions are embedded within the systemic structure of the ethics of knowledge and power.

5.1.1 Key Terminology

Epistemic Objectification and Epistemic Silencing. To explain epistemic objectification and epistemic silencing, Fricker (2007) delineates between *informants* and *sources of information.* To be a good informant is to be treated as an *epistemic agent* – a person who is respected as holding the credibility/power of knowledge/information. A source of information, in contrast, is not necessarily understood as a holder of knowledge. Importantly, the power to interpret and make sense of information falls upon the hearer, not the speaker. This is where epistemic objectification occurs as "the wrong that testimonial injustice inflicts" (Fricker, 2007, p. 6): speakers are merely treated as *sources of information* and "demoted from subject to object, relegated from the role of active epistemic agent" (Fricker, 2007, p. 132). Consider, for example, the biomedical approach to diagnosis: more often than not, the patient is merely treated as a source of information, answering the doctor's questions and describing their symptoms and experiences; it is the doctor who makes sense of the information and gives a formal diagnosis. Here, the patient is objectified as a source of information and is not respected as a contributor to the diagnosis. Instead, the doctor claims the role of good informant and assumes the sole position of the diagnosing subject.

Fricker views epistemic silencing as a phenomenon associated with epistemic objectification, occurring within the realm of testimonial injustice. She argues that, when an individual is not asked about their experiences and further, discredited when those experiences are shared, "the phenomenon of pre-emptive testimonial injustice in relations to social power" functions as "a mechanism of silencing" (p. 131). In Chapter 1, I discuss in detail these related constructs (e.g., testimonial injustice, hermeneutical injustice) along with testimonial sensibilities and hermeneutical resources – to invite readers to consider how to navigate epistemic in/justice and epistemic resistance in social work practice, education, and research (Lee, 2027).

Hermeneutical Resources. Hermeneutical resources refer to "our shared tools of social interpretation" (Fricker, 2007, p. 6). When there is a gap in hermeneutical resources, unequal social power distributions ensue, and different social groups are impinged upon. Notably, marginalized groups cannot often participate fairly in social inter/actions where social meanings are generated and through which norms are marked. Then, in a cyclical process, individuals in the disempowered group are "hermeneutically marginalized" (p. 6).

Willful Hermeneutical Ignorance and Contributory Injustice. Fricker (2007) notes that hermeneutical injustice occurs when one cannot comprehend and further communicate their experiences to others due to a gap in hermeneutical resources. According to Pohlhaus (2012), "willful hermeneutical ignorance" (p. 715) refers to the deliberate refusal to recognize alternative hermeneutical resources. Grounded in this concept, Dotson (2012) critiques Fricker's definition of hermeneutical injustice and argues that multiple hermeneutical resources exist; she suggests that marginalized groups indeed have situated knowledge/differentiated sets of hermeneutical resources available to them and can fully comprehend their own experiences. Yet, people in power may willfully consider these resources invalid or even treat them as non-existent, thus enacting epistemic injustice. Consequently, marginalized groups continue to be excluded, lacking access to contribute to the collective understanding of their experiences on structural levels, which Dotson calls "a third form of epistemic injustice, contributory injustice" (p. 25). Here, "the socio-epistemic structures that create and sustain situated hermeneutical inequality are the problem" (p. 30). Contributory injustice thus refers to a situation where:

> An epistemic agent's willful hermeneutical ignorance in maintaining and utilizing structurally prejudiced hermeneutical resources thwarts a knower's ability to contribute to shared epistemic resources within a given epistemic community by compromising her epistemic agency.
>
> (p. 32)

This construct is significant, as it invites us to critically reflect on the construction of social work knowledge and consider dismantling the willful hermeneutical ignorance that inhibits equal contributions of knowledge – that is, knowledge from marginalized groups, people with lived experiences, and our professional and scholarly expertise. In Chapter 14, Beresford (2027) critically discusses the potential for epistemic injustice in social work academia, even within epistemic injustice scholarship, from service user perspectives and their pioneering new social movement work.

Epistemic Status and Stance in the ***Epistemic Domain.*** The *epistemic domain* – that is, the territory of knowledge where we negotiate who has knowledge and how we go about getting it from others – is a driving force that underlies and structures everyday human inter/actions. In discussing the epistemic domain, Heritage (2012) distinguishes between two types: *epistemic status* and *epistemic stance*, which I find very useful in examining power dynamics in social inter/actions, and which will be detailed in the next section.

When engaging in various social inter/actions (e.g., making conversation, giving announcements, exchanging information through text and talk), each person holds different amounts of knowledge/power on a given topic; one person is typically more knowledgeable (coded by Heritage as "K+") and the other, less so ("K-"). A person's position on this "epistemic gradient" (Heritage, 2012, p. 4) – or continuum of knowledge – is defined by Heritage as *epistemic status*. He underscores that one's epistemic status is typically assumed, tacitly agreed upon, or even, to a certain extent, presupposed and taken-for-granted, thereby establishing differences in epistemic power within the inter/action. In contrast, *epistemic stance* refers to "the moment-by-moment expression" (Heritage, 2012, p. 6) of an epistemic status that can fluctuate, is more flexible, and often managed through turns at talk-in-action.

5.2 Negotiating with Epistemic Status and Stance to Counter Epistemic Injustice

A prominent conversation analyst, John Heritage, has been influential to me in understanding and interrogating a number of key themes: how social work inter/actions are constructed; how psychological, cultural, and sociopolitical factors can influence the implementation of our work; how social outcomes may be impacted by social work inter/actions (such as distributive in/justice of goods and services); and how social structures and power are produced and reified. Following the work of Goffman, Heritage examines *orders of social interaction* as a distinct and fundamental level of social organization with its own structural and moral dimensions. These orders refer to the organized, normative, and consequential nature of everyday human encounters – the patterned ways in which talk and action are coordinated – which provide the foundation for all social life (Goffman, 1983; Heritage, 1984). As a social worker, I believe that understanding these interactional orders is critical because they illuminate how micro-level exchanges – such as turn-taking, recipient design, and setting expectations in responses – are linked to broader social structures and power relations, shaping equity, access, and epistemic justice in practice. Although Heritage himself did not explicitly discuss the construct of epistemic in/justice in his work, I find that integrating his analyses of social interactional orders with epistemic injustice scholarship provides a powerful framework for social workers to critically reflect upon and reimagine social work practice.

For example, Heritage (2012) describes the significance of *epistemic congruency* in social interactions, where "the epistemic stance encoded in a turn at talk will normally converge with the epistemic status of the speaker" (p. 7). In his examination of social interactions in institutional health care settings (especially those between health care providers and patients), he finds that epistemic congruency is not always guaranteed: professionals may exploit their epistemic stance as experts in order to appear more knowledgeable and at times, more powerful than they actually are, creating what he calls *epistemic incongruency*. I think this is where epistemic injustice occurs: when social workers assert their professional power (i.e., projecting an elevated epistemic stance), a client's power as a knower may be deflated and, at times, denied and silenced. To equalize epistemic gradients between the participants in a social interaction, Heritage emphasizes the importance of attending to our epistemic stance moment-to-moment; in so doing, we can ensure a greater alignment between the epistemic stance and epistemic status in accordance with the knowledge possessed and shared by each speaker (thereby fostering epistemic congruency). We can also convey and meaningfully *demonstrate* our understanding of others' talk/experience, rather than *claiming* or even asserting our understanding/knowledge of their experiences (i.e., epistemic incongruency: Heritage, 2012).

Combining Heritage's theory of social interactional orders with epistemic injustice scholarship (Fricker, 2007; Dotson, 2012), I conducted a conversation analysis of videotaped social work encounters in a community mental health agency; I discussed how social workers accomplish empathic listening and convey understanding to clients and, correspondingly, how epistemic in/justice occurred in clinical social work practice (for detailed analysis, see Lee, Herschman et al., 2019). These findings highlight the importance of our own everyday discursive inter/actions in bringing epistemic justice into clinical social work encounters. I think this integrated framework can be applied not only to clinical settings to serve individuals and families but also to various other aspects of social work practice in community work. Below I will elaborate on how social workers negotiate their knowledge and power in theepistemic domain with various clients, families, and communities.

5.3 Knowledge, Power, and Epistemic Injustice in Social Work Practice

Who has knowledge of the issues at hand in social work practice? Clients and communities possess the power of knowing based on their own lived experiences: perhaps they tried to address their sufferings by troubleshooting them; they may hold accumulated knowledge of what works and what does not; they may have encountered various barriers and facilitators; and they may recognize who allies are and who must be approached with caution. To borrow Heritage's conceptualization of the status of knowledge (K) in everyday interactional power dynamics, clients and communities have the power of lived experience (K+), while social workers may not (K-). Conversely, social workers possess knowledge in the form of professional language to communicate with other professionals, assessment and intervention approaches, resources to help clients and communities, and affiliations with professional organizations and institutions that confer authority or power (K+), while most clients and communities do not (K-).

Notably, this asymmetric power dynamic in the working relationship is characterized by an epistemic gradient that is not static but fluctuating; at times, social workers implicitly or explicitly present themselves as having more epistemic power than they actually do (positioning themselves as K++). To illustrate this, I will share selected examples of social work practice with individuals, families, and communities from my own and other scholars' research. Although the selected case examples are analyzed in previous work focusing on topics relevant to negotiating Whiteness, racial microaggressions, and cross-cultural social work encounters (Lee & Bhuyan, 2013; Lee, Tsang, Bogo, Johnstone et al., 2018; Lee, Tsang, Bogo, Wilson et al., 2018; Lee, Herschman et al., 2019; Lee, Johnstone et al., 2019; Lee, Tsang et al., 2019), critically reflecting on these inter/actions from an epistemic injustice framework deepens our understanding of the multiple layers of epistemic domain in social work practice. All names have been changed and identifying information disguised to preserve confidentiality and privacy. Further, all line numbers in selected vignettes refer to speaking turns between the client and social worker in each session.

5.3.1 *Social Work Practice with Individuals: The Case of Manuel and Pat*

A client, Manuel, is a Latino father of two children in his mid-40s who currently attends individual counseling to address his depression at an outpatient family counseling agency. His therapist, Pat, is in her 50s, self-identifies as White, and has more than 20 years of post-graduate clinical experience. Manuel recently separated from his wife, who has full custody of their children, while he has biweekly visitation rights. He identified his main struggle as the loss of being the primary caregiver to his children, while his ex-wife had been the primary income earner for the family. In the middle of the second session, Pat asks what "going back to normal" in life means to Manuel, who then clearly shares his wish for "more frequent visits with my children." Here, Pat takes a not-knowing position/stance (K-) in her epistemic status with respect to Manuel's experience. Vignette 1 highlights the inter/actions that follow immediately after this conversation.

Vignette 1

145. Pat: OK. All right. OK. And-and so with stress, what more would you like to do? Because it sounds like you're terribly lonely without your children, and this is what it's like to be a parent when your children grow up in a different home or when you are in this kind of situation. So, what do we need to put in your life? Because you have a life: There's Manuel, the dad, and then there's Manuel, a person? So, Manuel, the dad, when he gets to be the dad, you sound very happy to be a dad? So, what can we put in your life as in Manuel, the person?

146. Manuel: I'm – I am trying to figure out, I dunno. I think it's OK to get involved in the community. And when I have a morning shift, I can go back to coaching soccer. [For brevity Lines 147–152 skipped]

153. Pat: And what about playing soccer for you?

154. Manuel: I stopped playing when I was 35 because I had lots of pain.... [For brevity Lines 155–174 skipped]

175. Pat: Everybody, I have the impression that everybody, all of you in South America, play soccer or are crazy for soccer?

176. Manuel: Yeah. Ever-every day, 3 or 4 hours of soccer. [Skipped for brevity]

177. Pat:	Very nice. So, do you follow, will you be following the World Cup in Germany?
178. Manuel:	Yeah, I hope so… I am not too fanatic, but I like it, yeah.
179. Pat:	You like to watch? Because some people are, they just love it so much that they are fanatics.
180. Manuel:	No. I think I'm a, I like, ah, all kinds of stuff. I am not too-too much on one thing… that's my only problem.
181. Pat:	Well, but I'm-I'm just thinking about your life as Manuel, the person, and it sounds like maybe soccer would be something to put back in your life because even in five years your children will be gone. If you start taking care of yourself now, not just over you being the dad, but as a person, then you'll be in much better shape than when they go off to university. Does that make sense?

In Line 145 Please ensure correct tagging is used and set 'Maneul' and 'Pat' as 'speaker' throughout the dialogue., Pat acknowledges Manuel's loneliness without his children; within the same turn, however, she equates his loneliness to that of other parents who do not live with their children and even introduces a new topic, self-care. Here, while Pat may have been trying to offer comfort by normalizing the client's grief, she appears to assume to "know" Manuel's loneliness (claiming herself as K+); notably, this loneliness is not uniquely experienced by him but is categorized as similar to that of other parents – although other fathers who live in different households from their children are not necessarily the primary caregivers. After Line 145, the conversation in Vignette 1 focuses exclusively on "self-care" and "soccer," topics initiated and then mainly driven by Pat that have little to do with what Manuel originally identified as his "normal": seeing his children more frequently.

This moment clearly exemplifies an alliance rupture since there is little agreement between the client and therapist about the goals and tasks of the therapy session – while Manuel expresses his grief, Pat pursues a self-care agenda. Clinical social work scholars highlight how a compatibility of goals, tasks, and emotional bonds between a client and therapist are the three components necessary for building a good working alliance; when there are disagreements or incompatibilities between them in any of these areas (i.e., goals, tasks, or bond), alliance ruptures occur (Lee, Johnstone et al., 2019; Tsang et al., 2011). Here, Manuel's voice and experiences are minimally heard and validated in his self-care planning; his epistemic stance is thus positioned by the social worker as K-, despite the fact that his epistemic status is, in reality, K+ as the knower of his own experience and future plans. This epistemic incongruency signifies epistemic injustice in clinical practice. Let's closely look into *how* this occurred, turn-by-turn.

Following Pat's question about his ways of caring for himself (Manuel as a person), Manuel initially hesitates ("I dunno") but comes up with the idea of "coaching soccer" as a potential means of "getting involved with the community" (Line 146). In the original research (Lee, Herschman et al., 2019), I interpreted his potential plan to get involved with the community as one way of addressing "not having enough involvement" with his children, which is consistent with his wish of "going back to normal," meaning to have a closer connection with his kids. Discursively, turn-by-turn, Pat changes the topic from his "normal" to "self-care": To Manuel, being "normal" is to be more involved with his kids and, alternatively, being involved with his community via coaching; this reflects a communal ideal of we-ness which contrasts Pat's notion of "self-care" (i.e., her recommendation that Manuel attend to himself, reflecting an individualized ideal of I-self). This topic change is achieved by shifting the focus from "coaching" to "playing" soccer (Line 153) and deploying a suggestion ("*how about* playing soccer for you?"). Conversational tactics, such as topic changes, suggestions, and over-explanations, are often forms of interactional coercion; they can be used to impose the speaker's power onto the hearer by gently overpowering them (Hall et al., 2014; Suonine & Jokinen, 2005).

At first, Manuel explicitly resists the idea of "playing soccer" with a clear answer ("I stopped playing … because I had lots of pain"), holding his epistemic stance as the knower of his own experience (K+). Then, a few lines later, Pat pursues her agenda – that Manuel ought to play soccer – this time deploying categorization and generalization of race and ethnicity ("all of you in South America play soccer or are crazy for soccer") in Line 175. Although the client goes along with her by staying with the topic, he again resists clearly, rebuking her generalization by noting "I am not too fanatic" (Line 178). Here, Manuel did not challenge her categorization/knowledge, perhaps because – I speculate – he does not want to contest her power; he may seek to preserve his relationship with his therapist while also trying to hold onto his epistemic status (K+) as the knower of his own experience. However, in Line 179, she appears to miss Manuel's effort to both comply with the therapist (i.e., staying on the topic of conversation) while simultaneously holding his own knowledge/power/dignity, and inserts her point again ("they *are* fanatics"). Manuel discursively works hard to retain his epistemic status, twice responding negatively to her comments ("*No.* …I am *not too-too much* one thing"). Nevertheless, Pat gives a long "explanation" to make her point in Line 146, and again in Line 181. After imposing her message through this ongoing explanation, Manuel is further coerced discursively when Pat elicits his confirmation at the end of Line 181 ("Does it make sense?").

In this vignette, we may speculate about three areas of Pat's unconscious racial and gender biases – what Fricker (2007) describes as "identity prejudice" (p. 4): (1) Essentializing all South American men as "crazy and fanatic about soccer"; (2) Normalizing Euro-centric views by (a) emphasizing an individualistic I-self by focusing on self-care, which is a commonly promoted clinical intervention, and (b) privileging the American nuclear family life cycle common to upper-to-middle class families, in which pursuing and accessing higher education is the presumed norm ("even in five years your children will be gone"); and (3) A presumably gender binary view around who is normalized as a primary caregiver. Because the therapist quickly suggested that Manuel replace the loss of being the main caregiver with self-care – especially by playing soccer like other South American *men* – I wonder if Pat would propose the same activity if the client were a mother – rather than a "Latino" "father" – who recently lost her caregiver identity. Clearly Pat's essentializing racial, class-based, and gender biases are deployed to guide her treatment recommendation (i.e., self-care by playing soccer), despite Manuel's clear and repeated resistance to this idea. Meanwhile, Manuel's plausible view of family-centered values, his identity of being the primary caregiver, and the notion of a familial-self characterized by close ties to family and community, appear to be pre-empted from the conversation. Consequently, Pat (and thus we, as readers) have little information about these themes – i.e., pre-emptive hermeneutical resources – and are left with a limited understanding of his views and life experiences.

5.3.2 *Social Work Practice with Families: The Case of Makoto, Naoki, and Eden*

The next case is from another dataset that includes audiotaped social work encounter (Lee, Tsang et al., 2019). The client, Makoto, is a single, second-generation Japanese-Canadian. The social worker, Eden, self-identifies as White, has a Master of Social Work degree, and possesses over a decade of post-graduate practice experience in community mental health settings. Both are in their 40s. Makoto has been in and out of an inpatient unit due to his mental health issues and now lives in a basement suite in his parents' house. In the next vignette, Eden, Makoto, and his father, Naoki, discuss how to secure Makoto's disability-related assistance to be self-sufficient. Makoto has a history of jeopardizing his income assistance since he accumulated assets over the eligibility boundary.

Vignette 2

71. Makoto:	And I went without money [meaning income assistance] for about a year,
72. Naoki:	Yeah
73. Makoto:	And I didn't need any money.
74. Eden:	Was it because he couldn't get to the office?
75. Naoki:	We got him there, but he wouldn't answer the questions that he thought…

76. Makoto: But I didn't want anything, I didn't. I was sick for a while, so I was thinking of getting better, and I didn't want to take government money at the time, because that was like 6 or 7 years ago. But I mean I refused the money at first because I didn't need it, I had food and … I was sick, I didn't get better, and now I don't know what's going to happen with my health, like I can continue with what's happening,

77. Eden: Well hopefully we'll get as much money as you're entitled to, until you're able to do.

Helping clients to secure income assistance is part of routine case management for many social workers, yet what we are interested in here is *how* this task is accomplished in ways that dis/respect the client and consequently dis/honor his dignity. In this vignette, Makoto repeatedly states that he does not need money using multiple I-statements in Lines 71, 73, and 76 – that is, he discursively informs both Eden and his father about *his* personal experience and preference for financial independence. Initially, Makoto's epistemic stance (K+) and epistemic status (K+) are congruently aligned. However, Makoto's position is promptly dismissed discursively by both Eden and the father: instead of asking Makoto a question directly in Line 74, Eden asks the father instead ("Was it because *he* couldn't get to the office?"). Why does the social worker do this? We may speculate that Eden may consider Makoto to be sick and incompetent to the degree that there is no reason to ask him directly. Eden's conversational gesture seems to set into motion the inter/actions of the next turn, in Line 75: the father discursively joins with Eden by deploying the pronoun "we" (i.e., referring to himself and his wife/Makoto's mother) and aligning himself with Eden, who tacitly established a division between normal (father) and abnormal (Makoto) in the previous turn. Embedded within the father's "we" is the implicit suggestion that "we" (normal people) understand the importance of ensuring financial security/obtaining income, while Makoto, the ill person, is too incompetent to comprehend this need; consequently, Makoto did not answer the questions required to receive income assistance, despite the fact that "we got him there." Not only are Makoto's statements about his needs in Lines 71 and 73 totally dismissed and discredited (i.e., testimonial injustice) but also, his presence in the session is disregarded and ignored (i.e., his existence as a human being deserving of respect), as if he were not there!

Fricker (2007) notes the deeply detrimental and disturbing impacts of epistemic ignorance and oppression on a human being:

> To be wronged in one's capacity as a knower is to be wronged in a capacity essential to human value.… No wonder, then, that being insulted, undermined, or otherwise wronged in one's capacity as a giver of knowledge is something that can cut deep. No wonder too that in contexts of oppression

> the powerful will be sure to undermine the powerless in just that capacity, for it provides a direct route to undermining them in their very humanity.
> (p. 44)

I argue that this critical point is exemplified discursively in Line 76: Initially, Makoto tries to maintain his epistemic status by endeavoring to legitimize his reasons for not needing income assistance using I-statements (i.e., "I didn't want" twice, "I refused," "I didn't need") while negotiating with the view of others ("I was sick for a while"). However, toward the end of this turn at talk, Makoto adopts the gaze of "we" (that of Eden and the father) and describes himself as being ill and incompetent ("I was sick, I didn't get better, and now I don't know"); clearly Makoto's epistemic stance is now shifted to K-.

Instead of inviting Makoto to expand upon his conflictual discourse and how it relates to his experiences in Line 77, Eden omits the initial part of Makoto's speech and selectively hears the latter part, which he deploys to legitimize his initial agenda of obtaining income assistance ("we'll get as much money as you're entitled to…"). Here, Eden elevates his epistemic stance from K- to K+, claiming he *knows* what is better for Makoto. What if Eden invited Makoto to share his experiences in this turn instead? The social worker, for example, could ask: "what was it like for you to go without income assistance?"; "what do you mean you did not need money?"; "what is it like for you to hear from both of us that you need money?"; "it sounds like you have strong feelings about receiving government money, would you mind sharing your thoughts about it? Where do you think this idea comes from?" Unfortunately, no such invitations were initiated, not only in this session but throughout the intervention recorded (i.e., a total of 19 sessions). In these inter/actions with the social worker, what is it like for Makoto to be reminded of being incompetent? How did it feel for him to be ignored while present in the room? How might he have felt to be viewed as dependable now and in the future? In the end, Eden and the father (and thus, we as readers) have little understanding of how Makoto constructs meaning around receiving income assistance from the government. His experience/knowledge is pre-emptively silenced.

5.3.3 Social Work Practice with Communities: Two Cases of Environmental Justice Work and "Hard-to-Reach" Communities

Social work practice with communities occurs in community organizations, through advocacy and/or activism to address local concerns, and via systemic impacts on people in and beyond a given community. Here, I will examine two examples: one focused on environmental justice work and the other on "hard-to-reach" communities. Social work has actively engaged with issues concerning environmental justice (e.g., climate change, ecological degradation, overconsumption of resources, natural disasters, pollution, and sustainability) together with issues of displacement, poverty, industrialization, and colonialism that have impacted numerous communities around the world (Shajahan & Sharma, 2018). The current call for action for social workers in environmental justice is also aligned with the United Nations' *2030 Agenda for Sustainable Development* (UN, 2015).

Various theoretical guidelines have promoted environmental justice in social work practice, education, and research, such as eco-social work, green social work, political ecology, Indigenous knowledge, and community resilience (Dominelli, 2019). Critical environmental justice scholars, however, invite us to pause and reflect on their underlying ontological and epistemic positions (Martin et al., 2013; Svarstad & Benjaminsen, 2020; Vermeylen, 2019). They argue against marking Euro-centric environmental justice discourse from the Global North as a "universal" and "liberal" approach that can be applied to the Global South without consideration of local knowledge and contexts; these contexts often involve impoverished communities impacted by environmental disasters, described in homogenous ways, and expected to adopt "dominant ways of knowing nature and living with nature" (Martin et al., 2013, p. 123). Thus, Vermeylen (2019) warns against the slippage of environmental justice into "an act of epistemic violence" (p. 89) when the knowledges and worldviews of people in the Global South are not respected and recognized, and their local contexts not considered and valued.

In their work in both Uganda and Tanzania, Svarstad and Benjaminsen (2020) found that "marginalized people were not really recognized as actors with independent voices by scholars and activists who were speaking for them instead of listening to them" (p. 6). This finding exemplifies how the voices of local communities can be discredited (i.e., testimonial injustice), how their epistemic status (K+) as conveyers of knowledge on local environmental issues can be silenced (K-), and how these groups can be excluded from contributing to broader knowledge production on environmental justice work (i.e., hermeneutical injustice). Therefore, in collaborating with communities, a prominent green social work scholar and activist, Lena Dominelli (2019), underscores that:

> environmental issues and their impacts on communities involve a complex web of relationships that have to be coordinated and orchestrated to bring people together who can engage with communities to co-develop their resilience and co-provide solutions to problems that they identify.
>
> (p. 242)

This point truly highlights the importance of crediting communities and centering their knowledge when addressing environmental issues at hand and viewing community members as the experts with lived experiences when engaging in community work; doing so embodies both testimonial and hermeneutical justice.

Having worked with various communities impacted by HIV, critical social work scholar, Carmen Logie (2021), examines the framing of certain groups as "hard-to-reach," particularly those involving multiple, marginal, intersectional identities (e.g., Black, Indigenous, and people of color, gender and sexually diverse individuals, etc.). These communities are continuously sidelined and even rendered "hidden" within dominant knowledge frameworks, while simultaneously being overlooked as "deserving" recipients of resources and services. She demonstrates the detrimental impacts of labeling communities impacted by HIV, noting how the "hard-to-reach" designation further places the onus for reaching out on the clients/communities themselves – even blaming them for not doing so – while conveniently excusing our own failure to reach out, listen to, and collaborate with them.

Drawing upon scholarship on the *epistemology of ignorance*, Logie (2021) attests that ignorance is not a passive stance that can be attributed to a lack of information, but rather "an active engagement in practice" (p. 15) that is strategically promulgated to structurally maintain it, thus characterizing ignorance as "a form of epistemic injustice" (p. 15). To combat this, Logie (2021) disrupts the pervasive "hard-to-reach" discourse, and poses an important question: "what if instead of looking outside for the problems that create barriers for people to engage with us, we start looking inside ourselves to our own actions and beliefs" (p. 1). In endeavoring to balance the epistemic gradient, each chapter of her book thus elaborates how she and her team worked with community partners – such as Indigenous youth in the Northwest Territories in Canada, internally displaced women in post-earthquake Haiti, LGBTQ communities in the Global North and Global South, and communities of people at the intersections of these identities – intentionally as co-participants in various community projects. Although she did not explicitly frame her work through the lens of epistemic domain, I found this stance (i.e., positioning herself as K-, seeking greater epistemic congruency between researchers and community practitioners) in her research and practice with various HIV-impacted communities as a step toward epistemic justice. Similarly, in Chapter 4 of this book, Tang Yan (2027) invites us to critically examine our research process, including in community-based participatory research (CBPR) and participatory action research (PAR), where collaboration with communities can be co-opted if researchers do not critically interrogate interlocking systems of power and oppression; such omissions may lead to performative enactments of seemingly equitable knowledge co-creation.

5.4 Discussion: Reflecting on Epistemic Ignorance of Epistemic Injustice in Social Work

Guided by critical feminist scholars' work on the ethics of knowing, power, and social discrimination, this chapter examines various forms of social work practice where epistemic injustice occurs. Using Heritage's work on epistemic status and stance in particular, I examined how the epistemic gradient can fluctuate as social workers claim to know clients' experiences (positioning themselves as K+), while clients who are discredited and silenced are relegated to the margins (K-) despite being the true knowers of their own experiences (K+). Significantly, the epistemic domain is a site where power and knowledge are negotiated in social work relationships, shaping our daily inter/actions with clients and communities in subtle and mundane ways. I have discussed this epistemic domain with both social work students and social workers in the field using selected case examples – much like I did in this chapter – and invited them to critically reflect on different ways we may empower clients: by carefully listening to them, giving clients full credit as the knowers of their own experience, and changing how we work to expand our hermeneutical resources (e.g., professional knowledge) so that it may be integrated with clients' knowledge. More often than not, social work students and practitioners respond to the case examples with comments such as, "Oh, this is bad practice – you are sharing extreme cases" or "You selected only a few minutes of the session! We cannot accurately interpret it based on a small segment."

Initially, I tried to support my points by sharing more examples; indeed, I have many! As was demonstrated in the case of Manuel and Pat, experiences of invalidation among many immigrants of color are often replicated and reactivated during therapeutic encounters (see Lee, Johnstone et al., 2019; Lee, Tsang et al., 2019). Elsewhere, I shared different case examples demonstrating epistemic injustice between individual clients and social workers: one involving a Mexican immigrant mother who struggled to understand and manage her teenage daughter's acting-out behaviors while working with a social worker at a family counseling agency (Lee & Bhuyan, 2013); and another involving a single, second-generation Vietnamese immigrant woman with a history of psychosis who worked with a social worker to address various case management matters in a community mental health agency (Lee, 2022).

Like the family therapy case example involving Eden, Makoto, and his father, elsewhere I shared another case consisting of a 17-year-old daughter and her 40-year-old mother, who were originally from Pakistan and immigrated to Canada when the daughter was a toddler (Lee et al., 2018b). They attended family counseling with a social worker after the daughter got suspended from her high school. The analysis elaborated how the social worker either joined with the family or ruptured the relationship by selectively listening to certain themes, especially those related to generational gaps, cultural customs, and cultural expectations. In one session, for example, the social worker directly asks the mother:

> what we're told by a lot of people from different cultures, like privacy wasn't, you know what I mean, some cultures it's more like everybody lives

> in the same room, did you have a concept like when you were growing up, privacy?
>
> (Lee et al., 2018b p. 17)

Based on her limited hermeneutical resources ("what we're told…"), the social worker (like Pat and Eden) pretends to *know* the clients' experiences and cultures and, consequently, elevates her epistemic status (K+). Meanwhile, the mother – who speaks English fluently and has lived in Canada for years – is assumed to be less intelligent (presumably unfamiliar with the concept of privacy) and her culture characterized as primitive (because "everybody lives in the same room" without any respect for "privacy"). As the sessions progress, the social worker discursively splits the daughter's culture (Canadian) from the mother's (Pakistani) despite their initial testimony that they share the same roots and culture, thus committing testimonial injustice (for detailed analysis see Lee et al., 2018b).

Furthermore, examples of social work's complicity with intentional and unintentional acts of epistemic injustice within various communities around the world sadly abound in both the past and present. For example, Canadian social workers participated in and perpetuated state violence by removing Indigenous children from their families and communities; this occurred via the residential school system, the Sixties' Scoop, and even the present-day foster care system, where Indigenous children are still disproportionately represented (Blackstock, 2009). Social work historian Yoosun Park (2008) traced the contributions of social workers to the internment of Japanese-Americans during World War II. As her provocative title, *Facilitating Injustice*, notes, social workers indeed facilitated all aspects of the internment process. A recent edited volume, *Social Work's Histories of Complicity and Resistance* (Ioakimidis & Wyllie, 2023), also includes a collection of articles detailing our profession's involvement in and complicity with wrongful actions and prejudicial stances toward marginalized communities in the past: these include Jewish communities in Nazi Germany (Kuhlmann, 2023); the oppressive mental health system in England (Moth, 2023); apartheid against Black communities in South Africa (Harms-Smith & Turton, 2023); and adoption practices in Ireland (McGettrick, 2023), among others.

Also, given my over 25 years of clinical experience in practicing and supervising clinicians, the ongoing negotiation of epistemic status versus stance has been inevitable; I have frequently experienced and observed how easily we traverse the boundaries between epistemic justice and injustice. Despite social work's claim to be a helping profession, it is ironic to frequently see myself and others overpower and silence clients in everyday practice.

Returning to the questioning I receive about my research findings, I still respond to such comments by providing more examples, to let readers see how pervasive epistemic injustice is in everyday social work practice. Now, I'd also like to pause and reflect on this ongoing experience of *being questioned.* It could be understood in several ways: perhaps it can be attributed to my social location as a person of color, immigrant, and woman who may be taken less seriously than a White, male scholar with a similar research focus. Maybe it has to do with my research methods; qualitative approaches (such as critical discourse analysis, conversation analysis, and reflexive thematic analysis) may be regarded as less credible than quantitative methods (like the so-called gold standard of research, randomized controlled trial experimental designs), which are more privileged as hermeneutical resources in academia. Or, it could be that my research focus on culture, race, and social justice is less valued in the scholarly economy than other topics which deal with outcomes, cost-efficiency, and measurable behavioral indicators in social work practice. These reflection points are not new, and several feminist, antiracist, and social justice-oriented scholars have drawn our attention to these matters for years.

What I would like to add here, however, is an invitation to us, as social workers, to look inside – specifically, to face our own tendency to avoid or even disavow the fact that we do commit epistemic injustice in our practice. I am aware of how uncomfortable and challenging it is to accept the "bad" or more ugly aspects of our profession while also retaining its goodness as being "worth fighting for" (Ioakimidis & Wyllie, 2023, p. 4). If we continue to deny our enactments of epistemic injustice altogether, attempt to relegate it to the past, or attribute it to a few "bad" social workers, I think this very gesture would constitute "willful hermeneutical ignorance" (Pohlhaus, 2012, p. 715). Without acknowledging and confronting the "bad" and the ugly, our hopes of cherishing the good in social work practice will be incomplete (Finch et al., 2025). To me, considering social workers' inter/actions with individuals, families, and communities through the lens of the epistemic domain is not intended to incriminate some social workers' practice in the past; instead, it can be used to inform our practice for the future by learning from their/our mistakes and being vigilant about not slipping into epistemically oppressive practices. To align our practice with epistemic justice, Chapter 1 details how the social worker, as an "epistemic agent," can resist epistemic injustice at various levels of social work practice and provides some recommendations in terms of how to expand hermeneutical resources for marginalized populations.

References

Beresford, P. (2027). Challenging epistemic injustice through more inclusive discourse: A standpoint from service users' lived experiences. In E. Lee, R. Hu, & A. Greenblatt (Eds.), *Epistemic injustice and resistance in social work: Rethinking social justice in practice, education, and research.* Routledge.

Blackstock, C. (2009). The occasional evil of angels: Learning from the experiences of aboriginal peoples and social work. *First Peoples Child and Family Review*, *4*(1), 28–37. https://doi.org/10.7202/1069347ar

Dominelli, L. (2019). Green social work, political ecology and environmental justice. In S. A. Webb (Ed.), *The Routledge handbook of critical social work* (pp. 233–243). Routledge. https://doi.org/10.4324/9781351264402-21

Dotson, K. (2012). A cautionary tale: On limiting epistemic oppression. *Frontiers: A Journal of Women's Studies, 33*(1), 24–47. https://doi.org/10.5250/fronjwomestud.33.1.0024

Finch, J., Crivatu, I., & Howells, A. (2025). The good, the bad and the ugly – the experiences of social work practice educators in three organisations in England. *Social Work Education*, 1–17. https://doi.org/10.1080/02615479.2025.2531862

Fricker, M. (2007). *Epistemic injustice: Power and the ethics of knowing*. Oxford University Press.

Garfinkel, H. (1967). *Studies in ethnomethodology*. Prentice-Hall, Inc.

Goffman, E. (1983). The interaction order: American Sociological Association, 1982 presidential address. *American Sociological Review, 48*(1), 1–17. https://doi.org/10.2307/2095141

Hall, C., Juhila, K., Matarese, M., & van Nijnatten, C. (2014). *Analysing social work communication: Discourse in practice*. Routledge Press.

Harms-Smith, L., & Turton, Y. (2023). 5 Colonial and apartheid South Africa: Social work complicity and resistance. In V. Ioakimidis & A. Wyllie (Eds.), *Social work's histories of complicity and resistance: A tale of two professions* (pp. 73–94). Policy Press. https://doi-org.myaccess.library.utoronto.ca/10.56687/9781447364306-008

Heritage, J. (1984). *Garfinkel and ethnomethodology*. Polity Press.

Heritage, J. (2012). Epistemics in action: Action formation and territories of knowledge. *Research on Language and Social Interaction, 45*(1), 1–29.

Ioakimidis, V. & Wyllie, A. (2023). Learning from the past to shape the future: Uncovering social work's histories of complicity and resistance. In V. Ioakimidis & A. Wyllie (Eds.), *Social work's histories of complicity and resistance: A tale of two professions*. Policy Press. https://doi.org/10.1332/policypress/9781447364276.003.0001

Kuhlmann, C. (2023). 6 Social services in Nazi Germany and the role of social workers between complicity and rare resistance. In V. Ioakimidis & A. Wyllie (Eds.), *Social work's histories of complicity and resistance: A tale of two professions* (pp. 97–108). Policy Press. https://doi-org.myaccess.library.utoronto.ca/10.56687/9781447364306-009

Lauer, S., Wong, K. L. Y., & Yan, M. C. (2025). Social infrastructure, community organizations, and friendship formation: A scoping review. *Community Development Journal, 60*(2), 267–285. https://doi.org/10.1093/cdj/bsae023

Lee, E. (2022). Fact construction and categorization in assessment: Cultivating epistemic justice and resistance in social work assessment. *Social Service Review*, 96(3), 534–571. https://doi.org/10.1086/721273.

Lee, E. (2027). Understanding epistemic domain in social work to foster social justice. In E. Lee, R. Hu, & A. Greenblatt (Eds.), *Epistemic injustice and resistance in social work: Rethinking social justice in practice, education, and research*. Routledge.

Lee, E., & Bhuyan, R. (2013). Negotiating within whiteness in cross-cultural clinical encounters. *Social Service Review, 87*(1), 98–130. https://doi.org/10.1086/669919

Lee, E., Herschman, J., & Johnstone, M. (2019). How to convey social workers' understanding to clients in everyday interactions? Toward epistemic justice. *Social*

Work Education: International Journal, 38(4), 485–502. https://doi.org/10.1080/02615479.2018.1539070

Lee, E., Johnstone, M., & Herschman, J. (2019). Negotiating goals and tasks in cross-cultural encounters. *Journal of Social Work Practice, 33*(4) 447–462. https://doi.org/10.1080/02650533.2018.1504288

Lee, E., Tsang, A. K. T., Bogo, M., Johnstone, M., & Herschman, J. (2018). Enactment of racial microaggression in everyday therapeutic encounters. *Smith College Studies in Social Work, 88*(3), 211–236. https://doi.org/10.1080/00377317.2018.1476646

Lee, E., Tsang, A. K. T., Bogo, M., Johnstone, M., & Herschman, J. (2019). Clients and case managers as neoliberal subjects? Shaping session tasks and everyday interactions with Severely Mentally Ill (SMI) clients. *European Journal of Social Work, 22*(2), 238–251. https://doi.org/10.1080/13691457.2018.1529662

Lee, E., & Tsang, A. K. T., Bogo, M., Wilson, G., Johnstone, M., & Herschman, J. (2018). Joining revisited in family therapy: Cross-cultural encounters between a therapist and an immigrant family. *Journal of Family Therapy, 40*, 148–179. https://doi.org/10.1111/1467-6427.12148

Logie, C. (2021). *Working with excluded populations in HIV: Hard to reach or out of sight?* Springer.

Martin, A., McGuire, S., & Sullivan, S. (2013). Global environmental justice and biodiversity conservation. *The Geographical Journal, 179*(2), 122–131.

McGettrick, C. (2023). 17 Adoption social work practice in Ireland: Critical reflections on present-day injustices. In V. Ioakimidis & A. Wyllie (Ed.), *Social work's histories of complicity and resistance: A tale of two professions* (pp. 261–277). Policy Press. https://doi-org.myaccess.library.utoronto.ca/10.56687/9781447364306-020

Moth, R. (2023). 11 Institutionalisation and oppression within the mental health system in England: Social work complicity and resistance. In V. Ioakimidis & A. Wyllie (Eds.), *Social work's histories of complicity and resistance: A tale of two professions* (pp. 165–182). Policy Press.

Norcross, J. C. (Ed.). (2011). *Psychotherapy relationships that work: Evidence-based responsiveness*. Oxford University Press.

Park, Y. (2008). Facilitating injustice: Tracing the role of social workers in the World War II internment of Japanese Americans. *Social Service Review, 82*(3), 447–483.

Pohlhaus, G. (2012). Relational knowing and epistemic injustice: Toward a theory of willful hermeneutical ignorance. *Hypatia, 27*(4), 715–735.

Shajahan, P., & Sharma, P. (2018). Environmental justice: A call for action for social workers. *International Social Work, 61*(4), 476–480. https://doi.org/10.1177/0020872818770585

Sudbery, J. (2002). Key features of therapeutic social work: The use of relationship. *Journal of Social Work Practice, 16*(2), 149–162.

Suonine, E., & Jokinen, A. (2005). Persuasion in social work interviewing. *Qualitative Social Work, 4*, 459–487.

Svarstad, H., & Benjaminsen, T. A. (2020). Reading radical environmental justice through a political ecology lens. *Geoforum, 108*, 1–11. https://doi.org/10.1016/j.geoforum.2019.11.007

Tang Yan, C. (2027). Epistemic injustice in community-based participatory research: Toward embodying decolonial ethical relationality, sentipensante, and accountable praxis in social work. In E. Lee, R. Hu, & A. Greenblatt (Eds.), *Epistemic injustice and resistance in social work: Rethinking social justice in practice, education, and research.* Routledge.

Tosone, C. (2004). Relational social work: Honoring the tradition. *Smith College Studies in Social Work, 74*(3), 475–487. https://doi.org/10.1080/00377310409517730

Tsang, A. K. T., Bogo, M., & Lee, E. (2011). Engagement in cross-cultural clinical practice: Narrative analysis of first sessions, *Clinical Social Work Journal, 39*(1), 79–90. https://doi.org/10.1007/s10615-010-0265-6

United Nations (UN). (2015). *Transforming our world: The 2030 agenda for sustainable development.* https://sdgs.un.org/2030agenda

Vermeylen, S. (2019). Special issue: Environmental justice and epistemic violence. *Local Environment, 24*(2), 89–93.

Watts, L., & Hodgson, D. (2019). *Social justice theory and practice for social work: Critical and philosophical perspectives.* Springer.

Part II

Interrogating Epistemic Injustice in Social Work Practice with the Marginalized

Chapter 6

Epistemic Injustice and Youth Mental Health

The Role of Social Workers in Promoting Epistemically Just Practice

Andrea Greenblatt

6.1 Introduction

Is it conceivable that young people face prejudice based on their age? It can be argued that many societies hold an "adultist" worldview, prioritizing adult thinking, doing, and being (Prilleltensky et al., 2001). Consequently, some may be hesitant to support children and youth in their decision-making (Delgado, 2006). As Murris (2013) aptly notes, "adults often put metaphorical sticks in their ears in their educational encounters with children. Hearers' prejudices cause them to miss out on knowledge offered by the child, but not heard by the adult" (p. 245). Youth facing mental health concerns may experience enhanced skepticism around their credibility, thus facing prejudice due to *both* their young age and their experience of mental health issues (LeFrançois, 2008; Liegghio et al., 2010; Mishna et al., 2004). More specifically, this group of youth may experience certain forms of *injustice*. One form of such injustice is *epistemic injustice*, a concept developed by philosopher Miranda Fricker (2007), describing prejudice against a group that ultimately leads to a *credibility deficit* or a questioning of their credibility.

Utilizing this concept as the premise for this chapter, I will first summarize key forms of epistemic injustice that youth with mental health concerns may face, drawing on examples from a qualitative study (Greenblatt, 2022; Greenblatt et al., 2024) exploring the experience of mental health care among a group of ten Canadian young people. In this study, I used Critical Narrative Analysis methodology to establish how narratives demonstrate both *implicit* and *explicit* experiences of testimonial and hermeneutical injustice during encounters with healthcare providers, peers, and the education system. I then consider how youth-facing social workers can practice in more epistemically just ways and conclude with personal reflections on how Fricker's (2007) theory and concepts have impacted my own work.

6.1.1 Key Terminology

Testimonial Injustice. Fricker (2007) explains that testimonial injustice occurs when "prejudice causes a hearer to give a deflated level of credibility to a

DOI: 10.4324/9781003639046-9

speaker's word" (p. 1). In this chapter, testimonial injustice refers to the denial or dismissal of youths' credibility when sharing their mental health experiences with healthcare providers, family members, and teachers.

Pre-emptive Testimonial Injustice. It is a form of "prejudicial deficit" (p. 130) that silences testimony even before a person can or tries to share their point of view. In this chapter, youth reveal instances where mental health dialogue is silenced in anticipatory ways through implicitly understood rules that govern interactions. For instance, youth may adhere to unspoken conversational dynamics that preclude discussions of mental health, which effectively act as silencing mechanisms that inhibit expression before they can "come to the table" for dialogue.

Hermeneutical Injustice. Fricker (2007) describes hermeneutical injustice as "a gap in collective interpretive resources [that] puts someone at an unfair disadvantage when it comes to making sense of their social experiences" (p. 1). In this chapter, hermeneutical injustice describes how youths' experiences with interpretive resources may differ from dominant medical discourse. For instance, the *Diagnostic and Statistical Manual of Mental Disorders* (*DSM*) (American Psychiatric Association, 2022) criteria may not resonate with their own understandings of their depression or anxiety.

Hermeneutical Marginalization. When certain individuals are subject to unequal participation in meaning-making, they experience hermeneutical marginalization (Fricker, 2007, p. 153). In addition to hermeneutical injustice, youths' narratives indicated simultaneous barring from hermeneutical participation with their healthcare providers – specifically, their lived experiences and conceptualizations of mental health were excluded from how the medical system collectively understood their experiences.

Hermeneutical Resources. Fricker (2007) describes this concept as the "shared tools of social interpretation" (p. 6). In this chapter, hermeneutical resources are understood as the means by which youth make meaning of their mental health. Youth report relying on their individual lived experiences to understand their mental health or cultivating a shared approach to coping with mental health among like-minded peers (i.e., use of humor). These resources may differ from dominant ones, like medical criteria (i.e., *DSM*), or resources typically drawn upon by parents or teachers.

6.2 Epistemic Injustice and Youth Mental Health

Fricker's (2007) theory of epistemic injustice describes two primary forms of injustice: *testimonial injustice* and *hermeneutical injustice*. Testimonial injustice occurs when one's testimony or knowledge is denied credibility. For youth with mental health concerns, this can occur when they access care and are determined to be lacking in credibility by healthcare providers based on their age and/or having a mental health concern (Ritunnano, 2022). Another form of *testimonial injustice* is *pre-emptive silencing,* which occurs when individuals are pre-emptively excluded from contributing their knowledge (Fricker, 2007). For instance, youth may be present at medical appointments but their perspectives are not meaningfully elicited, thus barring them from collaborating in medical decision-making and treatment planning. Indeed, research indicates that youth engaged in the mental health system report little latitude in decision-making regarding their care and that their "input [is only] taken up if their suggestions [are] were consistent with practitioners' pre-arranged plans" (Gondek et al., 2017; LeFrançois, 2008, p. 215).

Hermeneutical injustice occurs when certain groups are denied access to resources that would facilitate sense-making of their own life experiences. Groups with social power tend to assign credibility and, thus, determine with whom they wish to develop shared meanings. Groups without power may lack access to meaning-making resources through which they might join in these shared understandings. Fricker (2007) provides an excellent example whereby a woman experienced unwanted attention from her superior. Despite knowing this behavior was wrong, she did not have the *language* to name her experience as harassment and, therefore, was unable to act on her own behalf. In this case, she did not have access to the meaning-making resources needed to understand and name her experience. Youth may encounter *hermeneutical injustice* when they lack access to resources that could support their understandings of their own mental health struggles and related experiences. Alternatively, youth may indeed draw on hermeneutical resources of their own, but these may not be recognized by others. For example, a youth may understand their experience of depression, anxiety, or psychosis in ways that are different from those defined by medical discourse. Without exploration and collaboration with healthcare providers, this youth may miss opportunities to contribute to shared understandings of depression and anxiety as they proceed through their treatment; they are thus excluded from "hermeneutical participation" (Fricker, 2007, p. 153) or from contributing to collective hermeneutical understandings about youth's experiences with mental health (Dotson, 2012; Tate, 2019). Instead, healthcare providers may single-handedly determine a youth's capacity for understanding and decision-making (LeFrançois, 2008) and act on their *behalf* instead of *alongside* them (Liegghio et al., 2019; Mishna et al., 2004).

6.3 Qualitative Research on Youth's Own Words of Mental Health Experiences

To contribute to research integrating youth mental health with Fricker's work, my doctoral dissertation focused on understanding how youth make meaning of their mental health. Recruitment occurred at children's mental health agencies and among mental health practitioners in private practice throughout the Greater Toronto Area in Ontario, Canada. Inclusion criteria were youth between the ages of 13–19 years and who were connected with a mental health professional. Youth self-identified as having a mental health concern regardless of formal diagnosis. Exclusion criteria were youth experiencing an acute mental health or substance use crisis and who were not currently connected with a mental health professional. Youth under the age of 16 required parental consent. During individual interviews, youth were asked about their experiences of mental health (i.e., symptoms, healthcare, etc.) as well as their interactions with others related to this theme. The objective of the dissertation was to capture youth voices and position them as experts in making sense of their own experiences with mental health. Full study details can be found in previous publications (Greenblatt, 2022).

6.3.1 *Positionality*

Generally speaking, I identify as a Canadian-born woman who obtained a PhD in social work and continued with further post-doctoral training. As I engaged in the process of analyzing and reflecting on the data presented in this chapter, however, I considered my *own* positioning and identities more deeply. These include belonging to various academic and/or clinical contexts, along with the epistemic privileges these positions hold, including access to concepts like those of Fricker. As I reflect on both my past and present work within systems and institutions, I can identify a constant need to navigate systemic barriers that sometimes contradict epistemically just practice. I, thus, do not present these findings or the discussion that follows as any "blueprint" for how to do this work, but more as an opportunity to reflect on our own positionalities, take steps to mitigate our own prejudice, and truly *listen* to our youth.

6.3.2 *Participants and Data Analysis*

A total of ten youth aged 13–19 participated in this study. The participants included five female-identifying youth, three male-identifying youth, and one youth identifying as they/she/he; demographic information was missing for one participant. Youth were asked to describe their cultural backgrounds and mental health concerns as they saw fit. Youth reported having depression, anxiety, borderline personality disorder, eating disorders, Post-Traumatic Stress Disorder, suicidality, somatization, autism, Attention Deficit Disorder, trichollitomania, and "no label." They also reported being of White, Jewish, Italian, Jamaican, French, Canadian, and Scottish backgrounds.

Critical Narrative Analysis (CNA: Souto-Manning, 2014) was chosen as a suitable method given its attempt to bridge critical discourse analysis with narrative analysis, essentially allowing for inquiry into both micro and macro level narratives. Souto-Manning (2014) asserts that CNA facilitates "analysis of narratives in the lifeworld – the everyday stories people tell – within the context of institutional discourses" (p. 163). In using this method, I was able to see how youth drew on broader discourses to make meaning of their experiences, while also identifying how institutions incorporated everyday narratives into their discourse (Souto-Manning, 2014). While transcripts of all ten interviews were analyzed in the original study, a selection of five transcripts was included in this chapter as these narratives were deemed to clearly illustrate otherwise complex concepts of epistemic injustice.

The following analysis and findings were initially presented in my doctoral dissertation (Greenblatt, 2022) and in a prior publication (Greenblatt et al., 2024). While this current chapter draws on analyses from these previous works, it differs in two key ways: (1) The primary audience here is social workers, and not general groups of healthcare providers. While findings can certainly be relevant to many professionals, it was conceptualized with social workers at its center. Thus, implications and recommendations for practice are shared within the context of the field; (2) It incorporates the author's more recent reflections on Fricker's concepts, years after previous publications, and in the context of the current edited compilation. More specifically, how have these concepts impacted my own learning and practice as I moved through my work? How can these reflections support others in the field working with youth, and who may be interested in learning about epistemic injustice? Next, analysis revealed instances of both epistemic injustice and justice across youth's narratives.

6.4 Youth Experiences of Epistemic Injustice in Mental Health Services

Under epistemic injustice, the following themes will be described below: pre-emptive silencing, explicit silencing, and institutional ignorance.

6.4.1 *Pre-emptive Silencing: "Don't Ask, Don't Tell"*

Through analysis, it appeared that youth experienced both implicit and explicit silencing of their mental health experiences. Some youth appeared to be *pre-emptively* silenced. For example, one youth reported: "I've grown up… in a family that's kind of don't ask, don't tell. Or, like, fake it till you make it about mental health. I would really train myself to just not talk with any of that, anyone about it" (Participant #1). This youth describes an anticipatory form of silencing, where even the opportunity to discuss certain topics, like mental health, is understood to be unwelcome. Fricker (2007) characterizes this as a type of *testimonial injustice* that precludes individuals from even being *asked* about their experiences – they are effectively "barred entry to the community of informants" (p. 130). Thus, this form of implicit injustice occurs in silence. In this example, a personal experience of mental health is "barred" from the family's general discourse. In addition to clear messaging around pre-emptive silencing on a personal level, this youth also draws on broader discourses of "don't ask, don't tell" and "fake it till you make it" when discussing mental health. For instance, cultural discourse around "Don't ask, don't tell" can be traced back to a historical policy in the United States that prevented LGBTQ+ military service members from disclosing their sexual orientations (Human Rights Campaign, n.d.). This youth appears to invoke this broader discourse to give meaning to her personal experience.

Another youth described an instance of silencing that was both *non-verbal* and *pre-emptive* in nature. After a visible somatic response to anxiety, one youth stated that her friend would no longer make eye contact with her, saying, "that bothered me for a long time because we were such close friends and now you can't even look at me" (Participant #2). This youth experienced a non-verbal form of silencing, which she understood to indicate that her experience is not to be shared with her friend.

6.4.2 *Explicit Silencing: "Don't Let Anyone See You Like That"*

Youth also experienced more overt forms of silencing. One youth described how her response to the COVID-19 pandemic was explicitly stifled by her family:

> …I know this sounds pretty melodramatic, but it [COVID-19] has been the worst thing of my life, and a lot of people are like, especially my mother [say]…there's people who've lost their jobs, whatever, whatever, and it's like, well, everybody experiences things a) differently and b) even though someone is affected and somebody else is affected they both feel the negative effects in the same way, but differently.
>
> (Participant #2)

Here, this youth experiences a *testimonial injustice* when her hardships during the pandemic are dismissed. Instead, challenges faced by adults during the pandemic, like unemployment, are identified as worthy of pain – supporting stereotypes of younger people being entitled or selfish (Baumtrog, 2018). It should be noted that such responses – like the mother's, in this example – should not necessarily be disparaged; perhaps the mother attempted to imbue optimism or offer perspective by helping her daughter to understand struggles faced by others during the pandemic. However, such comparisons also run the risk of dismissing her daughter's valid reaction to her own experience of upheaval in her life.

Another youth described overt messaging around his mental health and symptom expression. When discussing his experience of anxiety attacks, for example, this youth recalls being told to not "let anyone see you like that" (Participant #3). Adults in his life typically guided him to leave the classroom as soon as possible during a panic attack because "if someone sees you crying in ninth grade or eighth grade it's like, it's not good." Interestingly, this youth chose not to internalize this messaging, instead asserting his belief that "people kind of understand" and that he does not need to hide himself if he is struggling. More broadly, this youth challenges larger stigmas around concealing mental health concerns, which can be framed as an example of *epistemic resistance* (Medina, 2013) – an enactment of resistance to an unjust assumption related to mental health and silencing.

6.4.3 *Institutional Ignorance: "Your Own Feeling Is Your Feeling and That's What's Most Important"*

Youth shared experiences of epistemic injustice within healthcare institutions on a systemic level. For instance, biomedical discourse was described as inadequately capturing the spectrum of mental health experiences; one youth spoke of the limited *hermeneutical resources* provided by the *DSM*:

> it's not something that's … quantifiable … it's so individual to each person … diagnosis is really important in the mental health field, but it also makes it really difficul t… *your own feeling is your feeling, and like, that's what's most important*, not what, like, the *DSM* is telling you that you have or you don't have.
>
> (Participant #4)

Another participant shared a similar sentiment:

> this is kind of what I wish a couple of mental health professionals understood … sometimes, you don't really have, like, a set condition that you can really diagnose someone with. Just a bunch of different ones that will, like, overlap. But, having depression and anxiety isn't the same as having depression and anxiety, if that makes any sense? Like, I'm anxious and, sometimes separately, I'm also depressed. But often, they're the same thing.
>
> (Participant #1)

Both these quotes reveal how dominant medical discourses can result in a hermeneutical injustice if medical constructs do not resonate with youth's experiences. In these quotes, youth state that their own individual feelings are how they primarily make meaning of their experiences and that these should play a more prominent role in medical dialogue and treatment planning. They also describe conceptualizing depression and anxiety as "overlapping" and not always as separate constructs – perhaps differing from medical constructs. These youth experienced a "hermeneutical marginalization" – where their hermeneutical resources are not drawn upon by their providers to aid in making meaning of their mental health experiences.

6.5 Youth's Experiences of Epistemic Justice in Mental Health Services

The findings also revealed two themes of epistemic justice, including clinical discourse as a sense-making resource and validation.

6.5.1 *Clinical Discourse as a Sense-Making Resource: "I'm Not Crazy, I'm Not Making This Up"*

While some youth struggled to connect with medical discourse, others found it helped them to make meaning of their mental health. Some youth felt that medical criteria resonated with their own symptoms and helped them make further sense of their experiences. One youth described her diagnosis as "a huge weight off my shoulders" and that "it got me the help I needed" (Participant #5). This demonstrates *hermeneutical justice* in that youth's experiences are meaningfully integrated into institutional practice. Another youth echoes this sentiment when referring to the support she received from her therapist: "OK! I'm not crazy, I'm not making this up" (Participant #1).

6.5.2 *Validation: "We're Able to Talk about the Ins-and-Outs of It" due to Shared Experiences*

Some youth encountered *testimonial justice* when their experiences were overtly validated by others, including friends and certain adults in their lives. One youth stated that, among friends who also experienced mental health concerns, they can "make jokes about it, we're very open about it, and we're able to talk about the ins-and-outs of it because, you know, similar experiences," as opposed to others "who've never experienced that, kind of pity us" (Participant #5). The capacity to find humor (instead of pity) in their experiences exemplifies what Fricker (2007) calls "indicator properties" (p. 130) that help determine who deserves credibility. In this case, youth who share similar experiences can identify these indicators in each other and help validate each other's experiences.

Another youth mentioned certain teachers who also validated their experiences. For instance, one reported that "some teachers would like really like try to make an effort to try to make things easier for me and like understand that, hey, this kid has this thing that means he has to do things like differently..." (Participant #3). These are examples of *testimonial justice*, where youth's experiences are not only validated but also responded to appropriately. In the first example, the youth recalls how peers with similar mental health experiences understand *how* to discuss their experiences and how best to cope (i.e., humor vs. pity). They can validate one another's experiences in ways that others may not be able to because they assign credibility to each other's testimonies. In the second example, this youth experiences their teachers as listening to their needs and making efforts to accommodate them based on these needs (i.e., "do[ing] things differently"). Again, these teachers *trust* youth's reports of their experiences and, further, act based on this trust.

6.6 Toward Epistemic Justice in Social Work Practice with Youth

While social workers may understand concepts of epistemic injustice on a theoretical or abstract level, it can certainly be more difficult to identify them in practice. How, then, can we as social workers working with young people ensure our interactions are grounded in the validation of youth's experiences? Findings from this study offer a number of opportunities to reflect on how we can better meet this standard as a profession. This final section will provide some recommendations for practice and close with some reflections on both the personal and professional impacts of Fricker's (2007) work on epistemic injustice on the author of this chapter.

As a first step, even the most experienced social workers may benefit from regular check-ins around their own biases, assumptions, and social positionings as clinicians, researchers, or professionals holding power. What have we been conditioned to believe or disbelieve about youth credibility? What about the credibility or incredibility of youth with mental health concerns? How does our positioning within systems (i.e., healthcare, education, child welfare, etc.) impact how we interact with youth? As privileged hearers of youth's narratives, often presenting to us at sensitive and vulnerable times, we have the opportunity to engage in critical reflection on how we can best *hear* their stories and ensure they have the hermeneutical space they need to engage in their own sense-making. At the most basic level, this involves simply and fundamentally *suspend[ing] judgment* regarding youth's credibility as speakers (Fricker, 2007, p. 92). Fricker (2007) describes that the *virtuous hearer* "neutralizes the impact of prejudice in her credibility judgements" (p. 92). For instance, youth may not see their symptoms as being potential mental health concerns (perhaps due to limited access to epistemic resources); thus, there may be a lack of shared experience between a youth and social worker as they navigate this discussion (Fricker, 2007). However, as social workers do daily as part of their roles, it is crucial to remain open-minded to youth's realities in order to establish rapport and validate their credibility. This may involve social workers collaborating with youth and mutually sharing information, ultimately resulting in a shared understanding of their experience, and determining possible next steps. This all stems from reserving judgment despite coming together without a foundation of shared experience.

Social workers across professional settings and contexts face high demands and low resources. We are tasked with balancing administrative and clinical responsibilities while also managing crises and high-risk situations as they arise. Fortunately, social workers are trained to engage in both reflexive practice (Mishna & Bogo, 2007) and the use of self in our work. We are thus well-suited to be leaders in epistemically just practice and uphold the principle described by Milner and Carolin (1999), that "to be heard and understood without judgement, to have another human being bear witness to both our suffering and our joy, is a basic human need" (p. xi). Our training also positions us to advocate for epistemic justice on multidisciplinary teams, where this level of reflection may not be readily practiced.

As a recommendation, we must remember that enacting hermeneutical and testimonially just work does not require *consensus* with youth on what is "truth." We do not need to interrogate the merit of their reality and, instead, this work "entails keeping an open mind to the origins, value and function of the patient's own interpretation of reality..." (Ritunnano, 2022, p. 250). Social workers must continually practice opening themselves to the awareness that youth may draw from hermeneutical resources that differ from dominant discourses and that efforts to understand these resources can only lead to positive outcomes (Ritunnano, 2022).

6.6.1 Reflecting on Epistemic Injustice Scholarship in Social Work Practice with Youth

As a learner of Fricker's concepts, this theory has impacted my perspective on my role as an academic, social worker, and person who identifies with varying levels of privilege. Working within various biomedical settings has, at times, placed me in a position of perceived "expert knowledge"; however, it has also revealed that there are clear hierarchies of knowledge that may subjugate subjective experience (Ashcroft & Van Katwyk, 2016; Crichton et al., 2017; Kidd & Carel, 2017), marginalize certain testimonies, and exclude those drawing on alternative hermeneutical resources to make sense of and communicate experiences. This observation aligns with research in which patients accessing mental health care report feeling the need to adopt "medical jargon" (Ashcroft et al., 2021, p. 1176) in order to secure credibility.

As I progressed in my career across various settings and roles, I have benefited from seeing Fricker's theory as a set of guiding principles that can both gently drive practice and research as well as support personal reflections on how we "show up" in interactions. We are encouraged to examine our own assumptions and biases. This particular compilation further supports this process by applying concepts to various subject areas.

How, then, in such settings can social workers help to promote hermeneutical justice for youth seeking care? I believe social workers hold unique and necessary roles on multidisciplinary teams where they can advocate for patient/client voices and create space for non-dominant perspectives to be integrated into what is considered "valid" knowledge. Social workers bring specialized training in these skills and are therefore excellent agents to both practice and lead others in recognizing bias, prejudice, and potential discrediting. As social workers become more familiar with these concepts and their applicability, they can attune to hearing narratives that may, for instance, indicate pre-emptive silencing around mental health concerns or a mismatch between the hermeneutical resources used by institutions and youth to understand diagnoses or treatment plans. Social workers may be in positions to provide psychoeducation to colleagues, educators, or parents to help them understand how youth may be making meaning of their mental health and how their approaches may differ from their parents or medical teams.

In closing, this chapter sought to explore Miranda Fricker's concepts of epistemic injustice through findings from a study examining these themes in the narratives of youth with mental health concerns. There is no prescriptive way for social workers to "perfectly" enact epistemic justice in their practice. Instead, this chapter hopefully serves as an opportunity for reflection on practice, the systems in which we work, and the youth we aim to support.

References

American Psychiatric Association. (2022). *Diagnostic and statistical manual of mental disorders* (5th ed., text rev.). American Psychiatric Publishing.

Ashcroft, R., Menear, M., Greenblatt, A., Silveira, J., Dahrouge, S., Sunderji, N., Emode, M., Booton, J., Muchenje, M., Cooper, R., Haughton, A., & McKenzie, K. (2021). Patient perspectives on quality of care for depression and anxiety in primary health care teams: A qualitative study. *Health Expectations*, *24*(4), 1168–1177.

Ashcroft, R., & Van Katwyk, T. (2016). An examination of the biomedical paradigm: A view of social work. *Social Work in Public Health*, *31*(3), 140–152.

Baumtrog, M. D. (2018). Navigating a necessary inequality: Children and knowledge-based injustice. *Alternate Routes: A Journal of Critical Social Research*, *29*, 294–306.

Crichton, P., Carel, H., & Kidd, I. J. (2017). Epistemic injustice in psychiatry. *BJPsych Bulletin*, *41*(2), 65–70.

Delgado, M. (2006). *Designs and methods for youth-led research.* Sage.

Dotson, K. (2012). A cautionary tale: On limiting epistemic oppression. *Frontiers: A Journal of Women Studies*, *33*(1), 24–47.

Fricker, M. (2007). *Epistemic injustice: Power and the ethics of knowing.* Oxford University Press.

Gondek, D., Edbrooke-Childs, J., Velikonja, T., Chapman, L., Saunders, F., Hayes, D., & Wolpert, M. (2017). Facilitators and barriers to person-centred care in child and young people mental health services: A systematic review. *Clinical Psychology & Psychotherapy*, *24*(4), 870–886.

Greenblatt, A. (2022). *Meaning-making and mental health: Capturing youth's voices* [Doctoral dissertation], University of Toronto.

Greenblatt, A., Lee, E., Ashcroft, R., & Muskat, B. (2024). Epistemic justice and injustice among youth with mental health concerns. *Children & Society*, *38*(4), 1039–1058.

Human Rights Campaign (n.d.). *Repeal of "don't ask, don't tell"*. https://www.hrc.org/our-work/stories/repeal-of-dont-ask-dont-tell

Kidd, I. J., & Carel, H. (2017). Epistemic injustice and illness. *Journal of Applied Philosophy*, *34*(2), 172–190.

LeFrançois, B. (2008). "It's like mental torture": Participation and mental health services. *The International Journal of Children's Rights*, *16*(2), 211–227.

Liegghio, M., Delay, D. C., & Jenney, A. (2019). Challenging social work epistemology in children's mental health: The connections between evidence-based practice and young people's psychiatrisation. *The British Journal of Social Work*, *49*(5), 1180–1197.

Liegghio, M., Nelson, G., & Evans, S. D. (2010). Partnering with children diagnosed with mental health issues: Contributions of a sociology of childhood perspective to participatory action research. *American Journal of Community Psychology*, *46*(1), 84–99.

Medina, J. (2013). *The epistemology of resistance: Gender and racial oppression, epistemic injustice, and the social imagination*. Oxford University Press.

Milner, P., & Carolin, B. (Eds.). (1999). *Time to listen to children: Personal and professional communication*. Routledge.

Mishna, F., Antle, B., & Regeher, C. (2004). Tapping the perspectives of children: Emerging ethical issues in qualitative research. *Qualitative Social Work*, *3*, 449–468.

Mishna, F., & Bogo, M. (2007). Reflective practice in contemporary social work classrooms. *Journal of Social Work Education*, *43*(3), 529–544.

Murris, K. (2013). The epistemic challenge of hearing child's voice. *Studies in Philosophy and Education*, *32*(3), 245–259.

Prilleltensky, I., Nelson, G., & Peirson, L. (2001). The role of power and control in children's lives: An ecological analysis of pathways toward wellness, resilience, and problems. *Journal of Community and Applied Social Psychology*, *11*, 143–158.

Ritunnano, R. (2022). Overcoming hermeneutical injustice in mental health: A role for critical phenomenology. *Journal of the British Society for Phenomenology*, *53*(3), 243–260.

Souto-Manning, M. (2014). Critical narrative analysis: The interplay of critical discourse and narrative analyses. *International Journal of Qualitative Studies in Education*, *27*(2), 159–180.

Tate, A. J. M. (2019). Contributory injustice in psychiatry. *Journal of Medical Ethics*, *45*(2), 97–100.

Chapter 7

Epistemic Injustice in the Context of Contested Diagnoses

Dismissal and Delegitimation in the Face of Complex Evidence

Ulla-Karin Schön and Noam Ringer

7.1 Introduction

Healthcare is often regarded as a specialized domain where patients place significant trust in healthcare providers to accurately diagnose and treat medical conditions. However, this trust can be severely undermined when patients encounter dismissal or misunderstanding of their experiences, particularly in the context of contested medical diagnoses. These interactions can be deeply disempowering, depriving individuals not only of effective care but also of their credibility and agency. Such experiences exemplify epistemic injustice (Fricker, 2007), a concept that addresses the ways in which individuals may be wronged in their capacity as knowers through mechanisms such as prejudice, dismissal, or a lack of shared interpretive resources.

Epistemic injustice manifests in two primary forms. Testimonial injustice occurs when an individual's credibility as a source of knowledge is unjustly diminished due to biases, which often arise from social power dynamics. Patients and caregivers often find themselves marginalized within these systems, with their experiential knowledge dismissed or undervalued. This dynamic is especially pronounced in the case of contested diagnoses such as PANS, when medical uncertainty compounds existing power imbalances. Hermeneutical injustice, conversely, refers to situations in which structural gaps in collective understanding prevent individuals from making sense of their own experiences (Fricker, 2007). Structural gaps in shared understanding leave individuals unable to articulate their experiences in ways that are recognized as legitimate. This form of injustice is particularly prevalent in contested diagnoses, where a lack of medical consensus exacerbates feelings of alienation and invalidation for both patients and caregivers. In healthcare, a patient's or caregiver's account may be dismissed or minimized because they are not perceived as legitimate sources of knowledge; this can be problematic since being heard and understood can significantly impact the course of treatment and recovery. Hermeneutical injustice arises when individuals' experiences fall outside of existing frameworks of knowledge, leaving them without the conceptual tools to interpret their realities.

DOI: 10.4324/9781003639046-10

This issue is particularly relevant for patients diagnosed with contested illnesses (such as PANS) and their caregivers, as the absence of a widely accepted medical framework for understanding the condition exacerbates their sense of alienation and misunderstanding (Gilbert et al., 2018). Healthcare systems, with their hierarchical structures and reliance on standardized knowledge, are particularly vulnerable to epistemic injustices. Addressing epistemic injustice is therefore essential for promoting more equitable and inclusive healthcare practices.

This chapter examines epistemic injustice in the healthcare experiences of children who were diagnosed with PANS, as well as the experiences of their primary caregivers, all of whom are the parents in the present study. Caregivers of children with PANS often encounter skepticism from healthcare providers, forcing them to assume dual roles as both caregivers and advocates. Drawing on qualitative research, this chapter explores how testimonial and hermeneutical injustice shape the experiences of patients and parents. It also considers strategies for mitigating epistemic injustice in healthcare settings, offering potential pathways toward more equitable and inclusive practices.

7.1.1 Key Terminology

Testimonial Injustice. In the context of this chapter, *testimonial injustice* occurs when patients or parents are not believed or taken seriously by healthcare professionals. When families attempt to share their observations of symptoms, histories, or treatment responses, they may be dismissed as exaggerating, misinformed, or overly anxious. Such practices not only undermine trust in the clinical relationship but also impose *epistemic harm*, since patients and families are wrongfully excluded from contributing valid knowledge about their own health experiences (Dunne & Kotsonis, 2025). Epistemic harm occurs when patients or families are unfairly discredited or dismissed, undermining their ability to contribute knowledge about their own health experiences

Epistemic Marginalization. It arises when the perspectives and experiences of certain groups are systematically excluded from the dominant frameworks of understanding (Russo, 2023). This is especially relevant for families navigating contested or poorly understood diagnoses such as PANS. In these cases, the standard medical paradigms fail to adequately interpret or validate their lived experiences. Families find themselves at the margins of medical discourse, with little access to the interpretive resources necessary to make sense of what is happening to their children. This marginalization compounds the initial testimonial harms, leaving families both disbelieved and without a recognized language or framework to articulate their struggles within mainstream medicine.

Contested Diagnosis. It refers to a medical condition whose legitimacy, diagnostic criteria, or treatment is debated within the medical community (Harper et al., 2025). Pediatric Acute-Onset Neuropsychiatric Syndrome is discussed as an example of such a diagnosis.

Pediatric Acute-Onset Neuropsychiatric Syndrome (PANS). It is a clinical condition characterized by the sudden onset of obsessive-compulsive symptoms and/or severely restricted food intake, along with other behavioral and neurological symptoms. Its etiology remains unclear and is debated, leading to challenges in recognition and treatment (Pfeiffer et al., 2021).

Experiential Knowledge. It is defined as knowledge derived from personal experience (Dumez & L'Espérance, 2024). In the context of this chapter, it includes the lived experiences of children with PANS and their caregivers, which are often dismissed in clinical settings.

Person-centered Care. It refers to a healthcare approach that values and prioritizes the preferences, needs, and values of patients and their families (Zegarra-Parodi et al., 2024). It advocates for integrating patients' experiential knowledge into clinical decision-making.

7.2 From Diagnostic Uncertainty to Epistemic Marginalization

PANS is a clinical condition characterized by a sudden appearance of psychiatric symptoms and a loss of cognitive and motoric abilities (Sigra et al., 2018). Psychiatric symptoms often consist of separation anxiety, compulsive behaviors, tics, hallucinations, and eating disorders. Cognitive and motoric impacts can include, for example, losing the ability to bike, eat with a fork and knife, draw, and/or write. Not only do symptoms appear rapidly – typically developing within less than 48 hours – but they are also severe, leading to extensive consequences for the sick children and their families (Calaprice et al., 2017). The symptoms often negatively impact the child's school performance, social relationships, and homelife, including financial and marital challenges for caregivers (Tang et al., 2021). Frankovich and colleagues (2018) found that families with a child with PANS experience significantly higher levels of suffering and emotional strain in comparison to families with children who have other chronic illnesses. In addition, parents experienced substantial levels of burden related to caring for the ill child (Frankovich et al., 2018).

Being a relatively new diagnosis, there are many questions regarding the diagnostic procedure of PANS, as well as its etiology and treatment (Pfeiffer et al., 2021). Since PANS symptoms overlap with other psychiatric diagnoses (such as post-traumatic stress disorder, some anxiety conditions, and neurodevelopmental conditions), the diagnostic procedure of PANS is challenging, and the validity of the diagnosis is often questioned (Pfeiffer et al., 2021). The immunological hypothesis regarding the etiology of PANS is that infectious diseases and dysregulation of the immune system trigger the immune system to attack one's own nervous system, thereby impacting brain functioning (Cooperstock et al., 2017). This view comes into conflict with the psychiatric hypothesis, which emphasizes the role of underlying dynamics of acute stress and trauma as well as neurodevelopmental mechanisms (Prato et al., 2021). Consequently, disagreements exist regarding the appropriateness of treatments that aim to manage infections (e.g., antibiotics) or treatments that target the dysfunctional immune system (e.g., immunoglobulin therapy) to prevent it from attacking the body's own cells as alternatives to psychiatric medications and psychotherapeutic interventions (Prato et al., 2021).

This context predominated by a lack of knowledge – both scientific knowledge and knowledge among practitioners – is one in which children with PANS and their parents frequently find themselves in a position of epistemic marginalization; their accounts of their lived experiences are dismissed as exaggerated, anecdotal, or misinformed, while the lack of a unified medical framework for PANS complicates patient and family efforts to communicate their experiences in a way that resonates with healthcare providers. These challenges are not unique to PANS but are commonly found in other contested diagnoses, such as chronic fatigue syndrome (CFS: Allen, 2024), fibromyalgia (Hayes et al., 2010), and multiple chemical sensitivity (MCS), where medical uncertainty contributes to the devaluation of patient narratives (Armentor, 2017). Previous research on controversial diagnoses such as CFS or MCS illustrates how people who suffer from these syndromes often experience their illness as being questioned or denied (Armentor, 2017; Finell et al., 2018). Their symptoms are judged by healthcare providers to be psychosomatic, leading to psychiatric diagnoses in the absence of neurological consideration or examination (Finell et al., 2018; Kornelsen et al., 2016). Moreover, their motives for seeking care are questioned, their often complex needs remain unknown, and their right to care is denied (Finell et al., 2018; Montali et al., 2011).

Previous research highlights how patients with PANS and their parents are negatively impacted by the lack of relevant support and knowledge from the medical community (Dolce et al., 2022; Ringer & Roll-Pettersson, 2022). Parents have reported that one of their primary frustrations is the lack of support from healthcare professionals, often compounded by experiences of being turned away by doctors unfamiliar with PANS. Importantly, parents have expressed that having a healthcare provider who listens to their experiences and acknowledges PANS as a valid diagnosis is often the most crucial step in managing their child's illness (Dolce et al., 2022). Similar findings have emerged in other studies, with parents frequently noting that clinicians' initial explanations for their children's symptoms rarely include PANS, requiring the parents themselves to propose the diagnosis as a possibility (Ringer & Roll-Pettersson, 2022). These experiences of being dismissed or discredited are not confined to PANS but are also reported among patients with other contested conditions, such as CFS (Pilkington et al., 2020), MCS (Seppälä et al., 2022), and burnout (Heinemann & Heinemann, 2017). In these cases, individuals often face professional skepticism, a questioning of the legitimacy of their illness, and in some instances, blame for their perceived failure to recover, leading them to feel that their credibility is under threat (Pilkington et al., 2020; Seppälä et al., 2022).

Such experiences exemplify epistemic injustice (Fricker, 2007) between patients with contested illnesses and their healthcare providers, resulting in distrust toward the patient or their caregiver(s) and the subsequent failure to recognize or validate their experience-based knowledge (Blease et al., 2017; Buchman et al., 2017; Fricker, 2007). Fricker's theory of epistemic injustice provides a framework for understanding the moral dimensions of two fundamental practices: the transmission of knowledge to others (epistemic justice) and the validation of one's own experiences (hermeneutical justice) (Fricker, 2007). This theory offers a valuable analytical lens for studying the power structures and subtle mechanisms that determine who is believed and who is dismissed in healthcare settings.

7.3 Collecting the Lived Experiences of People Impacted by Pediatric Acute-Onset Neuropsychiatric Syndrome (PANS)

This chapter draws on a study that was conducted to deepen our understanding of the processes through which children with PANS and their primary caregivers acquire knowledge about the condition and communicate it to healthcare professionals. The study investigates the epistemic trajectories of children diagnosed with PANS and their primary caregivers, focusing on three interrelated objectives: (1) to identify the underlying factors that motivate patients and caregivers to pursue knowledge about PANS as an explanatory framework for the child's neuropsychiatric symptoms; (2) to examine the sources, strategies, and pathways through which this knowledge is acquired; and (3) to analyze how patients and caregivers perceive the reception and legitimacy of this knowledge within clinical encounters. By elucidating these knowledge-seeking processes, the study aims to contribute to a more nuanced understanding of how contested or emerging diagnoses are navigated in healthcare settings, thereby informing more responsive, person-centered communication practices and enhancing the inclusion of patients and caregivers as epistemic agents in treatment planning and decision-making.

7.3.1 Recruitment and Data Collection

After receiving ethics approval from the Regional Ethics Committee (2020-06554), participants were recruited online (i.e., through announcements posted on patient organization websites) and in the waiting areas of pediatric and youth medical clinics across Sweden. The announcements provided general information about the study and encouraged potential participants to contact the researcher via email or telephone. Parents who expressed interest in participating were provided with detailed written information about the study, including its purpose and the terms of participation. Informed consent to participate in the study was obtained both verbally and in writing from the participants.

Data collection occurred over two years, between 2021 and 2022. In-depth interviews were conducted with 10 adults with PANS and 13 parents of children diagnosed with the condition, totaling 23 participants (N = 23) in Sweden. The participating parents, five fathers and eight mothers, have children between the ages of 7 and 19 years and are not biologically related to the adult participants who have their own experience of PANS. Among the participants with personal experience of PANS, there were 5 women and 5 men aged 19 to 34 years. According to their accounts, all had experienced PANS-like symptoms during childhood or early adolescence. Additionally, they all reported recurring episodes of PANS symptoms into adulthood. A semi-structured interview guide was developed to explore and understand the lived experiences of individuals seeking and receiving healthcare related to a PANS diagnosis. This includes questions on the diagnostic journey, the context and emotions surrounding the diagnosis, perceptions of healthcare professionals' behaviors, and the nature and impact of communication during medical consultations and ongoing treatment. The interview guide was designed to serve as a flexible tool to promote the interviewees' deeper reflection and sharing. Follow-up probing questions were employed to further explore and enhance understanding of their experiences.

7.3.2 *Data Analysis*

To analyze the interview transcripts, thematic analysis was employed using an inductive approach, as outlined by Braun and Clarke (2022). Thematic analysis was deemed particularly suitable for systematically identifying and interpreting patterns (themes) within the extensive qualitative data. An inductive approach ensured that the themes emerged directly from the data, rather than being constrained by pre-existing theoretical frameworks. The data analysis was conducted in two main stages: open coding and subcategorization. In the first stage, the data were broken down into discrete components, parts, and properties, and examined for the actions, experiences, and meanings they conveyed. Each unit of meaning was coded based on its semantic content, with attention to what participants said and how they said it. This involved assigning descriptive codes to segments of the text that reflected significant concepts or expressions. The aim of this stage was to capture all relevant aspects of the content, ensuring that the range and diversity of experiences were comprehensively represented. In the second stage, the initial codes were organized, compared, and synthesized into higher-order groupings or subcategories. This process involved identifying patterns, similarities, and contrasts among codes. Importantly, categorization was guided not only by establishing the defining characteristics of a given subcategory, but also by what distinguished it from inclusion in other subcategories.

This comparative approach facilitated the development of analytically sound and conceptually distinct groupings, setting the foundation for the later construction of overarching categories or themes.

7.4 Findings: Striving for an Improved Knowledge of PANS

Three main themes emerged from the data analysis: (1) the triggers that prompted a search for further knowledge about PANS, (2) the ways patients and parents acquired knowledge about PANS; and (3) the responses of medical care professionals to patients and parents' knowledge. In the following, these three themes will be developed further, illustrated with direct quotes from the interviews. Given the relatively small number of participants and the limited number of children who receive this diagnosis, we have chosen to limit the contextualization of the participants in order to protect participants' anonymity.

7.4.1 The Triggers Which Prompted a Search for Further Knowledge about PANS

One of the most striking patterns in participants' accounts was their own observations of consistent dismissal by healthcare providers. Parents recounted how detailed descriptions of their child's symptoms were often met with skepticism or outright disbelief. This experience is illustrated by one of the parents:

> We got to see a new doctor, and I felt that he was mostly focused on showing us that we, as parents, shouldn't tell him what to do… that he was the one in charge and it didn't matter what we parents had to say. And it became very, very strange. We asked him to look at our child, at his tics, but no, he didn't want to.
>
> (Participant 4)

Many clinicians seemed to rely on standardized diagnostic frameworks that failed to accommodate the acute, varied, and multifaceted nature of PANS symptoms. This disconnect exemplifies hermeneutical injustice, as existing medical paradigms lacked the conceptual flexibility to recognize the legitimacy of families' experiences.

The participants with their own experience of PANS also reported on how they were extensively ignored by healthcare providers despite their embodied experience of this rare illness. They expressed that in healthcare encounters, *"it was made clear where the expertise lay and that healthcare staff clearly articulated that 'we have superior knowledge than you'" (Participant 15)*. This resembles the experiences of parents who frequently became knowledge seekers out of necessity, driven by dissatisfaction with initial diagnoses or treatments. Three key triggers for pursuing knowledge about PANS emerged from their experiences in healthcare: (1) a perceived mismatch between symptoms and diagnoses, (2) ineffectiveness of the standard treatments that were offered, and (3) a feeling of blame or judgment from healthcare staff.

7.4.1.1 Discredited Experiences due to a Mismatch between Symptoms and Diagnoses

The participating adults with their own experience of PANS described how their embodied suffering did not conform to the explanatory frameworks provided by healthcare providers. Years of intense searching for care and information for somatic and psychiatric support finally led to an understanding of the illness they suffered from, and an explanation for their behaviors and sudden inabilities. During this period, they received several different psychiatric diagnoses, all characterized by symptoms that did not fully align with their own, and underwent medical treatment that they did not perceive to provide any appreciable relief. Their narratives illustrated experiences of despair and a sense of being thrown around, as well as consulting with doctors who had not previously heard of PANS, as illustrated by the following description:

> Many doctors are not familiar with PANS. I don't know if that's because it hasn't been an established diagnosis for long. Or possibly, that I saw the wrong doctors?
>
> (Participant 19)

Also, many parents reported that their children's symptoms did not align with conventional diagnoses like anxiety disorders or obsessive-compulsive disorder. The unpredictable and acute nature of PANS symptoms often defies these diagnostic categories, leaving parents feeling unrecognized. This disconnect exemplifies hermeneutical injustice, as existing medical frameworks fail to capture their realities. Several parents noted that the symptoms assessed in questionnaires were either irrelevant or qualitatively different from their child's symptoms.

> I thought, this isn't the typical OCD [obsessive-compulsive disorder] they talk about. It must be something else. We had to do all those assessment scales, but hardly any of the questions matched.
>
> (Participant 2)

Some parents found that certain psychiatric diagnoses, such as neurodevelopmental disorders and anxiety disorders, for example, matched some aspects of their child's symptoms. However, many other experiences of their child – such as the unpredictability, varying character, and intensity of the symptoms, as well as the accompanying infections or other somatic conditions – were not addressed by these diagnoses.

The participants also talked about how they felt that there was an "emphasis on psychiatry" in the eyes of the healthcare workers where established diagnoses, such as autism and obsessive-compulsive disorder (OCD), were quickly put forward. Rather than remaining open to alternative diagnoses, the doctors appeared to have already formed a predetermined conclusion. One participant illustrates this point as follows:

> But doctors you see at the health center have difficulty understanding this thing about obsessive and compulsive actions. And [they don't understand] PANS at all. I should have come to a pediatrician's office straight away when I was 14, but I was sent to child psychiatry instead and was given antidepressants and such.
>
> (Participant 4)

The disconnect between the symptoms and diagnosis initially made by medical staff was further affirmed when parents encountered parents of other children with PANS. This experience was accompanied by feelings of loneliness, as well as a longing to recognize their own life situations in those of other parents.

> I started going to different forums and reading about OCD. I tried to be attentive and understand, but I couldn't relate, I just couldn't find it, like, "Your child sounds like my child." I never found it.
>
> (Participant 11)

Finding information about PANS – namely, the potential connection between symptoms and infections, combined with the rapid manifestation of symptoms – was described by many of the parents as an "*Aha!*-moment" or an "Eye-opening experience." It also enabled the parents to recognize their situation in that of other parents, and to develop an affinity with them. ***Enduring Ineffective Standard Treatments***

Parents often began questioning the validity of initial diagnoses when standard treatments – such as cognitive behavioral therapy (CBT) or psychopharmacological interventions – failed to improve their children's symptoms.

> *When we went to the child and adolescent psychiatric unit, he received CBT, but the treatment had no effect. You hope it gets better, but the treatment does nothing in comparison to other children. He actually got worse from the anxiety medication. And it was very frustrating. The psychologist adjusted the treatment to make it work better, but it didn't help. How he*

> *felt had nothing to do with the treatment itself. When he felt good, it didn't matter which method the psychologist used; when he felt bad, he felt bad. So, it didn't matter in any case. That's why it felt strange; it felt completely wrong. And then my wife and I thought it has to be something else.*
>
> (Participant 8)

These doubts frequently lead to testimonial injustice, as clinicians interpreted parents' skepticism as ignorance or resistance. When treatments had no effect or even worsened the child's condition, the parents started to doubt the validity of the treatments and searched for alternatives.

7.4.1.2 Getting Blamed and Judged

Some parents described feeling blamed for their children's conditions, with healthcare providers suggesting that symptoms were the result of poor parenting or environmental factors. This experience is described in the following quote:

> It's always that questioning. If she had worn long socks, she would have slept better. If you had disconnected the WiFi, she might have been happier. It's always about questioning. We never get out of there without being lectured about what we could or should have done. When your child is so ill, it's very difficult to be blamed. They do not focus on the child, do not take care of her. They focus on us. You two, what are you doing wrong? And if the child is so sick, you can't bear to be questioned. You need to learn as much as you can about what it could be.
>
> (Participant 5)

This blaming by professionals with authority not only undermined the credibility of the parents with lived experiences but also compelled them to seek knowledge with which to defend themselves and, more importantly, to advocate for their children. Several parents experienced that being blamed for their child's symptoms, as well as feeling disrespected by the care professionals, encouraged them to gain further knowledge about alternative causes for their child's behaviors. Knowledge about PANS, combined with an understanding of the corporeal mechanisms underlying its symptoms, allowed parents to manage and resist the blame.

7.4.2 Strategies for Knowledge Acquisition

When faced with these challenges, parents employed various strategies to build their understanding of PANS. They acquired knowledge about the condition, the meaning of the diagnosis, its treatments, and underlying etiology.

7.4.2.1 *Parents' Personal Observations*

One way to learn about PANS, particularly the possible connection between the psychological and somatic symptoms (e.g., infections or dermatological irritations), was through close observation and by paying intentional attention to this connection. Some parents reviewed old photos, read diaries they had written, and interviewed family members to investigate such connections. By meticulously documenting symptoms and patterns, parents created their own body of evidence. This experience is exemplified by the following quote:

> We had a teacher at school. And when she was going to do an educational assessment, she first observed him, and then when she interviewed me, she started asking lots of questions. And I answered, "No, he hadn't had any." But then I came home and started thinking, "Why did she ask all those questions?" So, I went back, looked at old pictures, and realized – right, he had impetigo. Which hadn't been a concern at all, and then he got sick. I remember exactly what day it was, where we were. We were at the park, and suddenly he started running around manically. And he had never done that before.
>
> (Participant 11)

While this knowledge was invaluable to parents, it was often dismissed by clinicians as anecdotal.

7.4.2.2 *Online Research*

The internet provides access to a wealth of information, from scientific articles to patient forums.

> What could it be? I didn't at all think that there could be a connection between the infection he had and the compulsion. And then I started reading and found some article in a neuroscience journal that mentioned some infection-inhibiting medication.
>
> (Participant 3)

However, healthcare providers frequently devalued these sources, framing them as unreliable or misinformed. From an epistemic injustice perspective, this dismissal reflects more than a professional judgment about the credibility of online materials. It also undermines the parents' efforts to engage critically and resourcefully with their child's condition. When the parents bring forward knowledge they have gathered, they are not only dismissed as lacking medical expertise but also positioned as incapable of contributing meaningfully to the clinical encounter. This dynamic constitutes epistemic harm, as their attempts at sense-making are devalued, and epistemic marginalization, as their contributions fall outside the recognized boundaries of legitimate medical knowledge. In effect, parents are silenced twice: first, by the absence of adequate medical frameworks for contested illnesses such as PANS, and second, by the discrediting of their attempts to fill that gap through independent inquiry.

7.4.2.3 Engagement with Parent Networks

A third way to learn about PANS was by joining local and national parent groups for parents of children with suspected or diagnosed PANS. Parent groups and advocacy organizations offered both practical advice and emotional support.

> We felt that we wanted to learn everything we could. We joined parent groups and learned a lot from other people's experiences. We are part of Facebook groups and read what others write.
>
> (Participant 2)

These communities helped to bridge the hermeneutical gap by creating shared understandings of PANS and its implications. This strategy was especially relevant after the parents started to become aware of the diagnosis. By joining a parent group, parents received general and theoretical knowledge about PANS, as well as specific and practical information (such as the treatment possibilities in their region, which clinics were recommended or to be avoided, and strategies that may help their child).

7.4.3 Responses from Providers

Participants recounted when their attempts to suggest alternative diagnoses or treatments were interpreted as overstepping boundaries. One of the parents described an experience in which they expressed to the clinical psychologist that CBT and exposure techniques would likely be ineffective in addressing their daughter's anxiety:

> Healthcare is just the way it is. If she has anxiety, then we do CBT. But there was nothing to expose her to. She just became terrified and ran out into the dark. We tried to explain to the psychologist that CBT would not be effective in this case, but they responded as if to say, "We know how to treat anxiety."
>
> (Participant 10)

This dynamic illustrates testimonial injustice, as the professional's assumptions about patients' and parents' lack of expertise undermined their credibility, effectively discounting their experiences and knowledge. The pervasive devaluation of patient and parental insights not only delayed effective treatment but also fostered feelings of powerlessness and frustration. Healthcare providers' responses to parents' knowledge-seeking efforts often fell into three categories: dismissal, discrediting, and sometimes validation and collaboration.

7.4.3.1 Dismissal of PANS as a Diagnosis

Some clinicians rejected PANS outright, framing it as speculative.

> I asked the Child and Adolescent Psychiatric Clinic about PANS, and they just said, "No, PANS doesn't exist, it's just popular science." And then half a year later I brought it up again, and they just said, "No, you have to give up and leave this PANS thing."
>
> (Participant 2)

This dismissal reflects hermeneutical injustice, as it denies parents access to a coherent narrative for their children's symptoms. Many parents experienced clinicians who dismissed the validity of PANS as a genuine diagnosis, suggesting that PANS was only an urban legend not recognized by the medical community. This invalidation pertained to both the existence of the diagnosis and the view that the psychiatric symptoms are related to autoimmune, infectious, and inflammatory states and can be treated with antibiotics, anti-inflammatory medications, and intravenous immunoglobulin.

7.4.3.2 Discrediting Children's and Parents' Knowledge

All participants, both patients and parents, wished (and in many cases, were still searching) for knowledge-based care when healthcare staff sought to collaborate with interdisciplinary colleagues, patients, and their parents. Some participants had previously undergone temporary treatments with antibiotics in neighboring countries (such as Norway or Denmark) which they felt had had positive effects on their wellbeing. These treatments had given them the experience of meeting a "knowledgeable doctor" (Participant 4) or an "expert on PANS" (Participant 20), which was a relief; they felt believed, for once, in their description of the syndrome, and had access to an effective intervention. A few of the participants had taken part in medical trials in Sweden, where they were offered medical treatment with rituximab and which made them feel much better. However, despite clear improvements in their health conditions, the treatment – which was funded through the research project – was discontinued once their participation in the project concluded.

However, suggesting possible diagnoses and treatment methods to doctors and other healthcare workers was not necessarily welcomed by medical health teams who often dismissed parents and patients' narratives despite their lived experience and knowledge. Several of the participants with their own experience of PANS expressed that their parents, most often mothers, had been badly treated by the healthcare system when they questioned diagnoses and expressed mistrust regarding treatment, especially in situations when they had tried to bring forward international and research-based knowledge about PANS and possible interventions.

> We got to see a new doctor and I felt that he was mostly focused on showing us that, "You parents, you shouldn't tell me what to do. Here, I am the expert," and it didn't matter what we parents were going to say. – And it gets very, very weird.
>
> (Participant 12)

Parents frequently encountered attitudes that devalued their insights, exemplifying testimonial injustice. This dynamic is particularly pronounced in hierarchical healthcare settings. With this type of response, the parents perceived the dismissal as occurring irrespective of their knowledge, focusing instead on the perceived role of their involvement in relation to the medical staff. This experience led to frustration and helplessness.

7.4.3.3 Validation and Collaboration

Despite these challenges, a few participants described moments where their experiential knowledge was acknowledged and valued. In rare cases, clinicians engaged in collaborative decision-making, validating parents' observations and integrating their insights into treatment planning.

> I called her doctor and asked, "Could it be PANS she has?" – "Yes, perhaps," she replied. And she listened and took samples, and even though I could tell it was new to her, she was responsive and tried to give her antibiotics and followed up with her. And it felt good to be able to trust her and to receive trust from her.
>
> (Participant 5)

These instances, while infrequent, highlight the potential for epistemic justice when healthcare providers recognized the legitimacy of experiential knowledge. Participants emphasized that such interactions restored their trust in healthcare systems and facilitated better service outcomes. These moments of epistemic justice demonstrate the possibility of more inclusive healthcare practices. When parents experienced that their knowledge was endorsed, they felt hopeful and encouraged.

7.5 Discussion: Social Workers' Roles in Addressing Structural and Cultural Barriers to Epistemic Justice in Healthcare

Social workers play a critical role in addressing epistemic injustices faced by families navigating contested diagnoses such as PANS by validating lived experiences, advocating for inclusive care, and bridging gaps in fragmented systems. By recognizing parents and children as legitimate knowledge holders, social workers promote person-centered, equitable healthcare rooted in social justice. In this chapter, the experiences of families navigating PANS highlight the pervasive impact of epistemic injustice in healthcare. Testimonial and hermeneutical injustices not only obstruct access to effective care but also erode trust and exacerbate suffering. Addressing these challenges requires a commitment to systemic change, where diverse forms of knowledge are valued and integrated into clinical practice. Medical hierarchies prioritize professional expertise, leaving little room for lay perspectives. Cultural differences further complicate these dynamics, particularly in diverse societies where patients and providers may have conflicting health beliefs. Addressing these barriers requires a structural rethinking of how knowledge is valued and shared in healthcare.

How can this epistemic injustice be counteracted? Mitigating epistemic injustice in healthcare requires both systemic reforms and cultural shifts. Recognizing families as essential contributors to knowledge is a crucial first step. Person-centered care models, which prioritize collaboration between providers, patients, and caregivers, offer a powerful framework for addressing testimonial injustice. By valuing experiential knowledge alongside clinical expertise, healthcare systems can create more inclusive and equitable environments.

7.5.1 *Implications for Knowledge Building in Healthcare Systems*

Expanding interpretive resources for contested diagnoses like PANS is equally important. Interdisciplinary collaboration among researchers, clinicians, and patient advocates can bridge gaps in understanding, fostering a shared language that captures the complexity of these conditions. Social workers, with their expertise in navigating systemic barriers and amplifying marginalized voices, play a critical role in this process. Their ability to facilitate communication between families and providers can help counteract the power imbalances that underpin epistemic injustice. To reduce the hierarchical positioning of social workers in treatment teams and expand interpretive resources for contested diagnoses like PANS, their epistemic expertise must be formally recognized within clinical decision-making. Integrative, interdisciplinary care models could position social workers as co-analysts alongside psychiatrists, not just as care coordinators. Their narrative and relational skills uniquely equip social workers to translate lived experience into clinically relevant insights, helping bridge gaps between families and providers. By explicitly addressing testimonial and hermeneutical injustices, social workers can advocate for the inclusion of marginalized knowledge as part of ethical care. Participatory research and cross-sector collaboration can further legitimize their role and democratize diagnostic knowledge.

Developing shared conceptual frameworks for conditions like PANS can bridge the gap between medical and experiential knowledge. This chapter has illustrated epistemic injustice in healthcare as a pervasive issue with profound ethical and practical implications. For parents of children with PANS, these injustices manifest in the dismissal of their knowledge and the absence of interpretive tools to validate their experiences. By addressing testimonial and hermeneutical injustices, healthcare systems can move toward a model of care that values all forms of knowledge, fostering equity and compassion in every interaction. This highlights the critical role of social workers in addressing epistemic injustices, particularly for families navigating contested diagnoses such as PANS. Social workers are uniquely positioned to advocate for person-centered care by amplifying the voices of patients and parents as essential contributors to healthcare decision-making. By actively listening to the lived experiences of parents and translating their narratives into actionable insights for interdisciplinary teams, social workers can counteract testimonial injustice. At the same time, they can foster hermeneutical justice by equipping families with the language, resources, and tools needed to articulate their struggles and engage meaningfully with the healthcare system and broader care networks.

7.5.2 *Implications for Epistemically Just Practice in Healthcare*

In practice, social workers can play a pivotal role in creating and maintaining support systems, guiding families through complex healthcare landscapes, and advocating for collaborative knowledge-sharing practices. In contested cases like PANS, where distrust between families and healthcare providers may emerge, social workers can act as mediators. By building bridges between these groups, social workers help foster trust and reduce the misunderstandings that arise from hierarchical healthcare dynamics.

The findings of this study also point to the systemic barriers within healthcare systems that perpetuate epistemic injustice. Social workers' advocacy work in policy-making may help to address these barriers and ensure that caregivers' voices are meaningfully integrated into treatment planning, particularly in cases where collaboration is critical. Structural reforms should prioritize multidisciplinary care approaches that value diverse perspectives and acknowledge the contributions of caregivers. Policies must aim to standardize inclusive practices across all levels of healthcare, ensuring that families from diverse socioeconomic and cultural backgrounds receive equitable care.

7.5.3 Implications for Interdisciplinary Health Education

Educational initiatives for healthcare professionals must also address the gaps that perpetuate epistemic injustices. Training programs should emphasize the importance of listening to and validating patient and caregiver narratives, particularly in cases where traditional diagnostic frameworks fall short. By fostering a culture of humility and openness, clinicians can build stronger partnerships with families and improve care outcomes. Additionally, investments in training programs are essential for promoting healthcare systems that operate in epistemically just ways.

It is crucial for social work and healthcare training programs to incorporate the concept of epistemic injustice. Curricula should emphasize the systemic inequities that shape patient-provider dynamics, preparing future practitioners to recognize and counteract both testimonial and hermeneutical injustice. Case-based learning on contested diagnoses, such as PANS, can provide students with tangible examples of how these injustices manifest in real-world settings. By fostering interdisciplinary education that brings together social work, medicine, and allied health fields, educators can create a shared understanding of the value of experiential knowledge in shaping care practices. The findings of this study can serve as a foundational resource to illustrate the intersection of theory and practice, encouraging students to critically examine power dynamics and develop innovative strategies for addressing inequities in their professional roles.

7.5.4 Implications for Future Research

This study underscores the need for further research on contested diagnoses and the systemic factors that perpetuate epistemic injustices. Future research could explore how healthcare providers perceive their interactions with families of children with PANS, offering a more comprehensive understanding of the barriers to collaboration. Examining intersectional experiences, such as the ways race, socioeconomic status, and cultural background converge with epistemic injustice, would provide valuable insights into developing more inclusive care practices. Longitudinal studies on person-centered approaches in contested diagnoses could also demonstrate the practical benefits of integrating caregiver knowledge into healthcare systems. Social workers in healthcare settings can contribute as co-researchers, bringing their practice-based insights into these studies to ensure findings directly inform both policy and practice.

References

Allen, C. B. (2024). *You don't look sick: Epistemic injustice, ethos, and embodied expertise in narratives of chronic illness* (Paper 4289). [Doctoral dissertation, University of Louisville]. Electronic Theses and Dissertations. https://doi.org/10.18297/etd/4289

Armentor, J. L. (2017). Living with a contested, stigmatized illness: Experiences of managing relationships among women with fibromyalgia. *Qualitative Health Research, 27*(4), 462–473. https://doi.org/10.1177/1049732315620160

Blease, C., Carel, H., & Geraghty, K. (2017). Epistemic injustice in healthcare encounters: Evidence from chronic fatigue syndrome. *Journal of Medical Ethics, 43*(8), 549–557. https://doi.org/10.1136/medethics-2016-103691

Braun, V., & Clarke, V. (2022). Conceptual and design thinking for thematic analysis. *Qualitative Psychology, 9*(1), 3–26. https://doi.org/10.1037/qup0000196

Buchman, D. Z., Ho, A., & Goldberg, D. S. (2017). Investigating trust, expertise, and epistemic injustice in chronic pain. *Journal of Bioethical Inquiry, 14*(1), 31–42. https://doi.org/10.1007/s11673-016-9761-x

Calaprice, D., Tona, J., Parker-Athill, E. C., & Murphy, T. K. (2017). A survey of pediatric acute-onset neuropsychiatric syndrome characteristics and course. *Journal of Child and Adolescent Psychopharmacology, 27*(7), 607–618. https://doi.org/10.1089/cap.2016.0105

Cooperstock, M. S., Swedo, S. E., Pasternack, M. S., & Murphy, T. K. (2017). Clinical management of pediatric acute-onset neuropsychiatric syndrome: Part III—treatment and prevention of infections. *Journal of Child and Adolescent Psychopharmacology, 27*(7), 594–606. https://doi.org/10.1089/cap.2016.0151

Dolce, J. L., LaRusso, M. D., & Abadia-Barrero, C. (2022). Disruptions and adaptations in family functioning: A study of families' experiences with PANS/PANDAS. *Journal of Child and Family Studies, 31*(3), 790–806. https://doi.org/10.1007/s10826-021-02101-3

Dumez, V., & L'Espérance, A. (2024). Beyond experiential knowledge: A classification of patient knowledge. *Social Theory & Health, 22*, 173–186. https://doi.org/10.1057/s41285-024-00208-3

Dunne, G., & Kotsonis, A. (2025). Carving at the joints: Distinguishing epistemic wrongs from epistemic harms in epistemic injustice contexts. *Episteme, 22*(2), 425–438. https://doi.org/10.1017/epi.2023.62

Finell, E., Tolvanen, A., Pekkanen, J., Minkkinen, J., Ståhl, T., & Rimpelä, A. (2018). Psychosocial problems, indoor air-related symptoms, and perceived indoor air quality among students in schools without indoor air problems: A longitudinal study. *International Journal of Environmental Research and Public Health, 15*(7). https://doi.org/10.3390/ijerph15071497

Frankovich, J., Leibold, C. M., Farmer, C., Sainani, K., Kamalani, G., Farhadian, B., Willett, T., Park, J. M., Sidell, D., Ahmed, S., & Thienemann, M. (2018). The burden of caring for a child or adolescent with pediatric acute-onset neuropsychiatric syndrome (PANS): An observational longitudinal study. *The Journal of Clinical Psychiatry, 80*(1) 12091. https://doi.org/10.4088/JCP.17m12091

Fricker, M. (2007). *Epistemic injustice: Power and the ethics of knowing*. Oxford University Press.

Gilbert, D. L., Mink, J. W., & Singer, H. S. (2018). A pediatric neurology perspective on pediatric autoimmune neuropsychiatric disorder associated with streptococcal infection and pediatric acute-onset neuropsychiatric syndrome. *The Journal of Pediatrics, 199*, 243–251. https://doi.org/10.1016/j.jpeds.2018.04.035

Harper, I., Kenny, K., & Broom, A. (2025). Navigating the limits of diagnosis: Young adults' experiences of chronic living. *Sociology of Health & Illness, 47*, e13861. https://doi.org/10.1111/1467-9566.13861

Hayes, S. Myhal, G., Thornton, J. Camerlain, M., Jamison, C., Cytryn, K., & Murray, S. (2010). Fibromyalgia and the therapeutic relationship: Where uncertainty meets attitude. *Pain Research and Management, 15*(6), 361–400. https://doi.org/10.1155/2010/354868

Heinemann, L. V., & Heinemann, T. (2017). Burnout research: Emergence and scientific investigation of a contested diagnosis. *SAGE Open, 7*(1). https://journals.sagepub.com/doi/full/10.1177/2158244017697154

Kornelsen, J., Atkins, C., Brownell, K., & Woollard, R. (2016). The meaning of patient experiences of medically unexplained physical symptoms. *Qualitative Health Research, 26*(3), 367–376. https://doi.org/10.1177/ 1049732314566326

Montali, L., Frigerio, A., Riva, P., & Invernizzi, P. (2011). 'It's as if PBC didn't exist': The illness experience of women affected by primary biliary cirrhosis. *Psychology & Health, 26*(11), 1429–1445. https://doi.org/10.1080/08870446. 2011.565876

Pfeiffer, H. C. V., Wickstrom, R., Skov, L., Sørensen, C. B., Sandvig, I., Gjone, I. H., Ygberg, S., de Visscher, C., Idring Nordstrom, S., Herner, L. B., Hesselmark, E., Hedderly, T., Lim, M., & Debes, N. M. (2021). Clinical guidance for diagnosis and management of suspected Pediatric Acute-onset Neuropsychiatric Syndrome in the Nordic countries. *Acta Paediatrica, 110*(12), 3153–3160. http://doi.org/10.1111/apa.15875

Pilkington, K., Ridge, D. T., Igwesi-Chidobe, C. N., Chew-Graham, C. A., Little, P., Babatunde, O., Corp, N., McDermott, C., & Cheshire, A. (2020). A relational analysis of an invisible illness: A meta-ethnography of people with chronic fatigue syndrome/myalgic encephalomyelitis (CFS/ME) and their support needs. *Social Science & Medicine, 265*. https://doi.org/10.1016/j.socscimed.2020.113369

Prato, A., Gulisano, M., Scerbo, M., Barone, R., Vicario, C. M., & Rizzo, R. (2021). Diagnostic approach to pediatric autoimmune neuropsychiatric disorders associated with streptococcal infections (PANDAS): A narrative review of literature data. *Frontiers in Pediatrics, 9*. https://doi.org/10.3389/fped.2021.746639

Ringer, N., & Roll-Pettersson, L. (2022). Understanding parental stress among parents of children with Paediatric Acute-onset Neuropsychiatric Syndrome (PANS) in Sweden. *International Journal of Qualitative Studies on Health and Well-Being, 17*(1). https://doi.org/10.1080/17482631.2022.2080906

Russo J. (2023, February 9) Psychiatrization, assertions of epistemic justice, and the question of agency. *Frontiers in Sociology, 8*, 1092298.

Seppälä, T., Finell, E., & Kaikkonen, S. (2022). Making sense of the delegitimation experiences of people suffering from indoor air problems in their homes. *International Journal of Qualitative Studies on Health and Well-being, 17*(1). https://doi.org/10.1080/17482631.2022.2075533

Sigra, S., Hesselmark, E., & Bejerot, S. (2018). Treatment of PANDAS and PANS: A systematic review. *Neuroscience & Biobehavioral Reviews, 86*, 51–65.

Tang, A. W., Appel, H. J., Bennett, S. C., Forsyth, L. H., Glasser, S. K., Jarka, M. A., Kory, P. D., Malik, A. N., Martonoffy, A. I., Wahlin, L. K., Williams, T. T., Woodin, N. A., Woodin, L. C., Miller, I. K. T., & Miller, L. G. (2021). Treatment barriers in PANS/PANDAS: Observations from eleven health care providers. *Families, Systems & Health, 39*, 477–487. https://doi.org/10.1037/fsh0000602

Zegarra-Parodi, R., D'Alessandro, G., Baroni, F., Swidrovich, J., Mehl-Madrona, L., Gordon, T., Ciullo, L., Castel, E., & Lunghi, C. (2024). Epistemological flexibility in person-centered care: The cynefin framework for (Re)Integrating indigenous body representations in manual therapy. *Healthcare*, 12(11), 1149. https://doi.org/10.3390/healthcare12111149

Chapter 8

"Not Sick Enough"

How Willful Hermeneutical Ignorance and Agential Testimonial Injustice Shape the Clinical Care of Street-Involved and Homeless Youth with Eating Struggles

Christina Hyland

8.1 Contextualizing Eating Struggles among Street-Involved Homeless Youth from an Epistemic Injustice Lens

Eating disorders (EDs), also referred to as *eating struggles* in this chapter (Hyland, 2022), are known for having one of the highest mortality rates across all psychiatric challenges, with often debilitating mental and physical health outcomes (Miskovic-Wheatley et al., 2023). Youth are disproportionately impacted, with higher mortality rates among individuals ages 15 to 29 (Moreno et al., 2023). According to Kotilahti et al. (2020), a significant proportion of individuals develop severe and enduring eating struggles that require clinical treatment in healthcare systems. Until recently, eating struggles have been predominately conceptualized through a biomedical lens, where it is often perceived as a young, White, female, heterosexual person without disabilities and middle-to-upper class issue evidenced by physical emaciation (Halbeisen et al., 2022). Although this narrative has been shifting to include more diverse experiences, the dominant misconception of who and what constitutes as having an eating struggle remains; the pervasive biomedical discourse is often embedded in systems of policy, health/mental healthcare systems, and academic research, and is sadly evident through the lived experiences reported by diverse individuals such as the population I highlight in this chapter – street-involved and homeless youth (SIHY) who have eating struggles.

I would like to first share my subjectivity, social location, and positionality. While the intention of this chapter is to highlight the voices of those I have had the privilege of encountering and to illuminate the epistemic injustices they face in clinical contexts, I recognize that as a White, middle class, lesbian, person without disabilities and cisgender woman, both my Whiteness-centered education and related professional training as a therapist are inherently colonial and closely connected to the history of oppression. I also experienced an eating struggle myself and, due to my social locations, had access to care unlike most SIHY. Thus, I am cautious of how these aspects of my identity impact my lens

DOI: 10.4324/9781003639046-11

and understanding while discussing ways we address eating struggles among SIHY.

In addition, to highlight the voices of SIHY who have eating struggles, I will ground my discussion in the lived experiences of SIHY participants from my research. Eli (pseudonym) was a 26-year-old, White, Canadian, non-binary individual who experienced situations of homelessness and street involvement. Eli defined their eating struggle as eating disorder not otherwise specified (EDNOS), which presents as severe food restriction and, occasionally, binge-eating and purging. They struggled significantly with both their body image and body dysphoria related to their gender identity, and had extensive experience in accessing support, including publicly funded outpatient/inpatient treatment. With their permission to include their testimony in written texts, along with my experiences as a clinician speaking with other SIHY, this chapter aims to examine epistemic injustices that persist in the field of EDs and that directly impact SIHY who have eating struggles.

To critically reflect upon and address a longstanding history of silencing diverse knowledges and voices around eating struggles, the field has expanded to include them in the ED scholarship, specifically the associations between EDs, poverty, and food insecurity (FI) (Becker et al., 2018; Christensen et al., 2021; Hazzard et al., 2022; Rasmusson et al., 2019; Zickgraf et al., 2022). This research has primarily focused on EDs among individuals who are food insecure. However, the research on food and poverty often centered on FI only at the household level; thus, homeless individuals, such as SIHY, continue to be underrepresented within the literature (Hyland, 2022; Luongo, 2018). Moreover, the voices of Black, Indigenous, and People of Color (BIPOC) who overrepresent those enduring homelessness and poverty have been largely silenced within both the literature and clinical spaces on decision making regarding ED conceptualizations, treatment, and support.

This historical and even contemporary erasure of understanding of eating struggles among diverse individuals enduring homelessness, FI, and poverty in academic and clinical literatures is surprising given the strong evidence recognizing the link between systemic trauma and EDs (Livingston et al., 2019). Poverty, homelessness, and FI are devastating living conditions that are often enduring and thus inherently traumatic. Scholars note that trauma is often survived through embodied responses such as EDs (Burstow, 2003; Eli, 2018). Throughout my professional practice, working as a therapist in the ED field since 2014 with diverse youth (including SIHY and BIPOC individuals who have eating struggles), it has been overwhelmingly evident that the pervasive models of ED treatment within Canadian mental/healthcare systems remain largely devoid of trauma-informed, anticolonial care. Years of testimonies from SIHY, both in clinical and research settings, have revealed (1) how individuals are often not recognized or deemed ineligible for ED support due to not "fitting" into the dominant mental/healthcare conceptualizations of "who" and "what" constitutes as having an ED despite the severity of their suffering and (2) when accessing publicly funded health care, SIHY face treatment approaches that are devoid of accessible, anticolonial, and trauma-informed care; their experiences are often described as punitive, de-humanizing, re-traumatizing, non-inclusive, and incomplete. In the following, I share experiences from both clinical encounters and my doctoral thesis research conducted in this area (Hyland, 2022) to highlight two concepts that have evolved from Miranda Fricker's (2007) work on epistemic injustice known as (1) willful hermeneutical ignorance and (2) agential testimonial injustice.

8.1.1 Key Terminology

Eating Disorders (EDs) versus Eating Struggles. Throughout this chapter, I incorporate the terms *eating struggles* and *eating disorders* (*EDs*) interchangeably since research in the field tends to rely on the diagnostic characteristics and presentations that ED diagnoses imply. However, I seek to shift the discourse from "disorder" to "struggle" so as to de-pathologize and de-hierarchize the individual who is suffering with their relationship to both food and body. This was inspired by Thompson's (1996) use of the term *eating problems* which was used to "pathologize" the systemic traumas and oppressions that underlie the development of EDs (i.e., racism, classism, misogyny, sexism, homophobia, transphobia, ableism, etc.) rather than the individuals suffering from them. The aim in shifting the discourse toward "struggle" is to expand how we conceptualize who has and what constitutes as having an ED; thus, the term eating struggles acts as a reminder of the diversity that exists among those who suffer from eating and body related concerns (see Hyland, 2022 for more information).

Street-Involved Homeless Youth (SIHY). According to the United Nations (2019), there is no universally agreed upon definition of youth age range. In the context of both my clinical work and the sites where I conducted my research, I chose to closely align with the youth age range reflected in local youth organizations and thus define youth as individuals between the ages of 13 and 26. With regard to street-involvement and homelessness, according to Gaetz (2014), the homeless population in Canada is made up of approximately 20% SIHY, which translates to nearly 35,000 to 40,000 youth experiencing homelessness during the year; approximately 6,000 and 7,000 youth experience homelessness on any given night. In the context of this chapter, SIHY are youth who reside independently of their parents or caregivers in precarious housing, on the streets, in abandoned homes, in community shelters, and/or among various friends' couches (Hyland, 2022; Winter, 2021).

Willful Hermeneutical Ignorance. *Willful hermeneutical ignorance* is a concept that Pohlhaus (2012) first developed to expand upon Miranda Fricker's (2007) scholarship on epistemic injustice. It examines how dominant groups or individuals/institutions in positions of power willfully remain ignorant of marginalized individuals' knowledge despite it being accessible and often well known; this includes knowledge that should ultimately influence and inform best practices, policies, and procedures within various settings, including healthcare and mental healthcare spaces. Indeed, willful hermeneutical ignorance often involves a deliberate refusal by systems and dominant groups to examine and transform their practices, policies, and services despite being aware of what is needed by marginalized groups and service users to adequately support their needs.

Agential Testimonial Injustice. Expanding upon Fricker's (2007) seminal work on epistemic injustice – especially testimonial injustice, where one's testimonial agency is discredited – Jennifer Lackey (2020) brings our attention to *agential testimonial injustice*. This concept was further refined by Bortolotti (2025) to examine its prevalence in the mental health field. It is a concept that identifies the epistemic harm that occurs when individuals are treated as incapable of meeting their own needs or mitigating their own risks; they are thus coerced into making decisions that serve the priorities of those in power/institutions over their own while being denied full/truthful information about treatment options or processes (Bortolotti, 2025). This, at times, subtle act of harm undermines the individual and their capacity to act on their own behalf as decision-makers.

8.2 Epistemic Silencing and Epistemic Injustice of SIHY with Eating Struggles

The exclusion of diverse voices, including SIHY, from dominant narratives, research, and services related to eating struggles is not simply a representational oversight, but a deeper historical and structural epistemic erasure (Lee, 2024). Within healthcare and research systems, the knowledge and embodied experiences of marginalized groups are often unacknowledged or dismissed (Okoroji et al., 2023). For example, Smye et al. (2023) highlight how Indigenous service users accessing mental health support often find their narratives misinterpreted and, at times, redefined through clinical discourses that bypass the structural roots of their distress and trauma. This illustrates a cycle where the marginalized population's ways of knowing are excluded; the individual is prevented from contributing knowledge to the mental health field and its daily practices, impacting service provision in ways that perpetuate/compound the systemic trauma that underlies many individuals' mental health struggles.

These processes of silencing are shaped by what Fricker (2007) refers to as *epistemic injustice*, which is defined as the harm done to someone specifically in their capacity as a knower. Fricker (2007) identifies two key forms of epistemic injustice, which is important for contextualizing the erasure and silencing of the knowledge and experiences of SIHY. First, *testimonial injustice* occurs when identity prejudice causes a hearer to assign reduced credibility to a speaker's voice based on their social identity (Fricker, 2007). Too often, SIHY describe instances where, mainly due to their social locations, they are immediately dismissed in their testimonies of deep struggle with food and body; many SIHY with whom I've worked describe EDs as a "closeted" struggle, one that they rarely disclose to professionals due to the shared, lived experience among their community that it will be discredited.

A second component of epistemic injustice, known as *hermeneutical injustice*, refers to a structural issue in which a person "has a significant area of their social experience obscured from understanding owing to prejudicial flaws in shared hermeneutical resources" (Fricker, 2007, p. 155). This means that individuals may lack access to the language, concepts, or interpretive frameworks necessary to articulate their experiences, particularly when those experiences fall outside of dominant modes of understanding (Fricker, 2007). For example, since the pervasive discourse around EDs is mainly associated with middle-to-upper class, female-identified, White young girls, many professionals do not have hermeneutical resources to share these experiences with SIHY who present with EDs and eating struggles because SIHY do not fit into the conventional diagnostic criteria for ED. For SIHY, this experience further exacerbates their already deep-seated marginalization, since this hermeneutical injustice means not having access to language that legitimizes eating struggles as rooted in trauma, colonialism, displacement, or embodied survival-based responses.

8.3 Willful Hermeneutical Ignorance of SIHY with Eating Struggles

Despite increasing advocacy, education, and research that challenge dominant biomedical models of conceptualizing EDs, what I have found both compelling and deeply problematic in my years of working in the field among SIHY is the persistent silencing of their experiences (Luongo, 2018). In this context, I draw attention to a concept that extends our understanding of testimonial and hermeneutical injustice: *willful hermeneutical ignorance*. Pohlhaus (2012) first defined this form of epistemic injustice as the ignorance maintained by dominant groups of marginalized knowledge or experiences, even when this knowledge is accessible and well distributed. It goes beyond unexamined prejudice, exposing a deliberate refusal by systems to understand, acknowledge, adapt, or reform practices and policies in response to the needs identified by those who have lived experience.

There are two primary ways I have chosen to highlight how willful hermeneutical ignorance shows up in the lives of SIHY seeking support for their eating struggles. First, SIHY often report dismissal of their testimonies of eating struggles when pursuing healthcare support and, instead, are pathologized in other prejudicial and intersectional ways associated with homelessness and poverty. For instance, as a clinician requesting a referral to ED inpatient/outpatient treatment on behalf of a SIHY client, I can recall being met with confusion and disbelief by a general physician, leading them to redirect the referral request toward evaluating the possibility of substance use/abuse (despite substances not being a presenting concern). These youth described to me how several problematic, prejudicial assumptions surfaced in these interactions connected to their dismissal of support. Some felt that their physicians projected dominant, classist misconceptions of EDs which exclude impoverished individuals as a population who may endure or experience body image distress and struggles in their relationship with food; notably, these misconceptions occur despite the growing recognition of and training that links trauma with body-centered coping mechanisms, such as EDs (Thompson, 1996). Youth often shared with me how their relationship with food was impacted by deeply suffered trauma and yet, were often shut down by healthcare providers, not given the space to be heard or considered, despite the mental and physical health conditions that were presenting and described by the youth as potentially associated.

An additional, critical issue identified by both SIHY and most clients with EDs whom I have encountered over the years is the persistent and problematic biomedical emphasis on size and weight. This biomedical focus continues to dominate how eating struggles are conceptualized in both the *Diagnostic and Statistical Manual of Mental Disorders* (*DSM*) and within publicly funded ED treatment programs in Canada, despite the growing recognition that these markers are insufficient indicators of the complexity and severity of EDs (Eiring et al., 2021). Indeed, EDs manifest in all sizes, and while an individual may appear to be of a healthy or stabilized size, they very well could be enduring severe health complications and just as severe mental anguish as one whose size fits the biomedical criteria for ED diagnosis and treatment (Eiring et al., 2021).

For those trying to access publicly funded inpatient or outpatient programs, many in service need are denied treatment based on weight eligibility requirements. With regard to inpatient care, if you are not "thin enough" you are deemed ineligible; this often becomes an automatic denial of support for many individuals despite the presence of severe eating struggles and the corresponding health/mental health repercussions. As Eli states:

> you have to be in the very low BMI [Body Mass Index] in order to be inpatient. If you are still anorexic and you're over, like for me, over 95 pounds, you're just day patient but you can still be having the same struggles, um, as some of the inpatient programs or even like health wise. Cause, like, you could still be overweight [based on the BMI standard] but not eating enough and that's gonna cause problems with your heart, your lungs, your brain … they don't give the opportunity of being inpatient for people who are higher than the specific BMI.

Eli's comments mirror the experiences of participants from other studies that describe how patients in critical health and in need of life saving support are often denied even a referral from their family doctor due to their weight being insufficiently low (Babb et al., 2022).

This is often described as a polarizing paradox, as patients are taught to try not to focus on weight/size and overcome body image issues during treatment, while severely low weight/size is prioritized and imperative to getting the support they need. As a result, it is often the case that the denial of access to supports due to size only compounds body image distress and, in turn, often worsens eating struggles. Eli continues:

> if you're not sick enough, you're not perfect enough to get the funding, or you're not perfect enough to get the right program that you need. And then your eating disorder can get worse … they need to give the opportunity for people who are more than just underweight. That's what I think … Yeah, I think, umm, if they were to change one thing, letting people in inpatient no matter what size they are cause their health is more important than the way they look.

Just as Eli described, many of the clients I have worked with have, at some point, felt pressure to prove their need by paradoxically striving for greater weight loss to be taken seriously and receive the help they so critically require.

This archaic eligibility process has been challenged in many studies by advocacy groups and in other forms of writing, and yet, the current system persists (Armour et al., 2024; Kons et al., 2024; Mishra & Harrop, 2023). Many inpatient ED treatment programs effectively recognize that individuals are experiencing significant distress and need help but still deny them admission if they do not fall below a specific BMI threshold. This process not only delays critically needed care but also reinforces a harmful message that one is "not sick enough" to warrant treatment. Kons et al. (2024) note that patients with atypical anorexia nervosa (such as EDNOS) who may have experienced substantial weight loss but remain within or above normal BMI ranges are significantly less likely to be referred or admitted to inpatient treatment, despite a recognition among the staff that these clients possess equivalent medical and psychological risk. This signifies a willful hermeneutical ignorance, as these programs are aware of the risk but continue to perpetuate harmful weight-based eligibility processes. In fact, there have been several cases I have witnessed where, despite meeting the criteria for severe bulimia (8–13 episodes per week), clients are denied access to inpatient treatment due to not meeting BMI requirements (which vary greatly in cases of severe bulimia) and are offered day-treatment group sessions instead. This happens, again, despite the vast medical knowledge that bulimia is an ED with severe gastrointestinal, cardiovascular, and mental health implications, leading to extreme health problems and even an increase in mortality (Nitsch et al., 2021). As several clients have shared, although some staff in ED inpatient hospital programs advocate for or acknowledge the severity of eating struggles regardless of client size during intake, service accessibility remains limited by hospital regulations and a lack of available beds.

Despite there being a recognition of how severe EDs are to the health and mental health of those who struggle with them, publicly funded treatments for EDs are also known for having incredibly long wait-times (Armour et al., 2024). This is complicated by the potential fluctuations in one's weight/size during the waiting period. Once finally able to engage in evaluation and intake, some individuals are faced with a change in their eligibility status, which creates further delay as they are then placed onto other waitlists for alternative programs. As Eli states:

> I went into the program here, it wasn't suitable for me. So, the day patient one was the next one, and it took about two years for me to get into the program. Yeah it's a long wait, um, and got in, did the program, it's eight weeks … and then after that, six months later, I was back in the [hospital], so the program here, and that was the six-month outpatient program, didn't really work for me, so now I have to go back to the day patient one.

In addition to the sizist policies and treatment practices and confusingly long wait-times, SIHY report experiencing intersecting forms of prejudice due to stigmatizing and discriminatory discourses associated with the classism of being homeless, FI, and impoverished. As identified by another youth in my research, "you can't be homeless and fat," or else you face discriminatory assumptions about size and life circumstances associated with "laziness" and "poor eating choices." The SIHY I encountered describe how, despite suffering from extreme food restriction associated with their eating struggles and the intersections of FI, they often meet with physicians who lecture them about "healthy" eating choices and dieting approaches; not only are these options often inaccessible due to issues associated with FI (such as access to healthy, nutritionally adequate food, which is often costly), but also such comments discredit the pain and trauma SIHY endure due to their living conditions that impact their relationship with food. Indeed, it isn't uncommon for SIHY to undergo discussions with service providers in a variety of settings who have the tendency to pathologize or perceive their eating struggles as connected to poor eating habits, poor choices/judgment, lack of exercise, or health illiteracy. Notably, I found many of these youth to be extremely educated about and aware of nutrition and exercise information. In fact, some experienced a hyper-fixation on healthy eating and dieting (i.e., orthorexia nervosa) that they characterized as part of their suffering.

8.4 Agential Testimonial Injustice within Clinical Encounters

While publicly funded ED treatment programs are often inaccessible or not applicable to meeting SIHY needs, many of those who do gain access describe their lived experiences of inpatient and outpatient treatment as lifesaving, in some cases, or problematic, in others. This is because of how the system and the relational dynamics within it often mirror many of the elements underlying their eating struggles. This includes punitive and controlling practices/policies that, at times, replicate clients' experiences of trauma, which were characterized by mistreatment, suffering, and powerlessness over their own bodies and lives. Indeed, over the years, I have had several clients seek my clinical support to assist with advocacy and/or the subsequent processing of the traumatic treatment they themselves identify as having endured during their stays at various ED inpatient treatment programs. In the following, I share examples of these experiences, which highlight the agential testimonial injustice embedded within the processes of current publicly funded ED treatment programs and the dominant models used in ED psychotherapy in general.

Expanding upon Fricker's work on testimonial injustice, Lackey (2020) highlights the construct of *agential testimonial injustice* in the fields of criminology and law. According to Lackey, agential testimonial injustice refers to situations of false confessions, whereby credibility of testimony was given to coerced, false confessions resulting in criminalization and punishment. Bortolotti (2025) applied this concept to the mental health field, where agential testimonial injustice is defined as a form of epistemic harm in which individuals, particularly those from marginalized groups, are treated as incapable of understanding their own needs or risks; are coerced or subtly pressured into decisions that serve institutional priorities over their personal well-being; and are denied full or truthful information about treatment options or processes (Bortolotti, 2025). In clinical and social interactions, this often involves practitioners failing to genuinely engage with the patient's perspectives, pre-emptively dismissing their contributions, and undermining their capacity to act as competent knowers and decision-makers (Carel & Kidd, 2014; Fricker, 2007). Rather than being seen as a whole human being, the individual is reduced to their diagnosis, with practitioners relying heavily on behavioral treatment models (often required due to funding constraints and the current system policies/procedures). In my practice, I have come to understand the many ways that clients with eating struggles, especially SIHY, experience agential testimonial injustice in such spaces, which I describe below.

In Canada, the current "gold standard" therapeutic intervention used within inpatient/outpatient ED treatment is Cognitive Behavioral Therapy (CBT) and Enhanced CBT (CBT-e) (Atwood & Friedman, 2020; Couturier et al., 2020). The goals are behavioral monitoring, where patients are expected/required to refrain from ED "behaviors," and to restore weight. These goals are measurable and, from a capitalistic/neoliberal standpoint, marketable in terms of making such services eligible for funding access. Yet, the effectiveness of this approach in longstanding healing has been greatly disputed as there is extensive evidence reflecting low rates of remission (e.g., 21.8%) and high risk of mortality (Clague et al., 2024) despite it being an "evidence-based" treatment practice used within these settings (Miskovic-Wheatley et al., 2023). In contrast, I propose that a trauma-informed approach to treating EDs extends beyond an individualistic focus on EDs as primarily a set of behaviors; rather, it recognizes eating struggles as a response to the deeper psychological impacts of structural trauma and painful living conditions endured. This transition acknowledges that without addressing these underlying concerns and other multifaceted aspects, EDs often persist as one of the only felt options that some SIHY and other individuals struggling in this way feel they can rely upon to cope and survive.

Since most publicly funded programs do not include individual therapy or the trauma support essential to addressing the deeper struggles associated with the development of an ED, many of the clients I've worked with describe enduring multiple inpatient stays; they experience a "revolving door" of inpatient services which save their physical lives, but result in little (and at times diminished) internal, spiritual, emotional, and psychological relief and/or minimal changes in their harmful living conditions. In fact, a meta-synthesis recently documented that an overreliance on behavioral models devoid of anticolonial, trauma-informed care has resulted in a treatment system embedded in practices that are punitive and controlling in nature, one which often leaves patients feeling grossly misunderstood, stigmatized, and deeply impacted (Babb et al., 2022). This has been known to exacerbate the underlying factors associated with eating struggles. Consequently, it is not uncommon for symptoms to resurface soon after individuals are discharged. Other studies also note how it is common for individuals to describe inpatient ED treatment as "prison-like," relating to feelings of being punished (Joyce et al., 2019, p. 2075), and "locked up" (Escobar-Koch et al., 2012, p. 261). Individuals who have accessed ED inpatient/outpatient treatments describe how much of their self-agency is stripped away upon entering, including the loss of control over non-eating-related areas of everyday life.

Self-agency over decision-making in treatment is an imperative anticolonial, trauma-informed approach, especially when so much of the trauma underlying EDs relates to a severe loss of control, self-agency, power, and safety. For instance, SIHY and clients that I have encountered describe the dehumanizing and anxiety-provoking experience of having to use the washroom while supervising staff stand outside of the door and listen in to ensure they do not purge their meals. These clients shared how this portrays the message that they cannot be trusted and conveys a sense of being seen as an "illness" rather than as a human being. This mirrors other research findings in which participants identified with being "treated as an illness" (Joyce et al., 2019, p. 2078) and where untrained staff described patients "as an ED" (Patterson et al., 2017, p. 4). They often share how helpful it would be to, instead, shift the focus from policing their behaviors to providing individualized time with a therapist in which to process and understand the underlying trauma responses, experiences, somatic feelings, and origins of the urges to engage in their eating struggles that result in the response of purging. Although group therapy – the dominant form of psychological intervention used in inpatient/outpatient stays – is provided, individuals often note how the therapeutic interventions remain highly behavior-focused and intellectualized; instead, experiential and individualized approaches, such as providing in-the-moment guidance through challenging triggers and trauma responses, may be more meaningful. As Eli similarly states:

> I think if it was individualized, it would be better, or it would be different, um, but also because of, like, the lack of time that they have...The trauma support is definitely, I think, something that's necessary, too, and even like eating disorder programs, if they have some experience with it. But I don't know if they would even, I don't even know if I could say they are fully experienced with the PTSD and helping them through it, but you have to do it, you can't just be, like, slowly get into it. You just have to do it [eat the food that is required].

In this quote, Eli shares how it is common for staff in publicly funded treatment programs to be minimally trained in trauma-informed approaches, and thus, despite experiencing distress, patients are nevertheless forced to eat the food that is required without the space to process along the way.

Indeed, clients I have encountered described excruciating inner turmoil and somatic distress while being forced to complete a meal in the allotted time, with very little supportive guidance in unpacking and meaningfully understanding their experience of distress associated with food. The message is to ignore/suppress what is really being experienced and to bear the pain to achieve the required goal of treatment; once again, such experiences replicate the messaging that many individuals with eating struggles have internalized and which have contributed to the pain they endure in their relationships with food and their bodies. Moreover, the anxiety of the punishment they could receive should they not complete their meal in the given timeframe has been described as a compounding pressure that often mirrors self-punishment, which they already internally experience due to the nature of their eating struggle. While the fear of punitive consequences may temporarily shift the external behavior and physical weight of a patient, it does not address what is really requiring support for longstanding change.

Another problematic experience of agential testimonial injustice in the ED inpatient/outpatient space occurs when individuals are unable to meet the inflexible requirements of eating and refraining from ED symptoms (such as purging or restriction). Individuals report a dominant narrative that circulates in clinical encounters where punitive blame is placed back onto the individual (i.e., labeling patients as "noncompliant" or "treatment resistant"). Clients have often shared stories with me about being labeled as "manipulative" and "deceitful" when struggling deeply with the symptom abstinence required to remain in treatment. This framing pressures individuals to "self-monitor/self-police" or "confess" what providers want to hear in order to be taken seriously (i.e., owning up to ED behaviors and recognizing them as a "problem"); clients have shared how this approach often results in conversations devoid of any acknowledgment of the underlying trauma responses associated with their symptoms, further silencing their voices and diminishing their agency in care. In addition, clients have described how being defined in these ways often reinforces core, internalized ED-related beliefs about their sense of self as "defective," "a failure," "incapable," "deserving of punishment," and more.

A narrative I often hear from clients who were "unsuccessful" in inpatient care and subsequently prematurely discharged as a result is: "why am I getting kicked out for slipping up with my ED symptoms when the reason I am here is because I'm struggling with symptoms?" Indeed, there are several programs that have a very strict "no tolerance" approach to patients who turn to their eating struggles to cope, resulting in immediate discharge without aftercare support. While some programs argue that the purpose of such strict regulations is to prevent the triggering of other patients and to enforce control over the behaviors in an effort to "stop" the ED, the focus remains on the capacity of the individual within that environment (i.e., neoliberal approach to care); they do not question why the patient may be using their eating struggles to cope with the inpatient treatment space, or how the system itself may be influencing the individual and their capacity to be free from symptoms. As Eli disclosed, greater flexibility, patience, and understanding from staff while in inpatient/outpatient care is desired:

> they're taking away the biggest one … the eating disorder is the only one that I've ever used for like two years … it's just the eating disorder, and now that I'm in this program, it's like the whole thing is just coming out of me now and I have to deal with all my emotions without the last one … the last coping mechanism. It's hard … I cope by not eating … I use the eating disorder to cope with my other mental health problems.

This is especially important to consider when inpatient/outpatient treatment systems exert power and control over individuals, which is often why individuals draw on eating struggles to begin with – to regain a sense of control over their body. Many so-called "successful" clients who were subsequently discharged from treatment programs describe how this was achieved by reaching their "target weight" despite not feeling ready psychologically. As a participant of Ross and Green (2011)'s study described, "you feel alone, you put on weight and then you're told you can go when you're struggling the most with your weight" (p. 114). Even when staff do show care and empathy for challenges related to gaining weight, due to funding constraints that limit individual support and an individualized pace/approach to care, clients often leave the treatment settings with the dominant trigger(s) for relapse unaddressed (i.e., body image and trauma).

With regards to day patient and outpatient care, individuals are also forced to maintain a structured eating schedule/plan that includes specific foods accessed from specific locations (such as restaurants and grocery stores). Due to poverty and FI, however, many SIHY cannot "successfully" fulfill these requirements, which, in some cases, resulted in the forced termination of their care and sadly, being labeled as "noncompliant" or "having weak will or low motivation to change." Therefore, the prejudicial conceptualization that silences and erases marginalized populations who experience eating struggles is evident in the very structures of access to and treatment for EDs. As Eli describes:

> The way that some programs are, like, if you used to work before you went into the program, you're not allowed to work during the program. So, you can't access money which means you're not gonna have funds to pay for food. And if you can access food banks you're only gonna get certain kinds of food and that's not what the programs really want ... you have to have a certain amount of protein at every meal, a certain amount of, like, different food groups, but they have to be a specific amount each meal, and if they don't realize that most of the items that some people can get don't have a lot of the food groups in each item, like a can of soup [I get from food banks] doesn't really have enough protein or enough vegetable for that matter, so you have to add more of that one specific food group, but you don't have the funds to, so they don't understand and they don't really give funding for it either.

For Eli, FI impacted one of their treatment experiences when they were discharged from outpatient care due to being deemed "unsuccessful" at meeting the requirements of the program.

Despite this, Eli described trying to continue to apply to publicly funded treatments since they could not afford private treatment given their financial situation and the severe lack of affordable mental health support in Canada for EDs. As Eli states,

> I don't know of any individual [treatment] that doesn't cost anything ... I think also, like, the fact that there are people who struggle with eating disorders who use food banks and, like, soup kitchens, the government needs to realize that and put more funding out ... At-risk youth in eating disorder programs, as well. Like, how to help them find places to get their nutrients and things like that.

Indeed, while SIHY may be eligible for inpatient or outpatient care, FI and poverty are not considered and/or included in treatment and discharge planning. Thus, while some SIHY who attend these programs may fulfill the nutrition requirements, start to demonstrate changes in their eating, and experience weight restoration, they often return to living conditions of FI, poverty, and in some cases, homelessness upon discharge, which exacerbate and compound the likelihood of relapse. Although SIHY provide this knowledge directly to physicians, highlight the inappropriateness of publicly funded ED programs in meeting their needs, and emphasize the inaccessibility of maintaining the lifestyle that inpatient treatments model, the limitations of these programs persist. This exemplifies both agential testimonial injustice and the willful hermeneutical ignorance that upholds entrenched systems of discrimination – systems that grant access to care for those with privilege while rendering it inaccessible or even irrelevant to poor, BIPOC, and otherwise marginalized communities.

8.5 Discussion: Pathways to Epistemically Just and Trauma-Informed ED Care

In this chapter, I highlighted the epistemic injustices that are often experienced by individuals in general, and SIHY in particular, seeking support for their eating struggles within the current Canadian mental healthcare system. First, I elaborated on how willful hermeneutical ignorance has pervaded the ED field; that is, despite the growth of knowledge surrounding the diversity of those who struggle with EDs, there remain exclusionary treatment eligibility requirements which are inappropriate practices for SIHY, and other dominant misconceptions of who and what constitutes as having an ED. This chapter then delved more deeply into some common examples of how willful hermeneutical ignorance has enabled the construction of inpatient and outpatient treatment programs that result in agential testimonial injustices during clinical encounters (i.e., treatment practices that are controlling and punitive in nature).

There exists a long history of the pathologization of eating struggles – a history that has excluded diverse voices and experiences, and a history that has continued to shape the ways in which individuals who suffer are perceived and, in turn, treated. Eating struggles are responses; they are embodied reactions to suffering, to trauma, to living conditions, to disempowerment, to somatic distress, and/or to violence. They are complex, nuanced, and incredibly unique to the individual. Therefore, they require deep understanding, listening, adaptive, and individualized systems of care. Somatically negotiating with one's pain through restriction, purging, or other embodied eating-centered ways serves a function for many individuals that can be excruciatingly difficult to imagine relinquishing. Yet, there simultaneously exists a deep longing for freedom from the suffering that eating struggles inflict. Thus, genuine empathy and compassion are required to understand the function of EDs, along with greater attention to and support for the underlying suffering that leads one to develop an eating struggle in the first place.

To subject individuals who developed an ED due to feeling a loss of control to a treatment program riddled with issues of power-over, control, and punitive practices quite simply is not only an injustice of knowledge but also an injustice of human dignity and rights. We need to challenge old, historical narratives and current discourses of individuals with EDs, such as treating them as their illness; labeling them as manipulative, deceitful, and hysterical; and pathologizing the individual rather than addressing the systems of oppression that traumatize and call upon instinctual embodied reactions (such as eating struggles) to survive. It is imperative for social workers to hear diverse voices and to listen to those who have had direct lived experience: namely, those who have and continue to critique publicly funded ED treatments and our current "evidence-based" practices as incomplete and, at times, harmful.

Through this chapter, I hope to invite readers to pause for a moment of critical reflection by unpacking our current dominant, biomedical approaches to individuals with eating struggles, and to consider how to change these programs in ways that are more trauma-informed and anticolonial. Certainly, it would be naïve to ignore the reality that many of those entering inpatient treatment require intense physical support and lifesaving intervention. However, I want to acknowledge and center the voices of individuals who have been through these programs, and to recognize the role of control via staff at particular stages in the treatment process (e.g., when clients are severely incapacitated and unable to process decision making). That said, a greater balance with respect to shifts in control is required, necessitating collaborative approaches to treatment that honors one's individual healing journey and pace.

Indeed, the clients who shared positive and impactful experiences of inpatient/outpatient care encountered a few staff members who, despite the system, tried their best within the confines of the program requirements to integrate a more flexible, collaborative approach. This has often been described as more important than the type of therapeutic intervention provided. Collaboration, respect, and individualized care are trauma-informed; they enable the individual to take charge of their own recovery, respecting the pace and time that are required for healing. This also applies to other therapeutic spaces outside of publicly funded inpatient programming, such as one-on-one therapy and other clinical/healthcare areas. A more collaborative approach between service users and clinicians that acknowledges and centralizes individual needs, pace of treatment, empathy, and compassion is often described as empowering and, in turn, enhancing motivation for change. Most importantly, it is humanizing, ethical, and epistemically just, and so may counteract the struggles that such individuals often already face internally and externally.

References

Armour, C. Q., Feicht, B., & Gahagan, J. (2024). Improving adult inpatient eating disorder treatment: Perspectives of a sample of individuals in Canada with lived experience. *Journal of Eating Disorders*, *12*(1), 166.

Atwood, M. E., & Friedman, A. (2020). A systematic review of enhanced cognitive behavioral therapy (CBT-E) for eating disorders. *International Journal of Eating Disorders*, *53*(3), 311–330.

Babb, C., Jones, C. R., & Fox, J. R. (2022). Investigating service users' perspectives of eating disorder services: A meta-synthesis. *Clinical Psychology & Psychotherapy*, *29*(4), 1276–1296.

Becker, C. B., Middlemass, K., Johnson, C., Taylor, B., Gomez, F., & Sutherland, A. (2018). Traumatic event exposure associated with increased food insecurity and eating disorder pathology. *Public Health Nutrition*, *21*(16), 3058–3066.

Bortolotti, L. (2025). Agential epistemic injustice in clinical interactions is bad for medicine. *Philosophy of Medicine*, *6*(1), 1–19.

Burstow, B. (2003). Toward a radical understanding of trauma and trauma work. *Violence Against Women*, *9*(11), 1293–1317.

Carel, H., & Kidd, I. J. (2014). Epistemic injustice in healthcare: A philosophical analysis. *Medicine, Health Care and Philosophy*, *17*(4), 529–540.

Christensen, K. A., Forbush, K. T., Richson, B. N., Thomeczek, M. L., Perko, V. L., Bjorlie, K., Christian, K., Ayres, J., Wildes, J. E., & Mildrum Chana, S. (2021). Food insecurity associated with elevated eating disorder symptoms, impairment, and eating disorder diagnoses in an American University student sample before and during the beginning of the COVID-19 pandemic. *International Journal of Eating Disorders*, *54*(7), 1213–1223.

Clague, C. A., Conti, J., & Hay, P. (2024). Outcomes and associated clinical features of people with eating disorders participating in residential treatment facilities: A scoping review. *Eating Disorders*, *32*(3), 297–324.

Couturier, J., Isserlin, L., Norris, M., Spettigue, W., Brouwers, M., Kimber, M., & Pilon, D. (2020). Canadian practice guidelines for the treatment of children and adolescents with eating disorders. *Journal of Eating Disorders*, *8*(1), 4.

Eiring, K., Wiig Hage, T., & Reas, D. L. (2021). Exploring the experience of being viewed as "not sick enough": A qualitative study of women recovered from anorexia nervosa or atypical anorexia nervosa. *Journal of Eating Disorders*, *9*(1), 142.

Eli, K. (2018). Striving for liminality: Eating disorders and social suffering. *Transcultural Psychiatry*, *55*(4), 475–494.

Escobar-Koch, T., Mandich, C. C., & Urzúa, R. F. (2012). Treatments for eating disorders: The patients' views. *Relevant Topics in Eating Disorders*, *12*(1), 10–5772.

Fricker, M. (2007). *Epistemic injustice: Power and the ethics of knowing*. Oxford University Press.

Gaetz, S. (2014). *Coming of age: Reimagining the response to youth homelessness in Canada*. Canadian Homelessness Research Network.

Halbeisen, G., Brandt, G., & Paslakis, G. (2022). A plea for diversity in eating disorders research. *Frontiers in Psychiatry*, *13*, Article 820043.

Hazzard, V. M., Barry, M. R., Leung, C. W., Sonneville, K. R., Wonderlich, S. A., & Crosby, R. D. (2022). Food insecurity and its associations with bulimic-spectrum eating disorders,mood disorders, and anxiety disorders in a nationally representative sample of US adults. *Social Psychiatry and Psychiatric Epidemiology*, *57*(7), 1483–1490.

Hyland, C. E. (2022). *The lived experiences of street-involved and homeless youth who have eating struggles while living in situations of food insecurity* [Doctoral dissertation, University of Toronto]. University of Toronto.

Joyce, C., Greasley, P., Weatherhead, S., & Seal, K. (2019). Beyond the revolving door: Long-term lived experience of eating disorders and specialist service provision. *Qualitative Health Research, 29*(14), 2070–2083.

Kons, K., Essayli, J., & Shook, J. (2024). Comparing the knowledge, attitudes, and practices of pediatric and family medicine clinicians toward atypical anorexia nervosa versus anorexia nervosa. *International Journal of Eating Disorders, 57*(4), 993–1001.

Kotilahti, E., West, M., Isomaa, R., Karhunen, L., Rocks, T., & Ruusunen, A. (2020). Treatment interventions for severe and enduring eating disorders: Systematic review. *International Journal of Eating Disorders, 53*(8), 1280–1302.

Lackey, J. (2020). False confessions and testimonial injustice. *Journal of Crime, Law & Criminology, 110*, 43.

Lee, J. Y. (2024). The social epistemology of eating disorders: How our gaps in understanding challenge patient care. *Bioethics, 38*(4), 300–307.

Livingston, W. S., Brignone, E., Fargo, J. D., Gundlapalli, A. V., Maguen, S., & Blais, R. K. (2019). VHA-enrolled homeless veterans are at increased risk for eating disorder diagnoses. *Military Medicine, 184*(1–2), e71–e75.

Luongo, N. M. (2018). Disappearing in plain sight: An exploratory study of co-occurring eating and substance abuse dis/orders among homeless youth in Vancouver, Canada. *Women's Studies International Forum, 67*, 38–44.

Mishra, K., & Harrop, E. (2023). Teaching how to avoid overreliance on BMI in diagnosing and caring for patients with eating disorders. *AMA Journal of Ethics, 25*(7), 507–513.

Miskovic-Wheatley, J., Bryant, E., Ong, S. H., Vatter, S., Le, A., Touyz, S., & Maguire, S. (2023). Eating disorder outcomes: Findings from a rapid review of over a decade of research. *Journal of Eating Disorders, 11*(1), 85.

Moreno, D. A., Cao, Y., & Norris, C. M. (2023). Disparities in access to eating disorders treatment for publicly insured youth in Canada. *Journal of Eating Disorders, 11*(1), 113.

Nitsch, A., Dlugosz, H., Gibson, D., & Mehler, P. S. (2021). Medical complications of bulimia nervosa. *Cleveland Clinic Journal of Medicine, 88*(6), 333–343.

Okoroji, C., Mackay, T., Robotham, D., Beckford, D., & Pinfold, V. (2023). Epistemic injustice and mental health research: A pragmatic approach to working with lived experience expertise. *Frontiers in Psychiatry, 14*, 1114725.

Patterson, S., Bellair, R., Jeffrey, S., & Ward, W. (2017). Patients' perspective on inpatient treatment for eating disorders: A mixed-methods study of satisfaction, experience of care and perceived helpfulness of components of treatment. *Mental Health Addiction Research, 2*, 1–6.

Pohlhaus, G., Jr. (2012). Relational knowing and epistemic injustice: Toward a theory of willful hermeneutical ignorance. *Hypatia, 27*(4), 715–735.

Rasmusson, G., Lydecker, J. A., Coffino, J. A., White, M. A., & Grilo, C. M. (2019). Household food insecurity is associated with binge-eating disorder and obesity. *International Journal of Eating Disorders, 52*(1), 28–35.

Ross, J. A., & Green, C. (2011). Inside the experience of anorexia nervosa: A narrative thematic analysis. *Counselling and Psychotherapy Research, 11*(2), 112–119.
Smye, V., Browne, A. J., Josewski, V., Keith, B., & Mussell, W. (2023). Social suffering: Indigenous peoples' experiences of accessing mental health and substance use services. *International Journal of Environmental Research and Public Health, 20*(4), 3288.
Thompson, B. (1996). Multiracial feminist theorizing about eating problems: Refusing to rank oppressions. *Eating Disorders, 4*(2), 104–114.
United Nations (2019). *Global issues: Youth.* https://www.un.org/en/global-issues/youth#:~:text=There%20is%20no%20universally%20agreed,of%2015%20and%2024%20years.
Winter, P. A. (2021). *Homelessness count.* https://www.riverbankdevelopment.ca/wp-content/uploads/2021/04/2021-Prince-Albert-Winter-Homelessness-Count.pdf
Zickgraf, H. F., Hazzard, V. M., & O'Connor, S. M. (2022). Food insecurity is associated with eating disorders independent of depression and anxiety: Findings from the 2020–2021 healthy minds study. *International Journal of Eating Disorders, 55*(3), 354–361.

Chapter 9

The Absence of Gypsy, Roma, and Traveller Voices and Knowledge in UK Health and Social Work

Peter Unwin and Jackie Bolton

9.1 Introduction: Rethinking Social Work Complicity against Gypsy, Roma, and Traveller Communities in the UK from Epistemic Injustice Perspectives

This chapter is concerned with social work's failure to include Gypsy, Roma, and Traveller communities in the United Kingdom (UK) as an intrinsic part of their commitment to valuing diversity. There are very few policy or practice guides that even mention the needs of these communities, despite the disproportionate numbers of their children in state care (Allen & Hamnett, 2022) and a persisting mental health crisis in their midst (Unwin & Hulmes, 2025). Both authors are members of the Romani and Traveller Social Work Association, which was formed in 2020 to raise awareness of the needs of Gypsy, Roma, and Traveller communities by bringing together the small number of social workers from those communities alongside academic and other allies. The Association aims to challenge epistemic injustice by adopting a systemic approach to combat racism in social work; it seeks to co-produce models of social work that reflect, respect, and value Indigenous knowledge. The Association is small in size because very few members of the communities attain the degree level of education required to practise as a social worker in the UK, and the profession is not always an attractive career choice due to negative perceptions of social work within the communities. Since its formation, the Association has written a number of papers, presented at national and international conferences, and produced various practice guides – including an online training package for social workers (University of Worcester et al., 2023) – and developed the ROMA (Reflection, Objective, Movement and Action) model, a framework for restorative supervision when working with Gypsies, Roma, and Travellers (Allen et al., 2024).

Co-production is a way of working in research or service development which involves the inclusion of people from culturally diverse communities from design through to dissemination. Boyle et al. (2010) describe co-production as an approach which "overturns the conventional passive relationship between the 'users' of services and those who serve them" (p. 3). The *Care Act 2014*

DOI: 10.4324/9781003639046-12

guides social work with adults in England and Wales and is underpinned by the construct of co-production; guidance suggests that co-production should be used to develop preventative, strength-based services, support assessment, shape the local care market, and plan information and advice services (Social Care Institute for Excellence, 2022). Consequently, the local authorities that provide social work services are required to develop a local plan which adopts a co-production approach, involving user groups and people from diverse communities. However, these plans rarely mention Gypsy, Roma, and Traveller communities and the many social, economic, and health challenges they have faced historically and up to the present day. These challenges, which deserve scholarly attention from an epistemic injustice perspective, are most notably in the areas of children's social work practice and practice across the field of mental health.

There are disproportionate numbers of children from Gypsy, Roma, and Traveller families in state care (Allen & Hamnett, 2022) and this very fact suggests that the core principles of the Children Act 1989 – that the welfare of the child should be "paramount" (s. 1(1)); that the "no order" principle should prevail (s. 1(5)), denoting that legal statutes should be invoked only after all else has failed; and that children are best looked after by their own families (s.17(1)) – have not been followed. Child safeguarding policies and practice do not reflect the cultures and norms of these communities and have resulted in the high numbers of their children in state care via the poor practice evidenced in a number of child safeguarding reviews (Allen et al., 2025).

The mental health crisis in Gypsy, Roma, and Traveller communities (Sweeney & Dolling, 2020; Unwin & Hulmes, 2025) has been described as an epidemic (Bowers, 2025) and rates of suicide are among the highest of any ethnic minority in the UK (Knipe et al., 2014). Social work services in the UK hold very little accurate information about the presence of Gypsy, Roma, and Travellers in their communities, which means that culturally sensitive services for their particular needs are not developed. Many community members also conceal their identity because of (an often justified) fear of discrimination by professionals, thus further adding to the non-recognition of their social and health care needs (Unwin et al., 2025).

Coupled with the fact that so few social work professionals receive any training about the social care needs, health care needs, and cultures of Gypsy, Roma, and Traveller organizations, it is perhaps not surprising that the health and social care outcomes of communities are so poor on all aspects of physical and mental health care (Office for National Statistics [ONS], 2022). The areas in which social workers need training include knowledge about the different cultures within Gypsies, Roma, and Travellers; their distrust of authority; attitudes toward shame and stigma; gendered roles within families; and a lack of knowledge around mental health. Additionally, the lack of relevant data collection mechanisms that allow Gypsy, Roma, and Travellers to identify themselves via ethnic monitoring systems (Unwin et al., 2025) leads to the epistemic erasure of these communities from any consideration by social work and other professions. This erasure conflicts fully with the International Federation of Social Work's (2014) definition of social work, which cites principles of social justice, human rights, and respect for diversities as being core to all social work practice.

The social work profession has largely ignored the plight of Gypsies, Roma, and Travellers and has been complicit in the epistemic injustice that their communities have suffered. This injustice is compounded by there being very few voluntary sector organizations across the UK that provide specialist support and guidance to Gypsy, Roma, and Traveller families, meaning that many families have nowhere to turn when help is needed (Hulmes & Unwin, 2024). The social work profession still shares many of the prejudices of the general public about Gypsy, Roma, and Travellers, and consequently discredits their knowledge and lived experience of family life – thus participating in testimonial injustice. Furthermore, Unwin et al.'s (2025) review of ethnic data categorization in the National Health Service (NHS) demonstrated that access to supportive health and social care services is often not made available to Gypsy, Roma, and Traveller communities, which constitutes distributary injustice.

The Romani and Traveller Social Work Association intends that its lobbying, training, conference presentations, website, and academic/practice publications will bring about not only a raising of awareness among social workers, but also a new form of practice that addresses the epistemic injustice of the past; it seeks to give a voice to Gypsy, Roma, and Traveller communities. The co-productive work of the Association offers a platform for these communities to make sense of and convey their experiences in ways that challenge the historical inequities that have silenced their voices (i.e., hermeneutical injustice) and led to distributive injustice in terms of social work support and an absence of customized resources. This chapter illuminates the above epistemic injustice by discussing social work practice with Gypsy, Roma, and Traveller communities, with particular focus on the fields of child protection and adult mental health.

9.1.1 Key Terminology

Gypsy, Roma, and Travellers. Gypsy, Roma, and Travellers have been part of the UK's population for hundreds of years and range from groups that originally came from India to groups that have only ever lived in the UK. These different groups include English Gypsies, Welsh Gypsies, Scottish Gypsy Travellers, and Irish Travellers, as well as Travelling Showmen and Circus communities. There are also groups which have more recently adopted nomadism, such as New Travellers and Van Dwellers, some of whom may trace their history over several generations.

Co-Production. Co-production is an approach to services or research undertakings that involves professionals and community members working in authentic partnership from the design through to delivery, analysis, and evaluation of any enterprise (Sealey et al., 2021). A co-production approach challenges epistemic injustice in ways that better help achieve equitable and reciprocal outcomes.

English Child Safeguarding System. The English child safeguarding system refers to the law and procedures that govern social work practice under the *Children Act 1989*. This seminal *Act* provides the framework for safeguarding children in England, under which health services, social work services, and the police are obliged to work together in protecting and promoting the welfare of children, including responsibilities to identify and support children at risk of harm (National Society for the Prevention of Cruelty to Children [NSPCC], 2024).

State Care. State care refers to the framework through which the UK government (via local councils) provides protection and support for children who cannot live with their parents due to issues of neglect, abuse, parental ill-health, or family breakdown. Also known as being "looked after" or "in care", there are currently 81,000 children in state care in England, approximately two thirds of whom live in foster care. A further 141,000 live in kinship care, whereby a relative or close adult friend cares for them (Foster & Mackley, 2025).

National Health Service (NHS). National Health Service is the collective term for the publicly funded healthcare systems of the UK.

9.2 The Historical Context of Epistemic Injustice Experienced by Gypsy, Roma, and Traveller Communities in the UK

Despite the historical presence of a majority of Gypsy, Roma, and Traveller communities in the UK, these groups have continuously suffered from systemic forms of discrimination across the fields of health, housing, education, and employment (House of Commons Women and Equalities Committee, 2019; Unwin & Hulmes, 2025). Negative stereotypes, fuelled by mainstream and social media as well as public TV programmes – such as *Big Fat Gypsy Weddings* (Wilkins, 2011–2015) – together with a history of repressive legislation, have all contributed to the epistemic injustice suffered. Gypsies and Travellers were once core to the rural economy, when their labour was an essential part of the agricultural workforce, which meant travelling around the UK with the seasons as crops were sown and then harvested. The mechanization of agriculture, however, alongside modern systems of labour which require high levels of education and computer literacy, has meant that many community members find themselves excluded from the workforce (Hulmes & Unwin, 2024). The recently arrived Eastern European Roma are largely employed in cities and large towns, often in production and service industries.

The UK social work system operates under a strict set of inclusive values outlined in the *Code of Ethics* (British Association of Social Workers [BASW],

2021), which has underpinned social work since 1975. However, it was not until the formation of the Romani and Traveller Social Work Association in 2020 that Gypsy, Roma, and Traveller communities began to receive some of the professional advocacy, attention, and support they deserve. Despite the best efforts of the Romani and Traveller Social Work Association, levels of knowledge about this community among social workers remain low, and disproportionate numbers of children from these communities are taken into state care by social workers, many of whom have no real understanding of their culture and mores (Allen & Hamnett, 2022). This latter form of injustice accords with Fricker's (2007) construct of *epistemic injustice*, whereby wrongs are done to communities in their capacity as knowers.

Gypsy, Roma, and Traveller communities who become known to social workers bring with them a habitus, a set of ingrained dispositions, values, and practical orientations formed through their histories of mobility, communal living, and long-term experiences of marginalization (Bourdieu, 1990; Jesper et al., 2008). These factors conflict with the expectations of the social work establishment, which presumes clients to be literate, digitally aware, settled, and compliant with bureaucratic procedures. Such misalignment frequently results in exclusion, frustration, or resistance outcomes that are too often interpreted as individual shortcomings, rather than as evidence of epistemic injustice. Such injustice can be seen from the very beginning of any Gypsy, Roma, or Traveller family's contact with social work systems in that "catch-all" ethnic groupings, such as "Gypsy/Traveller" or "Other White", are part of the categorization systems used by social work services – categorizations which exclude distinct cultural identities and immediately lead to "othering".

Experiences of "othering" were commonly shared in focus groups composed of Gypsies, Roma, and Travellers, which were held across England; the focus groups were designed to explore attitudes towards the collection and use of their ethnicity data, with a view to developing recommendations for how this might be done in ways that fully reflect their ethnicities, rather than ignore or aggregate them (for details of the study, see Unwin et al., 2025). The quotes below are samples from these focus groups, which serve to illuminate epistemic injustice in the ways the NHS categorizes their different ethnicities:

> We are not the same as Roma ... [or] English Gypsies. ... We are Irish Travellers with our own traditions, our own Cant [language], our own history. But the system does not see that. ... It just calls us all the same thing, like we are interchangeable.
>
> (Female Irish Traveller, Focus Group 7)

> We struggle with speaking outside our community. We suffered decades of judgement, discrimination, not being listened to or understood. Even if we

> do speak out, we are often dismissed especially when trying to talk to health professionals. Instead of listening they dismiss us, invalidate us, and tell us how we are feeling. So, we shut down and suffer in silence.
>
> (Female Roma, Focus Group 10)

> They put 'Gypsy' and 'Traveller' on forms, but never Roma. It is like we do not exist. They just throw us in with 'Eastern European' or 'White Other'. But we are not just another Eastern European group. We are Roma. We have our own history, our own language, our own experiences. But the NHS does not care about that.
>
> (Female Roma, Focus Group 3)

The expression "it is like we do not exist" encapsulates the lived experience of categorical erasure. When bureaucratic systems fail to acknowledge Gypsy, Roma, or Traveller identities, they enact a form of epistemic injustice – i.e., hermeneutical injustice – a denial of the legitimacy of distinct groups deserving institutional recognition. Additionally, participants across the different Gypsy, Roma, and Traveller communities in Unwin et al.'s (2025) research revealed that many did not declare their ethnicities for fear of inevitable discrimination:

> If you put Roma on the form, you are treated different straight away. The moment they see it, their whole attitude changes. It is safer to just put 'White Other' and not bring trouble to yourself.
>
> (Female Roma, Focus Group 2)

> I would never state my ethnicity. It would only lead to bad things.
>
> (Female English Gypsy, Focus Group 5)

This invisibility is not coincidental but rooted in long-standing histories of exclusion and marginalization. Sarafian et al. (2024) note that Roma communities across Europe and the UK face systemic erasure that excludes them from services, while making them hyper-visible through surveillance. The absence of discrete Gypsy, Roma, and Traveller categories in many establishment systems reveals institutional priorities that acknowledge some minorities while erasing others. Top of Form

The social work profession, in common with the general UK public and their fellow professions, is guilty both of testimonial and hermeneutical injustice (Fricker, 2007) inflicted upon Gypsy, Roma, and Traveller families and communities. The authors' recent involvement in research projects across the UK is discussed below, where issues of mental health and child protection will be analysed through the lenses of both testimonial injustice and hermeneutical injustice.

9.3 Testimonial Injustice: Discrediting the Knowledge of Gypsies, Roma, and Travellers

Testimonial injustice occurs when the credibility of a speaker is unjustly undermined due to prejudice, leading to the dismissal or distortion of their knowledge and experiences (Fricker, 2007). For Gypsies, Roma, and Travellers, this form of epistemic injustice is evident in numerous areas of public life. These communities have long been stereotyped as untrustworthy or deceptive, often portrayed as criminals or scroungers by the media and popular discourse (see, Demianyk, 2022; Plunkett, 2012; Wilkins, 2011–2015). These harmful stereotypes create a biased framework that influences how their words and experiences are received. Such bias leads to the discrediting of their testimonies, making it harder for them to receive fair treatment in legal proceedings or to have their voices heard in public debates (Friends, Families & Travellers, 2025). Furthermore, their social and cultural knowledge, especially in relation to their traditional lifestyles, is frequently dismissed as primitive. This devaluation of their lived experiences prevents the community from fully contributing to societal discussions on issues that affect them, such as housing rights, education, and healthcare access.

With respect to the health, housing, education, and employment outcomes of Gypsies, Roma, and Travellers, these are variously acknowledged (e.g., Friends, Families & Travellers, 2022; ONS, 2022) as being poorer than any other ethnic minority group in the UK. While data on health outcomes for Gypsies, Roma, and Travellers are sparse, historical reporting (e.g., House of Commons Women & Equalities Committee, 2019; Sweeney & Dolling, 2020; ONS, 2022; Unwin et al., 2025) is consistent in its claims that their health outcomes are among the poorest of all ethnic minorities, with very high levels of mental and physical ill-health. Such reports and policy documents have recognized serious health inequalities, along with systemic discrimination, lack of education, and economic deprivation (Unwin et al., 2020). Despite multiple reports, the wider determinants of health – such as quality of life, literacy levels, limited employment opportunities, and economic conditions – for Gypsies, Roma, and Travellers continue to decline. Research recognizes the need for advocates to improve health outcomes, but no real-term progress has been detected in this regard. High levels of ill-health among this population are associated with their lower levels of accessing health services (Unwin et al., 2025).

For example, there is evidence that Roma children are more likely to have certain health conditions, such as partial deafness, but these issues may go undiagnosed or untreated due to a lack of cultural awareness among healthcare providers. Community perspectives on cultural competency within the health profession were reported from 11 focus groups exploring ethnic data collection held across Gypsy, Roma, and Traveller communities in the UK (Unwin et al., 2025), and illustrate cultures characterized by both hermeneutical and testimonial injustice:

> [NHS Staff need] … to understand that we are a travelling community, live in chalets and trailers, can't drop the work quickly to make appointments, especially in the summer months.
>
> (Female English Gypsy, Focus Group 2)

> That we have specific needs that differ from the wider public. That we have a language that when describing ill health may differ [*from professional language*]
>
> (Female English Gypsy, Focus Group 3)

> Need to listen to people/families. Try to have compassion for families. Understand that there is difference between 'Gypsy' and 'Slovak'.
>
> (Female Roma, Focus Group 10)

> My main issue is the stereotypes that are believed by some NHS staff members. No, we're not all violent and not everyone who is a Gypsy or a Traveller is 'traditional'.
>
> (Female English Gypsy, Focus Group 1)

The above quotes represent a form of epistemic injustice in that the voices of lived experience are either unheard, overlooked, or misunderstood. Also, it means that specific health and social care needs go unmet. Community members regularly report that health and social care professionals have no knowledge of their communities and cultures, even if significant populations of Gypsies, Roma, or Travellers live in their locality (Unwin et al., 2020, 2025).

The social, health, and economic challenges faced by Gypsy, Roma, and Traveller communities are not routinely included as part of the mandatory equality and diversity training that all health and social care staff undertake. This state of affairs might be seen as a deliberate hermeneutical injustice, which then leads to community voices not being valued or even listened to, thus constituting epistemic injustice and the perpetuation of the stereotypes referred to by community members above. The lack of understanding and insights held by health and social care professionals, who hold their own prejudices from the predominantly negative mainstream media portrayals of Gypsies, Roma, and Travellers, compounds families' experiences of ongoing epistemic injustice. The consequences of such injustice are not only moral but also physical; the refusal to listen to community voices about their beliefs, combined with the stigma around issues such as disability and mental health, has real consequences, leading to the deplorable health outcomes suffered by Gypsy, Roma, and Traveller families (ONS, 2022).

For example, it is taboo in some communities for women to receive any personal or medical care from male professionals, yet female professionals are rarely offered as a culturally acceptable option (Unwin et al., 2025). Additionally,

Roma families face language barriers and are often offered interpreters who speak only the Romani language, as opposed to the national language of the person's country of origin. Individuals are routinely denied the right to have a fluent, English-speaking family member speak on their behalf; while this may occur because social workers have safety concerns (i.e., that family members may be complicit in abusive situations), family can nevertheless be an important support system for marginalized populations (Durham Safeguarding Partnership, 2024). The authors' experiences have been that family interpreters are rarely, if ever, allowed by health professionals, at best leading to delays, and at worst, resulting in the engagement of interpreters who may not be able to best represent a person's needs.

The works of Allen and Riding (2018) and Allen and Hamnett (2022) demonstrate the disproportionate numbers of children from Gypsy, Roma, and Traveller families being taken into state care. Furthermore, the reality that there are only a handful of foster carers across the UK from Gypsy, Roma, and Traveller backgrounds means that, unlike most other ethnic minorities, the option of an ethnically matched foster placement is virtually non-existent. Thus, children from Gypsy, Roma, and Traveller communities who come into state care are doubly traumatized; not only are they taken from their families, but also, they are then subjected to being brought up in an alien culture in either foster or residential care. The quotes below are drawn from interviews with Irish Traveller women living in England who contributed to Unwin's (2025) work on the importance of same culture kinship care. They illustrate the hermeneutical and testimonial forms of epistemic injustice experienced by three different adult Irish Traveller women living in the south of England who had been fostered out-of-culture:

> I was encouraged to hide as a person; this had a huge impact on the rest of my life.
>
> (Female Irish Traveller A)

> I felt I had this double identity – 'not Traveller enough' for my own community and too 'Travellerified' for non-Travellers.
>
> (Female Irish Traveller B)

> I would talk to myself in my own language and got sent to a psychiatrist for what was my way of coping and holding on to my culture.
>
> (Female Irish Traveller C)

Kinship care has been the preferred option for children in need of care in recent decades, and there is general agreement in the research field that kinship placements provide children with more stability and a sense of identity through to adult life. A UK-wide review of kinship care by Wellard et al. (2017) found that outcomes for young people brought up in kinship care were more positive than those brought up in non-kinship foster care in terms of stability of placement, the likelihood of going on to higher education, and then onto employment. Gypsy, Roma, and Traveller families, however, are not routinely afforded the opportunity to become kinship carers. When a Gypsy, Roma, or Traveller family is brave enough to put their name forward as a potential kinship placement, they come up against a very bureaucratic process of assessment, one that epitomizes both hermeneutical and testimonial injustice. There are very few role models of Gypsy, Roma, or Traveller kinship carers, partly because they do not often have spare rooms, and the levels of literacy and computer competencies required in modern day kinship carer assessments preclude many good caring families from even applying.

The core tenet of the *Children Act 1989*, as discussed above, is that the welfare of the child is paramount and that its principle of "least intervention" is best served by making any necessary placement within extended family. That same legislation also encourages authorities to work in partnership with families and to help children feel a sense of stability, belonging, and self-worth. However, assessors can often turn recommendations into regulations, such as when the need to offer single bedrooms for kinship children can be interpreted by social workers as if it were a legal requirement. Such practice represents hermeneutical injustice, which disregards the cultural norms of many Gypsy, Roma, and Traveller young children, whose cramped living accommodations often offer no alternatives. Discriminatory attitudes held by social workers and other safeguarding professionals may also bring suspicion about a Gypsy, Roma, or Traveller family's motivation to become a kinship carer and can lead to a refusal to even consider a Gypsy, Roma, or Traveller family as a potential kinship carer (Allen et al., 2025). Social workers with such attitudes might unreasonably question a family's trustworthiness with respect to safeguarding any children in line with their care plan, especially regarding contact agreements, which are put in place by social workers to monitor contact with birth families. Such distrustful practices injure the communities deeply; disbelieving that a kinship carer from a Gypsy, Roma, or Traveller background will keep their word is a clear example of epistemic injustice.

While such epistemic injustice has arisen partly through the negative mainstream portrayals of Gypsies, Roma, and Travellers as untrustworthy, it can also be attributed to the failure of social work to include knowledge and training about the realities of these communities as part of their diversity and inclusion commitments. One can only imagine the trauma and mental health impact of growing up in a different culture to one's own, being prevented from speaking your own language, and, in the case of Gypsies, Roma, and Travellers, constantly seeing your community ridiculed and hated on an everyday basis. All children deemed to be in need of care outside of their immediate family should always be given the opportunity to live with extended kin or friends. It is, however, very rare that a Gypsy, Roma, or Traveller family comes forward to offer such a resource, mainly due to a lack of understanding of "the system" and because they expect to meet a wall of discrimination.

This situation must change and those making such life-changing decisions should always seek assurance that prospective families coming forward as kinship carers are given equal opportunity to prove themselves as good and safe carers. This will only come about if their assessors have professional understanding and insight into the norms and mores of the particular Gypsy, Roma, or Traveller community in which their assessment is taking place and give credibility to the narratives of the prospective Gypsy, Roma, and Traveller families.

9.4 Hermeneutical Injustice in UK Child Safeguarding

The following section illuminates hermeneutical injustice within the English child safeguarding system via an examination of all known Serious Case Reviews (SCRs) that involved a Gypsy, Roma, or Traveller family (Allen et al., 2025). Allen et al. are all members of the Romani and Traveller Social Work Association, whose aim is to improve social work approaches to Gypsy, Roma, and Traveller communities from inside the social work profession. SCRs are formal reports published after the death of or serious injury to any child in England; they are authored by professionals who are independent of any organization associated with the child's case in question, all such cases having been considered by a local safeguarding board to be sufficiently serious to warrant an independent review. The purpose of such reviews is not to apportion blame or punish, but to produce learning for future practice via independent scrutiny of all documentation associated with the case. The methodology adopted in this exploration of SCRs involving children from Gypsy, Roma, and Traveller communities was to conduct a literature review of all known cases fitting this criteria.

The National Society for the Prevention of Cruelty to Children (NSPCC) data base of all serious case reviews (NSPCC, 2025) was searched and revealed 13 cases involving Gypsy, Roma, or Traveller children. Analysis of these cases revealed multiple instances of *hermeneutical injustice*, where a person or community is excluded from the systems and opportunities that would ordinarily be afforded to other citizens (Fricker, 2007). Multiple examples of testimonial injustice were also found, such as when knowledge was shared by Gypsy, Roma, or Traveller community members but was disregarded.

The 13 SCRs reviewed involved families living in the community, including four cases that involved a fatality and evidence of neglect or abuse; one involved a fatality related to sudden unexpected death in infancy (that is, the death of a baby when there is no apparent cause); one involved the death of an infant through dehydration, due to an absence of care following the unlawful killing of her mother; one involved child sexual exploitation; two involved child sexual abuse; and four involved neglect or ill-treatment with harm falling short of death.

In one of the cases above, concerning an infant, "Child E" (Walters, 2015), the cause of death was determined by the coroner to have been sudden and unexpected, not due to neglect but impacted by co-sleeping. It was not known by the professional network that the infant, his carer, and other children had been sleeping on the floor in a caravan parked in the drive after being accidentally locked out of their house. The review stated: "the sleeping arrangements were chaotic" (Walters, 2015, p. 25), apparently blaming the carer for putting the infant and other children in this situation. However, as a short-term solution, and lacking access to cots and beds for the children, a member of the travelling community may see this as a logical, fairly risk-free solution, while duplicate keys were obtained or funds raised for a locksmith. This could be seen as an example of testimonial injustice, as the carer's Gypsy perspective was discounted; they were viewed with prejudice and judged for creating "chaos" by selecting a culturally appropriate form of accommodation. The carer does not seem to have been permitted to explain the rationale for her choices. Additionally, the carer may not have had the words or language necessary to convey her rationale or choices effectively in professional arenas, which would constitute hermeneutical injustice (Fricker, 2007).

9.4.1 *Missed Opportunities to Safeguard*

Analysis of the case reviews identified multiple missed opportunities for social workers and other professionals to have intervened and been proactive in lessening risks to the young people involved. Challenges related to the supervision of social workers were highlighted throughout the above reviews, noting that casework was often supervised by lead professionals who lacked any experience in working with Gypsy, Roma, and Traveller communities. Only one of the 13 SCRs facilitated family participation, despite the intention of such reviews to reflect the child's perspective and the family context; this suggests that the child protection system itself produces epistemic injustice due to the absence of any specific institutional mechanisms that could ensure that social workers consider culturally sensitive care for this population.

The challenges identified in each report were not attributed to professionals' lack of direct experience, but rather their inability to transfer their basic skills to the location and context of child protection practice with Gypsy, Roma, and Traveller children; notably, this difficulty may be partly related to professionals' own prejudices about Gypsy, Roma, and Traveller families whose cultures rarely form part of professional diversity training (Unwin et al., 2025).

A recurring theme throughout the reports was that social workers failed to apply "professional curiosity" – that is, observing, listening, and asking questions to verify information and comprehensively assess the lived experiences, perspectives, and realities of the child. Examples below illustrate how ethnicities were often conflated and further, how issues of ethnicity were incorrectly recorded and understood by social workers. Ward (2022) noted that most agencies working with families had recorded their ethnicity as White/British/Traveller. However, the parents from "Family B", who were the subject of Ward's (2022) SCR, disagreed with that ascription:

> Father, who describes himself as a settled Traveller, has said that the family does not strictly follow what are considered to be traditional Traveller ways and culture. They recognized the importance of their heritage but are more fully integrated into the local community. Mother has subsequently said that she is not a Traveller and is unhappy when professionals assume that she is. It appears that this was not known to the agencies working with the family. She does not remember completing any self-identification forms for agencies to identify the children as Travellers.
>
> (Ward, 2022, p. 14)

Three of the above 13 reports conflate ethnicity, describing the child as being from the "Gypsy, Roma, Traveller community", communities and cultures which are separate and distinct from each other. According to Ward (2022), for example, one parent identified the confusion amongst workers himself:

> Father has also now expressed concern that professionals do not understand the cultural and behavioural differences between Irish Travellers and English Travellers (he identifies as an English Traveller).
>
> (p. 14)

In the case review of "Child G", the child's ethnicity was never identified; instead, the umbrella term "Traveller" was used, and the family was described as belonging to the Gypsy, Roma, Traveller community (sic):

> The mother of Child G is from a Gypsy, Roma and Traveller heritage, it is unclear how father defines himself. Mother's partner is from a Gypsy, Roma and Traveller heritage. For the purpose of this review the families will be identified as Travellers because this is how they defined themselves.
>
> (Duncan & Griffiths, 2017, p. 5)

Several of the 13 SCR social worker reports identified a strong family orientation among community members, noting their tendency to live within large extended family networks who provided support, including childcare and social interaction. However, in the above-described examples, there is no indication that these family ties led to any serious consideration of kin as potential carers for the children concerned. Rather, there is evidence of failures to explore family history and culture with children and/or families, thus depriving children of the potential for kin-based care provision. Plans and decisions appeared to be based only on stereotypes and assumptions. This testimonial injustice is deeply unfair, especially when something as fundamental as an individual's view of their personal ethnic identity is ignored. In the case of "Family A" (Harrington, 2014), a local authority took seven children from the same family into state care; not one extended family member was assessed to be either available or suitable to be evaluated as a potential carer.

Such practice goes beyond marginalizing voices – it actually silences them by failing to recognize the legitimacy of family members as having the potential to be assessed as kinship carers and, as such, provides a profound example of hermeneutical injustice. By making assumptions and failing to check them directly with families, social workers systematically excluded children's and parents' voices, missed opportunities to assess more complex matters, and regularly failed to understand the day-to-day reality of Gypsy, Roma, and Traveller children. Such epistemic injustice marginalizes the lived realities of Gypsy, Roma, and Travellers, and is characterized by social workers making decisions which appear to be driven by stereotypical beliefs rather than authentic engagement and culturally humble, child-centric practice with the families concerned.

9.4.2 *Excluding Gypsy, Roma, and Traveller Perspectives*

Several of the 13 SCR reports suggested that parental ability to protect children from harm was affected by complex social factors that social workers did not fully explore or understand. Reports described families as possessing common "cultural traits", including low literacy, learning disabilities, limited parenting skills, experiences of violence and abuse, substance misuse, criminality, secrecy, self-imposed isolation, and reluctance to engage with social workers and other professionals. In the case of "Child G", for example, Duncan and Griffiths (2017) stated:

> ...some professionals felt scared and intimidated, whilst other professionals did not fully understand the culture of the Traveller community or had preconceptions, which they did not question. The knowledge of the professionals about the culture and values of the Traveller community appeared to be at a superficial level and was interspersed with 'stereotypical' views of how Travellers behaved.
>
> (p. 21)

Harrington's (2014) SCR on "Family A" notes: "It is clear that some staff accepted lower levels of care, and set aside evidence of abuse and neglect, because these children were Travellers" (p. 44). Furthermore, a majority of professionals recognized that they made decisions about "Family A" that they would not have made had the family not been part of the Traveller community.

There was little consideration of the accuracy of these aforementioned stereotypical "cultural traits". Instead, parents were stigmatized and blamed for disguised compliance or failure to engage with social workers. The Gypsy, Roma, and Traveller perspective was never sought from children or families, which could have provided a more comprehensive understanding of how poverty, marginalization, and racism impacted them and limited their choices. Instead, social workers' attention was diverted from the Gypsy, Roma, and Traveller children's perspectives by structural and systemic forces, their own personal reactions, and professional values (i.e., hermeneutical injustice).

When parents express high levels of need and display chaotic home conditions, social workers may become overwhelmed and distracted, especially when resources are scarce and there are complex procedures and practice guidelines to follow. In these instances, the child's voice can often be lost; in fact, analysis of the 13 SCR reports demonstrated that both the Gypsy, Roma, and Traveller perspective and voice of the child were often lost, particularly those living with child sexual abuse and exploitation. The case reviews showed that social workers "became too focused on verifying the accuracy of the information, losing sight of the child's lived and reported experience" (Allen et al., 2025, p. 7). Such examples of epistemic injustice can be seen to have compounded the children's exposure to abuse and trauma and increased their vulnerability.

This marginalization of the child's voice resulted in some professionals – including those responsible for overseeing cases and decisions – overlooking discriminatory value judgements about the family's ethnicity, reported cultural traits, identity, and heritage. Decisions appeared to be largely determined by a lack of professional curiosity and a reliance on unchallenged stereotypes. Every report noted the social workers' duty to promote the paramount welfare of the child; however, they did not consider how this duty could be met when the Gypsy, Roma, and Traveller perspectives were not incorporated into the assessment, decision-making, and review process. Excluding Gypsy, Roma, and Traveller perspectives was not confined to direct practice within child protection; Allen et al. (2025) also noted that, out of 13 reports, only two facilitated any participation of the family.

Although it is not uncommon for family members to be excluded from the review process, the low inclusion rate among Gypsy, Roma, and Traveller people in the review process could also indicate how racism works to silence the experiences of marginalized communities in their interactions with child welfare services. This exclusion can be seen to further constitute both hermeneutical and testimonial injustice; not only does it prevent Gypsy, Roma, and Traveller families from sharing their perspectives and voices, but also it reinforces structural inequalities and prevents a comprehensive understanding of the systemic failures that contribute to their children's disproportionate involvement in child welfare interventions (Allen & Hamnett, 2022).

9.4.3 *Fear and Helplessness in Both Service Providers and Users*

A common theme within the reports involved the feelings of mutual fear and helplessness between families and social workers. Social workers feared potential violence from families and had concerns for their own personal safety; at the same time, they held unacceptably low expectations for the standard of the children's care. Conversely, Gypsy, Roma, and Traveller families feared that their children would be removed by social workers and, as a result, some families moved away, missed social worker appointments, or in one instance, adopted various aliases to evade authorities. Every report suggested the relationships between professionals and parents became characterized by mutual fear and helplessness. As Duncan and Griffiths' (2017) SCR concerning "Child G" stated:

> Some professionals felt scared and intimidated, whilst other professionals did not fully understand the culture of the Traveller community or had preconceptions, which they did not question. The knowledge of the professionals about the culture and values of the Traveller community appeared to be at a superficial level and was interspersed with 'stereotypical' views of how Travellers behaved.
>
> (p. 21)

Eades's (2015) SCR regarding the "Baby John" case, commissioned by Essex Children Safeguarding Board, described both parents as having come from "a Gypsy, Roma, Traveller culture" (p. 3), illustrating a homogenized view of these groups which are actually distinct in terms of mores, language, and religion. This report goes on to describe how the professionals involved expected that the family would be nomadic and would lack consistency in education and health care. With such prejudicial mindsets, it is perhaps not surprising that, despite there being a large extended family, it was reported that no family members were "either available or suitable to be assessed as carers" (p. 17) for the four children. No details are provided regarding what efforts were actually made to assess extended family, although the wording used suggests that the extended family did not even merit assessment. It was also noted that legal advice recommended consulting a specialist in Gypsy, Roma, and Traveller culture to inform understanding parenting in this case; ultimately, however, this advice was not followed.

Harrington's (2014) review of "Family A" highlighted that the local authority in question had previously employed two specialist Gypsy, Roma, Traveller Officers, but terminated these posts with the following consequences:

> ...reduced knowledge of the communities, lifestyles and culture of the families living on the site amongst education staff. There was a reduced capacity to establish trust through the familiarity of the residents with a consistent

> person, sensitive to traveller lifestyle issues … [T]here was no longer an education specialist who could advocate for the relevance of education to children's futures and support parents in making decisions related to their children's education.
>
> (Harrington, 2014, p. 46)

The above findings from SCRs suggest that disempowerment and alienation are the inevitable outcomes when knowers are systemically disregarded or ignored, thus further compounding the neglect and abuse experienced by children.

9.5 Discussion: Toward Epistemic Justice in Child Welfare in the UK

This chapter illustrates how testimonial injustice (Fricker, 2007) occurs when a speaker's credibility – notably, the voices of Gypsies, Roma, and Travellers – is unfairly deflated due to the prejudice of social workers, social systems, and the public in the UK. From the authors' own research and other scholars' work, this chapter also highlights the ways in which both parents' and children's voices were systematically excluded from assessments, reviews, and decision-making processes (Allen et al., 2025). The doubting of children's own testimony and its undue scrutiny is a clear case of testimonial injustice, while the stereotypical assumptions – rather than engagement with families – resulted in life-changing decisions which clearly exemplify epistemic devaluation. Such injustice reduces the ability of Gypsies, Roma, and Travellers to engage as respected and valued knowers, which directly affected child welfare outcomes.

The lack of shared understandings about child protection concerns highlighted in Allen et al. (2025) and the authors' own research (Unwin et al., 2020, 2025) provides clear examples of hermeneutical injustice, with lived experiences being either excluded or not even sought, in contravention of both guidelines and law. Without sufficient intersectional knowledge about lifestyles, norms, poverty, racism, and history, social work and other professionals are not equipped with the basics needed to interpret and make critical decisions about Gypsy, Roma, and Traveller clients. Institutionalized language and protocols do not provide culturally sensitive environments, which means families are epistemically denied meaning-making interactions that impact deeply on their lives in what can be seen as a clear form of hermeneutical injustice.

Epistemic injustice can be seen to be more than an abstract or academic-only construct. As described earlier, the reciprocated feelings of fear and helplessness between families and social workers result in emotional distress for all parties. Families develop a cycle of mistrust and vulnerability which is reinforced by social workers who operate in a system that is different when Gypsy, Roma, and Travellers are involved, a system of practice that does not accord with their core values, and possibly brings them moral distress (Allen et al., 2025).

To address pervasive epistemic injustice across social work practice, we present the trauma-informed *Reflection, Objective, Movement & Action (ROMA) Model* for *Restorative Supervision* (Allen et al., 2024) as an excellent opportunity to change social work practice in a systemic way. This model recognizes social work's complicity in the historical and ongoing discrimination against Gypsy, Roma, and Traveller peoples; recognizes and challenges power and bias; makes space for lived experience, cultural humility, and reflection; supports accountability not blame; and seeks safe spaces for restorative practice. The ROMA model comprises a cyclical, structured approach for supervision that centres on emotional awareness, clarity of purpose, ethical growth, and culturally responsive action. The Reflection stage encourages social workers to think individually and structurally about what they bring to the work they do with Gypsy, Roma, and Traveller communities, and asks what might need to be unlearnt. The Objective stage explores ethics and dilemmas, while the Movement stage considers what shifts in knowledge and practice have taken place. This leads to the Action stage, which encourages social workers to build partnerships with their local communities and work differently from the ways reported above in this chapter. It is recognized that the ROMA model is not a panacea given the historical distrust between Gypsy, Roma, and Traveller communities and social workers but its restorative principles can go some way toward redressing the hermeneutical and testimonial injustices that run throughout social work history.

Adopting the ROMA model across social work would better guarantee that the values and ethics espoused by BASW (2021) are met, and that epistemic justice for all is more likely to be achieved. Co-production and working alongside families can itself be marginalized in a working environment ever-pressurized by managerial imperatives, targets, and deadlines but even the busiest social worker is of little value to their profession if such "busyness" is underpinned by fear and ignorance rather than knowledge and openness. The words below from a presentation by Chris Smith (2025), a Romany Gypsy who trains professionals and advocates for social justice on many fronts, emphasize why co-production is so important:

> When our communities come together, something transformative happens. It's not just about breaking down barriers or challenging discrimination – it's about telling our stories on our terms. It's about young Gypsies and Travellers seeing themselves reflected in places they may have thought were closed to them. It's about amplifying our lived experiences in ways that foster empathy and understanding.
>
> When health and social care professionals, they welcome us into their spaces, they open doors to new perspectives that enrich their teaching, research, and community work. They also take an important step toward becoming truly inclusive spaces where everyone belongs.

> This work matters because it goes beyond academic benefits – it's about paving the way for real change. By working together, we can challenge inequalities, celebrate diversity, and create a future where our children grow up in a society that values and respects who they are. For me, this partnership isn't just important – essential. It's a step toward healing, understanding, and building a better, more inclusive world for everyone.

Smith's narrative above emphasizes that future partnership between professionals and communities is essential. We must be open about the fact that social work, along with other professions, has colluded in the perpetuation of epistemic injustice that has excluded Gypsy, Roma, and Traveller communities from being able to access mental health services and to be treated equitably in child protection cases. The inequitable dismissal and devaluation of child and adult voices in Gypsy, Roma, and Traveller communities constitutes testimonial injustice. Future social work education and practice must address this unethical legacy of epistemic injustice if it is to remain true to its core value of being committed to the achievement of epistemic justice for all. The change must happen at the very beginning of social work education by including Gypsy, Roma, and Traveller community members in the co-production of training and research, and this practice should also become an intrinsic thread of post-qualifying training. There is a range of relevant reports, academic articles, and training materials available to help promote best social work practice with Gypsies, Roma, and Travellers. However, ingrained epistemic injustices are difficult to overcome without the meaningful epistemic inclusion of the actual community members. There still remains a long road to travel.

References

Allen, D., Bolton, J., Dove, J., Hulmes, A., Kidd, C., Moloney-Neachtain, M., Rees, I., Rogers, M., Smith, A., & Unwin, P. (2024). A scoping review of social work with Romani and Traveller communities: Introducing the ROMA model. *European Journal of Social Work, 28*(6), 1291–1305. https://doi.org/10.1080/13691457.2024.2424969

Allen, D., Bolton, J., & Kidd, C. (2025). Enhancing learning for the future: A document analysis of serious child safeguarding case reviews with Romani and Traveller communities in England. *Critical and Radical Social Work.* https://doi.org/10.1332/20498608Y2025D000000088

Allen, D., & Hamnett, V. (2022). Gypsy, Roma and Traveller children in child welfare services in England. *The British Journal of Social Work, 52*(7), 3904–3922. https://doi.org/10.1093/bjsw/bcab265

Allen, D., & Riding, S. (2018). *The fragility of professional competence: A preliminary account of child protection practice with Romani and Traveller children in England.* European Roma Rights Centre. https://www.errc.org/reports--submissions/the-fragility-of-professional-competence-a-preliminary-account-of-child-protection-practice-with-romani-and-traveller-children-in-england

Bourdieu, P. (1990). *The logic of practice*. Stanford University Press.

Bowers, J. (2025). *Reaching for the rope*. Jake Bowers. https://jakebowers.co.uk/reaching-for-the-rope/

Boyle, D., Slay, J., & Stephens, L. (2010). *Public services inside out: Putting co-production into practice*. Nesta. https://media.nesta.org.uk/documents/public_services_inside_out.pdf

British Association of Social Workers. (2021). *The BASW code of ethics for social work*. https://www.basw.co.uk/system/files/resources/basw_code_of_ethics_-_2021.pdf

Care Act 2014, c. 23 (2014). https://www.legislation.gov.uk/ukpga/2014/23/contents

Children Act 1989, c. 41 (1989). https://www.legislation.gov.uk/ukpga/1989/41/data.xht?wrap=true

Demianyk, G. (2022, February 22). Jimmy Carr condemned for 'vile' Holocaust joke about Gypsy, Roma and Traveller community. *HuffPost UK*.

Duncan, A., & Griffiths, S. (2017). *Child G: Serious case review (full overview report)*. Hertfordshire Safeguarding Children Board.

Durham Safeguarding Partnership. (2024). *Whole family approach*. Whole Family Approach Guidance

Eades, L. (2015). *A report of the serious case review of the Baby John case*. Essex Safeguarding Children Board. 2015essexbabyjohnoverview.pdf

Foster, D., & Mackley, A. (2025) *Kinship carers in England*. House of Commons Library. https://researchbriefings.files.parliament.uk/documents/SN02967/SN02967.pdf

Friends, Families & Travellers. (2022). *Health inequalities experienced by Gypsy, Roma and Traveller communities* [Briefing]. https://www.gypsy-traveller.org/wp-content/uploads/2022/11/Briefing_Health-inequalities-experienced-by-Gypsies-and-Travellers-in-England.pdf

Friends, Families & Travellers. (2025). *Trapped in the turnstile: Understanding the impacts of the criminal justice system on Gypsy, Roma and Traveller young adults and their families. Trapped in the Turnstile: Understanding the* impacts *of the* criminaljusticesystem *on Gypsy, Roma and Traveller* youngadults *and their*. Families – Friends, Families and Travellers.

Fricker, M. (2007). *Epistemic injustice: Power and the ethics of knowing*. Oxford University Press.

Harrington, K. (2014). *Serious case review: Family A*. Southampton Local Children Safeguarding Board.

House of Commons Women and Equalities Committee. (2019). *Tackling inequalities faced by Gypsy, Roma and Traveller communities* (7th Report of Session 2017–19). https://publications.parliament.uk/pa/cm201719/cmselect/cmwomeq/360/360.pdf

Hulmes, A., & Unwin, P. (2024). Rural social work with Romani and Travellers. In J. Pye & C. Turbett (Eds.), *Rural social work in the UK and beyond: Themes and challenges for the future* (pp. 91–112). Springer.

International Federation of Social Workers. (2014). *Global definition of the social work profession*. Global Definition of Social Work – International Federation of Social Workers

Jesper, E., Griffiths, F., & Smith, L. (2008). A qualitative study of the health experience of Gypsy Travellers in the UK with a focus on terminal illness. *Primary Health Care Research & Development, 9*(2), 157–165. https://doi.org/10.1017/S1463423608000613

Knipe, D., Moran, P., Howe, L., Karlsen, S., Kapur, N., Revie, L., & John, A. (2014). Ethnicity and suicide in England and Wales: A national linked cohort study. *The Lancet Psychiatry, 11*(8), 611–619.

National Society for the Prevention of Cruelty to Children. (2024). *Child protection system in England*. https://learning.nspcc.org.uk/child-protection-system/england

National Society for the Prevention of Cruelty to Children. (2025). *National case review collection: A repository of published reports*. NSPCC Learning.

Office for National Statistics. (2022). *Gypsies' and Travellers' lived experiences: Health, England and Wales*. Office for National Statistics (ons.gov.uk).

Plunkett, J. (2012, February). 'Big fat gypsy weddings' has increased bullying of Gypsies and Travellers. *The Guardian*.

Sarafian, I., Robinson, A., Christov, A., & Tarchini, A. (2024). In the margins of stigma: Health inequalities among Bulgarian Roma in a post-COVID-19 UK. *BMJ Global Health, 9*(11), e015686. https://doi.org/10.1136/bmjgh-2024-015686

Sealey, C., Unwin, P., & Fillingham, J. (2021). *Social policy, service users and carers*. Palgrave.

Social Care Institute for Excellence. (2022). *Co-production: What it is and how to do it*. SCIE.

Smith, C. (2025). *Presentation to the GRTSB into HE Pledge launch*. [Presentation]. University of Worcester.

Sweeney, S., & Dolling, B. (2020). *Suicide prevention in Gypsy and Traveller communities in England*. Friends, Families and Travellers.

University of Worcester, Worcestershire County Council, & Gypsy, Roma, and Traveller Association. (2023). *Gypsy, Roma, and Traveller e-learning training*. Training – Romani & Traveller Social Work Association.

Unwin, P. (2025). *The benefits of same-culture kinship care: A think piece*. Romani and Travellers' Social Work Association.

Unwin, P., & Hulmes, A. (2025). Inequalities in mental health services for Romani and Travellers: Time for social work to step up? *Critical and Radical Social Work*. https://doi.org/10.1332/20498608Y2025D000000088

Unwin, P., Meakin, B., & Jones, A. (2020). *The missing voices of disabled people in Gypsy, Roma and Traveller communities*. Disability Research on Independent Living & Learning. http://www.drilluk.org.uk/wp-content/uploads/2020/12/Missing-

Unwin, P., O'Driscoll, J., Hulmes, A., Hodgkins, S., McPhee, S., Cisneros, R., Bolton, J. A., & Molnár, G. (2025). *Equitable data collection for Gypsy, Roma & Traveller communities*. Understanding Patient Data. https://understandingpatientdata.org.uk/equitable-data-collection-gypsy-roma-and-traveller-communities-health-services

Walters, A. (2015). *Child E: Serious case review*. Bromley Safeguarding Children Board.

Ward, M. (2022). *Local child safeguarding practice review, family B*. Surrey Safeguarding Partnership.

Wellard, S., Meakins, S., Farmer, E., & Hunt, J. (2017). *Growing up in kinship care*. Grandparents Plus. https://kinship.org.uk/report/growing-up-in-kinship-care-experiences-as-adolescents-and-outcomes-in-young-adulthood

Wilkins, J. (Executive Producer). (2011–2015). *Big fat gypsy weddings* [TV series]. Firecracker Films; Channel 4.

Chapter 10

Reflecting on the Epistemic Silencing of People in the Sex Trades within the Anti-Trafficking Movement in the United States

Ran Hu

10.1 Introduction

In the longstanding global movement against human trafficking, *sex work* has been predominately positioned at the center of many policy debates and discussions on social intervention development; stories of people (especially children and women of color) trafficked into the sex trades have been widely shared and consumed in news, films, and public anti-trafficking campaigns. Despite being centralized in anti-trafficking debates and narratives, however, people in sex trading – whether by choice, force, fraud, or circumstance – are systemically excluded from or marginalized in the process of creating knowledge and developing policies and social interventions against trafficking.

My professional involvement in the anti-trafficking field began with my direct practice as a counselor advocate with an anti-trafficking organization in New York City in 2011. Coincidentally, this was a critical point in time in New York when the criminal courts that originally handled prostitution-related arrests were renamed from "prostitution diversion courts" to "human trafficking intervention courts." This "rebranding" stemmed from the belief that women in the sex industry should not be treated as defendants, but rather as potential victims of trafficking in need of opportunities for trafficking identification and access to services. At these courts, I represented one of several social service organizations that received referrals for women charged with prostitution-related offenses. Due to my Chinese migrant background and ability to speak Mandarin, I was hired to work with migrant women of Chinese descent, providing services to those referred to me for court-mandated counseling sessions. Through these sessions, my main duties were to identify signs of trafficking and connect women to services if necessary.

During my years of direct contact and work with many Chinese migrant women in massage parlor-based sex trading, I observed – and was often co-opted into – social service and criminal legal processes that failed to adequately account for the diverse and complex needs of migrant women involved in sex trades, whether by force, choice, or circumstance. In this chapter, I draw on my

DOI: 10.4324/9781003639046-13

direct work experience in anti-trafficking service provision, community-based knowledge, and scholarly literature to illustrate the ways epistemic silencing operates in the anti-trafficking movement in the United States (U.S.) and the consequent impacts on racialized and marginalized people in the sex trades.

10.1.1 Key Terminology

Sex Work, Sex Trafficking, and Sex Trade. In this chapter, the terms sex trade, sex work, and sex trafficking are used as distinct concepts. Specifically, among adults, *sex work* refers to the consensual exchange of sex for monetary or material gain, whereas *sex trafficking* occurs when the sex act is induced by force, fraud, or coercion (Stella, 2013; Trafficking Victims Protection Act, 2000). The *sex trade* refers to the broader industry within which a range of commercial sex acts take place. While I adopt these definitional distinctions, I acknowledge that these terms are somewhat categorical and static and often fail to capture the complex, dynamic lived realities in which adults may experience agency, choice, violence, and exploitation. Therefore, I use the term "people in sex trades" to describe those in the industry without assuming their experiences or how they self-identify (e.g., as survivors or sex workers).

Pre-Emptive Silencing. Drawing from Fricker (2007) and Medina (2013), *pre-emptive silencing* is a form of epistemic silencing where individuals are excluded from knowledge production processes due to the lack of existing frameworks or language to validate or interpret their lived experiences.

Epistemic Objectification. *Epistemic objectification* (Fricker, 2007), as another form of epistemic silencing, refers to situations where a knower is invited or allowed to participate in knowledge production activities but is only treated as a source of information rather than as a knower with the agency and capacity to analyze, think, and make sense of their lived experiences; in other words, their experiences are interpreted (and often misrepresented, intentionally or unintentionally) by others, who are frequently in positions of power.

Epistemic Agency. *Epistemic agency* refers to one's capacity to fully participate in knowledge production, especially the meaning-making of their own lived experiences, as an inquirer, an analyst, or an evaluator (Medina, 2013).

10.2 Theorizing Epistemic Silencing

To understand how injustice may be embedded in and occur through knowledge production, Fricker (2007) articulated two key philosophical concepts: hermeneutical injustice and testimonial injustice. In Fricker's (2007) own words, hermeneutical injustice occurs at the collective level of knowledge legitimization, an *a priori* stage where "a gap in collective interpretive resources puts someone at an unfair disadvantage when it comes to making sense of their social experiences" (p. 1). Testimonial injustice occurs "when prejudice causes a hearer to give a deflated level of credibility to a speaker's word" (p. 1). Hermeneutical and testimonial injustice can be further translated into two types of socio-structural silencing: pre-emptive silencing and epistemic objectification, respectively.

Building on the concept of hermeneutical injustice, pre-emptive silencing occurs when a knower is completely excluded from participating in any knowledge production activities because there is no recognized or legitimized framework to interpret or validate their lived realities (Fricker, 2007; Medina, 2013). For instance, when *migration for sex work* is defined *only* as a form of *transnational sex trafficking*, this interpretation limits our understanding of migrants in sex trades by reducing their experiences to a single narrative of trafficking victimization; in other words, it fails to recognize the possibility that some individuals might enter the work by choice or that others simply do not see themselves as trafficking victims. The definition consequently denies the epistemic existence of migrant *sex workers*, because it categorizes all as trafficking victims, leaving minimal room for alternative and more nuanced meaning-making as migrants in the sex trades.

While pre-emptive silencing involves the complete exclusion of a knower, epistemic objectification occurs when a person is included in the process of knowledge production but is treated merely as a source of information; their insights as contributions to knowledge inquiry are not valued (Fricker, 2007). Consider, for example, a racialized migrant woman who trades sex and is invited to join a community partnership meeting to share her lived experience in the sex trades. During the meeting she is not invited to make meaning of her experiences; instead, other knowledge inquirers, such as service providers and policymakers, who are often in positions of greater socio-economic and political power analyze or interpret (and sometimes misinterpret or purposefully distort) her experiences. Even if these inquirers have intentions to do justice to and equitably conceptualize her lived experiences, epistemic objectification still occurs if this migrant woman's own agency in inquiring, interpreting, or analyzing is not invited to exercise in the meaning-making and conceptualizing process.

Building on Fricker's (2007) notions of epistemic injustice and silencing, Medina (2013) expanded the concept of epistemic objectification (i.e., treating someone as a source of information only) by calling attention to the positional differences between a knower and an inquirer, as well as noted how power inequities embedded in communicative dynamics substantially influence the ways marginalized groups exercise their epistemic agency (that is, an individual's capacity to fully participate in knowledge production, acting as both an inquirer and evaluator of knowledge). First, Medina (2013) challenged Fricker's (2007) interpretation of epistemic objectification and argued that treating someone as an informant is insufficient; instead, to recognize one's full epistemic agency, informants should also be given equal opportunities to be "inquirers and evaluators of knowledge" (p. 93). Second, even when a person from a socially marginalized group is in the position of being an inquirer, they can still be silenced to varying degrees due to "the performative and pragmatic aspects of communicative dynamics" (p. 90). Communicative dynamics do not exist in a vacuum but are always situated in a larger socio-cultural-political context and consequently, are subject to positional and power differentials. Hence, when an inquirer is socio-structurally marginalized and vulnerable in a communicative setting, their capacity to negotiate for and participate in meaning-making activities can be compromised; due to the costs of exercising epistemic agency, socially oppressed and marginalized groups may sometimes even need to remain silent as a type of resistance and self-protection (Medina, 2013).

Drawing on the concept of epistemic silencing as discussed by both Fricker (2007) and Medina (2013), in the following sections, I focus on illustrating major types of epistemic silencing that people in sex trades have experienced both historically and presently in the anti-trafficking movement where knowledge is produced and legitimized. I demonstrate how pre-emptive silencing and epistemic objectification often work together to impose silencing effects, thereby perpetuating epistemic injustice across various domains in the anti-trafficking movement, such as the development and implementation of anti-trafficking policies, anti-trafficking storytelling, and the provision of anti-trafficking services and activism.

10.3 The Pre-Emptive Erasure of Sex Work in Anti-Trafficking Policies

The United Nations (UN) Trafficking Protocol, as a type of international law against trafficking, was officially passed and adopted by the UN General Assembly in 2000 (UNODC, n.d.). Although this protocol is now widely regarded as the "gold standard" for defining trafficking, the contentious negotiations among key state actors and non-profit actors that led to this universalized definition and framework have been largely overlooked. In fact, the issue of how *sex work* is (or should be) positioned in relation to trafficking was at the center of debate during the protocol drafting process (Doezema, 2002, 2005; Wijers, 2015).

As detailed by Doezema (2005), one dominant perspective, led by the Coalition Against Trafficking in Women (CATW) lobby group, considered *consent* to sex trading irrelevant when conceptualizing trafficking when people transnationally migrate and enter the sex trade. This perspective was supported by some government delegations but was opposed by a network of human rights groups and activists who were concerned that making consent to sex work irrelevant in the context of defining trafficking would fail to consider the diverse experiences of people involved in the sex trade (Doezema, 2005). Eventually, after a two-year-long debate over this disagreement, the definition of trafficking in the final version of the protocol was reconciled with a rather compromised stance on the legitimacy of *consent to sex work*; that is, the term "exploitation of prostitution" is ambiguously adopted to signify trafficking into the sex trade. Specifically, in the UN Trafficking Protocol, trafficking in persons is defined as:

> the recruitment, transportation, transfer, harbouring or receipt of persons, by means of the threat or use of force or other forms of coercion, of abduction, of fraud, of deception, of the abuse of power or of a position of vulnerability or of the giving or receiving of payments or benefits to achieve the consent of a person having control over another person, for the purpose of exploitation.
>
> (UN, 2000, p. 42)

Following this definition, it is further noted that "the consent of a victim of trafficking in persons to the intended exploitation," which includes "the exploitation of the prostitution of others or other forms of sexual exploitation," shall be considered "irrelevant where any of the means… have been used" (p. 43). Despite the inclusion of these details in this definition, certain important concepts, such as "sexual exploitation" and "the exploitation of the prostitution of others" (p. 43), remain undefined. These definitional ambiguities, although allowing an end to "an unnecessary yearlong debate over whether or not voluntary adult prostitution should be defined as trafficking" (Jordan, 2002, p. 32), leave much room for each government to make their own interpretation and consequently have "ended up rebounding on sex workers" (Doezema, 2005, p. 78).

Following the UN Trafficking Protocol, the U.S. government passed the Trafficking Victims Protection Act (TVPA) in 2000. In the TVPA, the term "sex trafficking" is chosen, and it refers to "the recruitment, harbouring, transportation, provision, or obtaining of a person for the purpose of a commercial sex act" (TVPA, 2000, § 7102(12)). Based on the literal meaning of this definition, "sex trafficking" is "simply involvement in any aspect of personnel recruitment for the sex industry" (Chapman-Schmidt, 2019, p. 174), which conflates trafficking for sexual exploitation (or "sex trafficking") with adult sex trading (by choice or circumstance). In fact, the TVPA adopted the phrase "severe form of sex trafficking" to refer to sex trading by force, fraud, or coercion (TVPA, 2000). In other words, according to the TVPA, *sex trading* is equivalent to *sex trafficking* and becomes a *severe* form of sex trafficking when force, fraud, or coercion is involved.

These two anti-trafficking policies are examples of pre-emptive epistemic silencing, demonstrating how both the rather ambiguous stance on sex work intentionally taken in the UN Trafficking Protocol and the definitional conflation of sex trafficking with sex work in the TVPA epistemically exclude the possibility of sex trading by choice or circumstance among adults. The complex social-economic and cultural contexts in which an individual gets involved in sex trading, according to these definitions, become completely irrelevant. This epistemic erasure of the contexts and circumstances of sex work directly leads to the systemic silencing of sex workers in many subsequent anti-trafficking policies; it does so by turning the issue of sex work into the main roadblock to solving trafficking, and people involved in sex trading become the main target group to be intervened with, surveilled, and rescued.

For instance, major sources of government funding supporting anti-trafficking efforts often explicitly set out restrictions on the use of funds for organization applicants to support sex work-related advocacy. The U.S. Department of Justice Office for Victims of Crime (DOJOVC), as one of many examples, requires service organizations, as grant recipients for victim housing assistance programs, to agree to two conditions: (1) the organization "does not promote, support, or advocate the legalization or practice of prostitution," and (2) the organization will not "use grant funds or program match funds to promote, support, or advocate the legalization or practice of prostitution" (U.S. DOJOVC, 2024, p. 25). This pledge required by applicants, first of all, epistemically reinforces a message that efforts toward anti-trafficking and supporting sex worker rights (i.e., policy advocacy) are mutually exclusive; and second, it practically excludes organizations that do support sex worker rights and advocacy from pursuing the funds. In 2018, under the Trump Administration, the Fight Online Sex Trafficking Act and the Stop Enabling Sex Traffickers Act (FOSTA-SESTA) were made into Public Law. FOSTA-SESTA were designed as anti-sex trafficking bills, primarily fighting against online sex trafficking through imposing severe penalties on websites for allowing content suspicious of promoting or facilitating trafficking for sexual exploitation. Since the passage of the bills, digital censorship of sex work-related content has been heightened resulting in the mass removal of online posts by sex workers who advertise online and producing even more financial precariousness and workplace safety barriers (Blunt et al., 2020; Blunt & Wolf, 2020; Chamberlain, 2019; Russo, 2019).

The pre-emptive erasure of sex work in anti-trafficking policies, intersecting with the criminalization of sex work, has legitimized the policing of sex workers. Ample empirical evidence has shown how policing sex workers has disproportionately targeted people of color and those with marginalized identities, such as migrants in sex trades who are undocumented or on temporary visas and gender and sexually minoritized sex workers (Dank et al., 2017; Fehrenbacher et al., 2020; Kaye, 2017; Pickering & Ham, 2013). For example, according to a report issued by the Urban Institute on an analysis of 1,400 prostitution-related arrests between 2015 and 2016, 98% of arrestees were women (93% cisgender women and 5% transgender women) with over one-third being migrants (Dank et al., 2017). Those who were arrested were first sent to the local criminal courts, Human Trafficking Intervention Courts (HTICs), and then referred to local service providers for mandatory counseling and trafficking identification assessments. During my own time taking client referrals from HTICs across different New York boroughs, I consistently observed the courthouse to be overwhelmingly filled with "defendants" who were marginalized women of color, in particular Black or Brown women, transgender women, or East-Asian migrants with precarious legal status (e.g., on a tourist visa, undocumented, etc.). Such an arrest-and-rescue process perpetuates a dichotomous lens whereby people in the sex trades are viewed as either defendants or victims. These empirical examples are rooted in the pre-emptive legal erasure of sex work which, in turn, perpetuates the non-existence and irrelevance of sex work in the dominant discussions and discourses of (anti-)trafficking.

10.4 Epistemic Objectification of People in the Sex Trades in Anti-Trafficking Storytelling

Although trafficking can occur in any industry that involves and relies upon human labor, trafficking in the sex trades, especially sex trafficking of women and children, has predominantly been portrayed in the narratives produced by and circulated in anti-trafficking campaigns, films, and news in North America (Andrijasevic, 2007; Andrijasevic & Mai, 2016; Baker, 2014; Cheng, 2008; Heynen & van der Meulen, 2022; Reynolds, 2021; Rodríguez-López, 2018; Uy, 2011; Wilson & O'Brien, 2016). Films and documentaries often link trafficking to migration for sex work, portraying "innocent" and "powerless" women or children living under extremely abusive and violent conditions in the sex trades (Andrijasevic, 2007; Plambech, 2016; Stiles, 2018). A similar patterned narrative, which portrays trafficking victims as foreign women "tricked" or coerced by their families or friends back-home into sex trades after migration, is observed in the storytelling of trafficking victims by anti-trafficking social service providers (Hu, 2019). Reynolds (2021) analyzed U.S. newspaper coverage of a major online platform, *Craigslist*, which had been used by many sex workers for marketing and advertising before the shutdown of *Craigslist Personals* due to FOSTA-SESTA. By critically analyzing 280 news articles published over a period of 13 years (2003–2016) from 7 major newspaper outlets, such as *The New York Times* and *The Washington Post*, Reynolds (2021) found that news stories often described sex workers as either "criminals" or "victims," portrayed *Craigslist* as "the Wal-Mart of sex trafficking," (p. 688) and noted that there was a narrative pattern of objectifying, stigmatizing, and othering sex workers. These narrative elements pervasively used in anti-trafficking stories can certainly be derived from some real lived experiences. However, when these narratives form a dominant pattern of trafficking storytelling and are much removed from socio-contextual concreteness, they become a type of epistemic objectification. Specifically, the complex socio-cultural conditions and life circumstances that lead individuals to become involved in sex trading are completely removed from the storytelling; some of those originally complex and dynamic life stories are omitted entirely, whereas some other lived experiences are treated as scattered pieces of information, subjected to a deliberate pick-and-choose process toward building a single, arguably imagined, dominant story of sex trafficking. The actual people in sex trades are epistemically objectified, as they are reduced to only selected "sources of information" (Fricker, 2007; Medina, 2013); their narratives are re-organized into completely new and ideologically charged ones by people with significant power to control and influence trafficking storytelling in public domains.

The aforementioned epistemic objectification of people in the sex trades in anti-trafficking storytelling has its epistemic roots in anti-sex work radical feminist ideologies, which have been deliberately promoted in the "end-demand" anti-trafficking movement (Kempadoo, 2015; O'Brien et al., 2013; Weitzer, 2007). Radical feminists take the stance that sex work industries are a form of patriarchal violence against women; hence, to end trafficking, the sex work industry must be abolished completely, with the focus on ending the demand for sex services (Ward & Wylie, 2017). This "end-demand" logic, as shown earlier, has been (re)produced and reinforced in major anti-trafficking policies, such as the UN Trafficking Protocol and the TVPA. The epistemic pre-emptive erasure of sex work produced by these policies becomes a philosophical foundation based on which the practices of epistemic objection are legitimized. The response from the CATW following the horrific shootings at Asian spas in Atlanta in 2021 is an example of how epistemic objectification and pre-emptive silencing very often work in tandem.

On March 16, 2021, a series of shootings committed by Robert Long, a 21-year-old White man, occurred at three different Asian spas and massage parlors in Atlanta, Georgia, resulting in a total of eight deaths, six of whom were Asian women (Homeland Security Digital Library, 2021). In a press release posted immediately after the shootings, the CATW, one of the international lobby groups that actively participated in the drafting of the UN Trafficking Protocol, called for an investigation into the Asian spas' "possible connections to sex trafficking" (CATW, 2021, para. 1). This urge for an investigation into trafficking was not surprising, given that Asian massage businesses have long been (mis)represented as the "hotspots" of "sex trafficking" by the "end-demand" anti-trafficking movement in the U.S. In this press release, Asian massage parlors, put in quotation marks, were referred to as "the highest risk venues for the sex trafficking of undocumented, immigrant women, who are often from Korea or China" (CATW, 2021, para. 3). Further in the article, the CATW stated the following:

> This case, like too many others across the country, serves as evidence that sex buyers are the primary source of violence against, and sometimes murder of, women and transwomen, mostly of color, in the sex trade. The U.S. federal definition of sex trafficking makes it clear that "patronizing" victims is a central element of sex trafficking. The most effective way for the state to prevent the sex trade from expanding and further harming vulnerable

> women is to hold sex buyers accountable and provide victims the services they need.
>
> (2021, para. 6)

In this statement, the CATW referenced the definition of sex trafficking constructed in the U.S. TVPA, which conflates sex trafficking with sex work, to further support their earlier claim that Asian massage businesses are "hotspots" of "sex trafficking" of migrant women from Korea and China, a claim that epistemically objectifies Asian migrant women in massage work. In fact, people with marginalized identities (e.g., women of color, migrant women, gender or sexually minoritized sex workers) in the sex trades are pervasively referenced in "end-demand" anti-trafficking storytelling, and elements such as traumatic exploitative events, minimal agency to think and make decisions, and reliance on external rescues from law enforcement and service providers are highlighted in the trafficking narratives. For instance, I conducted a critical discourse analysis to examine the representation of trafficking victims in the anti-trafficking narratives used for public education by "end-demand" lobby groups; the study found a patterned use of terms, such as "prostituted" and "bought and sold," to describe women and girls in "prostitution" (a term often used interchangeably with sex trafficking) (Hu, 2022, p. 456).

Although I, by no means, deny that forced or coerced labor could take place at any work venue, including massage businesses where sex services may be provided, the assumed link between sex trafficking and Asian massage businesses (or more broadly the sex work industries), again, has its roots in the epistemic conflations of sex trafficking and sex work – (re)produced and reinforced by the anti-trafficking international laws such as the UN Trafficking Protocol and U.S. policies such as the TVPA. Such an epistemic pre-emptive erasure of *sex work* has greatly directed both the focus of services and associated funding allocation for services while epistemically objectifying people in sex trades.

10.5 Dismissal of the Epistemic Agency of People in the Sex Trades in Anti-Trafficking Work

According to Medina (2013), one's epistemic capacity to negotiate in knowledge production is subject to communicative dynamics and contexts in which different roles and stakeholders are situated. In the communicative domain of the anti-trafficking field, the full exercise of epistemic agency in negotiating meaning-making has been rather challenging, if not impossible, for many in the sex trades; the epistemic capacities of people in sex trades are already constrained by the pre-emptive erasure of sex work and epistemic objectification in numerous international and domestic policies, as well as dominant trafficking stories. In the space of anti-trafficking and anti-violence, sex workers and sex worker rights activists have decades of experience and expertise in workplace violence and organizing for safety and rights (International Committee on the Rights of Sex Workers in Europe, 2020; Jackson, 2016). Ample scholarly publications and community-led reports have documented sex working communities' efforts to fight exploitation and violence in the sex industries, as well as their ongoing resistance to the epistemic inequities against them produced by and through the anti-trafficking movement (Blunt & Wolf, 2020; Global Network of Sex Work Projects, 2018; International Committee on the Rights of Sex Workers in Europe, 2020; Jackson, 2016; Lutnick, 2019; West & Horn, 2021). However, their voices and perspectives are often relegated to the margins in the anti-trafficking movement (Bergquist, 2015; National Survivor Network, 2023), and they are not viewed as credible inquirers in the space of anti-trafficking. In other words, the epistemic agency of people in sex trades (whether they identify as sex workers or survivors), sex workers and sex worker rights activists is unrecognized and dismissed. For instance, in a recent community report, jointly developed by Freedom Network USA and the National Survivor Network, anti-trafficking and survivor advocates called for urgent action to center the safety of sex workers. In this report, they documented common experiences of erasure and dismissal of people's consensual sex trading experiences as adults in the anti-trafficking space (National Survivor Network, 2023).

The dismissal of the epistemic agency of people in the sex trades has also been pervasive in anti-trafficking service provision, especially when it comes to serving communities with marginalized and racialized individuals. Anu, a South Asian Canadian migrant woman, offered her life stories in the sex trades, including experiences of sex working, being trafficked in the sex trades, and seeking support and services, via three powerful I-poems in a recently published case study (Raguparan & Raguparan, 2024). Through the I-poems, Anu shared how she found strength, agency, and empowerment in her involvement in the sex trades as a sex worker and how she also experienced sexual exploitation, rape, and violence in the industry; and static labels such as "sex trafficking victim" are certainly insufficient to capture her complex and dynamic lived realities. Anu further wrote about how she was not believed when she sought police and service support, because not only had she "failed" to meet an innocent victim profile (e.g., young, uneducated, traumatized, and weak), but also, she did not fit into the dominant cultural and gendered stereotypes of a South Asian woman (e.g., submissive, exotic). Echoing Anu's lived experience, I have observed similar patterns of epistemic agency dismissal during my direct work in anti-trafficking service provision with East-Asian migrant women arrested for "prostitution" in New York.

During my time providing HTIC court-mandated counseling to women, since I speak Mandarin, most of my clients referred by the courts were Chinese migrant women who were predominately arrested at massage parlors run by Chinese im/migrants (often women) across different boroughs in New York

City. During the clinical intake and assessment stage, referred clients were evaluated to determine if they met the criteria of trafficking defined by the TVPA – providing sex services by force, fraud, or coercion. Echoing the findings from empirical works consisting of interviews with Asian massage workers (Chin et al., 2019; Chin & Finckenauer, 2012), many of my clients did not recall the use of any fraud or coercive techniques on the part of their employers or managers forcing them to stay in the work against their will (massage, some kinds of sex services, or both). However, trafficking trauma and assumed "cultural barriers" (e.g., "Chinese cultural values of harmony and collectiveness") were often part of the clinical staff training and were used to justify clients' hesitancy to disclose "potential" abusive employers or traffickers. Hence, migrant women in sex trades were seen as "potential victims" who might not be ready to self-identify as survivors of sex trafficking. In other words, they were viewed as too traumatized to be epistemically capable of making "proper" sense of their own lived realities. They had to rely on actors in power who intervened in their lives (e.g., service providers, arresting officers, and legal representatives and judges at the court) to interpret and define their life experiences. The dismissal of their epistemic agency in telling and legitimizing their stories with service providers can have material consequences on service access. For example, many women that I worked with did disclose numerous challenges and issues that required attention and services. However, the service eligibility screening was too narrowly focused on meeting criteria for trafficking identification. Many services were only available with the presence of a so-called "solid" trafficking story, leaving many migrant women in the sex trades unable to access further support despite expressing critical needs and experiencing assault, robbery, pay disputes, and police harassment.

10.6 Reimagining Anti-Trafficking: From Epistemic Silencing to Epistemic Justice

As we (re)imagine approaches to and strategies for promoting epistemic justice for people with such diverse sex trading experiences and insider insights into anti-violence work, a first step is to critically examine what epistemic injustice and silencing may be like and to begin to address them. In this chapter, I draw on a range of examples to illustrate the ways in which people in the sex trades are epistemically marginalized and silenced in anti-trafficking work. These examples certainly do not exhaustively represent all aspects of how epistemic silencing has operated in the movement in the U.S., but they form a snapshot through which we recognize the material harms of epistemic exclusion and silencing of people in the sex trades.

Activists at the intersection of human rights and anti-trafficking efforts have called for the serious consideration of sex workers' rights and safety when developing anti-trafficking strategies (Freedom Network USA, 2021; National

Survivor Network, 2023). Many activists view sex work decriminalization as vital for decreasing trafficking to mitigate sex workers' vulnerabilities to force, violence, or coercion at work (Albright & D'Adamo, 2017). Criminalization, along with other forms of systemic oppression (e.g., stigma, racism, economic inequity, and homo/transphobia), also has a strong effect of epistemic silencing on people in the sex trades, especially those with marginalized identities, when they engage with anti-trafficking activities and knowledge production. For instance, when migrant sex trading remains criminalized, migrants in sex trades must navigate not only cultural and sometimes linguistic marginalization, but also social stigma and real legal risks due to criminalization, all of which place them in a rather disadvantaged and inequitable position in almost all forms of communicative settings in the anti-trafficking space. This leaves migrants in sex trades very little space to exercise their epistemic agency to offer their authentic interpretations of their lived experiences and to negotiate for equitable services, rights, and protections.

To minimize the costs and risks associated with exercising epistemic agency, one may choose to remain silent in certain communicative contexts for self-protection (Medina, 2013). Therefore, to promote the epistemic agency of people in the sex trades in anti-trafficking work, we must work alongside people with diverse and lived/living experiences to urgently address systemic forms of oppression and marginalization that impose and perpetuate silencing. Further, as was illustrated in this chapter, pre-emptive silencing and epistemic objectification, despite being conceptualized as distinct types of silencing, do not operate in isolation but work interdependently, reinforcing one another. The ideological assumptions, rooted in radical/carceral feminism and White supremacy, about sex trading that were mobilized to justify the legal definitions of trafficking and anti-trafficking frameworks must be revisited and confronted, in order to create an epistemically equitable conceptualization of trafficking and, more broadly, women's complex experiences in the sex trades.

References

Albright, E., & D'Adamo, K. (2017). Decreasing human trafficking through sex work decriminalization. *AMA Journal of Ethics*, *19*(1), 122–126.

Andrijasevic, R. (2007). Beautiful dead bodies: Gender, migration and representation in anti-trafficking campaigns. *Feminist Review*, *86*, 24–44.

Andrijasevic, R., & Mai, N. (2016). Trafficking (in) representations: Understanding the recurrent appeal of victimhood and slavery in neoliberal times. *Anti-Trafficking Review*, *7*, 1–10. https://doi.org/10.14197/atr.20121771

Baker, C. N. (2014). An intersectional analysis of sex trafficking films. *Meridians*, *12*(1), 208–226. https://doi.org/10.2979/meridians.12.1.208

Bergquist, K. J. S. (2015). Criminal, victim, or ally? Examining the role of sex workers in addressing minor sex trafficking. *Affilia*, *30*(3), 314–327. https://doi.org/10.1177/0886109915572844

Blunt, D., & Wolf, A. (2020). Erased: The impact of FOSTA-SESTA and the removal of backpage on sex workers. *Anti-Trafficking Review, 14*, 117–121. https://doi.org/10.14197/atr.201220148

Blunt, D., Wolf, A., Coombes, E., & Mullin, S. (2020). *Posting into the void.* https://hackinghustling.org/wp-content/uploads/2020/09/Posting-Into-the-Void.pdf

Chamberlain, L. (2019). FOSTA: A hostile law with a human cost. *Fordham Law Review, 87*(5), 2171–2212. https://ir.lawnet.fordham.edu/flr/vol87/iss5/13

Chapman-Schmidt, B. (2019). 'Sex trafficking' as epistemic violence. *Anti-Trafficking Review, 12*, Article 12. https://doi.org/10.14197/atr.2012191211

Cheng, S. (2008). Muckraking and stories untold: Ethnography meets journalism on trafficked women and the U.S. military. *Sexuality Research and Social Policy, 5*, 6–18.

Chin, J. J., Takahashi, L. M., Baik, Y., Ho, C., To, S., Radaza, A., Wu, E., Lee, S., Dulfo, M., & Jung, D. (2019). *Illicit massage parlors in Los Angeles County and New York City: Stories from women workers.* https://static1.squarespace.com/static/5e4835857fcd934d19bd9673/t/5e7fde8379950130737ed0f5/1585438345704/MassageParlorStudy.pdf

Chin, K. L., & Finckenauer, J. O. (2012). *Selling sex overseas: Chinese women and the realities of prostitution and global sex trafficking.* NYU Press.

Coalition Against Trafficking in Women. (2021). *The city of Atlanta must investigate recent shootings' potential connections to sex trafficking.* https://catwinternational.org/press/atlanta-investigate-shootings-potential-sex-trafficking-connections/

Dank, M., Yahner, J., & Yu, L. (2017). *Consequences of policing prostitution: An analysis of individuals arrested and prosecuted for commercial sex in New York City.* https://www.urban.org/sites/default/files/publication/89451/consequences-of-policing-prostitution.pdf

Doezema, J. (2002). Who gets to choose? Coercion, consent, and the UN trafficking protocol. *Gender and Development, 10*(1), 20–27. https://doi.org/10.1080/13552070215897

Doezema, J. (2005). Now you see her, now you don't: Sex workers at the UN trafficking protocol negotiation. *Social & Legal Studies, 14*(1), 61–89. https://doi.org/10.1177/0964663905049526

Fehrenbacher, A. E., Musto, J., Hoefinger, H., Mai, N., Macioti, P. G., Giametta, C., & Bennachie, C. (2020). Transgender people and human trafficking: Intersectional exclusion of transgender migrants and people of color from anti-trafficking protection in the United States. *Journal of Human Trafficking, 6*(2), 182–194. https://doi.org/10.1080/23322705.2020.1690116

Freedom Network USA. (2021, February 5). *Freedom network USA's input for the 2021 trafficking in persons report.* https://freedomnetworkusa.org/app/uploads/2021/02/FNUSA2021TIPReportInput.pdf

Fricker, M. (2007). *Epistemic injustice: Power and the ethics of knowing.* Oxford University Press.

Global Network of Sex Work Projects. (2018). *Policy brief: The impact of anti-trafficking legislation and initiatives on sex workers.* https://www.nswp.org/sites/nswp.org/files/impact_of_anti-trafficking_laws_pb_nswp_-_2018.pdf

Heynen, R., & van der Meulen, E. (2022). Anti-trafficking saviors: Celebrity, slavery, and branded activism. *Crime, Media, Culture, 18*(2), 301–323. https://doi.org/10.1177/17416590211007896

Homeland Security Digital Library. (2021, March 16). *Timeline: Atlanta spa shootings*. https://www.hsdl.org/c/timeline/atlanta-spa-shootings/

Hu, R. (2019). Examining social service providers' representation of trafficking victims: A feminist postcolonial lens. *Affilia, 34*(4), 421–438. https://doi.org/10.1177/0886109919868832

Hu, R. (2022). Problematizing the educational messaging on sex trafficking in the U.S. "end-demand" movement: The (mis)representation of victims and anti-sex work rhetoric. *Affilia, 37*(3), 448–465. https://doi.org/10.1177/08861099211058827

International Committee on The Rights of Sex Workers in Europe. (2020, November 24). *Missed opportunities and exclusion: Sex workers reflect on two decades of anti-trafficking*. https://www.opendemocracy.net/en/beyond-trafficking-and-slavery/missed-opportunities-and-exclusion-sex-workers-reflect-two-decades-anti-trafficking/.

Jackson, C. A. (2016). Framing sex worker rights: How U.S. sex worker rights activists perceive and respond to mainstream anti-sex trafficking advocacy. *Sociological Perspectives, 59*(1), 27–45. https://doi.org/10.1177/0731121416628553

Jordan, A. D. (2002). Human rights or wrongs? The struggle for a rights-based response to trafficking in human beings. *Gender & Development, 10*(1), 28–37. https://doi.org/10.1080/13552070215891

Kaye, J. (2017). *Responding to human trafficking: Dispossession, colonial violence, and resistance among Indigenous and racialized women*. University of Toronto Press.

Kempadoo, K. (2015). The modern-day White (wo)man's burden: Trends in anti-trafficking and anti-slavery campaigns. *Journal of Human Trafficking, 1*(1), 8–20. https://doi.org/10.1080/23322705.2015.1006120

Lutnick, D. A. (2019). The 'prioritizing safety for sex workers policy': A sex worker rights and anti-trafficking initiative. *Anti-Trafficking Review, 12*, Article 12. https://doi.org/10.14197/atr.201219129

Medina, J. (2013). *The epistemology of resistance: Gender and racial oppression, epistemic injustice, and the social imagination*. Oxford University Press.

National Survivor Network. (2023). *Re-centering sex worker safety in anti-trafficking work: Perspectives from the field*. https://nationalsurvivornetwork.org/wp-content/uploads/2023/11/Recentering-Sex-Worker-Safety-in-Anti-Trafficking-Work.pdf

O'Brien, E., Hayes, S., & Carpenter, B. (2013). *The politics of sex trafficking*. Palgrave Macmillan.

Pickering, S., & Ham, J. (2013). Hot pants at the border: Sorting sex work from trafficking. *British Journal of Criminology, 54*(1), 2–19. https://doi.org/10.1093/bjc/azt060

Plambech, S. (2016). The art of the possible: Making films on sex work migration and human trafficking. *Anti-Trafficking Review, 7*, Article 7. https://doi.org/10.14197/atr.201217710

Raguparan, M., & Raguparan, A. (2024). Anu's story: Unpacking the conflation of sex work and sex trafficking. *Sexualities, 28*(3), 1154–1172. https://doi.org/10.1177/13634607241246685

Reynolds, C. (2021). "Craigslist is nothing more than an internet brothel": Sex work and sex trafficking in U.S. newspaper coverage of Craigslist sex forums. *The Journal of Sex Research, 58*(6), 681–693. https://doi.org/10.1080/00224499.2020.1786662

Rodríguez-López, S. (2018). (De)constructing stereotypes: Media representations, social perceptions, and legal responses to human trafficking. *Journal of Human Trafficking, 4*, 61–72.

Russo, R. A. (2019). Online sex trafficking hysteria: Flawed policies, ignored human rights, and censorship. *Cleveland State Law Review, 68*(2), 314–345. https://engagedscholarship.csuohio.edu/clevstlrev/vol68/iss2/10

Stella. (2013). *Language matters: Talking about sex work.* https://www.nswp.org/sites/default/files/StellaInfoSheetLanguageMatters.pdf

Stiles, S. (2018). Good versus evil or "saying more": Strategies of telling in sex trafficking documentary films. *Journal of Human Trafficking, 4*(1), 35–47. https://doi.org/10.1080/23322705.2018.1423445

Trafficking Victims Protection Act of 2000, 22 U.S.C. § 7102(12). (2000).

United Nations. (2000). *Protocol to prevent, suppress and punish trafficking in persons especially women and children, supplementing the United Nations Convention against Transnational Organized Crime.* https://www-ohchr-org.proxy.lib.ohio-state.edu/en/professionalinterest/pages/protocoltraffickinginpersons.aspx

United Nations Office on Drugs and Crime. (n.d). *Signatories to the United Nations convention against transnational crime and its protocols.* https://www-unodc-org.proxy.lib.ohio-state.edu/unodc/en/treaties/CTOC/signatures.html

U.S. Department of Justice Office for Victims of Crime. (2024). *OCV FY24 anti-trafficking housing assistance program.* https://ovc.ojp.gov/funding/opportunities/o-ovc-2024-172033

Uy, R. (2011). Blinded by red lights: Why trafficking discourse should shift away from sex and the perfect victim paradigm. *Berkeley Journal of Gender, Law & Justice, 26,* 204–220.

Ward, E., & Wylie, G. (2017). Introduction. In E. Ward & G. Wylie (Eds.), *Feminism, prostitution and the state: The politics of neo-abolitionism* (1st ed., pp. 1–11). Routledge.

Weitzer, R. (2007). The social construction of sex trafficking: Ideology and institutionalization of a moral crusade. *Politics and Society, 35*(3), 447–475. https://doi.org/10.1177/0032329207304319

West, N., & Horn, T. (2021). *We too: Essays on sex work and survival.* The Feminist Press.

Wijers, M. (2015). Purity, victimhood and agency: Fifteen years of the UN trafficking protocol. *Anti-Trafficking Review, 4,* Article 4. https://doi.org/10.14197/atr.20121544

Wilson, M., & O'Brien, E. (2016). Constructing the ideal victim in the United States of America's annual trafficking in persons reports. *Crime, Law and Social Change, 65,* 29–45.

Chapter 11

Stigma as a Fundamental Cause of Epistemic Injustice

Case Studies on Forcibly Displaced Groups, Persons Living with Disabilities, and the LGBTQ+ Community

Luissa Vahedi

11.1 Introduction: Who Is Granted the Power of Knowing?

The power to be a storyteller, knowledge creator, interpreter of one's own or collective experiences, and recorder of so-called inalienable "truths" is not universal. To hold this power is to be recognized as credible and fully human, worthy of the collective audience or pen (Fricker, 2007). This power also involves the possibility (or intention) of shaping some of our core understandings: about the fundamental processes that structure our world, and about the policies that determine life course trajectories. This chapter situates epistemic injustice and stigma at the center of this essential discussion about power and knowing. In doing so, we deepen our understanding of why some people are not afforded the power of knowing.

Certain communities or persons are perceived to be less credible and are thus denied the possibility of knowing. This phenomenon is known as epistemic injustice and has been formally defined as being wronged in one's capacity as a knower; it means that one is harmed in a capacity essential to being human (Fricker, 2007). The connection between epistemic injustice and dehumanization is intentional. The ability to reason, interpret, and share in oral and written tradition is distinctly human. Yet, this capacity is not universally granted. Dehumanization is the ultimate culmination of status loss and strips a person of their innate capacity to know. There are profound harms, both palpable and philosophical, to not being heard.

At the heart of epistemic injustice is a process of devaluation or stigma. One of the most detrimental consequences of stigma is being discredited as human. One's lived experiences are stripped away, no longer wholly one's own; a person is not to be believed about the nature of what they have seen and felt. I argue that to fully understand epistemic injustice, we must first understand stigma. In other words, stigma is a fundamental cause of epistemic injustice. Without stigma, there can be no epistemic injustice. Conceptualizing the relationship

DOI: 10.4324/9781003639046-14

between stigma and epistemic injustice in this way offers a stepping-stone to developing strategies that ameliorate stigma, thus widening the horizon of who is deemed to be a knower and to what end.

11.1.1 Key Terminology

Stigma. Stigma is a social process by which individuals/groups are labeled, stereotyped, separated, and subjected to status loss and discrimination because of an attribute deemed undesirable, with power hierarchies facilitating the process (Link & Phelan, 2001).

Epistemic Injustice. Epistemic injustice refers to the harm done to someone in their capacity as a knower. It occurs via a credibility deficit (testimonial injustice) or a gap in collective interpretive resources (hermeneutical injustice) that renders a person's experience unintelligible (Fricker, 2007).

Evidence-Informed Policies. Evidence-informed policymaking is an approach where policy decisions are guided by systematic, transparent access to, appraisal of, and use of the best available research evidence and other relevant information (like lived experience and expert expertise), recognizing that values, resources, stakeholder interests, and context also matter (Ball, 2018).

Hard-to-Reach Populations. Hard-to-reach populations are groups for whom conventional service delivery, program engagement, or research recruitment is significantly impeded by structural characteristics and power hierarchies (such as geographic isolation, mobility, social marginalization, stigma, lack of formal sampling frames, or discrimination); these factors cause some scholars to question whether these populations are actually "hard-to-reach" or "out of our own sight" due to epistemic injustice (Logie, 2021).

Forcibly Displaced Populations. Forcibly displaced populations refers to individuals compelled to leave their homes, either within their country or abroad, due to conflict, violence, human rights abuses, or disasters (European Union, n.d.).

Persons Living With Disabilities. Persons living with disabilities refers to individuals who have long-term physical, mental, intellectual, or sensory impairments which, in interaction with various attitudinal and environmental barriers, hinder their full and effective participation in society on an equal basis with others (World Health Organization, 2025).

LGBTQ+ Community. The LGBTQ+ community refers to both persons and the social networks and movements to which they belong or self-identify who are lesbian, gay, bisexual, transgender, queer (or questioning), and other sexual orientations and gender identities beyond heteronormativity and cis-gender identity; membership is often grounded in a collective sense of identity, solidarity, and activism (LGBTQIA Resource Center, n.d.).

11.1.2 An Overview of Stigma

Stigma is a complex social and political phenomenon that has been discussed in the scholarly literature for decades (Goffman, 1984), with some texts dating back to Aristotle's ancient Greek writings on shame and moral virtue (Jimenez, 2020). How we understand stigma has been shaped over time and across different scholarly traditions and disciplines. Goffman's seminal work, *Stigma: Notes on the Management of Spoiled Identity* (1986), suggests that stigma is a deeply discrediting attribute that reduces an individual from a whole, usual person to a tainted, discounted one. Goffman identifies three primary types of stigma: abominations of the body (physical health ailments), blemishes of individual character (perceptions of one's moral character), and tribal stigma (pertaining specifically to groups based on ethnic or religious affiliations). Stigma, in this sense, is not simply a negative attribute but a negative embedded in a social context, where societal norms and values dictate what is considered "normal or desirable" and what is considered "deviant or undesirable": A stigmatized individual or group must navigate and cope with social interactions that are stained by avoidance, discrimination, or devaluation (Goffman, 1984).

Building on Goffman's seminal work, several scholars have expanded on some of his key ideas. For example, Link and Phelan (2001) argue that stigma goes beyond the negative labeling of individuals; they describe stigma as a process that involves four stages: (1) labeling, (2) stereotyping, (3) cognitive separation between "us" and "them", and (4) status loss and discrimination. This stigma process reflects, creates, and perpetuates social hierarchies (Link & Phelan, 2014). Power is central to establishing and maintaining such hierarchies. Fundamental to inequality and domination, power is both symbolic (operating invisibly through what appears natural) and relational (manifested through everyday interactions in families, workplaces, and social networks) (Bourdieu, 1991; Link & Phelan, 2014). The inequitable distribution of resources (economic, social, cultural) is sustained by a world view wherein some people are more deserving of full human rights and others are less deserving. Axes of identity (by race, gender, class) become legitimized and naturalized markers of hierarchies reproduced in our intuitions and social relationships. Power is then reinforced by silencing or sidelining alternative viewpoints that either center marginalization or question the assumptions that underlie the ideologies of oppression.

Adding a structural and political dimension, stigma involves both individual-level experiences and macro-level institutions that sustain inequities (Hatzenbuehler et al., 2013). Stangl and colleagues (2019) extend the works of Goffman and Link and Phelan by developing the Health Stigma and Discrimination Framework. This framework is unique in that it intentionally does not distinguish between the stigmatized and the stigmatizer. In other words, the framework situates broader social, cultural, political, and economic forces as stigma drivers and facilitators that shape stigma manifestations and outcomes, rather than emphasizing a binary where a person can either stigmatize or be stigmatized. Notably, the Health Stigma and Discrimination Framework situates stigma as dynamic. Persons can experience, internalize, anticipate, and enact stigma against others, thereby rendering a stigmatizer/stigmatized binary incomplete. Rather than focusing on interpersonal behaviors, we are reoriented to the power, norms, and systems that sustain stigma and related hierarchies both within and between groups. Thus, stigma is individually felt but structurally defined, reinforcing patterns of exclusion and inequality across the globe.

Stigma has also been analyzed from an intersectional perspective (Logie et al., 2011; Turan et al., 2025). Multiple social identities – including but not limited to gender, race, class, and sexual orientation – interact in ways that compound the status loss and discrimination experienced by stigmatized persons or groups (Logie et al., 2011; Turan et al., 2025). For example, women living with HIV in Canada face barriers to leaving relationships marked by intimate partner violence; internalized stigma related to HIV status results in the absorption of blame for being abused and consequently, women accept abusive relationships and fear leaving them (Logie et al., 2011). Yet, few HIV programs offer specific supports to women living in abusive relationships (El-Bassel et al., 2022).

11.1.3 An Overview of Epistemic Injustice

The scholarly discourse on epistemic injustice gained prominence with the publication of *Epistemic Injustice: Power and the Ethics of Knowing* (Fricker, 2007). However, elements of what we now understand as epistemic injustice were discussed in earlier works. For example, feminist philosophers and critical race scholars have long been concerned with how inequitable power structures diminish the legitimacy of knowledge and the authority of persons and communities that deviate from what bell hooks (2004) described as the Imperialist Capitalist White Supremacist Patriarchy. Feminist philosophers, like Sandra Harding in *The Science Question in Feminism* (1986), critiqued how women's knowledge and experiences are systematically excluded from dominant science and by extension, medical research (Harding, 1986). Similarly, Black feminists bell hooks (1986) and Patricia Hill Collins (2000) highlighted how Black women's voices were systematically dismissed or distorted in mainstream white feminism. In *The Racial Contract* (1997), critical race scholar Charles Mills examined how racialized knowledge stemming from the experiences and perspectives of people of color was systematically devalued within Western epistemology (Mills, 1997). These works collectively foreshadowed the later discourse on epistemic injustice.

Miranda Fricker, who popularized the term epistemic injustice, introduced two key forms: testimonial injustice and hermeneutical injustice (Fricker, 2007). The first, testimonial injustice, occurs when a speaker's credibility is undermined due to prejudices or stereotypes related to their social identity. This can lead to a complete disregard of testimony. The second, hermeneutical injustice, happens when a person or group lacks the resources needed to make sense of their experiences, often due to the dominant political group's control over knowledge production and dissemination. Fricker's work highlights that certain social identities are systematically denied the agency needed to share or interpret their own knowledge. Kristie Dotson's (2014) work on epistemic oppression adds further nuance to Fricker's concepts by considering how epistemic injustice is experienced at the intersection of multiple identities. Dotson (2014) argues that epistemic injustice is compounded by social identities (race, gender, and class), thereby yielding distinct types of epistemic violence.

11.2 Intersections between Stigma and Epistemic Injustice

As the previous sections of this chapter have demonstrated, stigma is a social judgment that discredits individuals based on certain salient attributes. Epistemic injustice is specifically concerned with how being perceived affects one's epistemic position. These concepts are not mutually exclusive; rather, the two are deeply interconnected. I argue that stigma frequently serves as a fundamental cause of epistemic injustice. The stigma process of (1) labeling, (2) stereotyping, (3) separation, and (4) status loss and discrimination has profound epistemic consequences (Link & Phelan, 2001). Stigmatized individuals are often perceived as being unreliable or incapable of contributing valuable knowledge, thereby increasing their vulnerability to epistemic injustice. Stigmatization is a primary process through which epistemic injustice occurs.

However, while stigma can culminate in epistemic injustice, the two concepts are distinct in terms of their specific focus. Stigma is a broader social judgment that marks individuals as inferior, whereas epistemic injustice specifically concerns how knowledge and credibility are distributed in society. Nevertheless, they rarely operate in isolation. The epistemic marginalization of stigmatized groups is not simply incidental; it is intricately woven into the broader social fabric of exclusion on the basis of power hierarchies. Stigmatized groups are more likely to experience both testimonial and hermeneutical injustices, reinforcing the idea that stigma and epistemic injustice are rarely mutually exclusive, but often work in tandem to uphold systemic inequalities. Consequently, addressing stigma is crucial in mitigating epistemic injustice and fostering a more inclusive and equitable worldview.

The relationship between stigma and epistemic injustice can be understood in terms of how stigmatized individuals are often systematically excluded from the epistemic community. In this way, stigma directly fuels epistemic injustice, as those who are stigmatized are more likely to be discredited or ignored in knowledge-producing processes, both formal and informal. This exclusionary dynamic is particularly harmful because it perpetuates the marginalization of entire communities, limiting the diversity of perspectives and lived experiences that are integral to a more comprehensive understanding of social realities. The denial of credibility and silencing of marginalized voices can reinforce existing power structures, thereby amplifying the very social inequalities that give rise to stigma in the first place. In other words, stigma is a fundamental cause of epistemic injustice because it creates the social conditions through which individuals or communities are rendered epistemically invisible. Those who experience stigmatization often face both testimonial injustice (being disbelieved) and hermeneutical injustice (having their social experiences misinterpreted or ignored). In the extreme, the underlying process of stigmatization can lead to profound dehumanization in the form of genocide and epistemicide: the worldwide destruction of knowledge systems (de Sousa Santos, 2015). Thus, stigma is a critical point of intervention in efforts to dismantle inequities in knowledge production, interpretation, and validation.

11.3 Three Case Studies on Stigma as a Fundamental Cause of Epistemic Injustice

Health research has been largely propelled by a data-driven biomedical model (Krieger, 1994). Further, the "evidence" in evidence-informed, scientific decisions is often assumed or expected to be quantitative. This quantification of disease and disability and related risk factors thereof (whether biological, behavioral, social, or political) leads to the construction of explanatory or predictive statistical models of causality. In turn, these abstracted statistical representations of reality are conflated with reality itself.

However, there are limits to quantification and statistical abstraction. Some psychological constructs, like distress or depression, for example, are difficult to quantify robustly, particularly across diverse cultural and geographical settings (McGrath, 2005). Other ways of knowing concerning the embodiment of risk factors and how disease and disability are experienced in the bodies of diverse people are pushed into the realm of the anecdotal or folkloric (Krieger, 2021). This tension between a data-driven research approach and qualitative lived experience is illustrated by the populations deemed "hard-to-reach".

Populations that are considered by researchers and policy makers as being "hard-to-reach" embody the double burden of stigma experiences and epistemic injustice. Social marginalization and stigma underlie the "hard-to-reach" label and can culminate in epistemic injustice. So-called "hard-to-reach populations" (e.g., sex workers, persons who inject drugs, trans women) are often excluded from research and policy due to competing demands, structural barriers, or historical harms inducing a resistance to participation (Logie, 2021). Indeed, the "hard-to-reach" label may be stigmatizing in and of itself because the label individualizes the social and political process of stigmatization, situating the lack of accessibility on characteristics of the population rather than the power systems of knowledge and policy production (Logie, 2021). In other words, the label places the responsibility of participation on communities, rather than the researchers, policy makers, and the institutions they represent.

I draw on three illustrative examples of "hard-to-reach" populations (i.e., forcibly displaced populations, persons living with disabilities, and the LGBTQ+ community) to describe how the stigma they experience circumscribes their ability to contribute to research and policy discourses. As the culminating stage of stigma, status loss and discrimination can justify life-threatening consequences like interpersonal or political violence (Dancygier et al., 2022; Jackson et al., 2022; Scoglio & Salhi, 2021; Wirtz et al., 2020). In parallel, the stigmatized group can also experience epistemological violence wherein researchers interpret data about marginalized or racialized groups in a manner that constructs these groups as inferior, even when alternative interpretations can be supported by the data (Teo, 2010).

11.3.1 Case Study 1: Forcibly Displaced Populations and Epistemic Injustice in Global Health Research

According to recent 2025 estimates from the United Nations High Commissioner for Refugees (UNHCR), approximately 123.2 million people have been forced to leave their homes. Of these, 43.7 million are refugees who have crossed international borders, and 4.4 million are considered stateless and have been denied a nationality, which is often a prerequisite to securing basic rights (UNHCR, 2025). Forcibly displaced populations, including refugees, asylum seekers, and internally displaced persons, face profound stigma during migration and upon relocating to a host country or community. In extreme cases, being forced to flee one's home equates to being stripped of one's own humanity.

This stigma reflects political, legal, and social structures, leading to the exclusion of forcibly displaced persons from lifesaving services and policies. For example, refugees are not recognized as credible sources of knowledge and are, in some cases, actively silenced by nationalistic policies. In some countries, refugees, as non-state actors, are often ineligible for public and social services. Refugee hosting countries, many of which are low- and middle-income countries with weak medical infrastructure, struggle to integrate refugees in national health plans, primary care, and hospital care. Though increasing over time, UNHCR research posits that, in 2023, 20% of host countries do not include refugees in national health plans and 17% report no or unequal access to hospital care among refugees (UNHCR, 2023). Further, among countries with health insurance plans, 53% of them do not include refugees as part of national health insurance schemes; refugees are often not authorized for employment which typically covers the cost of insurance premiums (UNHCR, 2023).

In cases where services are available to refugees, this group faces barriers to accessing quality public and social services wherein their experiences are heard and integrated into care plans. A 2022 systematic review on barriers to accessing mental health services among refugee women reported language challenges and a lack of culturally appropriate resources (DeSa et al., 2022). Related to both barriers were the use of language and cultural interpreters. Some refugee women relied on family member interpreters, leading to potential conflicts of interest and breaches of confidentiality surrounding the disclosure of sensitive mental health information (DeSa et al., 2022). There is also a risk that interpreters may not accurately represent refugee women's lived experiences or cultural mental health schemas, including traditional and religious beliefs outside of Western biomedical models.

Empirical research among African refugee families in Canada described experiences accessing the Interim Federal Health Program, which provides medical services for refugees in Canada (Woodgate et al., 2017). Language barriers emerged as a major theme, emphasizing the disconnect in communication and structural barriers in expressing one's medical needs. For example, a male participant from Ethiopia noted: "language the difficult thing. When you understand it, it makes it easier but sometimes you don't understand but you just say 'okay' and just leave, but you have no idea what, what they told you" (p. 7).

Further, an Ethiopian mother recounted her efforts to communicate with healthcare providers when her daughter was sick with pinworms: "I took her to the emergency and I wanted to tell them what's wrong with her, but they couldn't understand me, I couldn't really explain … so that language is really difficult sometimes to just get your message through to the next person" (p. 7).

A separate study conducted in the United Kingdom among refugees linked language barriers to feelings of embarrassment and an avoidance of health services:

> The doctor couldn't speak our language and, at that time, they had no interpreters. It was really bad. So, we hardly used to go. So, if we had like very pain, then we used to go. Because it was embarrassing, you know, telling doctors in a sign language. It made me feel like I had no self-esteem. I avoided going to the doctors.
>
> (Kang et al., 2019, p. 3)

Sovereign states maintain control over borders, mobility, and participation, reinforcing hierarchies between citizen and migrant. Even when invited into international spaces, refugees' voices are often tokenized. Given the focus on sovereign states and national identities, the unmet needs of forcibly displaced populations are often not captured or understood in ways that inform effective protection policies (Khan, 2024).The stigma surrounding forcibly displaced people is rooted in narratives that portray migrants as threats to national security, economic stability, and cultural identity. Media and political discourses often frame migrants as criminals, terrorists, economic burdens, or vectors of disease.

For example, right wing media in the United States promotes messages that migrants (and particularly migrants who are men and boys) are "here to destroy the country", "serial sexual predators", "invaders" who "disappear… only to be seen again when their faces are plastered on the news after they commit heinous crimes like murder, rape, human trafficking, assault, and drug dealing" (Simon & Dowe, 2024). At the intersection of gender and migration status, migrant men are stigmatized and dehumanized as being violent criminals who commit violent crimes, like assault and theft. Women and children, on the other hand, are less visible in mass media and reduced to being casualties or victims (Olier & Spadavecchia, 2022; Szczepanik, 2016). These stigmatizing views are enforced by institutional power structures, where immigration policies prioritize national interests over the protection of human rights. The legal status of refugees – often precarious or undocumented – further entrenches their exclusion from political and social processes, including research.

Both testimonial injustice and hermeneutical injustice occur in the context of forced displacement. Testimonial injustice is evident when the lived experiences of forcibly displaced populations are dismissed or undervalued. For instance, many mental health measurement and diagnostic tools have not been adapted or developed to capture the intersectional and multifaceted trauma experienced by forcibly displaced populations (Grupp et al., 2020). Refugees are seen as passive recipients of aid, their experiences marginalized by researchers who view them through a damage-centered lens, rather than sources of untapped potential for resistance. The provision of humanitarian aid is justified by the construction of a refugee identity that is vulnerable and passive. However, this framing delegitimizes political action and resistance. Refugees who act politically are often viewed as "threats", creating a dichotomy between "good" apolitical refugees and "bad" political ones (Khan, 2024). The distinction between "good" and "bad" refugees reflects the cognitive separation of the "us" and "them" stage of stigmatization, and has direct linkages for which type of refugee is seen as deserving of empathy, care, and service access. This politicized power silences dissent and transformational change.

Hermeneutical injustice manifests when forcibly displaced populations are unable to make sense of or communicate their experiences in ways that resonate within broader legal or academic frameworks. Refugees often lack the resources and opportunities to express the full impacts of their trauma, migration stress, and health needs due to both language barriers and the absence of culturally appropriate research tools. The hermeneutical gap in knowledge about refugee experiences results in the failure to design effective health interventions. For example, research on mental health in refugee populations often does not account for the trauma of displacement and its long-term effects, as these are not framed within the existing scientific understanding of mental health (Altunoz et al., 2016).

Further, health and social services may be gender blind in that they do not account for the caregiving responsibilities of women and girls. This gap contributes to the erosion of refugees' ability to meaningfully influence policy, as their lived realities are not fully understood or acknowledged. Refugees may develop a sense of disempowerment and disillusionment with the systems intended to support them. When refugees are excluded or supports are not integrated to support fuller participation in research and policymaking, they lose the opportunity to voice their own health concerns and needs, culminating in self-silencing. Power relations between researchers and refugee populations are evident in participatory research, where the use of academic or research jargon increases the complexity of interpretation. For example, the burden was often placed on interpreters or refugees to "ask researchers to clarify what it means to 'join the study' or 'participate in the trial' also what the safety protocol is, and to define PHQ-9" (Inge et al., 2024, p. 169). The absence or weak integration of refugee voices in research exacerbates global health inequalities, as policies continue to be crafted without considering the full complexity of the refugee experience, leading to ineffective and inequitable solutions. Even when included, researchers must weigh how their "methodological decisions have an impact on who gets to hear a refugee's story": What researchers ultimately do with "stories from forced migrants can contribute to social and political invisibility" (Saltsman & Majidi, 2021, p. 2522).

11.3.2 Case Study 2: Persons Living with Disabilities (PLWD) and Epistemic Injustice in Sexual and Reproductive Health (SRH) Research

An estimated 1.3 billion people live with moderate or severe disabilities due to underlying health conditions, representing 16% of the global population, or one in six people (World Health Organization, 2023). Ableist stigma renders people living with disabilities invisible in sexual and reproductive health research (SRH). Yet, persons living with disabilities (PLWD) experience many SRH adversities including HIV, unwanted pregnancies, and gender-based violence (Seidu et al., 2024). PLWD are often stigmatized as asexual, dependent, and incapable of engaging in sexual or reproductive activities. These stereotypes are deeply embedded in societal and medical attitudes, and they reinforce the idea that disability precludes sexual agency or autonomy. Historically speaking, people with disabilities have been desexualized and infantilized in healthcare encounters (Addlakha et al., 2017). Their capacity for relationships, sexual pleasure, reproduction, and parenting is often denied in patient-provider interactions (Ahumuza et al., 2014). Disability is rarely framed through a rights-based approach that acknowledges sexual diversity or autonomy.

At an extreme, due to the belief that PLWD cannot make decisions regarding their SRH and lack the judgment to behave in a responsible manner, women living with disabilities faced forced contraception and coerced sterilization, sometimes at the onset of menstruation (Steele & Goldblatt, 2020). Analyses of cases involving the sterilization of minor girls living with intellectual disabilities in

Australia noted that "non-consensual sterilization continues to be framed as a medical problem to be cured"; the Family Court of Australia can authorize the sterilization of girls under 18 years (Brady, 2001).

Disability is commonly understood from an impairment-based medical model, rather than a bio-psycho-social one that acknowledges the ways in which societal barriers limit access to participation and inclusion. In the context of HIV research, PLWD are frequently excluded because they are seen as less "at risk" for HIV, or their SRH needs are not adequately addressed or conceptualized (Groce et al., 2013; Hanass-Hancock & Nixon, 2009). Many HIV research studies focus on populations, such as men who have sex with men (MSM) or people who inject drugs, while failing to address the intersection of disability and HIV risk. As a result, PLWD's experiences with HIV prevention and care are not well documented or integrated into service delivery.

Disability and HIV are interrelated and bidirectional, including people living with HIV-impairments or episodic disability (e.g., neuronal damage, inflammation, cognitive impairment, opportunistic infections) and PLWD who later acquired HIV (Kuper et al., 2022). The higher risk of sexual violence places PLWD (and in particular, adolescents with intellectual disabilities) at a higher risk of HIV infection while also facing care access barriers and burdens (Kuper et al., 2022). PLWD experience a similar or higher HIV burden compared to persons living without disabilities (De Beaudrap et al., 2017; Doyle et al., 2020; Lunsky et al., 2017). Yet, global research signals that PLWD face under-addressed challenges for HIV prevention, testing, care, and treatment. Rotenberg et al. (2024) found that in low- and middle-income countries in particular, PLWD were less likely to have comprehensive HIV prevention knowledge and to know where to receive HIV testing, compared to persons without disabilities: Women living with disabilities were less likely to have been tested for HIV and to have knowledge about mother-to-child HIV prevention.

These forms of exclusion reflect testimonial injustice, where the voices and experiences of PLWD are undervalued and less acknowledged in HIV care. They also demonstrate hermeneutical injustice, where their lived experiences fall outside of the SRH guidelines and frameworks that were designed for persons without disabilities. These forms of epistemic injustice further limit the access of PLWD to appropriate SRH health interventions, thereby perpetuating disparities.

More specifically, testimonial injustice is evident when PLWD are excluded from studies or when their knowledge about their own health needs is ignored. PLWD who are excluded from HIV research experience worse health outcomes, including lack of access to disability-specific HIV prevention tools, sexual health education, and medical care. Their needs are not recognized, and they may not be given the opportunity to participate in health decisions that directly impact their lives. At the interpersonal level, PLWD may experience frustration and isolation when healthcare providers fail to take their needs seriously or fail to offer accessible health services. Communication with health care providers is a major barrier to obtaining care: health workers frequently lack training in how to interact with patients with disabilities; sign language interpreters are in short supply; and the availability of health information in accessible formats (such as Braille or audio) is limited (Ganle et al., 2020). Moreover, many providers hold prejudiced or dismissive attitudes toward PLWD, reinforcing a culture of discrimination within healthcare settings (Ganle et al., 2020). Privacy and confidentiality can also be compromised, with disabled individuals being denied the same dignity offered to other patients (Ganle et al., 2020). The hermeneutical injustice faced by PLWD in SRH research is evident in the lack of frameworks for understanding their specific experiences. The needs of PLWD, such as accessible health education or tailored prevention strategies, are often absent from HIV research because disability-specific challenges are not sufficiently explored or understood within existing research paradigms.

11.3.3 Case Study 3: The Erasure of the Embodied Experiences of Gender and Sexual Minorities

Gender and sexual minorities often face stigma due to intersecting axes of oppression: homophobia, transphobia, and heteronormativity. Society's dominant standard of heteronormative relationships between persons with binary and cis-gender identities marks members of the LGBTQ+ community as deviant threats. The stigma that LGBTQ+ individuals face is reinforced by legal, medical, and religious institutions that criminalize same-sex relationships or refuse to recognize non-binary or transgender identities. This systemic discrimination affects both the social and political recognition of LGBTQ+ people which, in turn, impacts their ability to contribute meaningfully to research or policy or to access public services.

For example, persons who are transgender experience what scholars term "identification-based injustice" – a specific form of epistemic injustice (Henckel, 2025, p.1). Here, a trans person's self-identification as a woman or a man is dismissed, doubted, or denied by those who operate from a cis-gender point of reference (Henckel, 2025). This denial of gender expression and transgender lived experiences is illustrated by the recent findings of the Supreme Court of the United Kingdom which, on April 16, 2025, ruled unanimously that womanhood is defined by biological sex. Here, trans women (even with gender recognition certificates of their affirmed gender) are excluded from this definition of womanhood (Al Jazeera, 2025). Consequently, transgender women would be prohibited from accessing refugee, sports, and health services specifically designed for women (Al Jazeera, 2025).

In addition, transgender women may be grouped together with MSM in research studies despite having different health needs; researchers have identified a relationship between gender-affirming hormone therapy and reduced rates of HIV seropositivity and viral non-suppression (Reisner et al., 2025). As a result, research data fails to reflect the lived realities of transgender individuals, and interventions are not designed with their specific needs in mind. Other research limitations concern the labels that are used to define human sexuality and their incongruence with the trans experience (Galupo et al., 2016). Transgender persons describe their sexualities in ways that counter traditional frameworks used in research (Galupo et al., 2016). For example, one study reported that trans persons characterize their sexuality in ways that highlight fluidity and the separation of sexual and romantic attraction (Galupo et al., 2016). While common sexuality categories used in research include heterosexual, homosexual, and bisexual, transgender participants expressed nuanced sexuality experiences:

> While I am gay and attracted 99% to men (I only want to have romance with men, only strongly desire or go out of my way for relationships with men) sexually I am more flexible and would fuck a girl, although I wouldn't want to commit to her etc. I don't have interest in specific females the way I do with male.
>
> (Galupo et al., 2016, p. 100)

Another participant, this time a transgender woman, described the fluid nature of her sexuality while transitioning:

> In the past, I was a man, attracted exclusively to women – aka heterosexual. Then I was in transition, expressing an appearance of being a woman while retaining male sexual parts and I was attracted to women – aka Bisexual. Now, I'm expressing being a woman, and having female sexual parts and am attracted to women – aka Lesbian. The labels don't work very well.
>
> (p. 98)

Hermeneutical injustice can arise when LGBTQ+ individuals lack the social and conceptual tools required to articulate their needs in healthcare settings. Medical professionals may not have the training or institutional support necessary to understand or address transgender health issues, leading to poor healthcare experiences. The training deficit is reinforced by informational erasure (insufficient knowledge by healthcare providers on transgender people and their health needs) and institutional erasure (insufficient policies related to trans identities and knowledge, including the lack of recognition that protection policies are needed) (Bauer et al., 2009). Further, hermeneutical injustice can also occur when educational curricula (at all levels) exclude or misrepresent trans experiences, denying students and learners the tools necessary to understand gender and sexual diversity (Martino, 2022). Empirical qualitative research of clinical encounters involving LGBTQ+ patients breathes life into these structural barriers. Data collected from Indiana, the United States of America among transgender women reveal the lack of medical training primary care physicians receive on feminizing hormone therapy and breast development; as stated by a 21-year-old, African American, transgender woman:

> A clinic doctor gave me hormones. [Afterwards] I started getting these lumps in my breasts… They were really tender and they hurt… I asked him [doctor], "Should I hurt this bad?" He said, "I don't know, go ask somebody who knows". And I thought, "Why is he giving me something that he doesn't know about?"
>
> (Hines et al., 2019, p. 89)

In a separate study conducted in the Southern United States, clinicians revealed not knowing how to inquire about a patient's gender, pronouns, or anatomy:

> I could tell by their appearance, that they were transitioning – one way or another, I was not confident which way it was. My nurse had gone in there and said, "Do you prefer to be addressed as Miss or Mr.?" and the patient answered "Miss". … So, I got a speculum and I went in the room to do my exam and I was like, "This is not what I was expecting". Actually, I don't know what I was expecting. And I was thinking, "I don't know how to appropriately ask a patient, 'What physical parts do you have?' so, I can do the correct exam".
>
> (Sileo et al., 2022, p. 7)

At the individual level, LGBTQ+ people who are excluded from research or whose experiences are misrepresented are at greater risk of lacking health care, legal protection, or social recognition. At the interpersonal level, healthcare providers, social workers, and legal professionals often fail to address the unique concerns of LGBTQ+ individuals due to their own biases or limited training, leading to microaggressions or outright discrimination. Ultimately, LGBTQ+ patients may self-censor due to the anticipation of being misunderstood, judged, or not believed, especially in culturally unsafe settings (Jonas et al., 2025). At the community level, the absence of LGBTQ+ voices in research and policy leads to poorly designed health services, legal protections, and social initiatives. At the societal level, the lack of representation in research and policy contributes to the widespread discrimination and stigmatization of LGBTQ+ people, further entrenching their marginalization in society.

11.4 Concluding Remarks on Knowing, Power, and Dehumanization with Linkages to Social Work Research and Practice

Stigma and epistemic injustice are interlinked processes of marginalization. At the heart of stigma is a process of dehumanization and devaluation, ultimately involving the silencing of voices and the hindering of one's capacity to fully know who one is. This chapter illustrated the interconnection between stigma and epistemic injustice by focusing on three so-called "hard-to-reach" populations. Drawing on the case studies of forcibly displaced persons, people living with disabilities, and the LGBTQ+ community, I described under-researched lived experiences that are not captured in dominant research and health frameworks. The stigmatization of such "hard-to-reach" populations creates social and political barriers to their expression and full participation in society, leading to exclusion, self-silencing, and epistemic injustice.

Social work research and practice occupy a focal position in confronting stigma and epistemic injustice, especially among populations deemed "hard-to-reach". Social workers are uniquely equipped to challenge power hierarchies and advocate for the recognition of marginalized groups as credible knowers. Through participatory research, trauma-informed and affirming practice, and policy advocacy, social work professionals can dismantle the social processes that devalue and silence marginalized voices. By integrating anti-stigma frameworks and centering lived experience, social work advances epistemic justice, ensuring that the worldviews of stigmatized populations inform research, policy, and service delivery. This transformative approach not only humanizes those who have been excluded but also strengthens the discipline's commitment to equity and social change.

Social work researchers can embed anti-stigma principles into participatory research methodologies, ensuring that forcibly displaced persons, persons living with disabilities, and LGBTQ+ individuals are not merely subjects but co-creators and leaders of knowledge generation. This involves recruiting marginalized voices, compensating lived expertise, and using culturally responsive tools that recognize testimonial and hermeneutical injustices. By doing so, researchers can counteract epistemic exclusion and produce findings that reflect the authentic experiences and needs of stigmatized groups.

Social work practitioners should adopt reflexive, anti-stigma approaches in direct practice: trauma-informed care, disability justice, and LGBTQ+ affirming frameworks. This includes ongoing training to recognize and challenge personal and institutional biases, adapting communication to honor clients' self-identification, and advocating for accessible, inclusive services. Practitioners must move beyond deficit-based models, instead foregrounding the strengths and agency of "hard-to-reach" populations in all interactions.

Both researchers and practitioners can leverage their roles to influence policy, ensuring that the lived realities of stigmatized groups are integrated into program design and evaluation. This means collaborating with community organizations, amplifying marginalized voices in policy forums, and using research evidence to challenge exclusionary practices. Anti-stigma interventions can be institutionalized in policy frameworks and clinical/social service delivery training, shifting from tokenistic inclusion to genuine power-sharing toward epistemic justice. Recognizing and challenging the stigma in epistemic injustice is an act of humanization, of breathing life into the experiences and stories cast into the shadows of power structures. If we expand our reach and range of inclusion in social work research and practice, nothing is hard to reach. *We* just have to get there.

References

Addlakha, R., Price, J., & Heidari, S. (2017). Disability and sexuality: Claiming sexual and reproductive rights. *Reproductive Health Matters*, *25*(50), 4–9. https://doi.org/10.1080/09688080.2017.1336375

Ahumuza, S. E., Matovu, J. K., Ddamulira, J. B., & Muhanguzi, F. K. (2014). Challenges in accessing sexual and reproductive health services by people with physical disabilities in Kampala, Uganda. *Reproductive Health*, *11*(1), 59. https://doi.org/10.1186/1742-4755-11-59

Al Jazeera. (2025, April 17). *Trans women aren't legally women: What the UK Supreme Court ruling means*. https://www.aljazeera.com/news/2025/4/17/trans-women-arent-legally-women-what-the-uk-supreme-court-ruling-means

Altunoz, U., Castro Nunez, S., & Graef Calliess, I. T. (2016). Mental health of traumatized refugees and asylum seekers: Experiences of a centre of transcultural psychiatry in Hannover, Germany. *European Psychiatry*, *33*(S1), S398–S398. https://doi.org/10.1016/j.eurpsy.2016.01.1433

Ball, L. (2018). *Explainer: What is evidence-informed policy-making?* ODI Global. https://odi.org/en/insights/explainer-what-is-evidence-informed-policy-making/

Bauer, G. R., Hammond, R., Travers, R., Kaay, M., Hohenadel, K. M., & Boyce, M. (2009). "I don't think this is theoretical; this is our lives": How erasure impacts health care for transgender people. *Transgender Health and HIV Care*, *20*(5), 348–361. https://doi.org/10.1016/j.jana.2009.07.004

bell hooks. (1986). *Ain't I a woman: Black women and feminism*. Pluto Press.

bell hooks. (2004). *The will to change men, masculinity, and love*. Atria books.

Bourdieu, P. (1991). *Language and symbolic power*. Harvard University Press. https://search.library.wisc.edu/catalog/999664935802121

Brady, S. M. (2001). *The sterilisation of girls and young women with intellectual disabilities in Australia: An audit of Family Court and Guardianship Tribunal cases between 1992–1998*. University of Queensland. https://humanrights.gov.au/our-work/sterilisation

Collins, P. H. (2000). *Black feminist thought: Knowledge, consciousness, and the politics of empowerment* (2nd ed.). Routledge.

Dancygier, R., Egami, N., Jamal, A., & Rischke, R. (2022). Hate crimes and gender imbalances: Fears over mate competition and violence against refugees. *American Journal of Political Science*, *66*(2), 501–515. https://doi.org/10.1111/ajps.12595

De Beaudrap, P., Beninguisse, G., Pasquier, E., Tchoumkeu, A., Touko, A., Essomba, F., Brus, A., Aderemi, T. J., Hanass-Hancock, J., Eide, A. H., Mac-Seing, M., & Mont, D. (2017). Prevalence of HIV infection among people with disabilities: A population-based observational study in Yaoundé, Cameroon (HandiVIH). *The Lancet HIV*, *4*(4), e161–e168. https://doi.org/10.1016/S2352-3018(16)30209-0

DeSa, S., Gebremeskel, A. T., Omonaiye, O., & Yaya, S. (2022). Barriers and facilitators to access mental health services among refugee women in high-income countries: A systematic review. *Systematic Reviews, 11*(1), 62. https://doi.org/10.1186/s13643-022-01936-1

De Sousa Santos, B. (2015). *Epistemologies of the South: Justice against epistemicide*. Routledge.

Dotson, K. (2014). Conceptualizing epistemic oppression. *Social Epistemology, 28*(2), 115–138.

Doyle, K. E., Sionean, C., Paz-Bailey, G., Hollis, N. D., Kanny, D., & Wejnert, C. (2020). High prevalence of disability and HIV risk among low socioeconomic status urban adults, 17 U.S. cities. *Disability and Health Journal, 13*(1), 100834. https://doi.org/10.1016/j.dhjo.2019.100834

El-Bassel, N., Mukherjee, T. I., Stoicescu, C., Starbird, L. E., Stockman, J. K., Frye, V., & Gilbert, L. (2022). Intertwined epidemics: Progress, gaps, and opportunities to address intimate partner violence and HIV among key populations of women. *The Lancet HIV, 9*(3), e202–e213. https://doi.org/10.1016/S2352-3018(21)00325-8

European Union (n.d.). *Forced displacement*. Retrieved October 24, 2025, from https://international-partnerships.ec.europa.eu/policies/migration-and-forced-displacement/forced-displacement_en#:~:text=Forced%20displacement.%20We%20refer%20to%20forced%20displacement,of%20climate%20change%2C%20environmental%20degradation%2C%20or%20disasters.

Fricker, M. (2007). *Epistemic injustice: Power and the ethics of knowing*. Oxford University Press. https://doi.org/10.1093/acprof:oso/9780198237907.001.0001

Galupo, M. P., Henise, S. B., & Mercer, N. L. (2016). "The labels don't work very well": Transgender individuals' conceptualizations of sexual orientation and sexual identity. *International Journal of Transgenderism, 17*(2), 93–104. https://doi.org/10.1080/15532739.2016.1189373

Ganle, J. K., Baatiema, L., Quansah, R., & Danso-Appiah, A. (2020). Barriers facing persons with disability in accessing sexual and reproductive health services in sub-Saharan Africa: A systematic review. *PLOS ONE, 15*(10), e0238585. https://doi.org/10.1371/journal.pone.0238585

Goffman, E. (1984). Stigma and social identity. In BlaikieA. , M. Hepworth, M. Holmes, A. Howson, D. Inglis, & S. Sartain (Eds.), *The body: Critical concepts in sociology* (pp. 116–146). Routledge Taylor and Francis Group. https://books.google.com/books?hl=en&lr=&id=dxQhGbIpBzUC&oi=fnd&pg=PA116&dq=Goffman+stigma+1963&ots=PXVsIvFZx0&sig=Ht5VR0sgjXTxfk2hboOvla0KQXE#v=onepage&q=discounted&f=false

Goffman, E. (1986). *Stigma: Notes on the management of spoiled identity*. Simon & Schuster.

Groce, N. E., Rohleder, P., Eide, A. H., MacLachlan, M., Mall, S., & Swartz, L. (2013). HIV issues and people with disabilities: A review and agenda for research. *Social Science & Medicine, 77*, 31–40. https://doi.org/10.1016/j.socscimed.2012.10.024

Grupp, F., Piskernik, B., & Mewes, R. (2020). Is depression comparable between asylum seekers and native Germans? An investigation of measurement invariance of the PHQ-9. *Journal of Affective Disorders, 262*, 451–458. https://doi.org/10.1016/j.jad.2019.11.055

Hanass-Hancock, J., & Nixon, S. A. (2009). The fields of HIV and disability: Past, present and future. *Journal of the International AIDS Society, 12*(1), 28–28. https://doi.org/10.1186/1758-2652-12-28

Harding, S. G. (1986). *The science question in feminism*. Cornell University Press.

Hatzenbuehler, M. L., Phelan, J. C., & Link, B. G. (2013). Stigma as a fundamental cause of population health inequalities. *American Journal of Public Health, 103*(5), 813–821. https://doi.org/10.2105/AJPH.2012.301069

Henckel, S. J. (2025). You think you know someone: Trans identities and epistemic injustice. *Hypatia*, 1–22. https://doi.org/10.1017/hyp.2025.4

Hines, D. D., Laury, E. R., & Habermann, B. (2019). They just don't get me: A qualitative analysis of transgender women's health care experiences and clinician interactions. *Journal of the Association of Nurses in AIDS Care*, *30*(5), e82–e95. https://doi.org/10.1097/JNC.0000000000000023

Inge, E., Sarkadi, A., Tökés, A., & Warner, G. (2024). Standard involvement is not enough: A mixed method study of enablers and barriers in research meetings with forced migrants. *Journal of Refugee Studies*, *37*(1), 157–180. https://doi.org/10.1093/jrs/fead062

Jackson, A., Hernandez, C., Scheer, S., Sicro, S., Trujillo, D., Arayasirikul, S., McFarland, W., & Wilson, E. C. (2022). Prevalence and correlates of violence experienced by trans women. *Journal of Women's Health, 31*(5), 648–655. https://doi.org/10.1089/jwh.2021.0559

Jimenez, M. (2020). *Aristotle on shame and learning to be good.* Oxford University Press. https://doi.org/10.1093/oso/9780198829683.001.0001

Jonas, L., Bacharach, S., Nightingale, S., & Filoche, S. (2025). Under the umbrella of epistemic injustice communication and epistemic injustice in clinical encounters: A critical scoping review. *Ethics, Medicine and Public Health*, *33*, 101039. https://doi.org/10.1016/j.jemep.2024.101039

Kang, C., Tomkow, L., & Farrington, R. (2019). Access to primary health care for asylum seekers and refugees: A qualitative study of service user experiences in the UK. *British Journal of General Practice*, *69*(685), e537–e545. https://doi.org/10.3399/bjgp19X701309

Khan, B. (2024, January). *Forging the path to meaningful refugee participation: Interdisciplinary analysis of power, agency, and participation.* Local Engagement Refugee Research Network. https://carleton.ca/lerrn/wp-content/uploads/WorkingPaper_22.pdf

Krieger, N. (1994). Epidemiology and the web of causation: Has anyone seen the spider? *Social Science & Medicine*, *39*(7), 887–903. https://doi.org/10.1016/0277-9536(94)90202-X

Krieger, N. (2021). *Ecosocial theory, embodied truths, and the people's health.* Oxford University Press. https://doi.org/10.1093/oso/9780197510728.001.0001

Kuper, H., Heydt, P., & Davey, C. (2022). A focus on disability is necessary to achieve HIV epidemic control. The Lancet HIV, 9(4), e293–e298. https://doi.org/10.1016/S2352-3018(21)00345-3

LGBTQIA Resource Center. (n.d.). *LGBTQIA Resource Center Glossary*. Retrieved October 21, 2025, from https://lgbtqia.ucdavis.edu/educated/glossary#:~:text=LGBTQIA+:%20Abbreviation%20for%20Lesbian,encompassed%20in%20the%20short%20acronym.

Link, B. G., & Phelan, J. (2014). Stigma power. *Social Science & Medicine*, *103*, 24–32. https://doi.org/10.1016/j.socscimed.2013.07.035

Link, B. G., & Phelan, J. C. (2001). Conceptualizing stigma. *Annual Review of Sociology*, *27*, 363–385.

Logie, C. (2021). *Working with excluded populations in HIV*. Springer. https://doi.org/10.1007/978-3-030-77048-8

Logie, C. H., James, L., Tharao, W., & Loutfy, M. R. (2011). HIV, gender, race, sexual orientation, and sex work: A qualitative study of intersectional stigma experienced by HIV-positive women in Ontario, Canada. *PLoS Medicine*, *8*(11), e1001124. https://doi.org/10.1371/journal.pmed.1001124

Lunsky, Y., Durbin, A., Brown, H. K., Bansal, S., Heifetz, M., & Antoniou, T. (2017). Health profiles and associated service use among adults with HIV and intellectual and developmental disabilities. *AIDS*, *31*(5). https://journals.lww.com/aidsonline/fulltext/2017/03130/health_profiles_and_associated_service_use_among.11.aspx

Martino, W. (2022). A transgender studies approach for educators in schools: Reflections on "cissexist pitfalls," bifurcated frameworks, and racial justice. *Teachers College Record*, *124*(8), 17–42. https://doi.org/10.1177/01614681221121514

McGrath, R. E. (2005). Conceptual complexity and construct validity. *Journal of Personality Assessment*, *85*(2), 112–124. https://doi.org/10.1207/s15327752jpa8502_02

Mills, C. W. (1997). *The racial contract*. Cornell University Press. http://www.jstor.org/stable/10.7591/j.ctt5hh1wj

Olier, J. S., & Spadavecchia, C. (2022). Stereotypes, disproportions, and power asymmetries in the visual portrayal of migrants in ten countries: An interdisciplinary AI-based approach. *Humanities and Social Sciences Communications*, *9*(1), 410. https://doi.org/10.1057/s41599-022-01430-y

Reisner, S. L., Pletta, D. R., Mayer, K. H., Deutsch, M. B., Poteat, T., Potter, J., Wirtz, A. L., Harris, A., Campbell, J., Keuroghlian, A. S., Hughto, J. M. W., Gonzalez, A., & Radix, A. E. (2025). HIV seropositivity and viral non-suppression in transgender, non-binary, and gender-diverse people in primary care receiving gender-affirming hormone therapy in the USA between 2013 and 2019 (LEGACY): An observational, longitudinal, cohort study. *The Lancet HIV*, *12*(4), e283–e292. https://doi.org/10.1016/S2352-3018(25)00004-9

Rotenberg, S., Chen, S., Hanass-Hancock, J., Davey, C., Banks, L. M., & Kuper, H. (2024). HIV knowledge and access to testing for people with and without disabilities in low- and middle-income countries: Evidence from 37 multiple indicator cluster surveys. *Journal of the International AIDS Society*, *27*(4), e26239. https://doi.org/10.1002/jia2.26239

Saltsman, A., & Majidi, N. (2021). Storytelling in research with refugees: On the promise and politics of audibility and visibility in participatory research in contexts of forced migration. *Journal of Refugee Studies*, *34*(3), 2522–2538. https://doi.org/10.1093/jrs/feab071

Scoglio, A. A. J., & Salhi, C. (2021). Violence exposure and mental health among resettled refugees: A systematic review. *Trauma, Violence, & Abuse*, *22*(5), 1192–1208. https://doi.org/10.1177/1524838020915584

Seidu, A.-A., Malau-Aduli, B. S., McBain-Rigg, K., Malau-Aduli, A. E. O., & Emeto, T. I. (2024). Sexual lives and reproductive health outcomes among persons with disabilities: A mixed-methods study in two districts of Ghana. *Reproductive Health*, *21*(1), 69. https://doi.org/10.1186/s12978-024-01810-4

Sileo, K. M., Baldwin, A., Huynh, T. A., Olfers, A., Woo, J., Greene, S. L., Casillas, G. L., & Taylor, B. S. (2022). Assessing LGBTQ+ stigma among healthcare professionals: An application of the health stigma and discrimination framework in a qualitative, community-based participatory research study. *Journal of Health Psychology*, *27*(9), 2181–2196. https://doi.org/10.1177/13591053211027652

Simon, C., & Dowe, N. (2024, September 8). *Right-wing media continue abhorrent racism and xenophobia as they try to push baseless "migrant crime" wave narrative.* Media Matters for America. https://www.mediamatters.org/immigration/right-wing-media-continue-abhorrent-racism-and-xenophobia-they-try-push-baseless?utm_source=chatgpt.com

Stangl, A. L., Earnshaw, V. A., Logie, C. H., Van Brakel, W., C. Simbayi, L., Barré, I., & Dovidio, J. F. (2019). The health stigma and discrimination framework: A global, crosscutting framework to inform research, intervention development, and policy on health-related stigmas. *BMC Medicine*, *17*(1), 31. https://doi.org/10.1186/s12916-019-1271-3

Steele, L., & Goldblatt, B. (2020). The human rights of women and girls with disabilities: Sterilization and other coercive responses to menstruation. In C. Bobel, I. T. Winkler, B. Fahs, K. A. Hasson, E. Arveda Kissling, & RobertsT. -A. (Eds.), *The Palgrave handbook of critical menstruation studies* (pp. 77–91). Palgrave Macmillan. https://www.ncbi.nlm.nih.gov/books/NBK565613/ doi: 10.1007/978-981-15-0614-7_8

Szczepanik, M. (2016). The "good" and "bad" refugees? Imagined refugeehood(s) in the media coverage of the migration crisis. *Journal of Identity and Migration Studies*, *10*(2), 23–33.

Teo, T. (2010). What is epistemological violence in the empirical social sciences? *Social and Personality Psychology Compass*, *4*(5), 295–303. https://doi.org/10.1111/j.1751-9004.2010.00265.x

Turan, J. M., Elafros, M. A., Logie, C. H., Banik, S., Turan, B., Crockett, K. B., Pescosolido, B., & Murray, S. M. (2025). Challenges and opportunities in examining and addressing intersectional stigma and health. *Focus*, *23*(1), 70–84. https://doi.org/10.1176/appi.focus.25023006

United Nations High Commissioner for Refugees. (2023). *Annual public health global review.* https://www.unhcr.org/sites/default/files/2024-04/annual-public-health-global-review-2023.pdf

United Nations High Commissioner for Refugees. (2025). *Figures at a glance.* https://www.unhcr.org/about-unhcr/overview/figures-glance

Wirtz, A. L., Poteat, T. C., Malik, M., & Glass, N. (2020). Gender-based violence against transgender people in the United States: A call for research and programming. *Trauma, Violence, & Abuse*, *21*(2), 227–241. https://doi.org/10.1177/1524838018757749

Woodgate, R. L., Busolo, D. S., Crockett, M., Dean, R. A., Amaladas, M. R., & Plourde, P. J. (2017). A qualitative study on African immigrant and refugee families' experiences of accessing primary health care services in Manitoba, Canada: It's not easy! *International Journal for Equity in Health*, *16*(1), 5. https://doi.org/10.1186/s12939-016-0510-x

World Health Organization. (2023). *Disability: Key facts.* https://www.who.int/news-room/fact-sheets/detail/disability-and-health

World Health Organization. (2025, October 25). *Disability.* https://www.who.int/health-topics/disability#tab=tab_1

Chapter 12

Unrecognized Truths

The Impact of Epistemic Injustice on LGBTQIA+ Communities

Vivien Roman-Hampton and Gio Iacono

12.1 Introduction

Epistemic injustice, a silencing and oppressive form of injustice, holds significant weight in helping us to understand the dynamics between knowledge, power, and marginalized voices. This concept acknowledges the systemic erasure and invalidation of individuals and communities, resulting in a society where the value or credibility of oppressed perspectives is systematically diminished. Fricker (2007) conceptualized epistemic injustice as encompassing two primary forms: *testimonial injustice*, where an individual's credibility as a knower is undermined due to prejudice, and *hermeneutical injustice*, where people lack the interpretative tools needed to understand and share their experiences. These concepts challenge social workers to examine how knowledge is constructed, legitimized, and shared while scrutinizing the mechanisms by which dominant norms exclude and diminish the voices of marginalized populations.

This framework becomes extraordinarily pertinent in understanding how certain groups – including our LGBTQIA+ populations – are rendered invisible or discredited. Epistemic injustice scholarship challenges our assumptions about whose voices are valued in constructing, disseminating, and interrogating the "truth", and whose perspectives are deliberately or inadvertently overlooked. Beyond personal interactions, this epistemic domain of injustice manifests systemically, embedded in policies, institutions, and learning environments that perpetuate inequities and reinforce pre-existing hierarchies in social structures. This injustice does more than undermine individual voices; it entrenches structural systems of oppression, ensuring that entire communities remain excluded from decision-making processes and from shaping the cultural and ideological frameworks that govern their lives.

Given the increasing socio-political hostilities toward LGBTQIA+ communities, particularly in the United States (U.S.), a focused analysis of epistemic injustice is imperative. Legislative attacks and regressive cultural norms demonstrate how deeply these injustices are embedded. In the following sections, we examine epistemic justice in relation to (1) diverse LGBTQIA+ communities

DOI: 10.4324/9781003639046-15

and their compounded effects through intersectionality, (2) its manifestations within social work education and practice, and (3) actionable strategies to address epistemic injustice and foster equity and belonging.

Unfair and unjust communicative structures, institutions, and practices have the potential to reproduce and further exacerbate existing socio-economic inequalities and injustices (Byskov, 2021). By situating these experiences within a broader socio-political and historical context, we aim to advance not only academic understanding but also meaningful advocacy and reforms in educational, social, and policy frameworks. Through this lens, epistemic injustice evolves from a conceptual framework to an urgent societal challenge that demands sustained attention and intervention.

12.1.1 Positionalities

As social workers, we see it as crucial to first identify how our social identities and intersecting places of privilege and marginalization can impact our work and writing.

I am Vivien Roman-Hampton (first author). As a second-year doctoral student and scholar-practitioner with a master's degree in social work, my research is profoundly shaped by my focus on the mental health and well-being of people with historically marginalized identities. Drawing from my Afro-Caribbean heritage, as someone of Puerto Rican descent, I navigate the complexities of oppression and exclusion stemming from my roots in a still-colonized island that has been deprived of its resources. This shared ancestral history, which includes the burden of oppression and exclusion, enhances my understanding of and empathy for the challenges faced by minoritized groups within the United States. Additionally, my multifaceted identities as a pansexual, veteran, and neurodivergent person enrich my perspective, fostering resonance with future study participants. Having lived in subsidized housing during my earliest years, enduring the impacts of divorce, and moving through various family dynamics, I am acutely aware of the diverse experiences of socio-economic instability. While I identify as cisgender and a person without a disability – identities I often take for granted – I recognize the privileges and disadvantages I navigate. These aspects of my identity, though not always visible, are integral to my approach as a researcher and practitioner, allowing me to acknowledge both my struggles and my advantages. This broad spectrum of experience informs my commitment to inclusivity and equity in my work, ensuring that diverse voices and experiences are acknowledged and valued. In confronting epistemic injustice, my positionality promotes a deeper awareness of the ways in which marginalization can distort knowledge production and recognition, compelling me to actively challenge dominant narratives and advocate for the voices of those who have been historically silenced within academic spaces. By centering lived experiences, I aim to dismantle barriers to understanding and contribute to a more equitable research environment that honors the complexity of marginalized identities.

I am Gio Iacono (second author). As an academic in social work at a large, research-intensive university in the Northeast United States, I am committed to advancing equity, inclusion, and belonging in research, teaching, and practice. I identify as a White, queer, cisgender man, and am a first-generation college graduate who immigrated to the United States. I am deeply committed to preparing social work students to practice with critical reflexivity and cultural humility, encouraging them to interrogate their own positions in relation to systems of power, privilege, and oppression. My pedagogical approach centers the importance of recognizing and honoring the lived experiences and knowledge of marginalized communities. My research focuses on community-based participatory approaches with LGBTQIA+ young people – I strive to address epistemic injustice by ensuring that diverse LGBTQIA+ voices and ways of knowing are elevated and valued, especially within systems that have historically marginalized or silenced them. Embracing both my places of privilege and marginalization, I remain dedicated to creating transformative spaces where all identities are valued, differences are celebrated, and the perspectives of those most often unheard are brought to the forefront of social work scholarship, education, and practice.

12.1.2 *Purpose of Critical Reflection*

In each section of this chapter, we include critical reflection questions. This inclusion serves several purposes. First, these questions provide an opportunity for readers to process and interrogate the concepts of epistemic injustice presented, moving from passive learning to active intellectual and emotional engagement. Second, they function as a tool for navigating bias and privilege, particularly when applied in professional or classroom settings. Lastly, these questions can foster productive dialogue, whether used individually for personal reflection or collectively in a group as part of educational programming or professional development.

Depending on the audience, these questions may be utilized differently. For example, in classroom settings, educators or facilitators can employ these questions to spark discussions on epistemic injustice and its impact, particularly in relation to LGBTQIA+ populations. Students may engage in peer dialogue, structured debate, or reflective journaling exercises based on these prompts. Critical questions can also serve as a basis for assignments, presentations, and case study evaluations. For individuals, readers might take time to personally consider these questions, reflecting on how their own positionality, beliefs, and practices align (or conflict) with the principles of epistemic justice. This reflection is an important precursor to cultivating cultural humility and promoting equity in professional settings.

12.1.3 Key Terminology

The following terms are central to understanding the dynamics of knowledge, power, and voice discussed throughout this chapter and provide a foundation for exploring how epistemic injustice manifests in LGBTQIA+ contexts.

Epistemic Injustice. The systematic exclusion, erasure, or undermining of the knowledge and credibility of marginalized individuals due to social and structural inequalities. First theorized by Miranda Fricker (2007), it includes testimonial and hermeneutical injustice.

Testimonial Injustice. This occurs when prejudice leads to the dismissal or devaluation of a speaker's credibility, discounting their lived knowledge and experiences (Fricker, 2007).

Hermeneutical Injustice. This manifests when marginalized groups lack access to the societal frameworks or language necessary to conceptualize, express, and understand their experiences (Fricker, 2007).

Intersectionality. A framework recognizing how overlapping social identities (e.g., race, gender, ability, sexuality) create unique modes of oppression and privilege. Coined by Kimberlé Crenshaw (1989), intersectionality highlights the compounded effects of multiple forms of discrimination.

Cultural Humility. An ongoing process of self-reflection and lifelong learning aimed at recognizing and addressing power imbalances and biases and fostering respectful engagement with diverse identities (Alessi et al., 2023).

Othering. The systemic marginalization of individuals or groups based on perceived differences, reinforcing hierarchical structures that exclude them from full societal participation (Powell & Menendian, 2024).

Belonging. A state of authentic inclusion and recognition within societal structures that validates and uplifts diverse experiences, voices, and identities (Powell & Menendian, 2024).

Critical Mass. The concept of achieving sufficient representation of marginalized groups so that individuals no longer feel isolated or tokenized but are empowered and included (Hagedorn et al., 2007).

Epistemic Exploitation. The phenomenon where marginalized individuals bear the burden of educating dominant groups about their experiences, perpetuating testimonial injustice and emotional labor (Berenstain, 2016).

12.2 Theoretical Framework: Epistemic Injustice and Its Relevance to LGBTQIA+ Populations

To understand epistemic injustice as it pertains to LGBTQIA+ populations, it is crucial to first examine its theoretical underpinnings. Miranda Fricker's seminal work, *Epistemic Injustice: Power and the Ethics of Knowing* (2007), laid the groundwork for understanding the role of power dynamics in shaping whose knowledge is deemed credible and whose is dismissed. Testimonial injustice, which occurs when prejudice influences the credibility assigned to a speaker's testimony, and hermeneutical injustice, which arises when individuals lack the societal frameworks necessary to interpret and articulate their lived experiences (Fricker, 2007), find practical applications across various domains, including education, healthcare, and policy.

In LGBTQIA+ contexts, testimonial injustice is evident when dominant groups dismiss queer voices as unreliable, biased, or incomplete. For instance, when social work educators or practitioners trivialize the lived experiences of LGBTQIA+ individuals, they perpetuate a culture of disbelief that invalidates the knowledge these individuals possess about their own realities. Hermeneutical injustice manifests when LGBTQIA+ people lack the language or institutional support needed to articulate their experiences – for example, when non-binary individuals grapple with rigid, binary gender frameworks within legal and social systems. These forms of epistemic injustice do not exist in isolation; they are deeply embedded in structural inequities that sustain systemic oppression. By applying these theoretical insights to LGBTQIA+ populations, this chapter underscores the broader implications of epistemic injustice. It reveals how societal norms regulating knowledge production and dissemination systematically disadvantage marginalized groups; in so doing, their voices remain contributory in shaping cultural and institutional narratives (Dotson, 2011).

12.2.1 Complexities within LGBTQIA+ Communities

Understanding LGBTQIA+ individuals as a monolith oversimplifies the realities and intersections within this diverse community. While the umbrella term "LGBTQIA+" encompasses a spectrum of sexual orientations, gender identities, and expressions, each subgroup within this community faces its own unique challenges and forms of epistemic injustice. Transgender and gender diverse individuals, for instance, experience intensified vulnerabilities due to linguistic, legal, and social constraints on their autonomy and visibility. Efforts to assert identity through pronouns are often met with resistance or ridicule, undermining these individuals' epistemic authority as knowers of their own experiences (Ahmed, 2006).

The broad categorization of LGBTQIA+ populations itself brings challenges of representation and equity into focus. It is often the case that within an attempt to address systemic injustices, injustices are unintentionally multiplied, layered upon those already facing exclusion and marginalization. For instance, lumping trans and gender diverse individuals into LGBTQIA+ discussions without careful consideration of their unique experiences may perpetuate epistemic injustice. Similarly, individuals within LGBTQIA+ communities who also identify as disabled, neurodivergent, or Black, Indigenous, and People of Color (BIPOC) encounter an even broader scope of baseline inequities. Their voices are further drowned out within the intersections of race, ability, gender, financial inequity, and other identifying factors – all compounded by societal norms (Powell &

Menendian, 2024). These norms, largely found across the globe, including the United States, prioritize White, cisgender heterosexuality as dominant, and sideline diverse perspectives into the realm of "irrelevant" or "other".

One of the most visible arenas of epistemic injustice for LGBTQIA+ populations is healthcare. LGBTQIA+ individuals often face significant challenges regarding mental health that are exacerbated by epistemic injustice. For instance, many LGBTQIA+ individuals may feel isolated or misunderstood within traditional mental health frameworks that predominantly reflect heteronormative values and experiences. When seeking support, they may encounter mental health professionals who lack the necessary understanding of their unique struggles, leading to a sense of dissonance between the professionals' perspectives and their own lived realities. This gap can result in epistemic injustice – feelings of invalidation where their experiences are dismissed or misunderstood, contributing to further distress and confusion. Moreover, healthcare providers may dismiss or question self-reported experiences, thereby denying these individuals' testimonial credibility. The current rollback of legal protections for gender-affirming care in several U.S. states (Dawson & Kates, 2025) further aggravates these challenges, sending a clear message that LGBTQIA+ voices are unworthy of recognition within medical discourse. Policy frameworks exacerbate these issues by enshrining systemic exclusions into law. Legislation banning discussions of LGBTQIA+ topics in classrooms illustrates how epistemic injustice is codified at institutional levels. These policies (*Map*, n.d.) do more than restrict access to resources or spaces – they delegitimize LGBTQIA+ identities, reinforcing societal narratives that deny the value of queer voices. Addressing these injustices requires not only challenging these laws but also advocating for policies that actively promote equity, inclusion, and representation. The impact of these epistemic injustices can be profound, as it not only negatively impacts LGBTQIA+ individuals materially and beyond, but also undermines their confidence in articulating their feelings and experiences. This struggle is encapsulated in the words of Miranda Fricker (2007), who notes:

> When you find yourself in a situation in which you seem to be the only one to feel the dissonance between received understanding and your own intimated sense of a given experience, it tends to knock your faith in your own ability to make sense of the world, or at least the relevant region of the world.
>
> (p. 163)

Knowing who you are in your lived experience and being told otherwise, sometimes oppositionally so, leads one to second guess their sense of self, others, and the world; it is a feeling that can leave someone shaken to the core and moving through life with a sense of uncertainty.

Critical Reflection Questions

How might epistemic injustice be experienced differently by a transgender person of color compared to a White gay man? What does this suggest about the need for intersectional approaches in your practice?

12.3 Epistemic In/Justice: DEI, Intersectionality, Othering, and Belonging

In understanding the connection between diversity, equity, and inclusion (DEI) in addressing and dismantling epistemic injustice and promoting equity and belonging, we believe that (1) an in-depth look at what we currently know of the application of DEI, and 2) an openness to new conversations and trajectories in the work are required. We cannot continue to do what we have already been doing and expect different results. Our current climate of epistemic injustice is spreading, and to stem the growth we must be ready to "see" in new ways. Notably, DEI policies have allowed us to move forward as a whole in many ways – and yet, at times, those initiatives can move certain members of specific groups forward while leaving many behind. Further, the few who do move forward may often be tokenized in their advancement and, as such, never truly belong but instead be put on display. What changes do we need to make to see a more universal movement for groups to belong? In the following sections we explore how the concepts of intersectionality, othering, and belonging relate to epistemic injustice and DEI strategies to address epistemic injustice.

12.3.1 Intersectionality

Intersectionality encompasses groups facing multiple forms of oppression, suggesting that various social categories intersect at the individual level, reflecting multiple intertwined systems of privilege and oppression at the broader societal level (Collins, 2015).

The LGBTQIA+ umbrella encompasses communities with vastly different relationships to power, privilege, and oppression. LGBTQIA+ people of color face compounded credibility loss, with their knowledge discounted through both racism and queerphobia. Disabled LGBTQIA+ people experience hermeneutical injustice when dominant narratives about disability ignore queer-specific needs and relationships. Women-identified LGBTQIA+ persons navigate layered patriarchal, heteronormative, and cisnormative biases, even within queer spaces. Intersectionality, as conceptualized by Crenshaw (1991), amplifies these challenges by revealing how overlapping identities – such as being a queer person of color or a trans person with a disability – magnify vulnerabilities to epistemic injustice. In such cases, the compounded effects of racism, ableism, and heteronormativity, for example, further erase individuals' voices from societal discourse. In her essay "La Guera", Moraga (1983) succinctly captures how intersectional oppression contributes to epistemic injustice:

> In this country, lesbianism is a poverty – as is being brown, as is being a woman, as is being just plain poor. The danger lies in ranking the oppressions. The danger lies in failing to acknowledge the specificity of the oppression. The danger lies in attempting to deal with oppression purely from a theoretical base. Without an emotional, heartfelt grappling with the source of our own oppression, without naming the enemy within ourselves and outside of us, no authentic, nonhierarchical connection among oppressed groups can take place.
>
> (p. 26)

Moraga personalizes the concept of othering as a form of epistemic injustice, illustrating how it intersects with ideas of intersectionality and showing that othering can occur within groups, from external forces, and internally.

The prioritization of White, cisgender, and heterosexuality as dominant norms creates environments where diverse LGBTQIA+ voices are relegated to the margins. Policies and curricula often exclude the contributions of LGBTQIA+ individuals, particularly those from racialized or disabled backgrounds, further entrenching inequities. Addressing these disparities requires not only acknowledging the diversity within LGBTQIA+ communities but also developing inclusive and intersectional frameworks that uplift all voices, identities, and experiences.

Critical Reflection Questions

In what ways might your own social location and identity influence how you receive and evaluate knowledge from LGBTQIA+ clients or colleagues? How can you actively work to recognize and interrupt your own epistemic biases?

12.3.2 Othering

Central to the experience of epistemic injustice within LGBTQIA+ populations are the dynamics of othering and belonging. Othering operates as a systemic process that marginalizes groups based on perceived differences, reinforcing hierarchies of power and exclusion. It is not merely an interpersonal phenomenon; othering is more than interpersonal bigotry – it is the expression of broad prejudice in law, culture, and norms, and the condition of group subordination and marginality (Powell & Menendian, 2024).

The lens of othering helps us see the commonalities among the tropes, laws, customs, and stories that all convey a message about who belongs, who doesn't, and the grounds for such claims (Powell & Menendian, 2024). It manifests structurally through laws, policies, cultural attitudes, and institutional practices. For LGBTQIA+ individuals, othering involves being cast as "deviant" or "other" against a backdrop of cisheteronormative ideals, leading to systemic exclusion from societal participation.

12.3.3 Belonging

Belonging, by contrast, represents the potential for inclusion, equity, and recognition within societal systems. For LGBTQIA+ populations, achieving belonging goes beyond surface-level inclusion; it requires systemic changes that validate LGBTQIA+ voices as equally credible and deserving of authority. In essence, belonging necessitates a reimagining of societal norms to prioritize equity and representation. Consider how belonging plays out in educational systems. When LGBTQIA+ experiences are excluded from classroom discussions, or when queer students face ridicule for expressing their truths, they are implicitly taught that their voices do not matter. Conversely, inclusive policies and practices – such as validating pronoun use, incorporating intersectional queer literature, and fostering safe spaces – can transform oppressive systems into ones that nurture belonging and empowerment.

12.4 Reimagining DEI: Dismantling Epistemic Injustice

DEI initiatives offer valuable entry points for addressing epistemic injustice, but to be effective they must go beyond representation (Omodan, 2023) and address the underlying structures that sustain testimonial and hermeneutical inequities. A justice-centered approach anchors DEI in the redistribution of both voice and interpretive authority (Hatch-Tocaimaza & Oliver Andrew, 2025). Testimonial justice begins with credibility recalibration, redesigning decision-making processes so that lived experience is valued alongside traditional credentials. LGBTQIA+ individuals must be included on curriculum committees, hiring panels, and governance boards with equal decision-making power. Bias must be interrupted in real time by equipping leaders, facilitators, and educators with techniques to identify and address moments when LGBTQIA+ people's contributions are undermined, ignored, or appropriated.

In exploring the concept of testimonial injustice, Dotson's (2011) notion of *testimonial quieting* stands out, particularly within academic spaces. This form of injustice occurs when listeners fail to perceive the speaker as a credible source of knowledge. In our community, this dynamic often reinforces the marginalization of LGBTQIA+ voices, devaluing their contributions to education and discourse. Over time, this can lead to what Dotson called *testimonial smothering*, where marginalized individuals, conditioned by repeated dismissals of their knowledge, self-censor and withdraw their voices in spaces that fail to validate their experiences or insights.

Hermeneutical justice requires the creation of a shared vocabulary in partnership with LGBTQIA+ communities and the ongoing development of conceptual resources that accurately reflect lived realities. Participatory knowledge-making ensures that programs, research, and institutional narratives are designed *with* LGBTQIA+ stakeholders, guaranteeing that interpretive frameworks are generated from within the community itself. For instance, in our community-based participatory research (CBPR) with LGBTQIA+ youth, these individuals are co-researchers, actively involved in the development and evaluation of mental health interventions (Iacono et al., 2024) and engage in a process of collaboratively creating language and frameworks that authentically articulate their mental health experiences. This CBPR approach ensures that program curricula and group discussions reflect perspectives and concepts meaningful to the youth themselves, rather than defaulting to dominant, adult-centric narratives.

Further, DEI can support the revision of educational curricula (Ahmed, 2007) to reflect diverse perspectives, adopt inclusive practices, and create legal frameworks that protect rather than marginalize LGBTQIA+ identities. Also, structural supports for DEI entail the integration of equity impact assessments into initiatives with explicit attention to intersectionality and the measurement of belonging through qualitative indicators (e.g., influence, safety, recognition) rather than simple headcounts. These assessments take an active role in disrupting testimonial quieting – the process by which individuals are dismissed as credible speakers due to societal biases (Dotson, 2011). By uncovering hidden inequities, such assessments work to ensure that all voices are considered legitimate contributors to knowledge and decision-making processes.

When implemented together, these strategies transform DEI from a symbolic gesture into a mechanism that actively dismantles embedded epistemic hierarchies.

Critical Reflection Question

How can allies effectively challenge epistemic injustice without speaking for marginalized communities or inadvertently perpetuating the very dynamics they seek to address?

12.5 Working Toward Epistemic Justice in Social Work Education and Practice

Epistemic injustice is particularly visible within educational systems, especially in social work education, despite its efforts to promote social justice (Council on Social Work Education [CSWE], 2022). For instance, the CSWE *2022 Educational Policy and Accreditation Standards* (EPAS) explicitly foreground anti-racism and DEI as fundamental guiding principles for professional preparation. Nevertheless, institutionalized practices in social work education often perpetuate an imbalanced preference for dominant voices, reinforcing testimonial and hermeneutical injustice for marginalized populations. Curricula that prioritize dominant perspectives (Freire, 2017; Kumashiro, 2001) send clear messages regarding whose knowledge is seen as valuable and whose is deemed extraneous. For social work educators, the role of the teacher is not to be the epistemic authority about a certain subject matter, but to be the facilitator or midwife for the student's learning (Kotzee, 2017). Educational systems perpetuate epistemic injustice by centering cisheteronormative narratives and excluding queer perspectives.

The absence of diverse cultural narratives in social work educational curricula exemplifies hermeneutical injustice, which occurs when marginalized groups lack access to the societal collective understanding necessary for articulating their identities. The exclusion of LGBTQIA+ perspectives (Duarte et al., 2023) not only creates a hermeneutical gap but also limits students' abilities to grasp the complexities of these identities. When educational systems prioritize dominant narratives, the experiences and histories of LGBTQIA+ individuals are rendered invisible, perpetuating ignorance and prejudice and preventing a comprehensive understanding of their realities.

Testimonial injustice is also prevalent in educational settings, particularly when it comes to how the voices of marginalized students are perceived, "because teachers take learners' testimonies less seriously than they deserve" (Kotzee, 2017, p. 326). The teacher's prejudice is evident when those deemed "epistemically privileged" are consistently afforded more credibility and knowledge validation than LGBTQIA+ individuals. This systematic undermining of their credibility leads to a feeling among these students that their voices carry less authority, which further reinforces dominant narratives and ignores the validity of their experiences. The opportunity for seeing through different lenses is greatly diminished as the validated knowers, who all represent similar dominant voices, all see the same way (Kotzee, 2017).

Additionally, marginalized educators are often pigeonholed into roles that focus solely on their marginalized identities. Their status as "experts" stems only from their lived experiences, thus confining their credibility within the parameters of their profession (Kotzee, 2017). This act of testimonial injustice banishes these educators to a narrow definition of expertise based solely on their marginalized identities; the educational system devalues their knowledge and experiences outside that context. Consequently, their authority is diminished in other subject areas, reflecting an unfair assessment of their credibility based on social identity (Veldhuis, 2022). This reinforces structural inequities, limiting the capacity of educational systems to benefit from the holistic expertise of marginalized educators.

Critical Reflection Questions

If you were designing a social work curriculum, how would you move beyond "adding diversity" to fundamentally centering marginalized voices as knowledge producers? What would this look like in practice?

12.5.1 *Moving from Othering to Belonging in Social Work Education*

Incorporating queer theoretical perspectives in social work education works toward inclusive knowledge and the expansion of belongingness. It challenges binary conceptions of sexuality and gender, promoting research inclusive of minority populations within sexual and gender minority groups (such as racialized and gender diverse individuals) (Iacono, 2017). Engaging in institutional recruitment – including employee, faculty, and student representation – that moves the LGBTQIA+ demographic from one of tokenization to "critical mass" can further help build inclusiveness and belonging. This concept of "critical mass" (Hagedorn et al., 2007) takes into consideration what an intended demographic needs to no longer feel isolated or spotlighted, which is often what happens when underrepresented groups are placed in spaces they do not normally appear, and dominant voices assume that enough has been done. Belonging occurs when everyone feels as if they are not only welcomed but also empowered and have a stake and a say – you are fully able to participate in the norms, setting, and ideally, in co-creating the culture and life of the organization (Powell & Menendian, 2024). As detailed above, achieving epistemic justice in education requires more than representational changes.

Here, we illustrate how these concepts can be implemented in classroom practice. Education operates as either a replicator or dismantler of epistemic injustice. Aligning pedagogy with justice requires systemic redesign, not merely curriculum add-ons. Decolonizing the curriculum means that LGBTQIA+ scholarship becomes integral to core theory across programs such as social work, psychology, law, and public health. To effectively address epistemic injustice, pedagogy must intentionally integrate the concepts of testimonial and hermeneutical justice into educational practices and processes. Pedagogical transformations must explicitly disrupt epistemic injustice (i.e., testimonial and hermeneutical), positioning LGBTQIA+ students and educators as authoritative knowers rather than subjects of study. Practical measures, such as structured positionality exercises, enable learners to critically evaluate unconscious biases, fostering a culture of reflexivity, ethical engagement, and credibility realignment. These exercises, combined with authentic case studies co-created with LGBTQIA+ communities, ensure that narratives are affirming and accurately represent diverse lived experiences. Reflective writing and peer dialogue may also help learners interrogate unconscious biases that contribute to epistemic injustice. This pedagogical approach ensures that students recognize LGBTQIA+ individuals as authoritative producers of knowledge about their own lives. For example, in our teaching, we regularly utilize critical reflective writing journals and structured peer dialogues in which social work students are invited to examine their biases related to diverse LGBTQIA+ communities (e.g., trans and gender expansive communities of color), share moments when they felt challenged by unfamiliar perspectives, and collaboratively analyze the tensions that arise when individual experiences do not align with dominant cultural narratives; these approaches can lead to deeper insight, greater empathy in the classroom, and directly challenge epistemic injustice.

Critical Reflection Questions

(1) Consider a time when you lacked adequate language or tools to describe an experience. How did this hermeneutical gap affect understanding or action, and what resources could have helped?

(2) What would achieving "critical mass" rather than tokenistic representation look like in your organization? How would you know when this transformation has occurred?

12.5.2 Moving from Othering to Belonging in Social Work Practice

In an effort to address epistemic injustice and move from othering to belonging in social work practice, social workers must undergo LGBTQIA+ cultural humility and responsiveness training to ensure affirming care (Cruciani et al., 2024) that centers the lived experiences of LGBTQIA+ clients as valid sources of knowledge. Furthermore, collaborative care models that integrate interdisciplinary relationships enhance overall access to and delivery of gender-affirming treatments and mental health services.

Providers must adopt trauma-informed care practices to acknowledge and validate these complex lived experiences (Scrutton, 2017). Trauma-informed care recognizes the pervasiveness of trauma (particularly among marginalized communities) and seeks to address clients' concerns with dignity – an important part of the concept of belonging – while recognizing the impact of social and medical systems-based injustices. This may help create better engagement and outcomes for LGBTQIA+ populations.

A significant barrier within mental health care for LGBTQIA+ communities, particularly transgender and gender diverse individuals, is the lack of culturally competent providers, particularly in rural or conservative areas. This leads to what we understand as *epistemic erosion*, where clients are burdened with educating providers about the nuances of their identities and care needs. We see this concept of epistemic erosion in many marginalized groups that are the minority in terms of representation; such individuals may experience the multiple challenges of being tokenized, regarded as a spokesperson, or viewed as representative of their identified population while simultaneously subjected to testimonial injustice.

Epistemic injustice within social work and mental health care for LGBTQIA+ communities also impacts their ability to access and receive affirming care. Historical pathologization and systemic biases often lead LGBTQIA+ individuals, particularly transgender individuals, to avoid seeking health and mental health care, as their self-reported experiences are frequently dismissed (Dickey et al., 2016). This constitutes testimonial injustice. Moreover, reliance on diagnostic frameworks (such as gender dysphoria) further perpetuates hermeneutical injustice, as it pathologizes diverse gender expressions without proper acknowledgment of societal discrimination and environmental stressors as root causes of mental health distress. To address these inequities, social work and mental health care settings must become inclusive spaces, where, for example, transgender individuals feel safe to openly discuss both gender-related and general mental health concerns without fear of stigma (Dickey et al., 2016).

Addressing epistemic injustice in social work practice then requires a systemic shift toward trauma-informed, culturally responsive, and collaborative practices. Providers must challenge the structures that perpetuate stigma, pathologization, and invalidation of LGBTQIA+ individuals' lived experiences. Affirming care assumes that transgender and gender diverse individuals are knowledgeable participants in their healthcare journey, and such care must prioritize dignity, respect, and inclusivity at individual, institutional, and societal levels (Dickey et al., 2016). By dismantling epistemic injustice, care systems can better serve the health and mental health needs of LGBTQIA+ communities and create transformative pathways toward equity and healing.

Critical Reflection Questions

(1) When working with LGBTQIA+ clients, how do you balance your professional expertise with recognition of their lived experience as a form of knowledge? Can you identify moments when you might inadvertently engage in testimonial injustice?
(2) Examine your workplace or educational institution's policies, procedures, and informal practices. Where do you observe testimonial or hermeneutical injustices operating against LGBTQIA+ individuals, and what specific changes could address these?

12.5.3 Multiple Layers of Consideration When Working toward Epistemic Justice in Social Work

Addressing epistemic injustice in our daily actions within education and practice requires layered action. At the individual level, professionals must invest in ongoing self-education and actively challenge bias – including settings where no LGBTQIA+ individuals are present. Organizationally, regular DEI and equity audits with community oversight and overhauled language in all forms and materials are essential. Systemically, advocacy for inclusive law and policy, as well as funding for LGBTQIA+-led research and archives, solidifies belonging as lived reality rather than merely symbolic inclusion.

In both social work education and practice, there is guidance on addressing the challenges of epistemic injustice. The American National Association of Social Workers' (NASW) *Code of Ethics* (2021) provides foundational principles that emphasize the responsibility of social workers to be part of the solution rather than perpetuating systemic inequities. This involves exploring our own conscious and unconscious biases, speaking up for those who are not in positions to do so for themselves, and sitting with the discomfort of our own personal and professional transformation. Ethical principles – such as "Service", "Social Justice", and "Dignity and Worth of the Person" (NASW, 2021) – highlight the critical importance of equity, belonging, and inclusion. These values challenge social workers to prioritize the dignity and belonging of all individuals, especially those from marginalized communities, by respecting the unique layers of identity that shape their experiences. Such differences should not be viewed as grounds for othering but rather as invitations to center belonging in our work, a commitment reinforced by the principle of "Importance of Human Relationships" (NASW, 2021).

Systemic reforms are equally critical. Policy interventions must address both immediate threats to LGBTQIA+ rights and broader structural inequities. This includes overturning discriminatory legislation, expanding anti-discrimination protections, funding LGBTQIA+ community programs, and actively promoting diverse representation in policymaking processes. Ultimately, dismantling the systemic hierarchies that sustain epistemic injustice requires sustained efforts across education, practice, and policy. Sustained progress against epistemic injustice for LGBTQIA+ communities also requires research that is both intersectional and action oriented. Comparative global research, such as examining models for gender-affirming care or anti-discrimination policies across diverse nations, can reveal local and international innovations, while longitudinal studies should track the lived outcomes of inclusivity and belonging over time. For true transformation, LGBTQIA+ individuals, especially those multiply marginalized, must play a central role in envisioning, governing, and evaluating DEI and justice agendas. Collaboration between education, health, and social services can develop cohesive strategies to address structural inequities and foster a society rooted in inclusion and belonging. Only by aligning these efforts and centering LGBTQIA+ voices can lasting equity and justice be achieved. These partnerships must be intentional, unified, and driven by both research insights and lived experiences.

Limitations also exist in that we write from one geographic vantage point and this topic would benefit from a multiplicity of geopolitical voices. What does epistemic injustice look like in other countries for LGBTQIA+ populations? What are the ways that we are challenging these issues and creating belonging elsewhere? Additionally, we recognize that our discussion did not specifically address many groups within LGBTQIA+ populations (e.g., asexual, intersex, pansexual) concerning epistemic injustice. This omission was not due to a lack of interest but rather the constraints of a single chapter, which would not suffice to adequately provide detailed information on these multiple diverse experiences. Our intention was to offer a broader-level approach, rather than risk creating a sense of invisibility among particular LGBTQIA+ subgroups.

The United States often stands out as a manufacturer of epistemic injustice in relation to its interactions with other countries globally. We routinely send the message that what happens here is preeminent, and as such, the innovations, ideas, and changes within other countries do not carry the same weight. As a result, we regularly enact testimonial and hermeneutical injustices as common practice. However, there have been several notable international collaborations that actively work to center diverse LGBTQIA+ voices and challenge these epistemic hierarchies. The International Partnership for Queer Youth Resilience (INQYR), led by Shelley Craig, a professor at the University of Toronto, exemplifies such efforts by bringing together over 40 international academic partners across multiple countries to understand and support LGBTQIA+ youth resilience in diverse global contexts (Craig et al., 2021). This collaborative approach ensures that knowledge production about LGBTQIA+ experiences is not dominated by Western perspectives but instead emerges from authentic partnerships with local communities and researchers worldwide. Future exploration must prioritize global collaboration to develop frameworks that account for the varying manifestations of epistemic injustice across diverse cultural contexts. By engaging with international LGBTQIA+ communities and scholars, we can collectively uncover innovative approaches and shared strategies for fostering equity and belonging worldwide. These partnerships must be intentional, unified, and driven by both research insights and lived experiences from multiple cultural contexts, moving beyond extractive research models toward truly reciprocal knowledge exchange.

As writers living in the United States, we may be engaging in an "epistemic" narrowing of sorts here, in our writing. We are confined to the restrictions of a focused chapter while also understanding that each chapter in this book deserves its own book; we want to plant seeds for a broader and global conversation and encourage LGBTQIA+ communities, social work scholars, and practitioners internationally to contribute perspectives from diverse cultural contexts that speak to epistemic injustice and pathways to dismantling its various manifestations. By centering DEI, belonging, and representation within social work education and practice, and societal systems, we can move closer to a world where epistemic justice is not only an aspiration but a lived reality for all.

Critical Reflection Questions

Consider a time when you, a colleague, or a client lacked adequate language to describe an experience. How did this *hermeneutical* gap affect understanding and action? What resources could have helped bridge this gap?

12.5.4 Strategies for Dismantling Epistemic Injustice: Pathways to Inclusion and Belonging

Epistemic injustice demands multifaceted solutions spanning education, organizational practice, and policy. Below, we offer targeted recommendations for social work education, practice, and institutional transformation, centering intersectionality and the authentic voices of LGBTQIA+ communities.

In social work education, we recommend (1) integrating queer and intersectional scholarship by moving beyond tokenistic content additions and embedding LGBTQIA+ scholarship and intersectional analysis into core curricula across disciplines; (2) decolonizing pedagogy by designing courses where marginalized voices are knowledge producers, not just subjects of study; (3) structuring positionality and reflexivity exercises that require students and educators to regularly examine how privilege and marginalization impact learning, testimony, and classroom dynamics; (4) co-creating curriculum and case studies by developing teaching materials in partnership with LGBTQIA+ individuals, ensuring authentic representation and inclusivity; and (5) facilitating participatory knowledge-making by creating opportunities for LGBTQIA+ stakeholders to help design research methods, institutional policies, and educational programs.

In social work practice, it is essential to adopt trauma-informed, culturally responsive, and competent care to ensure that practitioners understand and validate LGBTQIA+ individuals' lived experiences as credible sources of knowledge. Additionally, prioritizing collaborative and interdisciplinary models is key to fostering relationships among professionals in order to better address intersectional needs and improve access to affirming care. It is also important to emphasize cultural humility by training social workers in this approach while recruiting and supporting LGBTQIA+ staff, faculty, and students to achieve critical mass. This ensures sufficient representation for genuine inclusion, rather than settling for tokenism.

Organizational and systemic change requires recalibrating decision-making processes to include LGBTQIA+ voices in all governance bodies, such as curriculum committees, hiring panels, and boards, with genuine authority. Leaders and facilitators must also be equipped with tools to interrupt bias in real time, recognizing and disrupting moments when LGBTQIA+ contributions are minimized or appropriated. Collaborative efforts with LGBTQIA+ communities are vital for developing shared language and conceptual resources that authentically reflect lived realities. Additionally, implementing equity impact assessments is crucial, as these go beyond numerical representation to measure indicators of belonging, such as influence, safety, and recognition. Regular DEI audits should be conducted to ensure that policies, forms, and organizational language remain inclusive and affirming. Furthermore, advocating for inclusive laws and policies is essential, including support for anti-discrimination protections, equitable access to healthcare, and the right to participatory decision-making.

In the realm of research, policy, and cross-sector partnerships, it is vital to support intersectional and participatory research by funding and prioritizing studies led by LGBTQIA+ scholars, ensuring that lived experience remains central. Facilitating global and cross-sector collaboration is equally important, as building partnerships across education, health, and social services can help create comprehensive strategies to combat structural inequities. Additionally, monitoring outcomes longitudinally is essential for tracking progress in inclusion and belonging, enabling adjustments to initiatives as needed to achieve lasting transformation.

Critical Reflection Questions

(1) How do traditional research methodologies potentially perpetuate epistemic injustice? What alternative approaches might better center LGBTQIA+ voices and knowledge systems?
(2) Imagine a social work profession that had successfully addressed epistemic injustice against intersectional LGBTQIA+ communities. What would education, practice, and organizational culture look like? What concrete steps can you take to move toward this vision?

References

Ahmed, S. (2006). *Queer phenomenology: Orientations, objects, others*. Duke University Press.

Ahmed, S. (2007). The language of diversity. *Ethnic and Racial Studies*, *30*(2), 235–256.

Alessi, E. J., Kahn, S., Ast, R. S., Cheung, S. P., Lee, E. O. J., & Kim, H. (2023). Learning from practitioners serving LGBTQ+ forced migrants and other diverse groups: Implications for culturally informed affirmative practice. *Journal of the Society for Social Work and Research*, *14*(3), 609–631. https://doi.org/10.1086/716722

Berenstain, N. (2016). Epistemic exploitation. *Ergo*, *3*(22), 569–590. https://doi.org/10.3998/ergo.12405314.0003.022

Byskov, M. (2021). Unfair communicative structures and socio-economic inequalities. *Journal of Social Work*, *15*(2), 123–140.

Collins, P. H. (2015). Intersectionality's definitional dilemmas. *Annual Review of Sociology*, *41*, 1–20.

Council on Social Work Education. (2022). *2022 Educational policy and accreditation standards for baccalaureate and master's social work programs*. https://www.cswe

.org/getmedia/bb5d8afe-7680-42dc-a332-a6e6103f4998/2022-Educational-Policy-and-Accreditation-Standards-(EPAS).pdf

Craig, S. L., Eaton, A. D., McInroy, L. B., Leung, V. W. Y., & Krishnan, S. (2021). Can social media participation enhance LGBTQ+ youth well-being? Development of the social media benefits scale. *New Media & Society, 23*(9), 2503–2522.

Crenshaw, K. (1989). Demarginalizing the intersection of race and sex: A Black feminist critique of antidiscrimination doctrine, feminist theory and antiracist politics. *University of Chicago Legal Forum, 1989*, 139.

Crenshaw, K. (1991). Mapping the margins: Intersectionality, identity politics, and violence against women of color. *Stanford Law Review, 43*(6), 1241–1299.

Cruciani, G., Quintigliano, M., Mezzalira, S., Scandurra, C., & Carone, N. (2024). Attitudes and knowledge of mental health practitioners towards LGBTQ+ patients: A mixed-method systematic review. *Clinical Psychology Review, 113*, 102488.

Dawson, L., & Kates, J. (2025, August 11). *Policy tracker: Youth access to gender affirming care and state policy restrictions.* KFF. https://www.kff.org/lgbtq/gender-affirming-care-policy-tracker/

Dickey, L. M., Karasic, D. H., & Sharon, N. G. (2016, May 28). Mental health considerations with transgender and gender nonconforming clients. In M. B. Deutch (Ed.), *Guidelines for the primary care of transgender and gender nonbinary people* (2nd ed.). Gender Affirming Health Program, University of California San Francisco. https://transcare.ucsf.edu/guidelines/mental-health

Dotson, K. (2011). Tracking epistemic violence, tracking practices of silencing. *Hypatia, 26*(2), 236–257.

Duarte, M., Losleben, K., & Fjørtoft, K. (Eds.). (2023). *Gender diversity, equity, and inclusion in academia: A conceptual framework for sustainable transformation.* Routledge.

Freire, P. (2017). *Pedagogy of the oppressed.* Penguin Classics.

Fricker, M. (2007). *Epistemic injustice: Power and the ethics of knowing.* Oxford University Press.

Hagedorn, L. S., Chi, W. (YanFang), Cepeda, R. M., & McLain, M. (2007). An investigation of critical mass: The role of Latino representation in the success of urban community college students. *Research in Higher Education, 48*(1), 73–91. https://doi.org/10.1007/s11162-006-9024-5

Hatch-Tocaimaza, D. K., & Oliver Andrew, R. (2025). Charting new imaginaries for DEI: Lessons from a capabilities approach to justice. *Education Sciences, 15*(6), 754.

Iacono, G. (2017). Epistemic injustice: Towards uncovering knowledge of bisexual realities in social work research. *Advances in Social Work, 18*(2), 563–582.

Iacono, G., Holle, L., Loveland, E., Borel, C., Horton, E., Olson, H., Craig, S. L., & Bietsch, B. (2024). Community-based participatory action research with LGBTQIA+ youth during the COVID-19 pandemic: Reflections from a collaborative autoethnography. *Qualitative Social Work, 23*(6), 970–989.

Kotzee, B. (2017). Education and epistemic injustice. In I. J. Kidd, J. Medina, & G. M. Pohlhaus (Eds.), *The Routledge handbook of epistemic injustice* (pp. 326–336). Routledge.

Kumashiro, K. K. (2001). *Troubling intersections of race and sexuality: Queer students of color and anti-oppressive education.* Rowman & Littlefield Publishers, Incorporated.

Human Rights Campaign. (n.d.). *Map: Attacks on gender affirming care by state.* Retrieved November 6, 2025, from https://www.hrc.org/resources/attacks-on-gender-affirming-care-by-state-map

Moraga, C. (1983). *This bridge called my back: Writings by radical women of color.* Kitchen Table Press.

National Association of Social Workers. (2021). *Code of ethics.* https://www.socialworkers.org/About/Ethics/Code-of-Ethics/Code-of-Ethics-English

Omodan, B. I. (2023). Unveiling epistemic injustice in education: A critical analysis of alternative approaches. *Social Sciences & Humanities Open*, *8*(1), 100699.

Powell, J. A., & Menendian, S. (2024). *Belonging without othering: How we save ourselves and the world.* Stanford University Press.

Scrutton, A. P. (2017). Epistemic injustice and mental illness. In I. J. Kidd, J. Medina, & G. M. Pohlhaus (Eds.), *The Routledge handbook of epistemic injustice* (pp. 347–355). Routledge.

Veldhuis, C. B. (2022). Doubly marginalized: Addressing the minority stressors experienced by LGBTQ+ researchers who do LGBTQ+ research. *Health Education & Behavior*, *49*(6), 960–974.

Chapter 13

Tracing the Layers of Epistemic Injustice in Social Constructions of Aging and Older Adults

Implications for Gerontological Social Work

Manaal Syed

13.1 Introduction

In Western aging societies, the older demographic has remained under persistent public and policy scrutiny for decades (Fleras, 2024). Yet within social work and the social sciences more broadly, *aging* remains an undertheorized construct to explore how diverse older adults experience civic and social othering and exclusion (Torres, 2020). At the same time, while social work has an established critical and anti-racist consciousness in its practice and scholarship (Dominelli, 2017), it has inadequately considered how social prejudice seeps into theorizations of aging and how epistemic systems craft the ideological and material boundaries of exclusion and inclusion for minority older adults.

In order to address this knowledge gap, this chapter uses a purposefully expansive prose to lay the groundwork for aging studies to adopt an epistemic injustice lens to frame how older adults are wronged in their capacity as knowers. The chapter begins by unpacking how dominant sites of knowledge production in aging have privileged standardized and categorized models of normative aging, with insufficient space for alternative epistemologies. As part of this endeavor, the chapter traces the epistemological roots of the predominant narratives of aging, followed by an introduction of the key epistemic justice concepts being used in this chapter. Next, the discussion shifts its focus to one key epistemic site – the news media – which frequently influences, shapes, and/or reinforces the public discourse on older adults for a broader audience. The chapter concludes with the implications and benefits of an epistemic justice ethics framework for gerontological social work.

13.1.1 Key Terminology

Aging and Older Adults. Critical gerontological perspectives (e.g., Baars, 1991; Estes & Phillipson, 2007; King & Calasanti, 2006) de-center the definition of aging from a biological or physiological phenomenon to a socially constructed process in which structural forces (e.g., policies, institutions, and sociocultural

DOI: 10.4324/9781003639046-16

trends) shape aging lives. In this context, older adults are not narrowly conceptualized by finite chronological age markers, but by their advancement through time and space and the corresponding impacts on their bodies, minds, spirits, and experiences within their unique life conditions (Flores-Sandoval & Kinsella, 2020).

Contributory Injustice. Originally conceptualized by Dotson (2012), contributory injustice is a form of epistemic injustice that aims to exclude, distance, or minimize individuals from a knowledge creation process. This injustice is sustained when the epistemic contributions of dominant epistemic voices are privileged and left unchallenged (Nikolaidis, 2021).

Discourses. As a key concept in the critical and post-structuralist tradition, discourses can be defined as the larger social ideas and messages that people and systems rely on to effectively communicate underlying ideologies, values, and social standards (Hall, 2001). As such, discourses operate as integral tools of power given their capacity to construct, cement, and replicate widespread knowledge about any topic (Fawcett, 1998).

Epistemic Humility. Epistemic humility is a form of resistance to epistemic injustice. The approach promotes recognizing the limitations of one's own (or any privileged) epistemic insights and in turn, expressing a curiosity and openness to learning, interrelating, and engaging with new knowledge claims, particularly those from disadvantaged groups (Medina, 2013; Strahovnik, 2021).

13.2 Epistemological Roots of Predominant Aging Perspectives

At its core, the study of epistemology requires one to consider important questions such as who is the "knower" and what knowledge is "known." Neither of these questions is neutral nor banal. Rather, they point to the political nature and permeance of power dynamics that dictate which knowers and knowledge are deemed legitimate and authentic in society (McKinnon, 2016). These power dynamics are apparent in the foundations of academic and professional knowledge systems (including social work's) that were dominated by modernist, colonial, and Western paradigms and devalued Indigenous, racialized, and other minoritized intellectual bases (Howe, 1994; Maleku, 2025; McBeath & Webb, 1991). Philosopher Walter Mignolo (2002) calls this phenomenon the "geopolitics of knowledge" (p. 59), which reflects the inseparability of Western European modernity and coloniality from epistemology. Indeed, the spread of modernity or the modernism movement as a knowledge *system* across the world occurred through its claims of espousing the values of liberalism, order, reason, equality, and freedom (Escobar, 2007).

Theories of "age" and "aging" have also been influenced by several schools of thought, including biomedical, social, and critical perspectives, along with various subtheories within these broad camps (see, for example, Bengtson &

Settersten, 2016 for a fuller discussion of aging theories, including rich, historical theoretical developments and debates that are beyond the scope of this chapter). The life course perspective, for example, is one of the most central models of aging, which views the individual lifespan as an amalgamation of milestones or stages that are aligned with human development from birth to old age and are shaped by social, cultural, and/or political values in society (Kunkel & Settersten, 2021). The origins of this approach, to periodize the lifespan into different groupings (or life stages), are traced to the classical period and continuing through the 16th century (Carr et al., 2015). For example, during the Middle Ages, "age" and "aging" were seen as processes that fluidly transcended the entire lifespan, rather than being confined to narrowly defined, later stages of life (Pickard, 2023). As well, the era's overarching religiosity linked aging to a higher, spiritual elevation, awakening, and connection with God (Cole, 1992; Pickard, 2023).

The post-16th century era marked a shift in life course theorizing, where modernist themes began to emerge. For example, one's life came to be envisioned as a series of stages that move along a defined organizing principle (e.g., rise, peak, and decline) (Carr et al., 2015). An even more formalized approach to theorizing the life course framework in aging studies is attributed to around the 20th century (Elder, 1977). This process coincided with shifting economic and sociopolitical developments of the time – including the rise of industrialism, the emergence of a free-market labor system, and a work-centered life span – which played key roles in regulating the lifespan (Kohli, 2007). As such, government policy helped cement the definitional boundaries of a typical life course to espouse a linear life trajectory within pre-defined biological and socially-recognizable life milestones (Settersten, 2003).

Historically, pioneering theorists in aging also framed their approaches around the modernist values of reason, rationality, and objectivity, which helped to anchor aging theories within the biomedical model (Arxer & Murphy, 2012). The construction of aging as a medical problem stemmed from the earliest theories of gerontology, which bolstered the medical model as the dominant perspective for understanding the biological, social, and behavioral aspects of aging over other possible frameworks (Estes et al., 1984). Estes and Binney (1989) critiqued the biomedicalized roots of aging theories which have continued to link aging to a medical context among the scientific community, and within the realms of professional practice, policy, and public perception. As such, to a large extent, being old is still commonly associated with being ill and this disease-focused definition for aging continues to rely on discourses of undesirability, sickness, and dependency (Estes & Binney, 1989).

The epistemological roots of several major aging frameworks (e.g., social constructions of aging, urban aging, and the contemporary life course framework) that trace their origins back to the Chicago School of Sociology and European scholarship of the 1960s have also endured over the years. On one hand, these perspectives have facilitated the invaluable development of a formal, distinct intellectual base for aging that has offered rich, overarching insights to guide the field's progress to further theorize older adults' lives. At the same time, the prevailing impact of these perspectives often results in an ongoing theoretical and methodological tendency in the discipline to apply them across varied populations, settings, and geographies irrespective of identity and social differences within a fast-changing world (Marshall & Bengtson, 2011). For example, few aging theoretical frameworks have been able to sufficiently account for aging lives within the context of structural barriers or multi-layered systems of oppression (Ferrer et al., 2017).

Promisingly, however, aging studies continue to garner rich debate and evolution, grappling with its cemented principles and considering them in relation to lesser-pursued areas of social life. For example, recent aging scholarship notes an increase in research that adapts established aging frameworks to the contemporary social realities impacting older adults, including intersecting inequalities along gender, faith, and migration (e.g., Syed, 2021); racialization, ethnicity, and citizenship (e.g., Brotman et al., 2020); and transnationalism (e.g., Lauer & Wong, 2010).

13.3 Epistemic Injustice as a Theoretical Framework for Understanding Social Discourses about Older Adults

13.3.1 Epistemic Injustice as an Overarching Optic

Liberatory theories have long unpacked the politics of global knowledge production by illustrating how knowledge can be constructed, legitimized, and maintained by systems of power that simultaneously overlook and/or erase the experiences and identities of marginalized "knowers" and "knowledges" (Grosfoguel, 2005). This distribution of epistemic voices (unequally demarcated along the lines of authenticity, validity, and legitimacy for certain groups) is a key premise for the theorizations of epistemic injustice. In line with this optic that relies on the significance of power, seminal works of philosophers – such as Miranda Fricker (2007) and Kristie Dotson (2012) – center themselves within this liberatory agenda by providing a comprehensive philosophical framework for epistemic injustice and related concepts.

Broadly defined, epistemic injustice can be understood as the exclusionary outcome that results from practices that regulate the legitimacy of individuals, topics, or any phenomena in question (Kidd et al., 2017). While these practices can unfold at the "micro" or interpersonal level (in which a wrong is inflicted on individuals in their capacity as knowers), they are, in fact, closely tied to larger structural mechanisms of power that impact knowers' lives (Fricker, 2007). These power structures can span broader sociopolitical forces (e.g., neoliberalism, Eurocentrism) or specific epistemic systems (e.g., institutions such as education, policy, and media) (Pohlhaus, 2017). In this context, injustice occurs when systems are organized and upheld to be insufficient and incapable of meaningfully including non-dominant epistemic views (Dotson, 2012).

Along with its individual, sociopolitical, and structural manifestation, another important consideration of epistemic injustice is how it is operationalized. Byskov (2020), for example, proposes several general conditions that make an epistemic injustice an *injustice*. These conditions include: an unfair outcome experienced by a knower who has been discriminated against; an unfair, prejudicial judgment upon an individual's knowledge capacity; an unfair exclusion of a knower from contributing to a decision that impacts them; and an unfair rejection of knowers who are particularly disadvantaged in multiple areas. Collectively, these conditions indicate that an epistemic injustice arises when unwarranted exclusionary practices are invoked, which have a detrimental, harmful, and wrongful impact on the knower (Byskov, 2020; Fricker, 2007).

13.3.2 Contributory Injustice

Dotson (2012) introduces contributory injustice as a form of epistemic injustice that adds to Fricker's (2007) initial framework of two main subtypes (i.e., testimonial and hermeneutical injustice). Dotson (2012) defines the concept as follows:

> Contributory injustice is caused by an epistemic agent's situated ignorance, in the form of willful hermeneutical ignorance, in maintaining and utilizing structurally prejudiced hermeneutical resources that result in epistemic harm to the epistemic agency of a knower. Both the structurally prejudiced or biased hermeneutical resources and the agent's situated ignorance are catalysts for contributory injustice.
>
> (p. 31)

Through this definition, Dotson (2012) offers theoretical space for two important characteristics of contributory injustice. The first characteristic is one that contributory injustice shares with the broader concept of epistemic injustice, as both see themselves manifesting as an individual-level occurrence (i.e., injustice inflicted by a knower's epistemic ignorance towards others) while having a structural impact (i.e., where the individual-level injustice helps maintain people's exclusion from particular epistemic systems). However, the second characteristic of contributory injustice departs from the prevailing definition of epistemic injustice, which presupposes that all epistemic knowers are striving for access to the same pool of "hermeneutical resources" (e.g., language, oratory style, facts, or information) in order to generate knowledge. Instead, while being conscious of unequal power dynamics in society, Dotson (2012) makes a crucial point: that while there may be hermeneutical resources rooted in privilege that are widely accessible, there is a parallel presence of *alternative* epistemologies and hermeneutical resources belonging specifically to marginalized groups. In this regard, contributory injustice is inflicted when powerful epistemic agents display epistemic ignorance by neither acknowledging nor willfully engaging with marginalized, alternative knowledge bases for greater understanding or recognition of that perspective. This epistemic ignorance can, in turn, result in sustaining structurally prejudiced hermeneutical resources at the expense of marginalized knowers' agency to contribute to the epistemic knowledge space (Holroyd & Puddifoot, 2020).

Taken together, the theoretical framework presented above provides the key pillars that can be used to explain, unpack, and respond to the social discourses that inflict epistemic injustice (and more specifically, contributory injustice) upon minoritized older adults.

13.3.3 The News Media as an Epistemic Site: Applying an Epistemic Injustice Framework to Social Discourses of Aging and Older Adults

The news media is one type of knowledge base driving widespread social discourses about aging and older adults. Diverse older adults ultimately receive very little media representation in the Western press, and the few available representations frequently rely on discourses of ageism combined with biomedicalization, neoliberalism, colonialism, racialization, and citizenship dynamics. For example, studies analyzing media discourses about racialized older adults or older immigrants (see, for example, Lindblom & Torres, 2022) illustrate how these groups are portrayed as objects of public scrutiny and actively othered as human liabilities on Western economic and healthcare systems using xenophobic stereotypes. The expansive and repetitive nature of the media also helps replicate these themes in times of acute crises, which was evident during the COVID-19 pandemic and which posed disproportionate disease risks and fatalities for older adults. Yet recent scholarship (see, for example, Amundsen, 2022; Keeble, 2023; Morgan et al., 2021) found that older adults, especially those from diverse identity positionalities, were either absent or significantly underrepresented in pandemic-related news stories, and those that were represented were stigmatized as passive, burdensome, and vulnerable.

As such, the news media as an epistemic site is largely organized around the erasure or minimization of diverse older adults; that is, their voices on issues directly impacting them are either absent or associated with inferiorized messaging (Hilt & Lipschultz, 2013; Fealy et al., 2012; Schinkel, 2013). This has a two-tiered effect. Not only are minoritized older adults inferiorized in comparison to the general population, but they are also marginalized among their privileged counterparts from within their own age segment as well. As in times of crises, highly charged political moments in the news media are also instructive as they, too, make the underlying technologies of epistemic injustice more material. The following case example of a high-profile political saga serves as an apt illustration of epistemic and contributory injustice in news media coverage.

13.4 A Case Example of Mr. and Mrs. Khan: Negotiating Epistemic In/Justice through Silence

On July 28, 2016, Mr. Khizr Khan (aged 66) and his wife, Ms. Ghazala Khan (aged 65), appeared on stage at the United States (US) Democratic Party National Convention in Philadelphia, United States of America (USA). The Khans' appearance centered on their status as Gold Star parents of their son, US Army Capt. Humayun Khan, who was killed by a car explosion while serving in the US war in Iraq in 2004. The Convention was live-streamed and recorded and consequently, various versions of the Khans' video segment (including the complete segment and notable clips) were subsequently widely publicized across formal news media and public platforms which remain publicly accessible today (*C-SPAN*, 2016). The couple's appearance at the event came in the broader context of a heightened and charged political climate in the United States. The months leading up to the election in October 2016 were a pivotal, polarizing time in American politics, with instances of hyper-partisan and hostile social and political rhetoric towards many groups, including racialized, immigrant, and other minoritized populations (Bonikowski et al., 2021).

In their appearance, Mr. Khan was dressed in a dark suit while Ms. Khan was clad in a light blue *shalwar kameez* (a traditional outfit common to some parts of South Asia, including Pakistan and the state of Punjab in India) with a stole lightly covering her head as a *hijab* (a cultural and religious head covering). While Mrs. Khan did not speak during the appearance, she stood in close proximity to Mr. Khan with an active and involved presence. Mr. Khan delivered an impassioned speech about the sanctity of the Constitution and democracy, condemned hateful rhetoric in politics, and expressed a series of political critiques of the then-Republican presidential candidate as part of his endorsement of the Democratic presidential candidate, to resounding applause from the audience. This part of the speech followed Mr. Khan's emotional account about his son who had sacrificed his life while on active duty to protect his fellow soldiers.

The Khans' appearance was particularly notable as a media event as it was one of the first times that their story – as an older, racialized, Muslim, military Gold Star family of Pakistani-descent living in the United States for several decades – had entered the consciousness of the American public. It was also one of the only times that the public witnessed a couple holding multiple intersectional positionalities and lived experiences speaking as Americans to a large American audience during a political campaigning process.

Given that Mr. Khan's epistemic contribution was delivered in a format that facilitated archival preservation (i.e., a speech), its oratory dimensions have since received significant media and scholarly attention. For example, Kendall's (2017) narrative analysis of the speech indicates its effective use of emotion, personal narration, and channeling of personal and collective anger for public resonance. In this regard, Mr. Khan's persuasive use of collectively shared hermeneutical resources (Fricker, 2007), such as his display of a pocket-sized copy of the US Constitution and poetic eloquence in his speech pattern in a high-profile political space, established the couple's legitimacy as opinion-holders on American politics.

After their appearance at the Convention, the couple reported receiving significant racism from hate groups, as well as criticisms from some oppositional party leaders and affiliates (Swaine, 2016). Perhaps most notably, one major aspect of the political and hateful attacks on the Khans related specifically to Mrs. Khan, whose outward, recognizable appearance as a Muslim woman became the basis for insinuations that she was forced to stay silent during Mr. Khan's speech. For example, as part of a response in one interview, the Republican presidential candidate of the time noted: "If you look at his wife, the mother, she was standing there … she had nothing to say … Maybe she wasn't allowed to have anything to say. You tell me" (*BBC News*, 2016).

The substance of this political attack on Mrs. Khan as part of a larger media spectacle offers several epistemic injustice insights. As is the basis of epistemically unjust acts, the insinuation projected on Mrs. Khan, that she was *disallowed* by her family to speak publicly, relies on oft-noted broader ideologies of orientalist, gendered, Islamophobic imaginaries that simultaneously construct Muslim men in proximity to Muslim women (in this case, Mr. Khan in proximity to Mrs. Khan) as violent oppressors who regulate subjugated women's ability to speak (Razack, 2004). As well, in the absence of Mrs. Khan's verbal statements at the Convention, other visual markers of her identity, such as her cultural and faith-based sartorial choices, were then centralized to cast her within this oppressed Muslim woman archetype who is not allowed to speak publicly (). Importantly, these visual cues became the sites of epistemic or hermeneutical struggle (Medina, 2017) upon which Mrs. Khan's silence was misread and aimed to be discredited.

While the remarks attacking the Khans were met with outrage and broad condemnation from several political representatives from both major political parties and political analysts in the media, the topic itself continued to occupy heightened, sensationalized time and space in the media over several days (see, for example, Biressi & Nunn, 2017 for a comprehensive summary of the sequence of notable developments in the media frenzy that ensued after the Khans' first public appearance).

To participate in this media buzz in an effort to defend the Republican candidate's remarks, the party's affiliates and pundits also leveled their own criticisms towards Mrs. Khan. For example, as part of a media appearance in a *CNN News* segment from July 2016, one political worker stated: "Ghazala Khan – I mean, first of all, he [the Republican presidential candidate] didn't know her medical conditions. And if she was that sick, why they brought her on the stage to begin with? This politicizing and getting a political capital on it? That's not fair."

Through this statement, Mrs. Khan's epistemic contribution of silence was criticized through her positionality as an older woman using biomedicalized notions of aging (e.g., "medical condition," "that sick"). Kidd and Carel (2017) unpack the process of this type of epistemic injustice applied here by noting how bodies perceived to be ill are deemed epistemic failures given the stigma around their perceived deficient status and incapacity for meaningful contribution. In this regard, Mrs. Khan's contribution (i.e., her silence) and status as a valid epistemic knower was responded to with dismissiveness, with layered insinuations of her being passive, dependent, oppressed, and physically unwell. As such, from a contributory injustice lens specifically, statements by powerful epistemic agents (e.g., political leaders and allies) about Mrs. Khan revealed a hermeneutical ignorance and bias towards her epistemic contribution through exclusionary hermeneutical systems such as ageism, patriarchy, and orientalism (Anderson, 2017). The efforts to negatively frame Mrs. Khan's silence indicated a refusal to engage more deeply with her epistemic expressions.

In follow-up interviews with her husband, media representatives asked Mrs. Khan to comment on the insinuations made about her freedom to speak at the Convention. In response, Mrs. Khan refuted the false suggestions about her silence; she explained that her silence was not imposed but that she, herself, decided not to speak at the Convention, as she anticipated being too upset and pained to talk given the loss of her son (*ABC News*, 2016). She further stated:

> When I was standing there, all America felt my pain. Without saying a single word. … I was upset when I heard that I didn't say anything because I was in pain. … If you were in pain, you fight or you don't say anything. I'm not a fighter … so the best thing I do was [stay] quiet.

In contrast with Mr. Khan's verbal epistemic contribution, Mrs. Khan explained her deliberate choice to opt for *silence*, which played a pivotal role in the media event and provided a glimpse of alternative epistemologies of othered groups in practice. Contextualized with her explicit oratory clarification, Mrs. Khan's statement reframed her silence as an agentic practice that destabilized her perceived powerlessness and rejected the stereotypical projections assigned to her (Jangbar, 2022). Mrs. Khan's silence thus appeared as an alternative hermeneutical resource through which she expressed the maternal grief and sacrifice of an older, racialized, Muslim, and immigrant mother grieving her son killed in combat. Her silence and subsequent reply can be seen as instances of epistemic resistance (Medina, 2017), which added meaningful complexity to counter reductive political criticisms and media narratives about her and her family. Instead, Mrs. Khan's explanation indicated her positioning her grief as a necessary complement to Mr. Khan's verbal epistemic contribution about their family's values, sacrifices, and beliefs around democratic rights and freedoms and civic life.

13.5 Fostering Epistemic Justice in Social Work: Disrupting Epistemic Rigidity and Fostering Alternative Methods of Aging Epistemic Knowers

The preceding discussion of the dynamics of contributory injustice with an illustrative example provides important directions for both social work and gerontological practice. Overarchingly, the epistemic injustice optic in this chapter offers social workers a theoretical foundation that helps unpack how various forms of oppression, such as discrimination, exclusion, hatred, and disenfranchisement, are perpetuated by the deliberate erasure or delegitimization of individuals and groups in their capacity as knowers. The case example of the media and political frenzy surrounding the Khan family and specifically, Mrs. Khan, practically teases apart the layered interplay between contributory injustice practices inflicted through everyday platforms like the news media and importantly, the acts of resistance undertaken in response to these inflictions. As the case example shows, powerful epistemic actors relied on age, race, and faith-based social discourses to attempt to discredit Mrs. Khan's credibility as an older, racialized, religious minority woman knower. On the alternative side, Mrs. Khan's contextualization of the powerful use of her silence (and subsequent verbal and written statements) as her chosen modes of expression illustrate how non-dominant epistemic actors may adopt multiple tacit and nuanced practices to purposefully make space for their epistemic contributions in the public sphere.

A greater consciousness towards addressing epistemic injustice requires the social work profession to not only discourage the occurrence of such discriminatory acts against diverse communities but also develop a counter ethos of practice values that foster epistemic *justice*. In support of such an endeavor, Koh (2025), for example, proposes an alternative, intellectual "radical imaginary" and "epistemic ethics justice" (p. 286) through which social workers can respond to epistemic injustice by: decentering ethno- and Euro-centrism; focusing on altering cognitive and learned responses to racism; and undertaking power analyses. In Chapter 2 of this book, Koh (2027) further details how to expand epistemic ethics justice in social work.

Individual practice strategies can include viewing clients' and/or communities' issues through an epistemic injustice lens to explore the range of structural and individual epistemic harms they may face. This ties well with social work's ethical values that already prioritize a commitment to do no harm. In this regard, exploring the epistemic harms and injuries (Fricker, 2007) endured by clients can help to uncover how they express and make sense of their experiences. This approach connects well with existing foundational scholarship in social work, which has systematically synergized epistemic injustice theories with concrete, practical psychotherapy skills (see, for example, Lee et al., 2022) and other direct and indirect social work practice approaches as elaborated in Chapter 5 of this book (Lee, 2027). Overarchingly, this approach should first fundamentally craft a space through which marginalized knowers can express *how* they have faced epistemic injustice (Pohlhaus, 2017). Medina (2017) provides other practical strategies for creating such a space, such as introducing the necessity of a *virtuous listening* skill, which involves being open and aware of our own "hermeneutical openness" and "interpretive failures" (p. 48) when working with clients and encouraging them to pay attention to their own interpretative actions and expectations.

At the same time, Medina (2017) also stresses the importance of taking a structural approach to complement the above noted micro-strategies with macro, transformative work. Dotson (2012) refers to this work as "third-order" change (p. 34), which requires not only pushing back on discriminatory epistemic systems but also building new, alternative ones. Doan (2018) stresses the need for this structural work to be rooted in the recognition of knowers (not the perpetrators of injustice) and center their agency in addressing such acts.

This work can also be especially useful for gerontological social work in order to deconstruct problematic discourses about aging and older adults in the news media, which typically center elites' views of social reality (van Dijk, 1998). Reorienting media discourses from their supposed common sensibility (Capdevila & Callaghan, 2008) to their explicit shaping or enabling of discriminatory dimensions of minoritized groups can help expose problematic social constructions of people and groups that are sourced from larger, oppressive sociopolitical forces. As the preceding discussion illustrates, the news media could also be one site that is met with transformative work given its frequent complicity in upholding unequal epistemic opportunities for groups with unequal social capital. In this case, alternative avenues such as digital multimedia spaces (e.g., virtual villages/retirement communities, virtual reality social hubs) for marginalized older groups' creative expression could provide some effective counterbalance using grassroots epistemologies.

Within aging studies specifically, epistemic injustice remains a significantly underrepresented topic. However, a pocket of the literature within aging subtopics has illustrated how to challenge epistemic rigidities inflicted upon aging bodies. While focused on particular aging contexts, this scholarship does provide broader lessons for epistemic justice work within gerontological social work. For example, in the context of dementia, Bottenberg (2022) cautions against epistemic arrogance or the disregard of relevant views that face a particular lived experience. Instead, Bottenberg (2022) offers an epistemic humility approach, which recommends practices that are interpersonal (e.g., adapting new conversational codes with clients that take their linguistic impairment into account) and systemic (e.g., developing media campaigns that counter negative discourses in the news media) to rehumanize older adults in their personhood and knowledge. Similarly, Chazan's (2020) article presents the results of a project that used an Indigenous-centered model to disrupt the colonial-normativity and health-centric epistemic roots in aging theories. Chazan proposes alternative sharing methods, such as storytelling and critical writing, to facilitate work that can meaningfully challenge epistemically rigid narratives. These future practice directions are promising and encourage aging scholars to purposefully seek theories, methodologies, and pedagogies that create space for, and amplify the voices of epistemic agents whose personhood and epistemologies have consistently been delegitimized in social life.

As a researcher, educator, and practitioner in aging, an epistemic injustice perspective is a paradigm-shift for me in recognizing how marginalized older adult knowers can be systemically invalidated from speaking and contributing to the collective knowledge base about issues directly impacting their lives. In aging studies, greater attention to an epistemic injustice lens would be especially timely given our collective experience of a global pandemic, which had disproportionate health and social impacts on older, racialized, and low-income populations who also remain vulnerable to heightened hate and violence rooted in ageism, xenophobia, racism, and other forms of hostilities. As such, the epistemic injustice perspective provides a much-needed spotlight on the role of *justice* (beyond cursory inclusion) in directly addressing the inequity that results in systemic disproportionate harm to vulnerable communities in the first place.

This chapter concludes with a hopeful vision that social work will keep its gerontological optic at pace with a fast-changing world by asking the fundamental question: How do we come to understand and value the epistemic insights of aging lives in ongoing erratic global conditions? *By listening to those who live them*, we may at least begin to answer this question from an epistemic justice lens.

References

ABC News. (2016, July 30). Muslim family of fallen army captain responds to Trump. *ABC News*. https://abcnews.go.com/Politics/muslim-family-fallen-army-captain-responds-trump-shame/story?id=41022064

Amundsen, D. (2022). A critical gerontological framing analysis of persistent ageism in NZ online news media: Don't call us "elderly"!. *Journal of Aging Studies*, *61*, 101009.

Anderson, D. E. (2017). Conceptual competence injustice. *Social Epistemology*, *31*(2), 210–223.

Arxer, S. L., & Murphy, J. W. (Eds.). (2012). *The symbolism of globalization, development, and aging* (Vol. 7). Springer Science & Business Media.

Baars, J. (1991). The challenge of critical gerontology: The problem of social constitution. *Journal of Aging Studies*, *5*(3), 219–243.

BBC News. (2016, July 31). Fury as Trump mocks Muslim soldier's mother Ghazala Khan. *BBC News.* https://www.bbc.com/news/election-us-2016-36935175

Bengtson, V. L., & Settersten, R., Jr. (Eds.). (2016). *Handbook of theories of aging.* Springer Publishing Company.

Biressi, A., & Nunn, H. (2017). Transforming the politics of gender and voice: Strategies of expertise and experience. In R. S. Sabido (Ed.), *Representing communities: Discourses and contexts* (pp. 35–53). Palgrave Macmillan.

Bonikowski, B., Feinstein, Y., & Bock, S. (2021). The partisan sorting of "America": How nationalist cleavages shaped the 2016 US presidential election. *American Journal of Sociology, 127*(2), 492–561.

Bottenberg, F. (2022). Epistemic arrogance, moral harm, and dementia. *The Journal of Philosophy of Disability, 2*, 185–208.

Brotman, S., Ferrer, I., & Koehn, S. (2020). Situating the life story narratives of aging immigrants within a structural context: The intersectional life course perspective as research praxis. *Qualitative Research, 20*(4), 465–484.

Byskov, M. F. (2020). What makes epistemic injustice an "injustice"?. *Journal of Social Philosophy, 52*(1), 114–131.

Capdevila, R., & Callaghan, J. E. (2008). "It's not racist. It's common sense". A critical analysis of political discourse around asylum and immigration in the UK. *Journal of Community & Applied Social Psychology, 18*(1), 1–16.

Carr, A., Biggs, S., & Kimberley, H. (2015). Ageing, diversity and the meaning(s) of later life: Cultural, social and historical models to age by. *Contemporary Readings in Law and Social Justice, 7*(1), 7–60.

Chazan, M. (2020). Unsettling aging futures: Challenging colonial-normativity in social gerontology. *International Journal of Ageing and Later Life, 14*(1), 91–119.

CNN. (2016, July 31). CNN Newsroom 7-8pm ET Transcript. *CQ Roll Call.*

Cole, T. R. (1992). *The journey of life: A cultural history of aging in America.* Cambridge University Press.

C-SPAN. (2016, July 28). *Democratic national convention, Day 4* [Video]. https://www.c-span.org/program/campaign-2016/democratic-national-convention-day-4/449157

Doan, M. (2018). Resisting structural epistemic injustice. *Feminist Philosophy Quarterly, 4*(4), 1–23.

Dominelli, L. (2017). *Anti-racist social work.* Macmillan International Higher Education.

Dotson, K. (2012). A cautionary tale: On limiting epistemic oppression. *Frontiers: A Journal of Women Studies, 33*(1), 24–47.

Elder, G. H., Jr. (1977). Family history and the life course. *Journal of Family History, 2*(4), 279–304.

Escobar, A. (2007). Worlds and knowledges otherwise. *Cultural Studies, 21*(2–3), 179–210.

Estes, C. L., & Binney, E. A. (1989). The biomedicalization of aging: Dangers and dilemmas. *The Gerontologist, 29*(5), 587–596.

Estes, C. L., Gerard, L., Zones, J. S., & Swan, H. (1984). *Political economy, health and aging.* Little, Brown.

Estes, C. L., & Phillipson, C. (2007). Critical gerontology. In J. Birren (Ed.), *Encyclopedia of gerontology* (pp. 330–336). Elsevier.

Fawcett, B. (1998). Disability and social work: Applications from poststructuralism, postmodernism and feminism. *The British Journal of Social Work, 28*(2), 263–277.

Fealy, G., McNamara, M., Treacy, M. P., & Lyons, I. (2012). Constructing ageing and age identities: A case study of newspaper discourses. *Ageing & Society*, *32*(1), 85–102.

Ferrer, I., Grenier, A., Brotman, S., & Koehn, S. (2017). Understanding the experiences of racialized older people through an intersectional life course perspective. *Journal of Aging Studies*, *41*, 10–17.

Fleras, A. (2024). *Rethinking ageism: Age and ageing in an ageist world.* Brill.

Flores-Sandoval, C., & Kinsella, E. A. (2020). Overcoming ageism: Critical reflexivity for gerontology practice. *Educational Gerontology*, *46*(4), 223–234.

Fricker, M. (2007). *Epistemic injustice: Power and the ethics of knowing.* Oxford University Press.

Grosfoguel, R. (2005). The implications of subaltern epistemologies for global capitalism: Transmodernity, border thinking and global coloniality. In W. Robinson & ApplebaumR. (Eds.), *Critical globalization studies* (pp. 283–292). Routledge.

Hall, S. (2001). Foucault: Power, knowledge and discourse. In M. Wetherell, S. Taylor, & S. J. Yates (Eds.), *Discourse theory and practice: A reader* (pp. 72–81). Sage.

Hilt, M. L., & Lipschultz, J. H. (2013). *Mass media, an aging population, and the baby boomers.* Routledge.

Holroyd, J., & Puddifoot, K. (2020). Epistemic injustice and implicit bias. In E. Beeghly & A. Madva (Eds.), *An introduction to implicit bias* (pp. 116–133). Routledge.

Howe, D. (1994). Modernity, postmodernity and social work. *The British Journal of Social Work*, *24*(5), 513–532.

Jangbar, S. (2022). Silence of a Pakistani Muslim woman: The influence of culture on the meaning of silence. *Journal of International and Intercultural Communication*, *15*(2), 132–147.

Keeble, J. (2023). "They are not expendable": Older adults in British Columbia news media during the COVID-19 pandemic. *Canadian Journal of Media Studies*, *19*(1), 22–42.

Kendall, K. E. (2017). Why did Khizr Khan's speech at the 2016 democratic national convention go viral? Personifying collective values in an epideictic speech. *American Behavioral Scientist*, *61*(6), 611–623.

Kidd, I. J., & Carel, H. (2017). Epistemic injustice and illness. *Journal of Applied Philosophy*, *34*(2), 172–190.

Kidd, J., Medina, K., & Pohlhaus, G. (2017). Introduction. In I. Kidd, J. Medina, & G. Pohlhaus (Eds.), *The Routledge handbook of epistemic injustice* (pp. 1–10). Routledge.

King, N., & Calasanti, T. (2006). Empowering the old: Critical gerontology and anti-aging in a global context. In J. Baars, D. Dannefer, C. Phillipson, & A. Walker (Eds.), *Aging, globalization, and inequality: The new critical gerontology* (pp. 139–157). Routledge.

Koh, B. D. (2025). Epistemic ethics justice: A "radical imaginary". *Journal of Ethnic & Cultural Diversity in Social Work*, *34*(5–6), 286–294.

Kohli, M. (2007). The institutionalization of the life course: Looking back to look ahead. *Research in Human Development*, *4*(3–4), 253–271.

Kunkel, S. R., & Settersten, R. (2021). *Aging, society, and the life course.* Springer Publishing Company.

Lauer, S. R., & Wong, Q. (2010). Transnationalism over the life course. *Sociology Compass*, *4*(12), 1054–1062.

Lee, E., Greenblatt, A., Hu, R., Johnstone, M., & Kourgiantakis, T. (2022). Microskills of broaching and bridging in cross-cultural psychotherapy: Locating therapy skills in the epistemic domain toward fostering epistemic justice. *American Journal of Orthopsychiatry*, *92*(3), 310–321.

Lindblom, J., & Torres, S. (2022). Othering in media representations of elderly care: Using the social justice framework to make sense of public discourses on migrants and culture. *Social Policy and Society*, *21*(2), 275–291.

Maleku, A. (2025). Toward epistemic justice in social work research: (Re)imagining global knowledge production. *The British Journal of Social Work*, *55*(2), 613–620.

Marshall, V. W., & Bengtson, V. L. (2011). Theoretical perspectives on the sociology of aging. In R. Settersten Jr. & J. L. Angel (Eds.), *Handbook of sociology of aging* (pp. 17–33). Springer New York.

McBeath, G. B., & Webb, S. A. (1991). Social work, modernity and post modernity. *The Sociological Review*, *39*(4), 745–762.

McKinnon, R. (2016). Epistemic injustice. *Philosophy Compass*, *11*(8), 437–446.

Medina, J. (2013). *The epistemology of resistance: Gender and racial oppression, epistemic injustice, and resistant imagination.* Oxford University Press.

Medina, J. (2017). Varieties of hermeneutic injustice. In In I. Kidd, J. Medina, & G. Pohlhaus (Eds.), *The Routledge Handbook of epistemic injustice* (pp. 41–52). Routledge.

Mignolo, W. (2002). The geopolitics of knowledge and the colonial difference. *The South Atlantic Quarterly*, *101*(1), 57–96.

Morgan, T., Wiles, J., Williams, L., & Gott, M. (2021). COVID-19 and the portrayal of older people in New Zealand news media. *Journal of the Royal Society of New Zealand*, *51*(Suppl. 1), S127–S142.

Nikolaidis, A. C. (2021). A third conception of epistemic injustice. *Studies in Philosophy and Education*, *40*(4), 381–398.

Pickard, S. (2023). Neither the third nor the fourth age: Viewing old age through the philosophical lens of ambiguity. *The Gerontologist*, *64*(4), gnad113.

Pohlhaus, G. (2017). Varieties of epistemic injustice. In I. Kidd, J. Medina, & G. Pohlhaus (Eds.), *The Routledge handbook of epistemic injustice* (pp. 13–26). Routledge.

Razack, S. (2004). Imperilled Muslim women, dangerous Muslim men and civilized Europeans: Legal and social responses to forced marriages. *Feminist Legal Studies*, *12*(2), 129–174.

Schinkel, A. (2013). Justice and the elderly. In M. Schermer & W. Pinxten (Eds.), *Ethics, health-policy and (anti-) aging: Mixed blessings* (pp. 247–269). Springer.

Settersten, R. A., Jr. (2003). Age structuring and the rhythm of the life course. In J. Mortimer & M. Shanahan (Eds.), *Handbook of the life course* (pp. 81–98). Springer US.

Strahovnik, V. (2021). Epistemic injustice, shame, humility and sharing. In K. Skof & S. M. Hawke (Eds.), *Shame, gender violence, and ethics: Terrors of injustice* (pp. 91–104). Lexington Books.

Swaine, J. (2016, December 20). Khizr Khan on being vilified by Trump: "The far right feels that their voice has been heard". *The Guardian*. https://www.theguardian.com/us-news/2016/dec/20/khizr-khan-vilified-trump-far-right-voice-heard

Syed, M. (2021). An intersectional theoretical framework for exploring racialized older immigrant women's subjectivities. *Journal of Social Work, 22*(2), 1–20.
Torres, S. (2020). Racialization without racism in scholarship on old age. *Swiss Journal of Sociology, 46*(2), 331–349.
van Dijk, T. A. (1998). *Ideology: A multidisciplinary approach.* Sage.

Chapter 14

Challenging Epistemic Injustice through More Inclusive Discourse

A Standpoint from Service Users' Lived Experiences

Peter Beresford

14.1 Challenging Epistemic Injustice through More Inclusive Discourse

In her foundational analysis, Fricker (2007) highlighted two expressions of epistemic injustice: "testimonial injustice," meaning the devaluing of some forms of knowledge, and "hermeneutical injustice," meaning the inability to understand, acknowledge, or interpret certain kinds of experiences. Since then, other expressions of epistemic injustice have been identified and associated issues, like epistemological violence, examined. While epistemic injustice might be a relatively recent academic inquiry, not surprisingly, the more general framing of such discriminatory acts and behaviours has long been reported by individuals and groups experiencing oppression.

The problems they have identified as experiencing include:

- The powers that be not wanting to know (about such problems of epistemic injustice)
- Not being allowed to say (that there are such problems)
- Calling into question (such problems)
- Individualizing (knowledge and such problems)

While the terminology around "epistemic injustice" is relatively new, the issues it seeks to address are not. For example, the international disabled people's movement from the late 1960s onwards sought to address disability discrimination by gaining anti-disability discrimination legislation (Barnes, 1991; Charlton, 1998). The discussion the movement engaged in attempted to develop different understandings of knowledge discrimination; it built on the ideas of the liberatory new social movements (NSMs) of people facing this kind of oppression, particularly, as we have seen, the disabled people's and psychiatric system survivor movements, and the organizations they themselves established to achieve their goals. These *self-organizations* are democratically structured and controlled by the individuals and groups whose rights and needs they seek to

DOI: 10.4324/9781003639046-17

secure. This approach marks a radical shift from traditional charitable and public policy organizations where one (but usually more than one) privileged group acted on behalf of another. This change was summed up by the disabled people's movement as a transformation from organizations *for* disadvantaged people to organizations *of* such groups. These movements have highlighted *social* rather than individualistic and medicalized approaches to the issues they face – like the social model of disability. Instead of blaming and/or pathologizing people experiencing these issues, they also highlight their social relations and the barriers and discrimination in society associated with them (Charlton, 1998; Oliver, 1996). In these movements, the term *disabled people* is used rather than *people with disability*. Correspondingly, I use "disabled people" throughout this chapter intentionally to position disability as a social oppression, instead of the term "people with disability" which underlines individual impairment that the persons may have.

Further, pioneers in these movements have tended to reject narrowly focused discourses around disability (such as viewing disability as a problem of poverty, for example) and sought to explore the generally discriminatory nature of prevailing Western understandings of disability policy and practice (Charlton, 1998; Oliver, 1996). Pioneers, like the academic Mike Oliver who self-identified as "disabled," for example, rejected the strategy of conventional lobbies (i.e., the anti-poverty lobby) to define disability in such narrow terms, rather than as the result of more far-reaching disablist discrimination (Oliver, 1983). Prevailing understandings of disability tended to be based on medicalized, individualized notions, which framed disability as a personal problem or tragedy, rather than a form of social oppression (Oliver, 1996).

In this context, two related, socially based ideas emerged from the United Kingdom (UK) disabled people's movement which have had massive international, cultural, and political impacts: (1) the social model of disability and (2) the philosophy of independent living. The first drew a distinction between the individual (perceived) impairment (e.g., loss or lack of limb, sense, etc.) associated with a disabled person and a hostile and discriminatory societal reaction to this *impairment*. The second saw independence not in terms of the individual "standing on their own two feet" and coping alone, but in having the support and other social conditions necessary to enable disabled people to live on as equal terms to non-disabled people – or people without impairments – as possible (Oliver, 1990). We have seen similar developments in the psychiatric system survivor movement, such as the Mad Studies movement (LeFrançois et al., 2013), for example, encompassing a growing rejection of medicalized, individualized understandings, the emergence of survivor researchers, and increasingly articulated challenges to the exclusion of "them/us" and "their/our" modes of knowledge.

14.2 Epistemic Injustice within Epistemic Injustice Discourse: A Service User Perspective

This chapter explores the issues that emerge when a discussion about injustice, exclusion, and inequality seems to face and fall into some of the same difficulties in ensuring inclusion and equality as it identified and intended to address in its original subject matter. The specific context of the present discussion is discourse relating to "epistemic injustice" or injustice relating to knowledge. This concept emerged in the early 21st century to challenge the ways in which the knowledge of certain people and groups is routinely discounted, while that of others is privileged (Fricker, 2007). The damaging consequences of this discounting still haunt our unequal societies at every level, from devaluing a person's status as witness to a crime, to inequality, or even history (Beresford, 2025). My concern here is to explore the nature of the epistemic injustice debate and how some of the problems the epistemic injustice scholarship sought to raise have seeped into its own construction. This chapter also considers the efforts that have been and may be made to challenge this conundrum.

This author identifies as both a member of a group perceived as facing such "epistemic" inequality (i.e., disabled people/mental health service users/survivors) and as a member of the academy (an institution itself frequently facing accusations of such discrimination). The two overlapping welfare user groups I relate to – that is, groups significantly defined in terms of the policies and services they rely on – have faced particular problems as the subject of the others' judgements and analyses. Here, I want to explore this significant new development in knowledge production – the construct of epistemic injustice – and its complexities, with particular reference to both the critiques of it that are being developed by disabled people/survivors and their earlier analyses of knowledge and research production more generally, trying to maintain an intersectionalist perspective in doing so.

14.2.1 Challenging the Academicization of Epistemic Injustice

The growing interest in epistemic violence seems to come largely from academics and researchers, many of whom may lack lived experience of its extreme manifestations. In a way, the interest in epistemic injustice can be seen to reflect some scholars' efforts to "put their spin" on a pre-existing concern. The seminars, conferences, research and research grants, journal articles, books, and special issue journals have largely resulted from the initiatives of academics who do not write primarily from the position of lived experience or direct knowledge (for example, Fricker, 2007; Newbigging et al., 2024). Consequently, this lack of lived experience has been noted as an issue by some service user commentators, including myself. As Jasna Russo (2023), the survivor researcher, puts it, the concept of epistemic injustice "suddenly gave a name to the many struggles of psychiatrized people to have our knowledge count, not only in our individual lives, but also in our collective advocacy and research efforts" (p. 1). Whether this academic intervention has strengthened or weakened the challenge to existing oppressions and discrimination is open to question. As Russo put it, she subsequently realized, "How easy it is for a concept with the potential to become a change-making tool to be intellectualized to the point that it becomes an end in itself...Unfortunately this trend continues" (p. 1).

While some service users have welcomed the scholarly interest in epistemic injustice, others have critiqued the tendency to academicize the issue, as I found when I raised the question on the social media platform, Twitter/X. Although service users might incidentally gain insights from the academic interest in epistemic injustice, that is hardly the same as scholars initiating or prioritizing it based on their own lived experiences. Instead, we can see that the need to repeatedly challenge the external origins of epistemic injustice can serve as a diversion from oppressed groups' own action, agendas, and priorities. This is a particularly acute issue currently, where small state neoliberal politics and ideology, domestically and globally, have increased both health and poverty problems and reduced collective support to ameliorate them, including the resourcing of survivor and user-led organizations.

There are other difficulties, too. A key problem occurs when powerful others examine and analyse groups facing marginalization and oppression: the researchers tend to start from their own assumptions and prejudices. These assumptions, in turn, typically reflect prevailing dominant values and discriminations. Of course, this hegemonic standpoint raises problems since inequalities of power operate. From the women's and Black civil rights movements on, there has been a determination to challenge such co-option by trying to ensure that the standpoints and lived experience of marginalized groups are at the centre of analyses and understandings of such groups if this bias is to be avoided. An early example of this concern was highlighted by the new disabled people's organization, The Union of the Physically Impaired Against Segregation (UPIAS), in its *Fundamental Principles of Disability* (UPIAS, 1976) in the UK. There was also a growing effort to ensure that the diversity within people and groups facing discrimination was taken into account so as to avoid replicating dominant exclusions and prejudices (Beresford, 2013). Thus, it is not enough to include the most visible or determined members of any devalued group, but also to work to ensure that the viewpoints of all – regardless of age, impairment, class, culture, gender, ethnicity, sexuality, and so on – are represented. We can see – for obvious reasons – why this inclusion can be difficult to achieve in expert discussions, like those which have developed in relation to epistemic injustice. It is only likely to be when such "expert" discourses have more effectively challenged their own barriers and exclusions that we are likely to see major progress in this direction.

14.2.2 Reinforcing Exclusions in Epistemic Injustice Scholarship

In terms of status, credibility, education, relevant skills, confidence, and power, groups on the receiving end of stigmatizing policy and practice (like disability, mental health, and welfare benefits, for example), are often disadvantaged relative to those initiating such professional and "expert" debates. Processes of publication, conference presentations, and the rest are not the natural habitat of many of the people who are in the margin. Issues of accessibility – in terms of communication, environment, and culture – need to be central to how we work and do things. In the user-led organization I am involved with, for example, Shaping Our Lives (https://shapingourlives.org.uk/), avoiding jargon and prioritizing accessibility are fundamental to our agreed upon ground rules for how we work together. We can see how such routine exclusions from failing to do this may add to the challenges of ensuring that people and groups facing marginalization and discrimination are able to retain ownership of their own struggles, rather than being appropriated by more powerful others/experts.

It is not difficult to see how this appropriation can happen. Unfortunately, while it might be home for some, the academy is not an easy place for less advantaged groups to enter and operate in on equal terms. There is an unhelpful irony in seeking to advance an anti-oppressive argument in a bastion of inequality and elitism like the academy (although, of course, it may sometimes offer helpful opportunities and spaces through sympathetic individuals and its own resources). But it is unavoidably problematic to use a medium associated with exclusivity to "bang a drum" for inclusion and equality. Also, prioritizing such an essentially intellectualizing (NSMs: Todd & Taylor, 2004).

14.2.3 The Actual Centrality of Discrimination

From its beginnings, the whole strategy and worldview of the emerging disabled people's movement in countries like the United States and the UK was based on seeing discrimination as the central issue oppressing disabled people. This movement worked to highlight and overcome that discrimination through anti-discrimination and freedom of information legislation and supporting the self-organization of disabled people to achieve it (Charlton, 1998).

Notably, the disabled people's movement did not neglect issues of knowledge creation and development in seeking to address the core issue of discrimination. Nor did it attempt to isolate issues of knowledge creation and development from anti-discrimination and self-organization efforts as a separate area of focus or action (as those concerned with "epistemic injustice" have tended to) but instead raised the issue as one expression of a broader form of oppression. We may be sympathetic to the unstated agenda of disabled people about how helpful isolating, elevating and academicizing the construct of epistemic injustice is likely to be. While this academicization may have offered the field of philosophy a new lexicon and subject of study, however, it does not particularly seem to have strengthened self- and community-based organization. Disabled people and other welfare service users are unlikely to need others to tell them they are facing exploitation and discrimination and/or reconceiving it in their own terms. What they/we might value are allies supporting them/us in their/our own causes and priorities. Certainly, social justice movements (like the disabled people's and psychiatric system survivor movements, for example) have not marginalized the issue of knowledge production and knowledge discrimination in their struggles. Instead, these themes have been centre stage in their thinking and activities.

Disabled people segregated in welfare institutions and emboldened by the emergence of other NSMs began to challenge ruling assumptions held about them. Notably, one group living in a Leonard Cheshire "home" for disabled people rejected then-prevailing segregating practices based on the view that disabled people were incapable of living independently and required permanent residential support. They realized that they might not be believed on their own, so they sought out an independent research organization – the Tavistock Institute – to undertake a study to show that this was possible. When the research was finished, the group was shocked to discover that the researchers concluded that disabled people like them would always be "social parasites," as they were described (Miller & Gwynne, 1972).

The group, in turn, argued that it was the researchers who were parasites, basing their findings on conventional wisdoms rather than truly independent evidence (Hunt, 1972, 1981). The group set out to challenge mainstream disability research, determining instead to develop their own, which they and their international peers did. Not only did the group pioneer a different approach to knowledge development based on a set of key principles and processes, but the verdict of history confirmed both their beliefs and evidence; we have seen many more disabled people internationally live "in the community" and fulfil the responsibilities often previously denied them, including gaining employment, going to inclusive schools, undertaking higher education, forming relationships, and raising children. Although the Leonard Cheshire case is a historical example, similar cases of discrediting and discriminating against disabled people's voices have been documented to the present, particularly in relation to welfare benefits policy in the UK, for example, and social care policy more generally (see Beresford & Slasberg, 2023; Pring, 2024 for details).

14.2.4 The Importance of Service User-Led Research

The emancipatory disability research developed by the disabled people's movement represents an inherent challenge to epistemic injustice. This challenge becomes clear when we look at the principles underlying disability research, and in turn, those of survivor and user-led research which followed in its wake. Such user-led research is concerned with changing the roles and relations in research as a basis for changing the purpose of research. This effort is clearly political in nature, rather than nominally directed to a neutral process of information gathering. Such research is intended to help make change in line with people's rights and interests, as is reflected in its commitment to:

- Equalizing the relationship between researcher and research participant;
- Accountability to research participants;
- Seeking the personal empowerment of research participants;
- Working for broader political empowerment (Barnes & Mercer, 1997; Sweeney et al., 2009).

Such research is not limited to any particular research method. It may be qualitative, quantitative, or mixed methods, so long as the approach is adapted to support its participatory and emancipatory principles. What is explicit and powerful, though, is the commitment to action inherent in user-led research.

Indeed, this strong link to action means that user-led research has routinely been subject to adverse criticism, as being essentially political in nature. While traditional positivist research has stressed its objectivity and neutrality, user-led research is fundamentally at odds with this approach. The resulting tension between competing research philosophies highlights another potential problem between conventional academic and user-led research: the change-making focus of user-led research can actually be seen as incompatible with traditional positivist research values. Thus, if traditional research values drive research, rather than inspiration coming from the participants who directly face discrimination, then the knowledge produced is unlikely to be a strong force for change, and its impact will be diluted.

We should also add that it is not only that the knowledge of oppressed groups may be devalued; that of privileged groups may also be *over-valued* in terms, for example, of its reliability and rigour. The association of traditional research with positivist values of neutrality, objectivity, and distance also puts it in uneasy relation with people on the receiving end of such research, even though in recent years, there has been increasing interest in ideas like Patient and Public Involvement (PPI) and user involvement. However, the two – traditional research values and user involvement – do not necessarily sit comfortably together, as we have seen.

This tension has led to widespread criticism among service users and their organizations that the rhetoric of involvement has not been matched by the reality, which has been significantly manipulative and tokenistic. Critical scholars have been concerned about exclusion in research processes and outcomes, and it is encouraging to see Participatory Action Research (PAR) and Community-Based Practice Research (CBPR) approaches which attempt to be inclusive of research participants' voices (Fine et al., 2021; Johnson & Flynn, 2021; Wallerstein et al., 2017). However, as Chapter 4 reminds us, there is still a challenge around the centring of research participant/user voices (Tang Yan, 2027). This raises further concerns regarding the helpfulness or otherwise of professionally led debates like those about "epistemic injustice."

14.2.5 Resisting Epistemic Ignorance and Marginalization: Acknowledging What Has Gone Before

A long-time message from NSMs seems to be that serious problems can arise when old-style, top-down approaches to problem-solving control discussion and change-making, with only limited service user participation beyond that. The absence of user involvement is the antithesis of self-organizing; it tends to weaken the effectiveness of campaigning the lived experiences of service users and reinforce divisions and distrust between the professional community/academia and service users. My concern is that this marginalization of service user voices may be still happening with the issue of "epistemic injustice." I raised my worries about this with an editor of a special issue of a peer-reviewed journal focusing on epistemic injustice, suggesting that there needed to be more explicit recognition of and support for the role of service users and our movements in first raising the issue of epistemic injustice than was given in the call for papers. Despite assurances, the result consisted only of a reference in the editorial that disability and survivor movements had "long been concerned with inequalities in knowledge production, and with action to address these and support empowerment" (Newbigging et al., 2024, p. 1). This statement hardly seems to do justice to 50 years of recorded and unrecorded global struggle, some of which came at a heavy cost for many with lived experience, to bring about change and overcome the exclusion and devaluing of their knowledge. Instead, this editorial approach seems to express the same problem, "marginalizing" if not "ignoring" the work of the disabled people's and survivor movements to quote descriptors of epistemic injustice offered in the same editorial.

14.3 Discussion: Maximizing the Potential in Epistemic Injustice Work

While there may be problems in epistemic injustice work, there may also be ways forward. Focusing on epistemic injustice and associated inequalities and exclusions can be helpful and has at least concentrated professional attention on these issues. For example, such a focus has encouraged a consideration of a range of concerns, like increased patient involvement in psychiatric diagnosis, the importance of advocacy, helping to legitimate patient knowledge, and prompting professionals to challenge their own prejudices (Bueter, 2019; Fisher, 2023; Grim et al., 2019; Newbigging & Ridley, 2018). But, if we are to take epistemic justice forward in the most helpful ways, then there is much related experience to learn from; this experience points to the importance of finding strategies both to undertake research and work as practitioners in more inclusive and participatory ways. As Russo (2023) has observed, where psychiatrized people have adopted such a participatory approach, it has proved helpful as a simple and convincing way to frame the disqualification of our experiential knowledge and our truths both individual and collective.

14.3.1 Ways Forward

The experience of NSMs, especially the welfare user movement, highlights a range of criteria and steps that may be taken to maximize the helpfulness of epistemic justice as a construct and insight for action. As Russo (2023) suggests, epistemic justice discourse can only be helpful if it is reconciled and connected with disabled people's and service users' discussions. The concept of epistemic injustice casts a helpful and detailed spotlight on issues of exclusion and prejudice. There are many ways of taking this forward. First, it will likely be helpful to draw on wider learnings about participation and service user involvement to pursue this debate and develop it in as equal and inclusive a way as possible. We need to learn together. The professional discussion needs to support the broader, experiential discussion, but not take over or overshadow it. More generally, as Russo (2018) also argues, we need to know more about how such alliances can work; what are the different agendas involved, and how can they better connect.

At the heart of these issues lies the recognition and acceptance that if any strategy for tackling injustice and discrimination is to be successful, it must be truly participatory and egalitarian in its process, as well as its aims and aspirations. A key starting point for this is an approach to making change based on the praxis of *coproduction*. Coproduction essentially means that the different parties involved in any process of working for change – in this case, service users, practitioners, policymakers, and researchers – are in equal relationship with each other. This equality is unlikely to be the case initially, especially in as unequal a context as public policy; therefore, if the actual working process is constructed to be as equal, anti-discriminatory, and inclusive as possible, it will probably also demand a pre-process of empowerment to equip all parties with the skills and confidence needed to work together on as equal terms as possible (Carr, 2018; Needham & Carr, 2009). Chapter 2 of this book also highlights this anti-oppressive praxis as well (Koh, 2027).

The foundational step required to advance epistemic justice effectively is to implement a process that is committed to inclusive involvement. While this idea may "roll off the tongue" easily, inclusive involvement means a lot more than consultation, market research, or adding a few people with relevant lived experience into the professional mix. Instead, it should commit us to *a truly inclusive approach to involvement,* which takes into account the reality highlighted by the evidence: namely, that some groups tend to be routinely excluded from such initiatives. Often, those groups facing the highest levels of discrimination, oppression, or multiple difficulties are left out of the conversation. However, without their involvement, we will only ever secure a part of the whole picture. This inclusion will require a range of provisions to ensure effective access to and support for such groups (Beresford, 2013). These include:

- Renewed efforts to link discussion of such issues with action to bring about change;
- Ensuring environmental, communication, and cultural access;
- Ongoing support to all parties involved to improve understanding and skills for equal collaboration and co-working.

Communication access means supporting people to develop their communication skills, including challenging digital inequality, and much more. It involves avoiding jargon and recognizing different communication needs (i.e., from those who don't read or write, to those who communicate differently and have specific access needs).

Sadly, at present, much of the discussion about epistemic injustice is inaccessible to many who would benefit from being part of the challenge that demands to be made to it. *It's Our Lives*, the pamphlet I wrote in 2003, which was published by a service user-led organization, is about knowledge discrimination. It attempted to raise these issues in a more accessible way and has been widely cited but tended not to be drawn on in the subsequent professionally led discussion of epistemic injustice (Beresford, 2003). This is an example of what is included/excluded in broader knowledge production. Such sectarianism is unlikely to be helpful in this context.

Recognizing and encouraging the overlaps between service users, researchers, policymakers, and practitioners to support better understanding, build trust, and make possible more effective collaboration is also essential in cultivating inclusion. This is an insight that intersectionalism – that is, the recognition that few of us have monolithic identities but rather multifaceted and overlapping ones – has helped. Intersectionalism can foster a shared understanding, increase access to opportunities in both research and helping professions, and make collaboration more likely and more possible. Further, such initiatives must be adequately funded if they are to be carried out appropriately and inclusively.

Mad Studies may offer a helpful way forward in challenging such knowledge discrimination, but again, as commentators (Beresford & Russo, 2021) have highlighted, it is vulnerable to the same problems of academicization and co-option by psychiatric and other professionals. This is a threat that needs to be resisted. Epistemic resistance (Medina, 2013) is thus critical to epistemic justice, as described in Chapter 1 of this book (Lee, 2027).

14.3.2 *A Case Illustration of Epistemic Collaboration between Academic and Community Groups*

These principles apply to all aspects of activity aimed at challenging exclusion and discrimination, including what has come to be called epistemic injustice. This extends to practice, policy, organization, research, monitoring and evaluation, standard setting, and the rest. Much work has already been done in this regard, and there is considerable guidance forthcoming from it. One recent example that this author was involved with highlights how helpful such collaborations between academic and community groups can be, both in challenging epistemic injustice and inequality in its own process, and in helping advance inclusive and anti-discriminatory practice more generally. This relates to the efforts of the *British Journal of Social Work (BJSW)*, a respected, international, peer-reviewed journal, which recently put together a special issue on the "Voice and Influence of People with Lived Experience" (2023). This issue sought to prioritize the viewpoints of people with "lived experience" – that is, individuals who directly face the kind of problems that social workers encounter in their work and who receive social work support.

The *BJSW*'s approach was a carefully thought-through and coherent one. First, its editorial board decided to work in more participatory ways involving such lived experience. Second, they strengthened the editorial board itself by appointing a significant new tranche of members with relevant experience and skills. Third, they set up a diverse, international editorial group for this special issue which included three (of seven) people who identified with lived experience. We (since I was a member with lived experience) had frequent online meetings, and I can truly say that there was a sense of support and equality in our collaboration (Beresford et al., 2023). Certainly, there was no sense of hierarchy or heavy votes; instead, there existed a real feeling of finding our way together to inclusive and equal working and discovering solutions. This way of working led to a wholly fresh approach to our task.

I offer this case illustration as a real-life example, not as a model or blueprint. This experience included:

- A supportive approach to commissioning material, extending far beyond the usual impersonal, sometimes mechanistic academic model which often applies. People could have help in developing their ideas and articles;
- Payment to all with lived experience who wished to receive it, both as board members and contributors;
- The pursuit of three kinds of contributions: conventional academic pieces, reflective articles centring lived experience, and "creative artefacts" (which could include illustrations, poems, short films, music, etc.) to offer choice in line with people's potential skills, interests, and experience;

- A deliberately "kind" and sensitive response to suggestions and then contributions, framed in terms of helping, not judging, supporting, not negatively criticizing;
- Contributions developed as partnerships between professionals and people with lived experience, but with the process being led by the latter;
- A commitment on the part of the journal to incorporate the learning from this activity into its future working, to encourage more contributions from people with lived experience;
- A sense of support from the *BJSW* and its editorial board, and an ongoing commitment to its themes (i.e., including people with lived experience and their experiential knowledge and expertise on equal terms);
- A process of "taking stock" by the special issue editors, followed by further consideration on the part of the journal's editorial board. Additionally, one year after the issue, this subject was revisited in another editorial by the special issue's editors (Hughes et al., 2024);
- In the editorial, the *BJSW* set out in detail how it had gone about its tasks and achieved the results, to help other groups and organizations seeking to implement something similar (Beresford et al., 2023).

The initiative seems to have been a great success. The journal received 140 submissions and published a total of 81 articles, of which lived experience contributions accounted for 38. The special issue was made open access so that it could reach the largest possible number of people and has been treated as a watershed in the *BJSW*'s development. Of course, the key issue is to ensure that this initiative continues to have an influence on the *BJSW* and beyond. It certainly serves as a key precedent for challenging knowledge discrimination, and we know it has already had an impact on other journals.

If there's one lesson this experience taught me, which seems especially relevant here, it is that if we want to challenge epistemic injustice most effectively, then we first need to explore our own identities, behaviours, attitudes, and relationships. This can be seen as a helpful starting point for challenging such injustice and discrimination. We may come to have a good understanding of the discrimination we face, but that is best seen as a basis for empathizing and beginning to understand the discrimination faced by others and thereby avoid reinforcing it. The personal is very much political, and the political personal in this context.

References

Barnes, C. (1991). *People with disability in Britain and discrimination: A case for anti-discrimination legislation.* Hurst & Company.

Barnes, C., & Mercer, G. (Eds.). (1997). *Doing disability research.* The Disability Press.

Beresford, P. (2003). *It's our lives: A short theory of knowledge, distance and experience.* OSP for Citizen Press.

Beresford, P. (2013). *Beyond the usual suspects: Towards inclusive user involvement.* Shaping Our Lives. https://lx.iriss.org.uk/sites/default/files/resources/beresford.pdf

Beresford, P. (2025). *The antidote: How people-powered movements can renew politics, policy and practice.* Policy Press.

Beresford, P., Golding, F., Hughes, M., Levin, L., Mohamed, O., Schön, U-K., & Unwin, P. (2023). Editorial – Special Issue. *The British Journal of Social Work, 53*(3), 1275–1281. https://doi.org/10.1093/bjsw/bcad112

Beresford, P., & Russo, J. (Eds.). (2021). *The Routledge international handbook of mad studies.* Routledge.

Beresford, P., & Slasberg, C. (2023). *The future of social care: From problem to rights-based sustainable solution.* Edward Elgar Publishers.

Bueter, A. (2019). Epistemic injustice and psychiatric classification. *Philosophy of Science, 86*(5), 1064–1074.

Carr, S. (2018). Who owns co-production? In P. Beresford & S. Carr (Eds.), *Social policy first hand: An international introduction to participatory welfare* (pp. 74–83). Policy Press.

Charlton, J. I. (1998). *Nothing about us without us: Disability, oppression and empowerment.* University of California Press.

Fine, M., Torre, M. E., Oswald, A. G., & Avory, S. (2021). Critical participatory action research: Methods and praxis for intersectional knowledge production. *Journal of Counseling Psychology, 68*(3), 344–356. https://doi.org/10.1037/cou0000445

Fisher, J. (2023). Epistemic injustice: The silenced voices. *International Journal of Mental Health Nursing, 32*(4), 1186–1189.

Fricker, M. (2007). *Epistemic injustice: Power and the ethics of knowing.* Oxford University Press.

Grim, K., Tistad, M., Schön, U-K., & Rosenberg, D. (2019). The legitimacy of user knowledge in decision-making processes in mental health care: An analysis of epistemic injustice. *Journal of Psychosocial Rehabilitation and Mental Health, 6,* 157–173. https://link.springer.com/article/10.1007/s40737-019-00145-9

Hughes, M., Golding, F., Levin, L., Beresford, P., Unwin, P., & Mohamed, O. (2024). BJSW special issue on the voice and influence of people with lived experience: Our reflections one year on. *The British Journal of Social Work, 54*(5), 1783–1789. https://doi.org/10.1093/bjsw/bcae118

Hunt, P. (1972). Parasite people. *Cheshire Smile, 18*(3), 15.

Hunt, P. (1981). Settling accounts with the parasite people: A critique of 'A life apart' by E.J. Miller and G.V. Gwynne. *Disability Challenge, 1,* 37–50.

Johnson, H., & Flynn, C. (2021). Collaboration for improving social work practice: The promise of feminist participatory action research. *Affilia, 36*(3), 441–459. https://doi.org/10.1177/0886109920954424

Koh, B. D. (2027). Epistemic injustices: Anti-oppressive ethics praxis. In E. Lee, A. Greenblatt, & R. Hu (Eds.), *Epistemic injustice and resistance in social work: Rethinking social justice in practice, education, and research.* Routledge.

Lee, E. (2027). Epistemic injustice and epistemic resistance in social work. In E. Lee, A. Greenblatt, & R. Hu (Eds.), *Epistemic injustice and resistance in social work: Rethinking social justice in practice, education, and research.* Routledge.

LeFrançois, B. A., Menzies, R., & Reaume, G. (Eds.). (2013). *Mad matters: A critical reader in Canadian mad studies.* Canadian Scholars Press.

Medina, J. (2013). *The epistemology of resistance: Gender and racial oppression, epistemic injustice, and the social imagination.* Oxford University Press.

Miller, E. J., & Gwynne, G. V. (1972). *A life apart.* Tavistock Publications and Lippincott.

Mohamed, O., Schön, U.-K., & Unwin, P. (2023). Special issue title: Voice and influence of people with lived experience. *The British Journal of Social Work, 53*(3), 1275–1281. https://academic.oup.com/bjsw/issue/53/3

Needham, C., & Carr, S. (2009). *Co-production: An emerging evidence base for social care transformation.* Social Care Institute for Excellence. https://www.researchgate.net/publication/237126419_Co_production_An_Emerging_Evidence_Base_for_Adult_Social_Care_Transformation

Newbigging, K., & Ridley, J. (2018). Epistemic struggles: The role of advocacy in promoting epistemic justice and rights in mental health. *Social Science and Medicine, 219*(1), 36–44.https://www.sciencedirect.com/science/article/pii/S0277953618305690

Newbigging, K., Salta, A., Schön, U.-K., & King, C. (2024). Editorial: Addressing epistemic injustice in mental health. *Frontiers in Psychiatry, 15.* https://doi.org/10.3389/fpsyt.2024.1382528

Oliver, M. (1983). *Social work and people with disability.* Macmillan.

Oliver, M. (1990). *The politics of disablement.* Macmillan.

Oliver, M. (1996). *Understanding disability: From theory to practice.* Macmillan.

Pring, J. (2024). *The department: How a violent government bureaucracy killed hundreds and hid the evidence.* Pluto Press.

Russo, J. (2018). Commentary on: Happell, B., & Scholz, B. (2018). Doing what we can, but knowing our place: Being an ally to promote consumer leadership in mental health. *International Journal of Mental Health Nursing, 27*(6), 440–447.

Russo, J. (2023). Psychiatrization, assertions of epistemic injustice, and the question of agency. *Frontiers of Sociology, 8.* https://www.frontiersin.org/journals/sociology/articles/10.3389/fsoc.2023.1092298/full

Sweeney, A., Beresford, P., Faulkner, A., Nettle, M., & Rose, D. (Eds.). (2009). *This is survivor research.* PCSS Books.

Tang Yan, C. (2027). Epistemic injustice in community-based participatory research: Toward embodying decolonial ethical relationality, sentipensante, and accountable praxis in social work. In E. Lee, A. Greenblatt, & R. Hu (Eds.), *Epistemic injustice and resistance in social work: Rethinking social justice in practice, education, and research.* Routledge.

Todd, M. J., & Taylor, G. (Eds.). (2004). *Democracy and participation: Popular protest and new social movements.* Merlin Press.

Union of the Physically Impaired Against Segregation (UPIAS). (1976). *Fundamental principles of disability: Being a summary of the discussion held on 22nd November, 1975 and containing commentaries from each organization.* UPIAS/The Disability Alliance.

Wallerstein, N., Duran, B., Oetzel, J. G., & Minkler, M. (2017). *Community-based participatory research for health: Advancing social and health equity.* John Wiley & Sons.

Index

Page numbers in *italics* reference figures.

For Product Safety Concerns and Information please contact our EU
representative GPSR@taylorandfrancis.com
Taylor & Francis Verlag GmbH, Kaufingerstraße 24, 80331 München, Germany

www.ingramcontent.com/pod-product-compliance
Ingram Content Group UK Ltd.
Pitfield, Milton Keynes, MK11 3LW, UK
UKHW022350190926
475702UK00015B/2205
9781041071440